DOVES AND DIPLOMATS

Contributions in Political Science
Series Editor: Bernard K. Johnpoll

AMERICAN DEMOCRATIC THEORY: PLURALISM AND ITS
CRITICS
William Alton Kelso

THE CAPITOL PRESS CORPS: NEWSMEN AND THE
GOVERNING OF NEW YORK STATE
David Morgan

INTERNATIONAL TERRORISM IN THE CONTEMPORARY
WORLD
*edited by Marius H. Livingston with Lee Bruce Kress and
Marie G. Wanek*

DOVES AND DIPLOMATS

Foreign Offices and Peace Movements in Europe and America in the Twentieth Century

EDITED BY SOLOMON WANK

CONTRIBUTIONS IN POLITICAL SCIENCE, NUMBER 4

Greenwood Press

WESTPORT, CONNECTICUT ● LONDON, ENGLAND

Library of Congress Cataloging in Publication Data
Main entry under title:

Doves and diplomats.

(Contributions in political science ; no. 4)
Includes index.
1. Peace—Societies, etc.—History—20th century—
Addresses, essays, lectures. I. Wank, Solomon.
II. Series.
JX1952.D69   327'.172'0904   77-87969
ISBN 0-313-20027-0

Library of Congress Catalog Card Number: 77-87969
ISBN: 0-313-20027-0
ISSN: 0147-1066

First published in 1978

Greenwood Press, Inc.
51 Riverside Avenue, Westport, Connecticut 06880

Printed in the United States of America

10 9 8 7 6 5 4 3 2 1

For Barbara, Sarah and David

Contents

Preface

The aim of *Doves and Diplomats* is to bring to the discussion of peace movements and the opposition to them greater clarity and balance than has been the case. Until recently, traditional diplomatic history and writings on international politics have functioned within the idiom of established elites and of the political and international systems that are images of the elites' conceptions of foreign policy and national interest. As a result, the alternative views of foreign policy and national interest espoused by peace advocates have been ignored or trivialized.

After the debacle in Vietnam, the revelations of *The Pentagon Papers*, and one of the most successful antiwar campaigns in the history of any industrial nation, however, it is not quite so easy to view diplomats as "rational realists" and peace advocates as "naive utopians." If anything, the growing anachronism of traditional diplomacy—largely an extrapolation from the nineteenth-century experience of the European Great Powers—has imparted greater realism to the strategies of peace advocates. Perceptions of reality based on balance of power, unrestricted national sovereignty, armaments, and the autonomy of foreign policy are hardly adequate to cope with such untraditional and global problems as nuclear weapons, resource scarcities, population growth, food shortages, monetary reform and inflation, ecological deterioration, and harsh disparities in wealth and technology. For these problems, the plans of peace advocates, based on processes and devices of international cooperation and integration of interdependent nations into some kind of genuine world federation, seem far more relevant.

There is, of course, no guarantee that the peace advocates' solu-
tions will be adopted because they are relevant. Now, as in the past,
there are social and ideological forces opposed to major reforms
proposed by the peace movement. Nevertheless, given the turnabout
in the relationship of diplomats and peace advocates to current international and national problems, a historical reassessment of peace
and antiwar movements seems timely. The twelve chronologically
arranged essays in this collection, ranging from the beginning of the
century to the 1960s, are offered as a contribution to such a reassessment. The collection should prove useful to peace advocates, as well
as to historians, political scientists, and general readers.

These essays assume neither a naive utopian character generally
associated with peace movements nor the rational power considerations and cold rules of statecraft generally associated with foreign
policy. Rather, peace movements are seen as political phenomena
operating within specific political milieux. Foreign policy is seen as
interacting with domestic politics. From this dual perspective, the
essays examine the attempts of peace movements to influence official
policy and peace advocates' perceptions of their influence on the one
hand and, on the other, the responses of foreign office officials to
peace movements.

Not all of the essays have been able to deal directly with the interaction of peace movements and foreign offices. By virtue of their
social class affiliations and the attitudes of their members, as well
as by their moderate stance, some peace movements were, and still
are, more respectable than others in the eyes of professional diplomats and governing elites. Hence, some peace advocates had access,
and still do, to foreign offices and diplomats while others were very
distant from official policy makers. Inevitably, too, there are gaps
in the coverage. More than half of the articles deal with England and
the United States and none with smaller powers; only two of the
essays are set in the post-World War II period. Social and political
analysis of the kind customarily used by historians predominates as
a mode of investigation. Yet, taken together, the diversity of topics
and approaches and the comparative nature of the essays both
chronologically and geographically offer new interpretations based
on fresh research and new perspectives.

Several of the essays, notably those on Italy, France, Germany, and Austria-Hungary, break new ground in areas where the existing literature is very sparse. Important questions and issues are raised in all of the essays concerning the meaning and use of *pacifist* and *pacifism*, the diversity of peace movements and approaches to peace, the distinction between opposition to war by peace advocates and that by status-quo-oriented diplomats and statesmen, the power of executive authority to influence public opinion and foreign policy, and the social and ideological content of foreign policy before it is funneled into the diplomatic pipeline. Some of the essays raise the question of whether a peace movement can be respectable and moderate in the eyes of the establishment and still be effective in projecting and gaining support for alternative visions of foreign policy and relations between states. In short, the essays concern themselves with questions and issues that are very relevant to current thinking about peace movements and foreign policy and, in a broader sense, about peace and war. A separate bibliography has not been included since all of the essays provide ample bibliographical references.

This anthology was inspired by my association with the Conference on Peace Research in History, and I am grateful to several of its members for their encouragement, especially Charles Chatfield, Sandi Cooper, and Blanche Cook. Susan Rovi Mach, a graduate student in modern European history at Bryn Mawr College, generously performed several editorial chores, and I am happy to acknowledge my debt to her. I should like to thank Claudia Koonz of Holy Cross College for reading my essay and making helpful suggestions. Naturally I take full responsibility for the final result.

June 1977   Solomon Wank

DOVES AND DIPLOMATS

1
Introduction

SOLOMON WANK

I

"It is a curious commentary on the age," wrote the American diplomat Lewis Einstein one year before the outbreak of World War I, that "at a time when arbitration and peace movements have assumed an unprecedented importance . . . there should likewise be so vast an increase in armaments and military preparations."[1] What made the situation even more curious was the fact that both diplomats—in their public pronouncements at least—and peace advocates seemed to be engaged in the same task of ensuring international peace and stability. They differed, however, in their respective peace strategies. Diplomats saw the preservation of peace and stability almost exclusively in terms of maintaining the balance of power and the armed peace that was its corollary. Peace advocates, on the other hand, although not always consistent in their attitudes toward armaments, alliances, imperialism, and the balance of power, rejected in principle the notion of "peace in the panoply of war."[2] They pressed alternate strategies aimed at reducing, if not altogether eliminating, the likelihood of war: peaceful settlement of international disputes through arbitration, arms limitation, and various forms of international organization.

At times, tough-minded and realistic diplomats curried favor with the humanitarian sentiment of the age by supporting proposals emanating from the moderate upper-middle-class wing of the peace movement that committed them to do nothing of consequence, but in the main they condescendingly viewed the prescriptions of peace advocates as naive and muddled. The latter was undoubtedly true

in some cases, but in their criticism of the proposals of peace advocates, the diplomats were unable or unwilling to see how muddled
their own thinking was on the operation of the balance of power as
an actual or potential peace system.

Peace would be preserved, the diplomats argued, as long as the
Great Powers adhered to the requirements of maintaining the balance
of power—that is, as long as they recognized and avoided challenging the others' vital interests and met any threats of centralization of
power within the system. But the balance-of-power system was based
on power, and it assumed an aggressive and competitive character
of relations between states. It was dominated by the Great Powers,
who strove to expand, as well as preserve, their power. Peace then,
rested on the willingness of each of the Great Powers to resort to
war to preserve its status and vindicate its interpretation of its vital
interests. Periodic wars therefore were the logical and legitimate
means of adjusting the changing relations between states generated
by continuous competition for power; and in 1914 the periodic war
came.[3] Peace advocates predicted the coming of the war, but despite
the "unprecedented importance" of their peace movements, they
were not strong enough to prevent it.[4]

Today we are faced with a similar paradox. There is a live peace
movement in Europe and America that has a sophisticated understanding of modern technology and global interdependence.[5] In
general it has been successful in focusing attention on foreign policy
and defense issues and has contributed to making governments
possessing nuclear weapons more cautious in their approach to using
them. In the wake of the Vietnam war, the American peace movement has urged the necessity to curb executive discretion in the area
of foreign policy with some success, although it is still too early to
evaluate its long-term effects. The waning of Cold War pessimism
and the military détente among the Great Powers offer some hope
that, in the age of nuclear weapons, political and military leaders
are now convinced, as they were not before 1914 and in the interwar
years, that a general war would be too uncontrollable and insuffici-
ently limited to think of it as a means of achieving any rational objective. At the same time there is still a reliance on balance-of-power
thinking,[6] and new weapons continue to be developed even though
most new weaponry no longer adds real increments to national
strength and national security.[7]

Whether the peace movement will again not be strong enough to modify traditional and outmoded concepts of national interest and national security depends in part upon factors related to the peace movements and in part upon factors related to domestic social structure and politics that influence foreign policy in ways that are incompatible with the aims of peace movements. The essays in this collection probe both sets of factors. If they suggest that we should be wary of diplomats as "an advance guard of peace," there are caveats enough concerning the shortcomings of peace movements.

II

Peace movement is a rather loose rubric under which can be brought a variety of approaches to peace, some of them contradictory in aims and methods. This diversity ranges from absolute or integral pacifism (principled opposition to war and the use of violence under any circumstances on moral and/or religious grounds) to acceptance of interstate rivalries, remaining content to mitigate conflict within the nation-state system. Grasping the nature of this diversity is the key to assessing the historical significance and influence of peace movements. Therefore, some introductory remarks on the historical problem of defining peace movements, based chiefly on data scattered throughout the individual essays, may serve to tie them together.[8]

The articles in this collection fall in four periods: 1890-1914, World War I, the interwar years, and post-World War II. In none of these periods was there a single peace movement. Rather there were several such movements or organizations, each having its own membership and cultivating the support of a particular segment of public opinion. Each movement had its own distinctive approach to peace such as pacifism, disarmament, arbitration, international organization, and world government. This diversity led to a great variety of specialized plans and proposals that belie the general view of peace movement thinking as vague. Despite some overlaps, each peace movement or organization was defined by specific social or socially related characteristics such as being composed primarily of businessmen, the working class, intellectuals and scientists, Christians, women, or students. Ideologically the values and assumptions of peace movements are pacifist, liberal, or socialist.

These separate peace movements sought to exert their influence in different ways, which serve to define them further: lobbying, education, contacts with members of governing elites, private initiatives, and dramatizing issues through mass demonstrations or direct action. The influence of any one peace organization in a peace or antiwar coalition was historically and socially conditioned. For example, the working-class leadership of the antiwar movement in Italy during World War I, discussed by James Young, was a consequence of a much stronger internationalist socialist tradition than that found among the working classes in Anglo-Saxon countries and of the weakness of the Italian middle class relative to its counterparts in America and England.[9]

Historically peace movements also have been defined with respect to a predominate issue: the arms race and imperialism before 1914, the war and war aims during World War I, the breakdown of international order and the rise of totalitarianism in the interwar years, and the introduction of nuclear weapons after 1945. Each of these issues presented the peace movement with specific choices, which must be viewed in the context of the societies in which they operated. Peace movements are, as Roger Chickering points out, political phenomena, and they have advocated more than just peace. Furthermore, they must be distinguished from other groups to gain a clearer perspective on the strengths and weaknesses of peace movements: antinational leftists before 1914, social radicals and revolutionaries from 1914 to 1918, appeasers and isolationists in the 1930s, and communists after 1945. The blurring of such distinctions, as well as the commonplace view of the peace movement as a monolith, for example, has led many historians erroneously to posit an ambiguously defined pacifism as the reason why the National Government in Great Britain did not adopt a policy of rearmament and resolute resistance to fascist aggression before 1939.[10]

The diversity of aims, methods, social composition, and ideology has made it very difficult to build and maintain a single peace or antiwar coalition. A successful antiwar coalition, as shown by Howard Weinroth, Frank Myers, and Neil and Milton Katz, is inherently neutral ideologically and oriented toward a single issue (such as ending a war or halting nuclear testing). An antiwar coalition or peace campaign attracts people whose interests are not the same, and any attempt to use such coalition as a radical force in the sense of translating immediate issues into long-range alternatives generates dissension, which threatens the unity of the coalition. The anti-Vietnam war coalition of the 1960s succeeded in obtaining public support because of its ideological neutrality, but its ideological neutrality restricted its vision of peace to the achievement of the specific issue of ending American involvement in the war.[11]

The restricted scope of peace campaigns and antiwar coalitions is, in large measure, a consequence of the fact that the middle class, with which the rise of politically oriented peace movements in the nineteenth century is associated, is itself fragmented along religious and occupational lines. The split within the middle class has placed a premium on narrowly defined issues as a way of unifying diverse interests and has led to a preference for moral and humanitarian issues as opposed to domestic economic ones. The divergent interests of the middle class, as well as the markedly socially conservative orientation of the financial and industrial upper-middle class, also has implications for strategy. Most middle-class antiwar movements have been reluctant to engage in nonlegal methods of protest or to encourage mass movements, both of which have ideological implications of a radical, even revolutionary, kind in the eyes of many members of the middle and upper-middle class. The American upper-middle-class peace advocates in Michael Lutzker's article were more frightened by strong Socialist party statements against war with Mexico in April 1914 than they were by the prospects of war. In addition, their concern with respectability impaired their effectiveness. Similarly, by 1938, the middle-class led League of Nations Union in Great Britain was beginning to look a bit foolish because of its desire for respectability and its unwillingness to antagonize the government by recognizing and openly challenging government policies that conflicted with the League of Nations and collective security.[12] The articles suggest that the effectiveness of a peace movement depends on its willingness to oppose its own government and face the consequences. Few peace movements have passed that test, but in mitigation it should be said that the personal and political risks of that kind of opposition often are considerable.

One of the central themes of the essays is the failure of peace and antiwar coalitions since World War I to attract massive and consistent support within the working class and trade unions. Before World War I, the Socialist International was an outspoken and energetic antiwar organization with a mass following.[13] David Sumler's essay shows how effective the socialist working-class peace movement could be, but it also points out, as does the essay by Howard Weinroth, the close connection between working-class antiwar activity and its socioeconomic concerns. The war led to a fragmentation of the working class on the one hand and, on the other, the Bolshevik revolution, the social tensions of postwar reconstruction, and the rise of communist parties outside the Soviet Union frightened bourgeois peace advocates and made cooperation between bourgeois and working-class peace movements nearly impossible. A large part of the problem had to do with the socially conservative nature of the middle class, which was reflected in the tendency of most middle-class peace movements to avoid explicitly working-class issues. Although the working class, especially in England and America, is now largely deradicalized, it is still concerned with traditional demands centering around economic security and trade union issues. Clearly, if peace or antiwar coalitions are to develop a base of protest beyond the middle class, which they must do if they are to become strong enough to modify national policy and behavior, they must address domestic economic issues at the point where they intersect with peace issues. This strategy, however, is hindered not only by the fragmentation of the middle class but by the fact that the satisfaction of working-class desires requires a reconciliation of interests within the state. In this sense, the problem of peace movements and their dilemmas are those of society as a whole.

Although it is true that World War I is the central reference point for contemporary peace research, the failure of antiwar coalitions to attract significant working-class support may be traced back to the prewar period. In the mid-nineteenth century, middle-class liberals and radicals argued that lasting peace among nations could be achieved only by drastically transforming society along democratic lines,[14] but by the end of the century, the influential upper-middle class peace movement shifted the emphasis away from a connection between peace and internal composition of states. The argument linking peace with democratic social and political reform passed over into the socialist peace movement. Liberal internationalists in such prestigious organizations as the Interparliamentary Union, the Institute of International Law, and the Carnegie Endowment for International Peace maintained that peace could be attained through creating international legal forms for resolving disputes without war rather than through internal reform and arms limitation. The liberal internationalists did not deny that armaments constituted socially unproductive expenditures by governments that undermined domestic stability, but they assigned a higher priority to their international, legal, and organizational schemes, such as the Permanent Court of Arbitration at the Hague created in 1899 and the League of Nations and World Court created after World War I.[15]

Furthermore, even before World War I, the concern of the middle-class peace movement for respectability and moderation, rooted in a mixture of social class and political considerations, led to efforts on the part of middle-class peace advocates to distinguish their peace movement from that of the socialists. Thus an alliance with the socialist peace movement was difficult. The attitude of middle-class peace advocates toward socialists is revealed candidly in a letter from Alfred Fried to Heinrich Lammasch, a well-known Austrian advocate of international arbitration. Fried, also an Austrian, who was awarded the Nobel Peace Prize in 1911, wrote to Lammasch in February 1914 inviting him to become president of the twenty-first World Peace Congress scheduled to meet in Vienna in September. According to Fried, the congress not only would provide an opportunity to extol the peace work of Emperor Francis Joseph but it also would provide an opportunity to demonstrate the gulf that existed between it and the socialists. Fried wrote:

Precisely the fact that the International Socialist Congress meets just fourteen days earlier and will concern itself with the arbitration and disarmament questions—although with very different inclination from that of ours—will enhance the importance of the [World Peace] Congress for internal politics since it will provide an opportunity to expound the serious work of scientific and moderate pacifism as against Socialist endeavors.[16]

On those grounds, middle- and upper-middle-class antiwar advocates eschewed radical demands for a cessation of armaments and abolition of war because they "made a very bad impression on the diplomats of the old school which caused them to reject what was reasonable and attainable."[17]

10   SOLOMON WANK

The moderation of middle-class antiwar advocates gained them the
ear of diplomats and government officials. What they failed to see,
however, was that what "the diplomats of the old school" considered
"reasonable and attainable" had little effect on national sovereignty
and war and posed no threat to individuals and social groups, including some upper-middle-class antiwar advocates, whose power and
prestige were tied to high levels of military expenditures.[18] Governments, therefore, could make concessions that were hailed as victories by some peace advocates. Class and status attitudes also contributed, and still do, to the gap between the middle-class peace movement and the working class. Middle-class peace advocates have had
difficulty understanding the concerns of the working class. Class
distinctions and biases generally have made bourgeois peace advocates
feel uncomfortable with socialist and working-class spokesmen, who
in turn have resented the elitism and paternalism of the middle-class
peace movement.[19]

Another theme of the essays is the inconsistent and contradictory
usages of *pacifism* and *pacifist*. Before 1914, *pacifism* referred to the
general advocacy of peace and internationalism, which usually
meant minimizing the unilateral use of force. Very few of those who
are labeled pacifists really were pacifists in the absolute or integral
sense of religiously or morally based opposition to war and violence
under any circumstances. Pacifism before World War I was for the
most part a quietistic and passive faith held by members of certain
religious groups, such as Quakers, Methodists, Mennonites, and
Baptists.[20] If politically active at all, pacifists usually were associated
with the middle-class peace movement (such as English Quakers
who were associated with the antiwar wing of the Liberal party).[21]

The modern distinction between pacifist and nonpacifist peace
movements arose out of the experience of the peace movement in
World War I. The main body of prewar middle-class and socialist
antiwar movements either supported the war or did not openly
oppose it. The prowar peace advocates, especially liberal internationalists, were careful to distinguish themselves from those who
adhered to a strict pacifist refusal to fight or to cooperate in any
way in the waging of the war. After the war, the pacifist and internationalist peace movements developed along independent lines,
sometimes cooperating and sometimes conflicting. There also was a

considerable amount of ideological and political conflict between pacifists, socialists, and communists as a Ghandian perspective began to confront the Marxist perspective.[22] In the interwar years, pacifists tried to hammer out a coherent pacifist world vision. The process, as Thomas Kennedy's article shows, was a complex and painful one marked by internal dissension and disarray in the confrontation with fascism. In its evolution since 1920, pacifism has shed its quietistic and passive character and has joined its faith in peace and love with the quest for social justice. This vision of peace is more positive than the earlier, negative definition of peace as the absence of war. In the 1930s, pacifists began to experiment with nonviolent means of action involving nonviolent civil disobedience as a way of overcoming pacifism's objective political powerlessness in urging antiwar measures and bringing about social change. Nonviolent civil disobedience was further developed by conscientious objectors in prisons and Civilian Public Service camps during World War II as a means of protesting against poor conditions in those institutions and the deprivation of personal and civil rights. As the article by Neil and Milton Katz shows, nonviolent civil disobedience became an important ingredient in post-1945 peace movements, as well as a protest strategy going beyond the peace movement.

Although it is legitimate to use the terms *pacifist* and *pacifism* as they were used in a specific historical context, historians should make it clear that the terms mean something other than absolute or integral pacifism. Pacifists themselves were inconsistent in their opposition to war and the use of force; for example, during the 1930s the quest for social justice in the face of fascism led many pacifists to break with absolute pacifism and support, among other things, collective security under the League of Nations and the loyalist cause in the Spanish Civil War. Terms such as *peace advocate* or *antiwar advocate* may be more appropriate than *pacifist* for persons who are not pacifists but who promote ideas and publicly manifest a concern for eliminating, avoiding, or minimizing the use of unilateral force in the relations between states. Naturally, pacifists would be counted among peace advocates, but great care must be taken to distinguish between pacifists and other peace advocates on the one hand and, on the other, individuals and groups who may be opposed to a specific war or may support some arms limitation without being peace advocates, let alone pacifists, in any true sense of those descriptions.

A similar clarification is needed on internationalism. On the whole, most peace movements have accepted nation-states as the basic units of international relations and have worked for cooperation within the nation-state system. Although it is not clearly spoken, the internationalism of most active peace advocates involves at the very least the rejection of the idea of absolute national sovereignty in the sense of a willingness to yield a portion of national sovereignty to an international organization. Some peace advocates would even subordinate national power to the larger needs of the world community. By the above criteria, the internationalism of many political and military leaders and diplomats may be seen as a disguised way of pursuing narrow class and/or national interests and needs. This may be said of those State Department officials in Charles DeBenedetti's article, who in the 1920s were pursuing an early version of a Pax Americana under the banner of internationalism and those who, after 1945, saw the international arena as a place in which American institutions could expand and prosper.[23] From this perspective, the internationalism of multinational corporations and the potential for peace that they offer must be critically examined.[24] More recently, some peace advocates have begun to distinguish between internationalism and transnationalism or supranationalism. The former continues to imply acceptance of the nation-state system and national sovereignty, and the latter implies a belief in and a commitment to values and communities of interest that transcend the system.[25]

III

Several of the essays on foreign policy challenge conventional assumptions about international politics. For example, there is a general tendency to attribute international tensions in the twentieth century to the psychological force of nationalism. There is no denying that nationalism is a real phenomenon, but we must guard against taking it for granted as an independent variable, as diplomatic historians often do. James Young demonstrates that the Italian government entered World War I in May 1915 despite the overwhelming opposition of the Italian population. Clearly, there was no surrender in that case to a surge of nationalism in the sense of mass opinion.

Michael Lutzker's essay shows that, far from governments being forced by nationalistic pressures to do or not to do something, nationalistic pressures may be generated by government policies and actions. Lutzker examines how President Woodrow Wilson first created public opinion in favor of war with Mexico in April 1914 and then dampened it when he decided to avert war. These examples, along with those contained in other essays, reveal the domination of foreign policy by executive organs of the state, even in countries with well-developed deliberative bodies such as the United States and England.

The executive domination of foreign policy calls attention to the close connection between domestic and foreign politics, as well as the existence of ideological factors conditioning foreign policy preferences on the part of elite decision makers. Several of the essays, particularly those dealing with the period before 1914, show how unrealistic it is to separate domestic social and political issues from foreign policy and military issues.[26] The situation before 1914 is paradigmatic of how domestic political suppositions and international constellations are interwoven.

By the beginning of the twentieth century, state and society in Europe and America were caught up in intense and disruptive social conflicts generated by the rapid, continuous, and uneven economic growth of the previous fifty years. The formation of mass political parties during the depression of 1873-96 and the push toward democracy and urbanization raised fears of revolution and loss of power among dominant social classes and governing elites. The latter came under pressure from various social groups and interests to make far-reaching social and political reforms, if not to recast the entire society. As domestic tensions increased, especially in European countries where industrialism was taking place within still heavily traditional sociopolitical structures (such as Austria-Hungary, Germany, and Russia) the formulation of foreign policy became heavily influenced by domestic considerations and oriented toward domestic purposes. Insecure governing elites, particularly in Central and Eastern Europe, tended to project domestic tensions outward into the international arena, thereby making foreign policy objectives more diffuse and the relations between states less fluid. Governing elites became increasingly willing to turn to chauvinism, alarms about gaps in armaments, and war scares to restore national unity and defend their social power. The survival of domestic political systems became linked to economic growth as a barrier to a recurrence of domestic instability. Economic growth in turn became linked to a frantic imperialism associated with the transformation of the European state system into a global system. Diplomacy became increasingly concerned with economic questions, such as oil, arms trade, and trade routes, more so than its practitioners wanted to believe and despite the fact that diplomatic agents almost invariably saw economic questions in strategic terms. Many of the ententes and détentes of the early 1900s were founded on economic bargains.[27]

In the conflict between what Arno J. Mayer calls "the parties of order," which strove to preserve the status quo, and "the parties of movement," which pressed for reform (an interpretive framework I have used), decision making in such areas as military affairs, the formulation of foreign policy objectives, and diplomatic methods were drawn into the clash. All of these areas were traditionally considered to lie beyond partisan politics and were entrusted to professional and supposedly apolitical elites. The assumptions underlying the orientation of these "apolitical elites" also came under scrutiny: unrestricted national sovereignty, the balance of power in international relations, and the definition of national interests in terms of the amount of military power that could be displayed in relations with other states. As David Sumler shows these objectives and the foreign policy preferences derived from them were correctly seen by the parties of movement, especially the more radical wings, as supportive of the status quo. It was not war, armaments, secret diplomacy, or the balance of power that the parties of order defended but the allocation of resources and the specific internal distribution of social and political power that was rationalized and justified by the ever-present possibility of war, preparations for which constituted the paramount national interest. From this perspective, the efforts of the peace movement to bring about arms limitation, disarmament, and compulsory arbitration of international disputes threatened the internal material and ideological foundations of power and prestige of the parties of order.[28]

The above context partially explains the rapid revival of traditional concepts of national interest and national security after World

War I, the ineffectiveness of collective security under the League of Nations, and the persistence of the idea of the balance of power in the alliances and bloc politics of the post-World War II period. The deep social well-springs of the opposition to the peace movement and its objectives must be grasped in any evaluation of the issues and proposals raised by peace advocates.

In examining the actions of governing elites and foreign offices, it is important to understand that their fundamental opposition to peace and antiwar movements does not preclude opposition to war and additional armaments under certain conditions. The articles by James Young, Charles DeBenedetti, and Solomon Wank present cases of just that kind of opposition to war. However, if we are not to be misled, we must distinguish between opposition to a specific war or support for token arms limitation and arbitration proposals based on traditional controlling concepts of national interest and national security and a principled opposition to war and armaments that rejects those assumptions. Further, there is a considerable difference between the desire to preserve peace in the sense of preserving the established inequitable domestic and international order and making the peace in the sense of linking peace with social justice on the national and international level.

In essence, we already glimpse our present situation in the one that existed before 1914. This is true in the sense in which several political observers see the emergence of "low" politics, connoting a concern with the "less gaudy, but no less vital concern with monetary reform, population growth, energy, food and raw materials," as eclipsing "high" politics, which refers to "the grand game of balance of power diplomacy and interstate rivalry."[29] It is also true in the sense of the problems of low politics being out of reach of conventional diplomacy because they are an outgrowth of domestic politics of nation states. Indeed, low politics—involving numerous international agencies and their bureaucracies, such as the United Nations, the Common Market, the International Monetary Fund, and the organization of oil exporting countries (OPEC)—resembles more the constant manuvering and coalition building of domestic politics than it does conventional diplomacy.[30]

The failure of past efforts by peace movements to prevent war has not stemmed solely from their structural weaknesses or the inadequacies of their proposals. On the contrary, their major proposals and analyses have exposed the paradox of the twentieth century: continued mobilization of nation-states with ever-increasing armaments and psychological mobilization toward war on the one hand, and, on the other, as pointed out by peace advocate Norman Angell before World War I, the dependence of the welfare and prosperity of each nation upon common interaction, particularly in trade, finances, science, and technology.[31] Political leaders, military leaders, and diplomats before and after World War I, more or less blinded by domestic political anxieties and narrow national interests, failed to grasp the enormous destructive power accumulated by each Great Power. They may be accused of irresponsibility in not thinking through the consequences of modern technology and economic interdependence.

Today political and military leaders and diplomats are once again at the crossroads of responsibility and irresponsibility. The emergence of an international community that would put an end to world conflict is dependent on the reconciliation of national interests. A reconciliation of national interests is dependent, to a significant degree, upon the reconciliation of interests within states. In this regard we would do well to recall Jean-Jacques Rousseau's insight that international conflict is a safeguard for tyrants. They are secure when world peace is insecure.[32] The way is open to significant reductions in armaments and to alternative definitions of national strength in nonmenacing terms such as fulfilling societal needs and conserving valuable resources. A nation that projects that kind of strength would be able to cooperate confidently in the international arena in the interest of creating a just world order.[33] Even partial success along these lines would require drastic changes in domestic and foreign policies for which leaders and citizens must be educated. Peace movements, for all of their shortcomings, have been and still are the main agents in sensitizing leaders and citizens to explore and evaluate assumptions and foreign policy preferences different from those that have led to war in the past.[34]

NOTES

1. Lewis Einstein, "The United States and the Anglo-German Rivalry," *National Review* 60 (January 1913):736-41 in *Theory and Practice of the Balance of Power,*

1486-1914, ed. Moorhead Wright (Totowa, N.J., 1975), 128-34. The quotation appears on p. 130.

2. This description from an editorial in the British antiwar journal *Nation*, January 20, 1912, is quoted in Howard Weinroth, "The British Radicals and the Balance of Power, 1902-1914," *The Historical Journal* 13, no. 4 (1970):677.

3. For a summary of balance-of-power "rules," see Morton A. Kaplan, "Balance of Power, Bipolarity and Other Models of International Systems," *American Political Science Review* 51 (September 1957):686-87. For the multiplicity of balance-of-power meanings, see Martin Wight, "The Balance of Power," in Herbert Butterfield and Martin Wight, eds., *Diplomatic Investigations: Essays in the Theory of International Politics* (London, 1966), 149-75. For critiques of the balance of power, see Robert L. Rothstein, "On the Costs of Realism," *Political Science Quarterly* 87, no. 3 (September 1972):347-62, and Lancelot L. Farrar, Jr., "Importance of Omnipotence: The Paralysis of the European Great Power System, 1871-1914," *International Review of History and Political Science* 9, no. 1 (February 1972):13-44. For a recent study that disproves the deterrence theory that military strength reduces the probability of war, see R. Naroll, V. L. Bullough, and F. Naroll, *Military Deterrence in History: A Pilot Cross-Historical Survey* (Albany, N.Y., 1974).

4. Sandi Cooper, "Liberal Internationalists before World War I," *Peace and Change: A Journal of Peace Research* 1, no. 2 (Spring 1973):11-19. See p. 11.

5. Numerous articles in leading peace journals such as *Peace and Change* and *Journal of Peace Research* attest this. See, for example, Ernest J. Vanarella, "The 'Technological Imperative' and the Strategic Arms Race," *Peace and Change* 3, no. 1 (Spring 1975):3-16, and Lloyd J. Dumas, "Thirty Years of the Arms Race: The Deterioration of Economic Strength and Military Security," ibid. 4, no. 2 (Spring 1977): 3-9.

6. According to former Secretary of State Henry Kissinger, the most renowned latter-day representative of this kind of thinking, "If recourse to force has in fact become impossible, diplomacy too may lose its efficacy. Far from leading to a resolution of tensions, the inability to use force may perpetuate all disputes however trivial. . . . [In] a society of 'sovereign states' a power can in the last resort vindicate its interpretation of justice or defend its 'vital interest' only by the willingness to employ force." Quoted in Leslie Gelb, "The Kissinger Substance: Power Permits Diplomacy," *New York Times,* April 20, 1975, 17. Kissinger's defense of the unilateral use of force really applies only to the Great Powers and an international order which they legitimize. It might be noted that the use of force has not been precluded by peace advocates. Its use in the context of collective security associated with international organizations has been part of the thinking of peace advocates for a long time.

7. In addition to Vanarella, " 'Technological Imperative,' " and Dumas, "Thirty Years," see Lloyd J. Dumas, "National Insecurity in the Nuclear Age," *Bulletin of the Atomic Scientists* 32, no. 5(May 1976):24-35.

8. I also have relied on Charles Chatfield, ed., *Peace Movements in America* (New York, 1973), which may serve as a companion volume to *Doves and Diplomats*. Chatfield's introduction offers a survey of the history of American peace movements, which also casts light on their European counterparts.

9. For a structural analysis of this kind, see Frank E. Myers, "Dilemmas in the

British Peace Movement since World War II,'' *Journal of Peace Research* 6 (March 1973):81-90.

10. Donald Birn, "A Peace Movement Divided: Pacifism and Internationalism in Interwar Britain,'' *Peace and Change* 1, no. 2 (Spring 1973):20-24.

11. See Charles Chatfield, "Peace Research in History: The Ecology of Choice,'' *Peace and Change* 2, no. 2 (Summer 1974):4-6. In addition to some trenchant analysis of the anti-Vietnam war coalition, Chatfield offers some valuable general insights into the strengths and weaknesses of peace movements and the thinking of officials who supported and managed the war.

12. Birn, "Peace Movement,'' 23.

13. On the antiwar activities of the Socialist International, see Georges Haupt, *Socialism and the Great War: The Collapse of the Second International* (Oxford, England, 1972), 11-29, 79-82, and passim.

14. A. C. F. Beales, *The History of Peace: A Short Account of the Organized Movement for International Peace* (New York, 1931), 119-29.

15. On the liberal internationalists, in addition to several articles in this collection and Chatfield, *Peace Movements,* see the following: Cooper, "Liberal Internationalists"; Birn, "Peace Movement"; Michael Lutzker, "The Formation of the Carnegie Endowment for International Peace: A Study of the Establishment-Centered Peace Movement 1910-1914," in Jerry Israel, ed., *Building the Organizational Society* (New York, 1972), 143-61; and Michael Lutzker, "The Pacifist as Militarist; A Critique of the American Peace Movement, 1898-1914," *Societas* 5, no. 2 (Spring 1975): 87-104.

16. Alfred Hermann Fried to Heinrich Lammasch, February 22, 1914, in Stephan Verosta, *Theorie und Realität von Bündnissen: Heinrich Lammasch, Karl Renner und der Zweibund (1897-1914)* (Vienna, 1971), 636-37. On Fried and Lammasch, see the essays by Richard R. Laurence, Roger Chickering, and Solomon Wank in this anthology. See also Cooper, "Liberal Internationalists," 18.

17. Verosta, *Theorie und Realität von Bündnissen,* 3.

18. See Howard Weinroth, "Left-Wing Opposition to Naval Armaments before 1914," *Journal of Contemporary History* 6, no. 4 (1971): 116.

19. Ibid., 98, and A. J. A. Morris, "The English Radicals' Campaign for Disarmament and the Hague Peace Conference of 1907," *Journal of Modern History* 43, no. 3 (September 1971): 377.

20. On pacifism, see the trilogy by Peter Brock: *Pacifism in the United States: from the Colonial Era to the First World War* (Princeton, 1968), *Pacifism in Europe to 1914* (Princeton, 1972), and *Twentieth Century Pacifism* (New York 1970). See also Charles Chatfield, "Pacifism," in Alexander De Conde, *Dictionary of Foreign Relations* (forthcoming).

21. See A. J. Morris, *Radicalism against War, 1906-1914: The Advocacy of Peace and Retrenchment* (Totowa, N.J., 1972), passim.

22. For an early example of the confrontation between the Ghandian and Marxist perspectives, see David James Fisher, "The Rolland-Barbusse Debate," *Survey* no. 2/3 (91/92) (Spring-Summer 1974):121-59. Romain Rolland, the well-known French writer, was a pacifist intellectual and one of the earliest popularizers of Ghandi's ideas on the Continent; Henry Barbusse was a French communist intellectual.

23. On the various meanings of internationalism, see "Internationalism as a Current in the Peace Movement: A Symposium" in Chatfield, *Peace Movements,* 171-91. See also Roger W. Moorhus, "Three Varieties of European Socialist Internationalism before the First World War; Nieuwenhuis, Kautsky and Radek," *Peace and Change* 2, no. 1 (Spring 1974):36-41.

24. See Dennis Ray, "Pax Corporata: The Peace and Conflict Potential of Multinational Corporations," *Peace and Change* 2, no. 1 (Fall 1974):17-26. See also the published papers of the Fourth Biennial Conference of the Conference on Peace Research in History, August 30-September 1, 1974: "Toward a Historical Understanding of the Multinational Corporation," *Peace and Change* 3, no. 4 (Spring 1976), and 4, no. 1 (Fall 1976).

25. See Chatfield, ed., *Peace Movements,* xxviii-xxix.

26. In this regard, the reflections of W. W. Rostow, the economic historian, on his government experience as a "hawkish" adviser to President Lyndon B. Johnson during the Vietnam war are interesting: "And if there is anything I have to contribute from my experience as a public servant it is that such abstraction [of domestic from foreign politics] is unreal. Almost every chief of government I have heard speaking in private related instinctively and directly his foreign policy and military dispositions to his domestic political situation and problems." See Walt Whitman Rostow, *Politics and the Stages of Growth* (Cambridge, England, 1971), 354. For a useful discussion of the theoretical and methodological underpinnings of a structural analysis of foreign policy on the basis of large-scale economic factors, social forces, and domestic politics, as well as the debate among historians over that kind of analysis, see Hans Ulrich Wehler, "Moderne Politikgeschichte oder 'grosse Politik der Kabinett?' " *Geschichte und Gesellschaft* 1, no. 2/3 (1975):344-69.

27. In addition to several essays in this anthology, see Hans Rosenberg, *Grosse Depression und Bismarckzeit; Wirtschaftsablauf, Gesellschaft und Politik in Mitteleuropa* (Berlin, 1967). See 258-73 for the specific formulation of the link between economic fluctuation, domestic politics, and foreign policy. An early formulation of Rosenberg's hypothesis is found in "Political and Social Consequences of the Great Depression of 1873-1896 in Central Europe, 1873-1896," *Economic History Review* 13 (1943):58-73. See also Hans Ulrich Wehler, "Bismarck's Imperialism 1862-1890," *Past and Present* 48 (1970):119-155, and Solomon Wank, "Foreign Policy and the Nationality Problem in Austria-Hungary, 1867-1914," *Austrian History Yearbook* 3, pt. 3 (1967):37-56. The articles by Rosenberg and Wehler have been reprinted in James J. Sheehan, ed., *Imperial Germany* (New York, 1976).

28. In addition to the literature cited in the essay by Solomon Wank, see Arno J. Mayer, *Wilson vs. Lenin: Political Origins of the New Diplomacy, 1917-1918* (Cleveland, 1964), 1-14, and his *Dynamics of Counterrevolution in Europe, 1870-1956* (New York, 1971), esp. chap. 6, "Internal Causes and Purposes of War in Europe, 1870-1956." See also Robert J. Scally, *The Origins of the Lloyd George Coalition: The Politics of Social Imperialism, 1900-1918* (Princeton, 1975).

29. These definitions of "high" and "low" politics, originally made by Raymond Aron, are found in James Chace's review of George W. Ball, *Diplomacy for a Crowded World* in *New York Times Book Review,* July 11, 1976.

30. For some suggestive comments along these lines and on the imperative need to create a world order, see Stanley Hoffmann, "Toward World Order," *The New Republic,* March 19, 1977, 10-12.

31. Norman Angell, *The Great Illusion: A Study of the Relations of Military Power in Nations to their Economic and Social Advantages* (London, 1911). For a more recent statement of the paradox see Barbara Ward, *Spaceship Earth* (New York, 1966), esp. 141.

32. For Rousseau's views on international relations, see Stanley Hoffman, "Rousseau on War and Peace," in *The State of War: Essays on the Theory and Practice of International Politics* (New York, 1966), 54-87.

33. The eminent philosopher and sociologist George H. Mead discussed this kind of national strength in an article written in the 1920s that is still valuable. See his "National-Mindedness and International-Mindedness," in Andrew J. Reck, ed., *Selected Writings of George H. Mead* (Indianapolis, 1964), 355-70.

34. For brief discussions of some of these alternative assumptions and foreign policy preferences see Charles Chatfield, "Peace Research Is History: The Ecology of Choice," *Peace and Change* 2, no. 1 (Spring 1974):56-58.

2
The Peace Movement in Austria, 1867-1914

RICHARD R. LAURENCE

A survey of the efforts made over the years 1867-1914 to initiate and sustain a peace movement in Austria uncovers two broad categories of thought and action. First, there were those, such as the Liberals and the Marxist Social Democrats, who chose to work within the established parliamentary process to change the domestic and international conditions they felt were responsible for militarism and war. Second, there were others, such as Bertha von Suttner, Alfred Hermann Fried, and the Austrian Peace Society, who, lacking a political base or effective political organization, sought to achieve their goals by remaining outside politics and exerting moral pressure on the institutions of Austrian and European society. Some, such as the international jurist Heinrich Lammasch, were active in both categories. Each of these individuals and groups represented different socioeconomic strata, and all operated on the basis of their characteristic perceptions of the problem and the reforms they felt were necessary to achieve peace.[1]

From the outset all sections of the Austrian peace movement labored under extensive restrictions placed by the government on their political and civil liberties. This meant that effective pacifistic agitation was very difficult to organize, even for groups that were otherwise quite conventional and in no way subversive or politically radical. These restrictions derived from the fact that the Austro-Hungarian compromise, or Ausgleich, of 1867 had left the old system of monarchical absolutism essentially intact. Even though the

Crown made certain democratic concessions, such as the introduction of a constitution establishing a limited form of parliamentary
government in both the Austrian and the Hungarian halves of the
monarchy, it never relinquished control of its fundamental prerogatives, above all, those of determining the military and foreign policy
of the empire. Any challenge to these the Crown would not tolerate.

The Austrian Parliament was thus restricted by the 1867 Constitution to determining essentially domestic matters.[2] The only way
the Parliament could affect military policy was by voting, or refusing to vote, military credits and numbers of recruits, their length of
obligatory service, and the jurisdictional range of military courts.[3]
The internal procedures and organization of the army were never
subject to parliamentary law. Paragraph 14 of the 1867 Constitution,
moreover, provided the Crown a way around any serious parliamentary difficulty, for all the emperor needed to do in the event of
an impasse was declare a national emergency to exist and proceed
to rule by decree, entirely without Parliament.[4] As to foreign policy,
the major decisions were simply presented to the Parliament as faits
accomplis.[5]

Neither did the post-1867 constitutional system accord Austrian
citizens a generous latitude of personal liberty. True, a bill of rights
was included, which granted all citizens equality before the law,
the right to a jury trial, and basic liberties, such as freedom of speech,
press, assembly, and religion.[6] Yet a closer examination of the Constitution and its ancillary legislation reveals that all of these civil
rights and liberties, so generous in principle, were in fact very closely
circumscribed by the authority of the Crown and its bureaucracy.[7]
Administrative officials, for example, could refuse to charter, or
they could disband, organizations they considered "illegal or subversive."[8] This included any group—political, religious, or other—
whose members violated, or threatened to violate, the penal code or
other laws, including those pertaining to the military obligation.[9] In
like manner, officials enjoyed vast authority of censorship over the
press, being empowered to delete, confiscate, or prevent publication of any material they deemed unlawful or dangerous to the state.[10]
Though there was redress in the courts against abuse of bureaucratic
fiat, it was in practice very difficult to prosecute a successful case
against the government,[11] and there was no judicial review of the
constitutionality of the laws themselves.

None of Austria's laws made provision for an individual's right to refuse military or war-related service, and conscientious objectors were treated as common criminals, a fact that served to keep their number at an absolute minimum. Stefan Zweig, an Austrian of pacifist sentiment who grappled with the agony of living under a system whose harsh statutes violated his deepest moral sense, recalled in his autobiography:

It struck me as a criminal anachronism to let myself be trained in the implements of murder in the twentieth century. The right thing for a man of my convictions would have been to declare myself a conscientious objector, a course which in Austria invited the heaviest punishments imaginable and would have demanded a martyr's steadfastness of soul.[12]

By such means of intimidation, every pacifistic or antimilitarist organization in Austria was kept under constant scrutiny and control by the state authorities. Any association that wished to exist legally and not be treated as subversive or conspiratorial had to knuckle under to the authorities and forswear all forms of agitation that might be construed as "illegal or subversive." This was a heavy price to pay, but it was in the end paid by the Liberals, the Social Democrats, and the Austrian Peace Society, groups that constituted the principal forces in the Austrian peace movement. It helps to explain, at least in part, why their actions proved ineffective in the long run. In exchange for the right to exist as legal entities, they had to renounce all radical activity against the state and its war-making system whose thoroughgoing reformation they regarded as a necessary precondition to the peace they sought so fervently.

To have changed these basic facts of the Habsburg system would doubtlessly have required a revolution more determined and more painful than those of 1848-49. Yet revolution in itself would have been no guarantee that a new regime would be any less warlike than the one it replaced. In any event, all of the Austrian peace groups forswore revolution as the means to their end and elected to work either through the existing political processes or through the medium of the public print to bring about the goals that they envisaged.

The earliest group to come forth as a spokesman against the dangers of war and armaments was the Austrian Liberal party. In social background it represented the propertied and well-educated German upper bourgeoisie, particularly those whose prosperity derived from industry, finance, and the learned professions. Though its members were by no means principled opponents of war as such, they did resent imperial absolutism and their own exclusion from the innermost decision-making circles of the monarchy, to which they believed that they, by virtue of their economic and educational achievements, rightly belonged. Nowhere were the evils of monarchical absolutism more bitterly obvious to the Liberals than in the military system, whose inner workings and privileged status they had no legal power to affect.

There were other grounds as well for the Liberals' antimilitarism. Many of them opposed the Crown's imperialistic adventures, such as the acquisition and military occupation of Bosnia-Herzegovina in 1878. They feared that the incorporation of more non-Germanic peoples into the monarchy would threaten German hegemony.[13] They also feared that extravagant adventures of this kind, coupled as they had to be with the maintenance of hugh armies, would overextend state finances and lead to bankruptcy at home. Since economic prosperity and financial gain constituted the basic principle of society for the Liberals, many voiced fundamental opposition to the politics of prestige conducted by their dynastic Great Power state.[14] The economic materialism basic to their weltanschauung tended thus to dictate their rather doctrinaire attitudes on most political issues. Since war and military spending could be bad for the economic health of nations, many Liberals professed to oppose both.

For such reasons the military budget became the target of repeated Liberal diatribes, especially during the 1860s and 1870s before the great arms race had gotten fully underway.[15] It was, in fact, the Liberals, or rather some of them, who introduced the peace movement as such to Austria.[16] Taking their inspiration from English Liberal parliamentarians who had initiated in the late 1860s a movement for cooperative worldwide armaments reduction, Austrian Liberals soon followed suit.[17] As early as 1875 Adolph Fischhof, a Liberal deputy in Parliament published a series of articles in Vienna's influential *Neue Freie Presse,* which were later reprinted in a pamphlet, *Zur Reduction der continentalen Heere.* In this work, Fischhof proposed a mutual, coordinated, and proportional reduction of the armies of all European nations. "For what purpose," Fischhof asked, ". . . are these gigantic military expenditures which, maintained by all, are equally useless for all? For what purpose exists this insatiable greed for wars and weapons, this over-extension of power, which ultimately leads to exhaustion and ruin?''[18] Clearly, the answer to these rhetorical questions was that no valid purpose exists. Therefore all excessive and useless military expenditures must be opposed.

Fischhof, to be sure, was neither an opponent of war nor did he advocate unilateral disarmament. His suggested remedy for the international impasse on armaments was to propose the invocation of a series of general interparliamentary conferences from among the elected representatives of every nation that wished to attend. The purpose of these meetings would be to find ways, through discussion and coordination of government policy, to control and reduce the expenditure and manpower size of armed forces everywhere.[19]

In addition to their contribution to the inauguration of the Interparliamentary Union, which officially commenced in 1889, Fischhof and other Austrian Liberals were instrumental for nearly twenty years in keeping the Austrian military budget and number of recruits at a lower level than that desired by the emperor and the high command.[20] Though the Liberal opposition to increased armaments spending began to die out during the 1880s because of fears of war emanating from the Balkans, conclusion of the Triple Alliance, and other circumstances, Liberal antimilitarism was, along with national dissatisfaction in the empire, a major factor in curtailing military outlays. It is significant to note that ''during a period when all Europe was arming feverishly, the Austro-Hungarian military budget remained the lowest of the major powers.''[21]

Even though in Austria Liberal strength in domestic politics began to wane after the 1880s, the antimilitarist idea continued to spread in all countries. The person most responsible for initiating an organized peace movement in the Habsburg lands was Bertha von Suttner, an Austrian noblewoman of Liberal persuasion whose ideas were formatively influenced by the British pacifist Hodgson Pratt. In her memoirs Suttner recalled that from a friend she learned for the first time in 1887 that there existed in London a so-called International Arbitration and Peace Society, whose avowed purpose was to bring into existence, through the creation and organization of a favorable public opinion, an international court of arbitration, which in place of armed might would have the right to decide the outcome of international conflicts. Her reaction was one of complete amazement: "What? Such a thing really existed? The idea of international justice, the striving for abolition of war, had actually acquired shape and life? The news electrified me."[22]

The result of Suttner's enthusiasm for this idea was the publication two years later of her famous novel, *Die Waffen nieder*. "I wanted to do a service to the peace movement," she recalled, "and how could I do that better than by undertaking to write a book which would spread its ideas? . . . And so I sat down and wrote *Die Waffen nieder*."[23]

Contrary to all expectations her novel became a spectacular best seller almost overnight, was soon translated into many languages, and was sold throughout the world. Though overly sentimental and extremely contentious, this Victorian novel about the horrors of war bore one message loud and clear: exert yourself to the fullest to bring about an end to war. To the question, What must I do to effect this? Suttner answered, join your nearest peace society. Help it work to achieve its goal, which is "to move governments by the pressure of public opinion . . . to relegate their future conflicts to an international court of arbitration" and thus "to establish once and for all justice in place of brute force."[24]

These words announced the main direction of Suttner's practical program and can in effect be taken as the motto of her entire lifework as a crusader for peace. The ideas on which she based this program derived mainly from English sources and comprised essentially a mixture of liberalism and utilitarianism. She believed in basic human reasonableness and goodness and did not think war was an ineluctable given of man's condition. Wars result, Suttner believed, from human ignorance; enlighten the public and they will disappear.[25] To abolish war, goodwill and hard work are sufficient. Progress and therefore peace are irrepressible.[26]

In line with these ideas, in 1891 Suttner established the Austrian Peace Society and shortly thereafter a monthly periodical, *Die Waffen nieder,* both devoted to the effort to convince governments and public opinion of the necessity of international arbitration. Thus the peace movement in Austria, already launched by the Liberals through the governmentally sanctioned activities of the Interparliamentary Union, was now augmented by the Austrian Peace Society, whose membership consisted essentially of private citizens rather than politicians.[27]

From the very beginning Suttner sought to make the Austrian Peace Society both nonpolitical and noncontroversial: its goals were to be "purely humanitarian," devoted solely to the aim of "furthering the principle of lasting world peace."[28] To this end she sought support from all political groups and envisaged a massive public response based not on partisan politics but exclusively on the desire in everyone's heart for peace.

The support she sought was never forthcoming, for, among other reasons, the social base of her movement was much too narrow to elicit a broad response. The membership of the Austrian Peace Society derived mainly from a thin stratum of the upper bourgeoisie and liberal aristocracy, as a glance at the names of its executive committee will serve to indicate.[29] Bankers and factory owners, lawyers and writers, university professors and certain aristocratic notables were preeminent in the leadership of the society, and their outlook and politics were scarcely representative of the aspirations of either the ruling elite or the broader masses. Suttner and her colleagues did achieve some success in enlisting members of the Habsburg ruling elite as honorary sponsors of various peace-movement projects, but most of this support was only pro forma.[30] On the whole Austria's ruling classes preferred to rely on traditional power politics rather than on arbitration and disarmament to keep the peace.

In her effort, moreover, to make her program palatable to everybody, Suttner made it so bland that it appealed to virtually nobody. Except for a few people from the Liberal party, now falling rapidly into political oblivion, Suttner's movement gained the support of no major political grouping in Austria: neither the Christian Social party, nor the Social Democrats, nor any of the nationalist parties. All had political goals their members viewed as more important than international arbitration; Suttner's program, however, made no place for the realization of any partisan aspirations. "We have nothing against working for the improvement of political and economic conditions," she wrote, "but not on our platform. We are not here to hold a Socialist congress. . . . The establishment of world law is our only goal."[31]

Suttner's program was not based on any principle of absolute pacifism (a categorical rejection of warfare or violence). For all her desire for peace, she could not bring herself to denounce the notion of a just defensive war.[32] Nor did she or her society ever advocate refusal of military service on grounds of conscience. In this she quarreled with Tolstoy, who had criticized her whole movement for just these reasons.[33] Suttner's defense against this criticism was to reply that

peace societies who adopted this program [advocating refusal of military service] would be entirely unable to exist. Their by-laws would receive no approval from the authorities. Rather, they would fall under a very special paragraph of the law prohibiting "incitement to refusal of service." And those who followed up this exhortation would be brought before a court martial.[34]

Though Suttner was correct, her statement also reveals the limitations of her movement and the degree to which it was intimidated by the Austrian authorities and statutes.[35]

Nevertheless, Suttner persisted with unshaken determination in her efforts to prepare public opinion to accept the idea of arbitration. With the help of her industrious colleague Alfred Hermann Fried, she undertook to sponsor the founding of new peace societies throughout Austria-Hungary and Germany and sought, especially through her periodical *Die Waffen nieder*, to propagate the ideas of the peace movement. During this time she was also instrumental in persuading Alfred Nobel, the Swedish dynamite magnate for whom she had earlier worked as his private secretary, to establish a Nobel Peace Prize out of his estate.[36] She even gained an audience with Emperor Francis Joseph in 1897 and presented him with a document drawn up and signed by 170 English prelates petitioning from the heads of state of every major government in the world favorable attention to the concept of arbitration. The emperor's reaction was not enthusiastic.[37]

Such efforts and accomplishments, however praiseworthy in themselves, nevertheless embodied a strong element of political naiveté, namely, the wishful thinking that meaningful reform could be accomplished through goodwill and rational argument alone. Nowhere was the political vacuity of these dreams more harshly revealed than in the results of the Hague Conferences of 1899 and 1907.

Despite much publicity and well-wishing by the peace movement, the Hague Conference of 1889 produced little in the way of note-

worthy results, for the nations represented there effectively dodged
the two central issues of disarmament and arbitration. Although an
international court of arbitration was established for the first time
in history, no nation was obliged to submit its disputes to the court
or, if submitted, accept its decisions. The 1907 Hague Conference
was, if anything, even less willing to consider disarmament or obligatory
arbitration of international disputes, and both issues were laid to rest
by the unanimous adoption of bland noncommittal resolutions as
to the mere desirability of these goals.

The attitude of the Vienna Foreign Office was typical. In 1899
Foreign Minister Agenor von Goluchowski instructed Austria-
Hungary's delegates to the first Hague Conference that "existing
relationships do not permit any essential results to be achieved. On
the other hand, however, we ourselves would scarcely wish that anything could be achieved, at least in so far as military and political
questions are concerned."[38] As to arbitration, Goluchowski declared
that there could be no consideration of the issue of compulsory
adjudication of international disputes. However, diplomatic necessity dictated that Austria-Hungary be willing to accept a system
entailing some form of arbitration on a purely voluntary basis.[39]

The position of Austria-Hungary at the second Hague Conference was no different. Delegates were instructed, this time by Foreign
Minister Alois Lexa von Aehrenthal, that acceptance of a system of
fully obligatory arbitration was completely out of the question and
that discussion of the issue was to be strictly avoided, if at all possible.[40]
On the issue of armaments limitation, the best solution, Aehrenthal
declared, would be to dispose of it by "a platonic declaration,"
just as had been the case in 1899.[41]

Such were the stark realities that the peace movement faced at
the conclusion of the two Hague conferences. It was obvious that
the methods of Suttner and the peace societies were not equal to the
task at hand, for they had no power to compel governments to accept their ideas. Neither were their ideas themselves (at least heretofore) sufficiently persuasive, either to the ruling class or to the wider
masses. Despite the fact that new societies continued to be founded
and that Suttner kept on writing, lecturing, and organizing until her
death in June 1914, it became ever more clear that the movement
lacked élan and had, in fact, become moribund. Even Suttner, in her

private diaries, confided a pessimistic awareness of this. "For a long time already," she noted, "I have felt the Austrian Peace Society to be a misery." "All [is] slumber, lethargy, and death in the Society." "There is nothing more to be expected from our Society; an entirely new star must rise."[42]

A similar fate also overtook the government-favored branch of the Austrian peace movement, the Interparliamentary Union. In the aftermath of the two Hague conferences, it too had nothing new or significant to contribute. The spirit of the interparliamentary organization had always been liberal, and most of the deputies associated with it hailed from the Liberal party and represented its viewpoint. From about the 1880s on, however, the Liberals, who represented the German point of view in Habsburg politics, grew increasingly frightened at the specter of emergent Slavic power, both within the monarchy and without. The majority of them thus threw in their support with the Crown, including its military and foreign policy.

The politics of Ernest von Plener, one of the Liberal party's foremost spokesmen and from 1906 to 1914 leader of the Austrian interparliamentary group, illustrates this trend concisely.[43] Despite his associations with the Interparliamentary Union, Plener was an outspoken proponent of a strong military policy based on the Triple Alliance and a powerful Austro-Hungarian army.[44] The idea of "the people in arms . . . as it is in Germany" was his ideal.[45] His conception of peace was the distinctly imperialistic one of an international order dominated by German (and Austro-German) might.[46] After World War I began, Plener became one of the leading proponents in Austria of a military annexationist policy aimed at the creation of a German-controlled Central Europe.[47] His association with the peace movement as leader of Austria's chapter of the Interparliamentary Union is therefore indicative of the ambiguous, class-bound, and nationalist character of much of the peace movement in Austria during the last years before the war.

Despite the demise of the peace societies and Liberals such as Plener as effective contenders against the war-making system, new ideas were not long in coming from other quarters. One of the most impressive efforts to think through the strengths and weaknesses of the peace movement from the point of view of the realistic possibilities of arbitration was undertaken by the learned jurist and scholar,

Dr. Heinrich Lammasch.[48] Widely known in Austria and abroad for his erudition in international law, Lammasch, a distinguished professor of law at the University of Vienna, had been chosen by the Vienna Foreign Office to be its legal adviser at both Hague conferences. Among his many public honors, Dr. Lammasch was named four times to serve on the bench of the Permanent Court of Arbitration at the Hague, and there he functioned as a justice until the outbreak of World War I in 1914. Lammasch was, however, more than a detached scholar and jurist; he became Austria's most informed advocate of the idea of international arbitration.

Lammasch was unique in the Austrian peace movement because of his close ties both to leading peace advocates, such as A. H. Fried, and to the highest circles of government. As a devout Roman Catholic, a monarchist, and a moderate conservative in politics, Lammasch did not offend the old-school diplomats, who sought his judgment and his expert legal advice on questions of international law. Even Archduke Francis Ferdinand considered him a trusted adviser. Lammasch's vision of world peace was not predicated upon radical or utopian demands; instead it embraced the principles of national interest and power politics as the key factors in international relations, principles that the majority of delegates of the nations assembled at both Hague conferences agreed upon implicity.

In light of the results of the two Hague conferences, the future Lammasch saw for arbitration was the subject of his searching scholarly study, *Die Lehre von der Schiedsgerichtsbarkeit in ihrem ganzen Umfange* (1913-14), and shorter works of a similar nature. Lammasch accepted incontestably the principle that state sovereignty is the sole basis for an effective system of arbitration. "Not through their own desire, only through the exercise of their sovereignty," will arbitration of any kind ever work.[49] Therefore there can be no such thing as compulsory arbitration (except, perhaps, specific limited disputes that do not involve national honor or "vital interests"), for no powerful nation would accept such a system or abide in good faith by its verdicts.[50]

Given this assessment of the situation, what then was to be hoped for in the way of progress toward preventing wars among nations? At this question, Lammasch grew optimistic and pointed to the fact that since the establishment of the Hague Court in 1899, on whose bench he so proudly served, there had been over a hundred disputes, many of them quite bitter, successfully adjudicated before the international tribunal. This proved quite clearly, he felt, that most nations were gradually coming to realize that it was in their own self-interest to refrain from war in settling their disputes. The immediate task, therefore, was to seek firm agreements from states at the third Hague Conference, tentatively scheduled for 1915, by which the jurisdiction of the world court could be enlarged to cover disputes not now submitted.[51] Even this, to be sure, would not provide a guarantee that wars would not occur. "Not even I," Lammasch wrote, "am of the opinion that wars can be banished from the world through resolutions by societies, through acts of parliaments, or through state treaties. . . . All historical experience tells us that it will never be possible to abolish war entirely."[52]

Nevertheless, Lammasch remarked on the very eve of the war, "We may allow ourselves one sure hope: that war is becoming an extraordinary rarity."[53] Responsible statesmen were coming more and more to renounce armed conflict as an implement of state policy, he believed. To reach the goal of a safe and peaceful world required a still enormous task of civic education. The best means to that end, Lammasch concluded, was the court of arbitration itself. Only through its existence and the extension of its functions could the rational and moral capacity of states for self-limitation be demonstrated to mankind.[54] It was doubtless his firm and unshakable belief in this principle, which, together with his active Christian conscience, enabled Lammasch to withstand the war hysteria in 1914 and emerge from the earliest days of the conflict as a steadfast opponent of the war. "Let us not let all hope sink," he wrote in September 1914; the work for peace must go on, now stronger than ever.[55]

Though Lammasch was Austria's most knowledgeable expert on arbitration, it was Alfred Herman Fried who proved to be the most energetic force in the Austrian peace movement from 1899 to 1914. Fried had begun his work as a close associate of Suttner, but his career departed significantly from hers toward the end of the 1890s as he grew ever more aware of the inadequacy of Suttner's analysis of the situation and her program for reform of it. Most basically, Fried rejected Suttner's emotional approach to the problem of peace: not sentimentality (*Gefühlspazifismus*) but realpolitik, he contended,

must be the basis of an effective peace movement. Cold dispassion-
ate reason, he believed, would show man that war is bad for the
health and prosperity of nations. It is a postulate of pure reason, a
cardinal tenet of realpolitik, that the civilized nations of the world
stood only to lose from war and would therefore seek peace.[56]

To elucidate these tenets more clearly, Fried sought to create a
"science of peace" (*pazifistisch Wissenschaft*), a scholarly discipline
that would be entirely objective—"just as neutral as physics,
chemistry, or medicine."[57] It need have nothing to do with human
sympathies or antipathies, emotions or values. The practitioner of
this science would be called a *Friedenstechniker* (peace technician).[58]
When such a person, Fried argued, analyzed the condition of nation-
states dispassionately, reason would lead him to the incontrovertible
conclusion that there is only one cause of war: international anarchy.
Remove that cause and you will have removed its worst effect, which
is war.[59]

From this Fried inferred the somewhat curious corollary that it
was not necessary for a pacifist even to oppose war, for war is only
an effect, not a cause. The proper concern of pacifism, he concluded,
was not antagonism toward war as such (armies, compulsory military service, militarism, and so forth); rather, the task was to construct a workable system of world law.[60]

But how—by what methods—could such a system of world law
be realized? That, to Fried's mind, was the fundamental question.
He answered it with the words that from January 1906 became the
motto of his entire program: *"Organisiert die Welt!"* (Organize [or
unite] the world").[61] World peace would come through world government, through the creation of a superstate (*Übernation*).[62] This plan,
more concretely, called for the federation of Europe into a political
entity patterned along the lines of democratic republics like Switzerland and the United States.[63] Such a superstate, of course, would
possess armed might sufficient to enforce its laws vigorously and
with determination.

Statism was thus the dominant element in Fried's political and
moral philosophy. This stance, incidentally, put Fried at the opposite pole from Tolstoy and his followers, who saw the state as the
chief enemy of mankind and of peace.[64] Fried, however, with overtones of Hegel, praised "the state as the pinnacle of civilization" and

proclaimed, "We can say with confidence that the state, with its scientific academies, its parliaments and its universities, cannot assume the role of a criminal or highwayman."[65]

Though one can today but wince at such optimism, it was an important component of the zeitgeist of Fried's era, particularly among those in the peace movement. World peace, Fried believed, could only be synonymous with world democracy—that is, world-wide representative government on the pattern of America and the republican states of Western Europe. The solution to the problem of peace, he wrote in 1911, "rests . . . in the victory of Liberalism and democracy."[66] It was the same illusion to which Wilson and the makers of the Versailles Treaty would later fall prey.

With these ideas Fried set forth to remold the world in their image. His means to this end was the printed word. As the author of numerous books and articles and as editor and principal contributor to his bimonthly journal, *Die Friedenswarte*, which began publication in 1899, Fried succeeded in raising the ideas of the peace movement to the level of academic respectability. In Austria-Hungary and in Germany, his theories gained significant acceptance among many scholars and leading university professors.[67] In Europe and America, he was regarded as one of the leading thinkers and organizers of the entire peace movement. In recognition of his many achievements, Fried was awarded the Nobel Peace Prize in 1911.

Two essential Austrian groups, however, which Fried had hoped to win over to his ideas remained fundamentally unpersuaded: the policy-making circles of government and the Marxian Social Democrats. Though the reluctance of the former to accept Fried's remedies can be understood against a background of opposing political ideologies (such as unwillingness of the monarchical elite to share power by allowing greater "democratization," especially of the army and foreign policy), the adamant refusal of the latter requires some explanation.[68]

The Austrian Social Democratic party, formed in 1889 at the Hainfeld party congress, had from the start professed its allegiance to a strong policy against militarism. Thus paragraph 6 of the party's Hainfeld Declaration of Principles read as follows:

The cause of the continual danger of war is the standing army, whose constantly increasing burden is estranging the people from its duties to civilization. Therefore we must support a general armament of the people [*allgemeine Volksbewaffnung*] as a substitute for the standing army.[69]

Seven months later, at the first congress of the Second International at Paris, a similar resolution was adopted as an integral part of the program of the International. It held that the standing army was an instrument of the ruling class, that it was used to oppress the laboring class, that its interests were aggressive and not peaceful, that its costs were ruining the economy and thwarting necessary social legislation, and that it should be abolished and replaced by a popular militia.[70] Two years afterward at the Brussels congress, the peace program of the Second International was worked out in the basic details that were to remain in operation until World War I. Of key significance was the following section of that program: "All those who wish to abolish war have the obligation to join the international Social Democratic Party, the only party with peace as its fundamental doctrine."[71]

It was precisely this point, which the Austrian Social Democrats insisted upon dogmatically and unremittingly, that spelled the end of any cooperation between them and the nonsocialist peace groups. Although on a practical level the two movements had much in common, they were in reality separated by a wide ideological gulf reflecting both political attitudes and class resentments.[72] The Social Democrats of Austria simply regarded the movement of Fried, Suttner, and the Interparliamentarians, which they contemptuously called "bourgeois pacifism," as a tool of the capitalist-ruling class and refused to cooperate with it.

Despite continuous efforts by Fried and others to reconcile the socialists of Austria (and Germany) with the broader "bourgeois" peace movements, no success ever was achieved.[73] Even though the socialists of France, Belgium, England, Italy, and Switzerland sent delegates to the Interparliamentary Union and coordinated their agitation with bourgeois groups, the German and Austrian Social Democrats remained aloof and apart to the end.[74]

True to their revisionist Marxist principles, Austria's Social Democrats believed that the best way to peace lay through the introduction of universal suffrage into the Habsburg monarchy. This change, they thought, would place power into the hands of a proletarian majority and lead to a peaceful transformation of the monarchy.

Thus domestic social reconstruction by legal methods carried a higher priority with the party leadership and its rank and file than did the international effort at preserving world peace. More radical methods of agitation, such as the general strike or refusal of military service, were emphatically rejected.[75] When after the electoral reform of 1907 hopes in the magic power of universal suffrage proved to be illusory, the socialist program for peace turned out to be just as bankrupt as that of the bourgeois.

By 1914 all the ideas of the Austrian peace movement proved ineffective in envisaging a practical way to prevent war in general or World War I in particular. Admittedly, no very radical methods, such as widespread civil disobedience or refusal of military service, were ever advocated or tried by the peace groups and parties.[76] Among those who professed allegiance to pacifistic ideals, only the anarchists, themselves notoriously divided between those who rejected and those who glorified violence, attempted such measures, but their numbers were too small and their movement too disunified to have any but a totally negligible influence on Austrian politics.[77] In addition, the anarchist movement was so thoroughly infiltrated by the police and so harassed by them that no effectively radical program of agitation could ever be mounted.

In the end all the significant peace groups in Austria, including the Social Democrats, were assimilated into the antiquated Habsburg system they had once hoped to change. The Liberals, needing the support of the Crown against the pressures of the non-German nationalities within the empire and fearing the possibilities of foreign invasion from without, acquiesced generally in the Crown's military and foreign policy. The Social Democrats, hoping to transform the monarchy via the ballot box, renounced revolutionary agitation against the established military and political system. Independent middle-class groups, such as the Austrian Peace Society, conservative by temperament and fearful of radical social change, reconciled themselves easily to the ongoing political establishment in return for being allowed moderate freedom of speech and of the press.

All these factions thus proved vulnerable to the time-tested Habsburg policy of divide and rule. Combining the threat of severe punishment for infractions of the law with the enticement of concessions for obedience and acceptance, the Crown was successful in obtaining the political submission of all the major peace groups in Austria.

In submitting to the statutes and political order of the prevailing system, the peace groups and parties gained legality, respectability, and freedom from persecution, but these very facts vitiated their movement and allowed events to be determined by others. None of the peace advocates had the vision or the determination to take risks that might have been necessary to change, even by nonviolent methods, the rules by which the game of politics in Austria was played. No one can say what would have been the results if they had taken those risks; one can only observe what happened when they did not.

NOTES

1. For studies of the peace movement in Austria, see Albert Fuchs, *Geistige Strömungen in Österreich* (Vienna, 1949), pp. 249-275; Heinrich Lammasch, "Zur Geschichte der Friedensideen in Österreich," *Österreichische Rundschau* 51 (April 1, 1917):1-5; Solomon Wank, "Introduction" to Hans Wehberg, *Die internationale Beschränkung der Rüstungen* (1919; reprint ed., New York: Garland, 1973), pp. 5-34; and Richard R. Laurence, "The Problem of Peace and Austrian Society, 1889-1914: A Study in the Cultural Origins of the First World War" (Ph.D. diss., Stanford University, 1968).

2. Parliament's competence was spelled out constitutionally in *Reichsgesetzblatt für das Kaisertum Österreich,* Nr. 141 (Dec. 21, 1867), paragraphs 11, 12 (hereafter cited as *RGB*). Cf. Ernest C. Hellbling, *Österreichische Verfassungs-und Verwaltungsgeschichte* (Vienna, 1956), pp. 374-383.

3. *RGB,* Nr. 151 (Dec. 5, 1868). See the discussion of this statute in Edmund Bernatzik, ed., *Die österreichischen Verfassungsgesetze mit Erläuterungen,* 2d ed. (Vienna, 1911), pp. 690-691. See further Ferdinand Schmid, *Das Heeresrecht der österreichisch-ungarischen Monarchie* (Vienna and Leipzig, 1903), pp. 11-24. For the larger context, see Joseph Redlich, *Austrian War Government* (New Haven, 1929), and Gunther E. Rothenberg, *The Army of Francis Joseph* (West Lafayette, Indiana, 1976).

4. *RGB,* Nr. 141 (Dec. 21, 1867), paragraph 14. Such provisions, it should be noted in fairness, were by no means unique to Austria-Hungary. For a study of similar provisions in other countries, see Clinton Rossiter, *Constitutional Dictatorship: Crisis Government in the Modern Democracies* (1948; reprint ed., New York and Burlingame, 1963).

5. F. R. Bridge, *From Sadowa to Sarajevo: The Foreign Policy of Austria-Hungary, 1866-1914* (London and Boston, 1972), p. 10; Oscar Jászi, *The Dissolution of the Habsburg Monarchy* (1929; reprint ed., Chicago, 1961), p. 115.

6. *RGB,* Nr. 142 (Dec. 21, 1867), art. 2, 4, 5, 8, 9, 10, 11, 12, 13, 14, 17, 19, and ibid., Nr. 144 (Dec. 21, 1867), art. 9, 11.

7. Article 20 of *RGB,* Nr. 142 (Dec. 21, 1867), provided for suspension, under emergency conditions, of articles 8, 9, 10, 12, and 13 of the same statute. *RGB,* Nr. 66

(May 5, 1869), spelled out the conditions of emergency legislation pursuant to paragraph 14 of *RGB*, Nr. 141 (Dec. 21, 1867). The law of May 23, 1873, *RGB*, Nr. 120, provided for suspension of jury trial during emergency periods and *RGB*, Nr. 119 (May 23, 1873) established the legal basis for the imposition of martial law on civilians (see paragraphs 429ff.). For further details, see Alexander Koller, *Ausnahmsgesetze und Verordnungen für den Kriegsfall in der österreichisch-ungarischen Monarchie* (Vienna, 1914).

8. *RGB*, Nr. 134 (Nov. 15, 1867), paragraphs 4, 6, 12; ibid., Nr. 135 (Nov. 15, 1867).

9. Ibid., Nr. 134 (Nov. 15, 1867), paragraphs 17, 20-22, 24; ibid., Nr. 135 (Nov. 15, 1867), paragraphs 6, 13-17; ibid., Nr. 137 (June 28, 1890).

10. *Pressgesetz vom 17. December 1862, Nr. 6 RGB. für 1863,* paragraphs 3, 10, 11, 16, 19, 25, 26. This statute was later supplemented by *RGB*, Nr. 161 (June 9, 1894) and ibid., Nr. 261 (Dec. 27, 1899). See Franz Storch, "Presserecht," in Ernst Mischler and Joseph Ulbrich, eds., *Österreichisches Staatswörterbuch. Handbuch des gesamten österreichischen öffentlichen Rechtes,* 2d ed. (Vienna, 1907), 3:973-983; and Kurt Paupié, *Handbuch der österreichischen Pressegeschichte 1848-1959* (Vienna and Stuttgart, 1960), 1:1-82.

11. Henry Wickham Steed, *The Hapsburg Monarchy,* 4th ed. (London, 1919), pp. 98-105.

12. Stefan Zweig, *The World of Yesterday: An Autobiography* (New York, 1943), pp. 228-229. The relevant statute was *RGB*, Nr. 137 (June 28, 1890).

13. See William A. Jenks, *Austria under the Iron Ring, 1879-1893* (Charlottesville, Va., 1965), p. 51.

14. Georg Franz, *Liberalismus. Die deutschliberale Bewegung in der habsburgischen Monarchie* (Munich, 1955), p. 321.

15. Cf. Elfriede Jandesek, "Die Stellung des Abgeordnetenhauses der im Reichstrat vertretenen Königreiche und Länder zu Fragen des Militärs 1867-1914" (Ph.D. University of Vienna, 1964).

16. Lammasch, "Zur Geschichte der Friedensideen in Österreich," pp. 1-5; Hans Wehberg, *Die internationale Beschränkung der Rüstungen* (Stuttgart and Berlin, 1919), pp. 104-114.

17. Merze Tate, *The Disarmament Illusion: The Movement for a Limitation of Armaments to 1907* (New York, 1942), pp. 32-55. For background, see Sandi E. Cooper, "Liberal Internationalists before World War I," *Peace and Change* 1, no. 2 (Spring 1973):11-19.

18. Adolph Fischhof, *Zur Reduction der continentalen Heere. Ein Vorschlag,* vol. 1 (Vienna, 1875), p. 3.

19. Ibid., pp. 6ff. For a history of the Interparliamentary Union, see Christian Lange, et al., *The Interparliamentary Union from 1889 to 1939* (Lausanne, 1939). On Fischhof, see Richard Charmatz, *Adolf Fischhof: Das Lebensbild eines österreichischen Politikers* (Stuttgart and Berlin, 1910).

20. See Alfred von Wittlich, "Die Rüstungen Österreich-Ungarns von 1866 bis 1914," *Berliner Monatschefte* 10 (1932): 861-79; Franz, *Liberalismus,* pp. 321-22; Jenks, *Austria under the Iron Ring,* chap. 2; and Rothenberg, *Army of Francis Joseph,* p. 78.

21. Gunther E. Rothenberg, "The Habsburg Army and the Nationality Problem in the Nineteenth Century, 1815-1914," *Austrian History Yearbook* 3, pt. 1 (1967); 84.

22. Bertha von Suttner, *Memoiren* (Stuttgart and Leipzig, 1909), p. 176. Cf. A. H. Fried, *Handbuch der Friedensbewegung,* 2d ed. (Berlin and Leipzig, 1911-1913), 2:90.

23. Suttner, *Memoiren,* p. 180. The best study of Suttner is Beatrix Kempf, *Bertha von Suttner. Das Lebensbild einer grossen Frau* (Vienna, 1964).

24. Bertha von Suttner, *Die Waffen nieder: Eine Lebensgeschichte* (Dresden and Leipzig, 1892), 2:304-305.

25. Bertha von Suttner, *Inventarium einer Seele* (Leipzig, 1883), pp. 113, 177-179.

26. Ibid., pp. 69-71, 114.

27. Fuchs, *Geistige Strömungen in Österreich*, pp. 252-253.

28. Suttner, *Memoiren*, pp. 208-210.

29. A list of these names is contained in the periodical *Die Waffen nieder* 2 (1893): 424 (hereafter cited as *DWN*), and regularly thereafter in subsequent issues.

30. For example, the meeting of the Twenty-first Universal Peace Congress, scheduled to take place in Vienna from September 15-19, 1914, but never held because of the outbreak of the war, was to have had Foreign Minister Count Berchtold as its honorary president and cabinet ministers (such as Austrian Prime Minister Stürgkh, Joint Finance Minister Bilinski, and others) as members of its honorary executive committee. See report in *Die Friedenswarte* 16 (1914):158-160 (hereafter cited as *FW*), and Stefan Verosta, *Theorie und Realität von Bündnissen. Heinrich Lammasch, Karl Renner und der Zweibund 1897-1914* (Vienna, 1971), pp. 454-455.

31. *DWN*, 1, nr. 7/8 (Aug. 15, 1892):51-52.

32. Suttner, *Memoiren*, pp. 354-355. See also her article in *FW* 7 (1905):19, where she wrote that "Gewalt, bewaffnete Gewalt, ist nötig—aber nur um vor Gewalt zu schützen" (Force, armed force, is necessary, but only to protect yourself from force).

33. Leo Tolstoy, *The Kingdom of God Is within You* (1893; reprint ed., London, 1936), chap. 6.

34. *DWN* 3 (1894):310.

35. The pertinent statute was *RGB*, Nr. 137 (June 28, 1890), paragraphs 1-8. Cf. Georg Lelewer, *Die strafbaren Verletzungen der Wehrpflicht in rechtsvergleichender und rechtspolitischer Darstellung* (Vienna and Leipzig, 1907), and Suttner, *Memoiren,* pp. 520-521.

36. Suttner, *Memoiren,* pp. 270ff.; Kempf, *Bertha von Suttner,* pp. 58ff.

37. Suttner, *Memoiren,* p. 380.

38. Haus-, Hof- und Staatsarchiv, Vienna, P.Λ. X/144 (hereafter cited as HHSA).

39. Ibid.

40. HHSA, A. R. 60/67.

41. Ibid. On Aehrenthal's views, see Solomon Wank, "Varieties of Political Despair: Three Exchanges between Aehrenthal and Goluchowski, 1898-1906," in Stanley B. Winters and Joseph Held, eds., *Intellectual and Social Developments in the Habsburg Empire from Maria Teresa to World War I: Essays Dedicated to Robert A. Kann* (Boulder, Colo., 1975), pp. 203-239.

42. Bertha von Suttner, "Tagebücher," manuscript, United Nations Library, Geneva, entries of July 20, 1906, May 6, 1909, and March 11, 1913. See Kempf, *Bertha von Suttner,* pp. 92-94.

43. For Plener's account of his activities in the Interparliamentary Union, see his *Erinnerungen* (Stuttgart and Leipzig, 1921), 3:333-346.

44. Ernst Freiherr von Plener, *Reden von Dr. Ernst Freiherrn von Plener, 1873-1911* (Stuttgart and Leipzig, 1911), p. 466.

45. Ibid., p. 461.

46. See ibid., pp. 459-467, 1032-1037. Cf. Fuchs, *Geistige Strömungen,* pp. 5-17.

47. Cf. Henry C. Meyer, *Mitteleuropa in German Thought and Action, 1815-1945* (The Hague, 1955), pp. 160, 231.

48. On Lammasch, see Marga Lammasch and Hans Sperl, eds. *Heinrich Lammasch. Seine Aufzeichnungen, sein Wirken and seine Politik* (Vienna and Leipzig, 1922), and Verosta, *Theorie und Realität von Bündnissen.*

49. Heinrich Lammasch, *Die Lehre von der Schiedsgerichtsbarkeit in ihrem ganzen Umfange* (Berlin, Stuttgart, and Leipzig, 1913-1914), p. 2.

50. Ibid., p. 10; Heinrich Lammasch, *Die Rechtskraft internationaler Schiedssprüche* (Kristiania, 1913), pp. 91ff.

51. Heinrich Lammasch, *Die Fortbildung internationaler Schiedsgerichtsbarkeit* (Berlin, Stuttgart, and Leipzig, 1914), pp. 4-5.

52. Ibid., pp. 6-7.

53. Ibid., p. 7

54. Ibid.

55. *FW* 16 (1914):298-299.

56. It is noteworthy that Fried agreed completely with the ideas of Norman Angell, as expressed in the latter's book, *The Great Illusion.* See *FW* 12 (1910):61-64.

57. Ibid. 13 (1911):130.

58. Ibid. 12 (1910):8.

59. Ibid. 7 (1905):145-149.

60. Ibid., p. 147.

61. Ibid. 8 (1906):1.

63. Ibid., p. 3.

63. Ibid., pp. 1-3.

64. For Fried's views on Tolstoy, see ibid. 12 (1910):8, 221-223.

65. A. H. Fried, *Friedens-Katechismus. Ein Compendium der Friedenslehre zur Einführung in die Friedensbewegung* (Dresden, Leipzig, and Vienna, 1895), p. 57.

66. *FW* 13 (1911):220.

67. Roger Chickering, "A Voice of Moderation in Imperial Germany: The 'Verband für internationale Verständigung' 1911-1914," *Journal of Contemporary History* 8, no. 1 (January 1973):151-164. See also Roger Chickering, *Imperial Germany and a World without War: The Peace Movement and German Society, 1892-1914* (Princeton, 1975), pp. 89ff.

68. For a more complete explanation of this situation, see Laurence, "Problem of Peace," chap. 7. See also Norbert Leser, *Zwischen Reformismus und Bolschewismus. Der Austromarxismus als Theorie und Praxis* (Vienna, Frankfurt, and Zürich, 1968), esp. pp. 263-271.

69. *Verhandlungen des Parteitages der österreichischen Sozialdemokratie in Hainfeld. Abgehalten vom 30. Dezember 1888 bis 1. Jänner 1889* (Vienna, 1889), p. 4.

70. The full verbatim text of the resolution is reprinted in Ludwig Brügel, *Geschichte der österreichischen Sozialdemokratie* (Vienna, 1922-1925), 5:129-130.

71. Reprinted in ibid., p. 130.

72. Cf. Wank, "Introduction," p. 22.

73. See *FW* 2 (1900):133-135; 5 (1903):101-102; 8 (1906):151-152, 166ff.; 10 (1908): 92-93, 177-178, 203-207; 11 (1909):81-83; 13 (1911):129-132; 14 (1912):428-429; 16 (1914):228-229.

74. Cf. ibid. 8 (1906):151-152. See also Victor Adler's raillery at the bourgeois peace groups in *Protokoll der Verhandlungen des Parteitages der deutschen sozial-demokratischen Arbeiterpartei in Osterreich. Abgehalten in Wien vom 31. Oktober bis zum 4. November 1912* (Vienna, 1912), p. 114. For a fuller analysis, see Milorad M. Drachkovitch, *Les socialismes français et allemand et le problème de la guerre, 1870-1914* (Geneva, 1953).

75. See Victor Adler's speeches condemning the general strike in *Verhandlungen des vierten österreichischen sozialdemokratischen Parteitages. Abgehalten zu Wien vom 25. bis 31. März 1894* (Vienna, 1894), pp. 77-80, and in *Protokoll über die Verhandlungen des Gesamtparteitages der sozialdemokratischen Arbeiterpartei in Österreich. Abgehalten zu Wien vom 30. Oktober bis zum 2. November 1905* (Vienna, 1905), pp. 68-69, 125-132.

76. Occasionally nonpacifistic national groups, such as the Czechs and Hungarians, balked at heeding military demands. Such resistance, however, never led to the formation of a significant movement or reformation of the monarchy. See Rothenberg, "Habsburg Army," pp. 79-87.

77. For a fuller analysis of the anarchist place in the Austrian peace movement, see Laurence, "Problem of Peace," pp. 308-319.

3
Problems of a German Peace Movement, 1890-1914

ROGER CHICKERING

Peace movements are political phenomena.[1] Historically, their character, aspirations, tactics, and relative success have been vitally affected by the political milieux in which they have operated and by the social structures underlying these milieux. This is probably a truism, but it bears emphasis since many writers tend to exclude peace movements from the categories of social and political analysis customarily employed by historians in dealing with political movements. On the one hand, many pacifist commentators write as if the defining characteristic of peace movements were their communion with a higher moral truth, which would exempt them from conventional analysis. Much the same view underlies the writings of those who regard peace movements as havens for political lunatics whose activities can have no possible interest or relevance for serious social or political history. However, without minimizing the moral fervor that has animated peace movements and without overestimating the tangible successes they have enjoyed, one may safely reject as unhistorical any attempt to define unique categories for analyzing their history.

Perhaps no less obvious a point that bears emphasis is that historically peace movements have advocated far more than just peace. The assertion that warfare is in some way reprehensible is hardly

Note: Some of the material in this chapter appeared in *Imperial Germany and a World Without War: The Peace Movement and German Society, 1892-1914* by Roger Chickering, copyright © 1975 by Princeton University Press, and is reprinted by permission of Princeton University Press.

unique to peace movements; it reflects, one would like to think, the sentiments of most people who have ever lived. However, those active in peace movements have differed from most of their contemporaries in that they have developed specific analyses of the causes of war and then advocated reforms designed to eliminate it systematically. The political and social implications of these reforms have invariably been far-reaching. For example, in the sectarian pacifism of the early Christians or the millenarian movements of the late Middle Ages, warfare represented an intrinsic feature of a corrupt world order, and it would disappear only with the destruction of that world order itself.[2] Those who in the eighteenth and nineteenth centuries foresaw the coming of world peace generally believed in the perfectibility of the world order, but many of the changes they advocated for promoting this perfection and bringing peace, such as redrawing the map of Europe according to ethnic groupings, had revolutionary implications.[3] These implications—the fact that the reforms advocated by peace movements frequently clashed with the interests of important people—have been far more important than any general animosity to the idea of peace in explaining the minimal success of peace movements in the past.

The history of the peace movement that flourished in Europe and the United States during the quarter century before World War I presents an interesting case in point. The people who gathered annually at Universal Peace Congresses in these years proposed to resolve international disputes by means of a court of international arbitration. This proposal derived in turn from a more general credo, commonly called *pacifism*,[4] according to which the nations of the world constituted, or were coming to constitute, an international community linked by economic interest, ethical awareness, and eventually by international political institutions, which would render violence among nations as obsolete as the development of the modern states had, they believed, rendered organized political violence within their borders. By the turn of the century the peace movement had largely abandoned the religious motifs which had informed antiwar thinking and activity earlier in the century when the movement had been dominated by English and American Quakers. Secular, humanitarian, and liberal in emphasis, pacifism postulated the basic morality, rationality, and peace-loving character of all people and the ultimate compatibility of their interests.

Seen in this perspective, a court of international arbitration, or even an international political organization, was but the formal expression of wider social and political developments that the pacifists hoped to foster. The surest guarantee of peace, pacifists argued, would be democratic government and the growth of international contacts. The establishment of democratic regimes throughout the civilized world would enable the peace-loving masses to determine foreign policy, while the growth of international contacts, especially commerce, would serve to tie the nations more closely together in a community of interest. The product would be a liberal paradise. Not only would international peace be guaranteed, but domestic unrest would disappear, as the wasting of national resources on the military, which pacifists believed was the principal cause of poverty and social tension, would cease. With both international and domestic harmony ensured, the peoples of the world could look forward to peaceful interchange and cooperation.[5]

As these views suggest, the peace movement at the turn of the century was composed of people who were politically liberal, or even radical, but socially conservative—people whose pacifism stemmed in part from their fear that war would have revolutionary social consequences. With the exception of scattered liberal aristocrats in Central and Eastern Europe, the social composition of the movement was as a rule middle class or petit bourgeois. Schoolteachers, professional people, and businessmen, especially small businessmen—made up the largest occupational categories in the peace societies' membership.

By whatever standards used for comparison—the number and size of peace societies, support for them among important social and political groups, or their influence in governmental decision making—the peace movement was strongest, among the major powers, in the United States, England, and France. Part of the reason for this was that the aspirations of the movement were reasonably consonant with social and political reality in these countries. All three were political democracies. In all three political and economic liberalism survived well into the twentieth century and informed the programs of ruling parties. Moreover, all three countries were relatively immune to the domestic tension and conflict prevalent in much of Eastern and Central Europe. The influence of an illiberal aristocracy was no longer a major problem, either because the aristocracy had itself been liberalized, as in England, or purged from positions of power, as in France in the aftermath of the establishment of the Third Republic and the Dreyfus affair. In addition, large segments of the labor movement in all three countries had been successfully integrated into the political systems.

These factors combined to create a situation in which the program of the peace movement found resonance in important sectors of society. In the United States the leaders in the movements were Quakers and other Protestant churchmen, educators, and philanthropists, but pacifism enjoyed considerable support among business groups, progressive reform organizations, and leading political figures.[6] In England, Quakers remained probably the single most important group in the peace movement, but other nonconformist denominations were prominent. The English movement, like the American one, was strong among educators and business groups, while an important sector of the Liberal party was determined to put the peace movement's program into practice.[7] In France, the peace movement was inextricably connected to the groups associated with Radicalism—Masonic lodges, societies of *libres penseurs,* and local political committees of the Radical party. Particularly with the growth of Radicalism after the turn of the century, then, the peace movement became increasingly visible in French politics.[8] In all three of the Western democracies, reformist currents in the labor movement brought cooperation between working-class organizations and the peace movement, although this was far more the case in England than in France or the United States. In all three countries the peace movement thus represented a significant political force: its leaders were respected figures, its ideas were current among important sectors of public opinion, and the movement had important sympathizers in high political councils, as the names of Léon Bourgeois, Henry Campbell-Bannerman, and William Jennings Bryan attest.

However, one must resist the temptation to overestimate the significance of the peace movement in any of these countries, where a majority of politicians certainly regarded international arbitration with skepticism. Nonetheless, the situation in Germany was clearly different: the peace movement was pathetically weak and isolated, it enjoyed no political influence whatsoever, and its ideas were rejected by virtually every articulate sector of German society.

The German Peace Society was founded comparatively late, in

1892, and then by two Austrians, Bertha von Suttner and Alfred Hermann Fried. Although its headquarters was officially situated in Berlin until 1899, the great bulk of the society's membership was concentrated in local groups in the southwest, most notably in the state of Württemberg, where by 1913 fully half of all the *Ortsgruppen* were located.[9] Because of this concentration, as well as the hostility in the north to the peace movement, national headquarters was moved in 1899 to Stuttgart, where Otto Umfrid, a Lutheran pastor in a local parish, became the virtual head of the national society.

The social composition of the German Peace Society was as restricted as the geographical area in which the organization had any significant appeal. The society's membership was almost exclusively *kleinbürgerlich,* drawn primarily from small businessmen and low-level schoolteachers.[10] One of the most striking aspects of the peace society's membership was the nearly total absence of the kinds of people who were prominent in the movement in other countries: philanthropic businessmen, professors, and clergymen (Umfrid was practically alone in the peace society). It soon became clear that membership in the peace society was not at all an attractive proposition for anyone with much social or political status in Germany.

The leaders of the German Peace Society tried very hard to break through the social and geographical confines it faced. Like peace societies elsewhere, the German Peace Society was conceived as an agency of popular enlightenment, and, all objective evidence notwithstanding, its leaders hoped that influential sectors of German society could be persuaded to lend their support to the campaign in favor of international arbitration. In virtually every case, however, the pacifists found only isolated and insignificant pockets of support, and they discovered that churches, universities, newspapers, political parties, and governmental officials were very nearly at one in their hostility to the peace movement. In all, no one could argue with the conclusion reached by one member of the peace society, who wrote in 1922, "It would be a distortion of the facts to credit the German peace movement with any perceptible influence whatsoever on the fate of the German people in the . . . years before the war."[11]

The reasons for the peace movement's comparative weakness in Germany are largely the same as those that account for the movement's strength in the Western democracies, and they are directly linked to the domestic implications of the peace movement's program. In Germany, however, these implications clashed directly with social and political reality.

In order to pursue this argument, it is necessary to look more closely at the character of both prewar pacifism and the German political system. The German peace movement espoused the same liberal pacifism that had come to dominate most of the movement by the turn of the century, particularly on the European continent. As elsewhere, there was some tension in the German movement between those who based their beliefs on ethical considerations and those who appealed to social evolution as the eventual guarantee of peace. In Germany the principal representative of a moralistic condemnation of warfare was Bertha von Suttner. In her eyes, war was morally wrong; it contradicted the basic canons of human decency. Men were gifted by nature with the capacity for rational and ethical conduct; thus, she believed, there existed a community of ethical consciousness among all men, the dictates of which not only proscribed warfare but imposed an ethical obligation to work against it. Specifically, Suttner called for popular education in order to awaken this ethical consciousness.

The problem with Suttner's pacifism was that despite its idealism and moral conviction, it was vacuous as a theory of international relations. She assumed that once enough people had been enlightened, war would simply disappear. Moreover, she conveyed this message with a sentimentality that exposed her to the charge (not altogether unfounded) that she was colossally naive. In an effort to rescue pacifism from the discredit into which it had fallen in Germany, Alfred Fried began after the turn of the century to popularize a doctrine from which he claimed to have purged all vestiges of moralism.[12] Fried's "scientific pacifism," which was based principally on the theories of a contemporary Russian sociologist, Jakob Novikow, seemed considerably more plausible than Bertha von Suttner's incantations to morality and international harmony. Citing the development of a world economy, the expansion of international cultural and political ties, and the growth of a body of international law, Fried argued that these portended the establishment of an international political organization, in which all disputes would be settled by law rather than force. Moreover, Fried claimed that all this was demonstrably inevitable, determined by the laws of social and political evolution.

For all the rhetorical differences between moralistic and scientific pacifism, however, the two were similar in most fundamental respects. Most importantly, they both postulated a community of nations, the existence or emergence of which would make violent international conflict unthinkable. While moralists cited a community of ethical consciousness, which transcended national frontiers, Fried and his followers spoke of a community of material interest, in which the ties were becoming so inextricable that warfare was no longer a feasible instrument of policy. Beyond a common insistence on a community of nations, scientific and moralistic pacifism implied similar domestic reforms. Suttner's affirmation of man as a morally autonomous being corresponded to Fried's insistence that the masses, which were to be the beneficiaries of internationalization, were the best judges of their own interests. Both varieties of pacifism thus implied the need for democratic regimes as a prerequisite for a stable international order. As Ludwig Quidde, one of the leaders of the German Peace Society, put it, pacifism was "nothing other than the application of the fundamentals of democracy to international relations."[13]

In part because she was not a systematic thinker, in part because of her own aristocratic background, Suttner did not pursue the social implications of pacifism very far. Fried was under no such limitations. The process he described as the foundation of international community, the guarantee of world peace, was the internationalization of capitalism. The converse of this view was an analysis of the causes of war that would subsequently be called Schumpeterian: it emphasized the influence of illiberal, premodern sectors of society, which, threatened by capitalism and democracy, remained powerful politically and socially by virtue of their control of the military, which gave them a vested interest in the continuation of international conflict and tension.[14] The pacifists reasoned further that social conflict was also a product of this situation, which made necessary the squandering of national wealth on armies and navies while the lower classes suffered and became restive. The international community Fried and Suttner envisaged thus had as its corollary a world of democratic, capitalistic, yet socially harmonious states.

It is difficult to imagine a credo, short of anarchism, syndicalism, or revolutionary socialism, whose aspirations were more directly in contradiction to the social and political situation in the German empire. Here the social and political influence of the landed aristocracy remained decisive. The constitution was undemocratic in the most critical respects, notably in barring the Reichstag from any effective influence over the determination of foreign and military policy. In addition, the bulk of the articulate labor movement espoused an ideology that rejected the vision of social harmony under capitalism. The social and political tensions inherent in this situation explain, more than anything else, why the peace movement was so isolated in Germany.

Particularly during the last fifteen years, historians have been investigating these social and political tensions, and from their work a much more complete picture of the German empire has emerged. The conclusion seems inescapable that the imperial German political system was extremely troubled. At its top stood the Prussian aristocracy, its social and political survival made possible by constitutional contrivances, such as the three-class suffrage, a system of tariffs and subsidies to protect the grains its estates produced, and its continued domination of the top echelons of the army and civilian bureaucracies. Aristocratic domination was in turn resented and challenged by nearly all the other sectors of German society. In particular, liberal democrats, socialist workers, Catholics, and Poles were deeply alienated at one time or another from the system Bismarck had created. In fact, so basic were the antagonisms dividing the various groups that made up the imperial political system that it remained unintegrated in the sense that it failed to generate a consensus among the various groups even about the ground rules of politics.[15] Thus, political debate routinely drew into question the validity of the Bismarckian system itself and the claim to rule of the aristocratic elites who controlled it. Moreover, the threat to these elites appeared to become even more acute in the years shortly before the war, in view of the startling growth of the Social Democratic party.

The history of the German empire can be written largely in terms of the attempts of the traditional elites to parry the threat posed by this lack of integration in the political system. Specifically, these elites attempted to neutralize the forces that challenged their rule by creating a new consensus. In their efforts they displayed remarkable versatility and imagination. Among the devices to which they resorted were the social and political cooptation of the industrial bourgeoisie, the introduction of what was at the time the most progressive program of social insurance in the world, and the outright repression of assorted dissident groups.[16]

Just as important was the attempt to manipulate Germany's relations with other countries. In this case, the country's leaders hoped to compensate for the lack of internal consensus by fostering a common set of political orientations among Germans vis-à-vis the rest of the world. One need not subscribe unequivocally to Fritz Fischer's views on the origins of the war in order to appreciate how the pursuit of an active foreign policy—from Bismarck's decision to embark upon colonial ventures through Bernhard von Bülow's cultivation of weltpolitik—was designed to sublimate domestic antagonism into a new national consensus, born of a sense of pride in Germany's international stature and power.[17]

Pursuit of an active foreign policy was only one aspect of the attempt to promote domestic integration by invoking Germany's relations with the rest of the world. Another involved the systematic spread of military values and orientations throughout German society. The problem of German militarism has been well studied.[18] Here it is sufficient to note that the social and political prominence of soldiers, and the pervasiveness of military attitudes in society, led to a general acceptance of the proposition that international relations were, by their very nature, characterized by antagonism and violent conflict. This view in turn reinforced the assumptions on which an active foreign policy was based: that relations among nations were intrinsically governed by power, competition, antagonism, and armed conflict.

The obvious effect of such views was to justify the army's continued preeminence in society and politics. Beyond this, the threatening climate of international relations was invoked to resist pressure for liberalization, specifically demands that the Reichstag's competence be widened to include foreign and military policy, which would in turn challenge fundamental sources of the aristocracy's power. In this way, the emperor and his ministers could argue that the Reichstag was far too fractious and inefficient a body to control such vital matters in troubled times, which demanded national

unity. "Germany's position in the world is not secure enough,"
as Chancellor Bethmann Hollweg explained it to the Reichstag in
1912, "for us to dispense with our disciplined organization."[19]

Ironically, by such reasoning the imperial government implied
the validity of the pacifists' contention that there was a connection
between democratic government and international community, or
the absence of international conflict. Certainly the regime itself
recognized this connection in formulating its policy at the Hague
conferences; its determined opposition to the innocuous proposals
for a court of international arbitration make sense only in light of
the government's anxiety lest arbitration promote the impression
that peace was secure and thereby endanger what Bülow referred to
as "the fundamental principles of a conservative monarchy."[20]
Thus, one of the means the government used to resist democratization was to repudiate the idea of international community and to
promote the idea that antagonism and conflict were irremediable
aspects of international relations, and that war was, if not desir-
able, extremely likely. Because pacifism was the negation of this view,
the peace movement represented a potential threat to the domestic
order in imperial Germany. The pacifists challenged the specter of
international conflict as a source of domestic integration by denying
the desirability, necessity, or utility of such conflict and claiming
that their international reforms would eliminate the need to fear
external threats.

The most enlightening feature of the peace movement's experience in imperial Germany was the way it laid bare this connection
between resistance to liberalization and the perception of international conflict and demonstrated how effectively this perception
was promoted. As they approached political parties, churches,
schools, newspapers, and other sectors of German society that
they identified as important in shaping popular attitudes about
international politics, the pacifists discovered that these agencies
rejected not only the specific international reforms the peace movement advocated but the pacifists' most basic assumptions about the
reality of an international community. The result was to make the
inevitability or likelihood of international conflict a self-evident
proposition and to produce a climate of opinion in Germany which,
far more than any active harassment by extreme nationalists, para-
lyzed the peace movement. This general acceptance of international

conflict extended even to the Social Democrats. Committed, rhetori-
cally if not in practice, to revolution, German socialists felt compelled to attack the bourgeois peace movement, whose program
was such a paean to capitalism; when asked by pacifists for their
support, they responded that war was simply a fact of life—under
capitalism.[21]

In these circumstances the support the peace movement found
was limited to small clusters of bourgeois progressives and liberal
democrats, who were themselves practically as isolated as the pacifists. Politically, this support was restricted to the fragmented left-
liberal parties, especially the South German People party, which,
like the peace movement itself, was heavily concentrated in Württemberg. From the academic community a handful of progressive legal
scholars put together the *Verband für internationale Verständigung*
in 1911, but its influence, both within German universities and in
society at large, was negligible.[22] The German churches, particularly
the Protestant ones, denounced the peace movement for failing to
recognize that war was part of God's plan for man in the corrupt
temporal world; the few allies the pacifists found were Protestant
liberals who challenged the fatalism of Protestant orthodoxy.[23]
Excepting these sympathetic groups and a handful of free thinkers,
vegetarians, antivivisectionists, and other such reformers—who
were themselves generally dismissed as harmless eccentrics in Germany—the peace movement encountered only massive indifference
and hostility.

Writing in 1911, Alfred Fried suggested that international tension
was really the product of domestic conditions in Germany. "If
Germany were to develop into a democracy and carry on a democratic foreign policy, we would have peace in Europe," he predicted.
"The problem of peace is therefore a problem of domestic German
politics. It lies in the conquest of Junkerdom, in the victory of liberalism and democracy."[24] The value of this assertion as a prediction
is at best dubious. Popular enthusiasm in the opening phases of
World War I, in the Western democracies, as well as in Germany,
certainly casts doubt on the proposition that the "victory of liberalism and democracy" was going to lead to world peace. Yet there is
an important element of truth in Fried's analysis, insofar as it points
to the challenge the peace movement posed to the dominant elites

in imperial Germany. The program of the peace movement implied unambiguously the "victory of liberalism and democracy," while the German ruling classes were determined to resist it. Their efforts to forestall liberalization prominently included using their influence over agencies of political education to discredit the idea of an international community, in which arbitration was the appropriate means for resolving disputes.

The comparative weakness of the peace movement in imperial Germany can therefore be explained largely in terms of the domestic implications of its program. In France, England, and the United States there were no major contradictions between the constituted political systems and the domestic reforms implied by pacifism. In Germany, however, the reforms pacifists regarded as indispensable for a world without war were incompatible with the domestic realities of the Bismarckian system. In fact, the German political system depended on the repudiation of pacifism for its stability.

NOTES

1. This study represents a summary of themes dealt with at greater length, and with more complete documentation, in my book *Imperial Germany and a World without War: The Peace Movement and German Society, 1892-1914.*

2. David A. Martin, *Pacifism: An Historical and Sociological Study* (New York, 1966).

3. A. C. F. Beales, *The History of Peace: A Short Account of the Organized Movements for International Peace* (London, 1931), 45-277; F. S. L. Lyons, *Internationalism in Europe, 1815-1914* (Leyden, 1963), 309-61.

4. Alfred Fried, "Die Geschichte eines Wortes," *Die Friedens-Warte* 20 (1920): 60-61.

5. For a more extended discussion of the program of the peace movement at the turn of the century, see Sandi E. Cooper, "Peace and Internationalism: European Ideological Movements behind Two Hague Conferences (1899 to 1907)" (diss., New York University, 1967).

6. David S. Patterson, *Toward a Warless World: The Travail of the American Peace Movement, 1877-1914* (Bloomington, Ind., 1976); C. Roland Marchand, *The American Peace Movement and Social Reform, 1898-1918* (diss., Princeton, 1972).
Peace and Retrenchment (Totowa, 1972). See also Eric W. Sager's provocative "Pacifism and the Victorians: A Social History of the English Peace Movement, 1816-1873" (Ph.D. diss., University of British Columbia, 1975).

8. There is unfortunately no monograph on the French peace movement, although I have devoted a chapter of my book to it: *Imperial Germany,* 327-83. In addition, see the thorough biography of Paul Henri d'Estournelles de Constant by Adolf Wild, *Baron d'Estournelles de Constant (1852-1924): Das Wirkin eines Friedensnobelpreisträgers für die deutsch-französische Verständigung und die europäische Einigung* (Hamburg, 1973).

9. *Der Völker-Friede* 14 (1913):7.

10. See Alexander Dietz, *Franz Wirth und der Frankfurter Friedensverein* (Frankfurt a. M., 1911), 68-73.

11. Rudolf Goldscheid, ed., *Alfred H. Fried: Eine Sammlung von Gedenkblättern* (Leipzig, 1922), 32-33.

12. Alfred H. Fried, *Handbuch der Friedensbewegung* (Vienna and Leipzig, 1905).

13. Ludwig Quidde, "Wie ich zur Democratie und zum Pazifismus kam," *Frankfurter Zeitung,* 4 January 1928.

14. On the social views of the German pacifists, see especially Dorothee Stiewe, "Die bürgerliche deutsche Friedensbewegung als soziale Bewegung bis zum Ende des Ersten Weltkrieges" (diss., Freiburg, 1972).

15. M. Rainer Lepsius, "Parteiensystem und Sozialstruktur: Zum Problem der Demokratisierung der deutschen Gesellschaft," in Wilhelm Abel et al., eds., *Wirtschaft, Geschichte und Wirtschaftsgeschichte: Festschrift zum 65. Geburtstag von Friedrich Lütge* (Stuttgart, 1966), 371-93.

16. See Hans Rosenberg, *Grosse Depression und Bismarckzeit: Wirtschaftsablauf, Gesellschaft und Politik in Mitteleuropa* (Berlin, 1967); Wolfgang Sauer, "Das Problem des deutschen Nationalstaates," in Hans-Ulrich Wehler, ed., *Moderne deutsche Sozialgeschichte* (Cologne and Berlin, 1970), 428-36.

17. See Fritz Fischer, *Krieg der Illusionen: Die deutsche Politik von 1911 bis 1914* (Düsseldorf, 1969); Hans-Ulrich Wehler, *Bismarck und der Imperialismus* (Cologne and Berlin, 1969); Volker Berghahn, *Der Tirpitz-Plan: Genesis und Verfall einer innenpolitischen Krisenstrategie unter Wilhelm II* (Düsseldorf, 1971).

18. See especially Gerhard Ritter, *Staatskunst und Kriegshandwerk: Das Problem des "Militarismus" in Deutschland* (Munich, 1954-67); Gordon A. Craig, *The Politics of the Prussian Army, 1640-1945* (New York and Oxford, 1956).

19. *Stenographische Berichte über die Verhandlungen des Reichstages,* 13 L.P., 1 sess., 16 February 1912, 67, 283.

20. Bülow memorandum, 14 May 1899, in Johannes Lepsius, et al., eds., *Die Grosse Politik der Europäischen Kabinette, 1871-1914* (Berlin, 1926-27), 15:193-96, no. 4257, Anlage.

21. See for instance "Sonderbare Schwärmer," *Vorwärts,* April 4, 1900.

22. Roger Chickering, "A Voice of Moderation in Imperial Germany: The 'Verband für internationale Verständigung,' 1911-1914," *Journal of Contemporary History* 8, no. 1 (January 1973):147-64.

23. I have dealt with aspects of this problem in a short article: "The Peace Movement and the Religious Community in Germany, 1900-1914," *Church History* 38 (1969):300-11.

24. *Die Friedens-Warte* 12 (1911):219-20.

4
Diplomacy against the Peace Movement: The Austro-Hungarian Foreign Office and the Second Hague Peace Conference of 1907

SOLOMON WANK

I

Konstantin Dumba, the Austro-Hungarian diplomat who, in the summer of 1907, was in charge of the correspondence between the Foreign Office in Vienna and the Austro-Hungarian delegation at the second Hague Peace Conference, lamented in his memoirs: "Neither the [Foreign] Minister nor I, nor anyone else at the Ballplatz[1] gave proper attention to this Conference and its extraordinarily exacting deliberations; nor, completely engrossed as we were in the pre-war mentality, did we know how to evaluate correctly the damage that would accrue to us later in the public opinion of the Western democracies as a consequence of our negative attitude toward the disarmament[2] and compulsory arbitration proposals."[3] Dumba bemoaned the fact that Austria-Hungary acquired for itself the "doubtful glory" of opposing arms limitation and the principle of peaceful resolution of international conflicts and, together with its German ally, the "odium for dashing pacifist hopes" for agreements in these areas when in fact there was little chance of substantive, as opposed to academic, agreement among the Great Powers on either question.[4] Dumba gives the impression that Austria-Hungary merely displayed a lack of diplomatic tact, although his reference

to a "prewar mentality" hints at ideological and domestic sociopolitical factors that influenced the posture of the Austro-Hungarian
Foreign Office viv-à-vis the peace conference.

Dumba was right, in a way, that the second Hague Peace Conference was a diplomatic failure for Austria-Hungary, but it is important to distinguish between foreign policy and diplomacy, something Dumba himself did not do. From the beginning the second
conference, like the first one in 1899, was strictly a matter of diplomacy for the Austro-Hungarian Foreign Office. At both conferences, its policy aimed at preventing any substantial progress in
arms limitation and compulsory arbitration. However, in 1899, unlike in 1907, Austro-Hungarian diplomatic actions succeeded in
implementing its opposition in a manner not offensive to public
opinion.[5] But neither Austria-Hungary's diplomatic success in 1899,
nor its failure in 1907, tells much about why the Ballhausplatz opposed arms limitation and compulsory arbitration in the first place.
For the answer to that, one must go beyond the interpretive framework of conventional diplomatic history with its generally rigid
separation of domestic and foreign politics and its view that the
imperatives of foreign policy are imposed upon a state primarily
from without.[6]

Nearly half a century ago, Elie Halevy wrote that "no responsible
statesman would have said at the beginning of 1914 that he felt
safe against the perils of some kind of revolutionary outburst. . . .
What were the collective forces that made for revolution? One word
sums them up . . . 'socialism.' "[7] This feeling of sociopolitical anxiety
is revealed in a remark by Sir Edward Grey, the English foreign secretary, to Count Albert Mensdorff, the Austro-Hungarian ambassador at London, shortly after the outbreak of World War I: "It
[the war] is the greatest step towards Socialism that could possibly
have been made. We shall have labour Governments in every country
after this."[8] In this vein, I have suggested elsewhere that a more
fruitful way of understanding the opposition of European governing
elites to the peace movement is to see it as part of the pre-1914 Euro-
pean-wide social conflict engendered by rapid, continuous, and uneven economic growth.[9] Simply stated, although complex in reality,
the conflict—to use Arno J. Mayer's typology—was between the
"parties of movement" and the "parties of order," that is, between

social groups and interests that pressed for reform and those that strove to preserve the status quo.[10] The intensity of the domestic conflict and its effect upon the formulation of foreign policy and on international relations varied from country to country in relation to the adaptability of a given sociopolitical structure and governing elite to change.[11] Diplomats found themselves confronting modern political forces and public opinion without fully comprehending them and uncertain of what their image ought to be. Their response to the peace movement is indicative of their uncertainty and their confusion. They wavered between two alternatives that they dimly perceived. Either they simply opposed any "pacifist" proposals so as not to dignify them with their august support or appear to be weak, or they wished to appear to agree with "pacifist" proposals on the surface—to avoid the onus of being considered the archconservatives or reactionaries many of them were—while undercutting them in reality.[12]

II

The second Hague Peace Conference, called, like the first one, on the initiative of Czar Nicholas II, initially was scheduled to meet at the Hague in the summer of 1906. At the request of President Theodore Roosevelt, it was postponed until the next summer because of the Rio conference of Pan-American states scheduled for the summer of 1906.[13] On April 12, 1906, the Russian Foreign Office sent a circular letter to all of the participating powers containing the definitive program of the conference. The topics listed dealt only with improvements to be made in the convention of 1899 relating to the Court of Arbitration and to the technical regulation of war.[14] No mention was made of arms limitation, the question that occasioned the convening of the first conference, even though military expenditures and the size of armies and navies had increased appreciably. The arms limitation question, however, was not so easily disposed of. In May 1906, the British House of Commons, which had a large Liberal-Labour majority that included many peace advocates, passed a strongly worded resolution pledging the English government to raise the question of arms limitation at the next Hague conference.[15] However much government leaders and

diplomats, even in England, may have considered the arms limitation question impractical and inopportune, the English initiative
was a fact. No public figure could ignore the disarmament question
or reject it out of hand, although the German kaiser's frank statements in opposition to any discussion of arms limitation at the conference came close to doing just that.[16]

The Austro-Hungarian foreign minister at the time of the convening of the second peace conference was Baron Alois Lexa Aehrenthal. Most diplomatic historians see Aehrenthal's policy at the conference as guided by rational power-political considerations.[17] His
diplomacy, it is maintained, was directed toward preserving the
balance of power and preventing a further sharpening of the Anglo-
German rivalry. The Hague conference appeared destined to become another British diplomatic victory, destructive to both of
these objectives. Therefore, in order to avoid seeing his ally completely isolated and overwhelmed by England, Aehrenthal worked
to thwart the British desire to use the disarmament question "to put
Germany in a corner"[18] and have it bear the odium for the failure
of the great peace effort. Certainly such diplomatic considerations
played a role in Aehrenthal's thinking. At the end of August 1906,
Aehrenthal wrote to Count Agenor Goluchowski, his predecessor
as foreign minister:

It appears to me that the English policy, which becomes ever clearer, should
restrain the cabinets of Vienna and Berlin—especially the latter—from taking a position to these plans. . . .The convening of the Hague conference
will be a very interesting, important and, at the same time, *delicate* moment
for European politics in general but for Germany especially. . . . The Hague
conference can end up with a diplomatic success of England over Germany
or with a highly dangerous intensification of the international situation.[19]

Neither alternative offered Austria-Hungary much comfort. As a
way out, Aehrenthal recommended that Austria-Hungary, Germany,
and Russia form a united front at the conference. Such diplomatic
considerations, however, overlay far more complex motives that
sprang from deep social and ideological well-springs.

After 1900, Aehrenthal's political anxiety over the survival of
the Habsburg monarchy, like that of many conservative Habsburg

diplomats and members of the imperial political elite, began to increase.[20] Modern social forces—nationalist agitation throughout Austria-Hungary and growing demands for far-reaching social and political reforms that often interlocked with the nationalist movements—exerted great pressure on the monarchy's still heavily traditional dynastic sociopolitical structure.[21] Events in Russia, where Aehrenthal served as ambassador from 1899 until 1906, only heightened his political anxiety. He believed that the 1905 Russian revolution signaled the growth of a powerful movement of reform from below that would act as a catalyst on internal problems all over Europe: "The unparalleled defeats of Russia have hastened not only the Norwegian, but the Magyar crisis as well."[22] "Dualism in the long run is untenable."[23] Faced with actual revolution in Russia and the specter of it in Austria-Hungary, Aehrenthal's thinking became deeply influenced by counterrevolutionary motives and conspiratorial explanations of events with central roles assigned to Jews and socialists.[24] For Aehrenthal, the peace movement, almost synonymous in his view with the socialist movement, was part of the revolutionary tide threatening the established social order. It had to be defeated.

Aehrenthal's anxieties about Russia came to a head in the summer of 1906. In May of that year the first imperial Duma had met, and by mid-July the Czar and Duma were at loggerheads. In conservative circles in Russia, efforts were being made to persuade the Czar to dissolve the Duma. Aehrenthal was in favor of these efforts, and there is some evidence that he even abetted them.[25] He believed that the complete collapse of traditional monarchical authority in Russia would seriously weaken monarchical and conservative forces in Austria-Hungary in their efforts to master the social revolution before being overwhelmed by it. Aehrenthal saw a revival of the Three Emperors' League (Dreikaiserbund) of monarchical and conservative powers (Austria-Hungary, Germany, and Russia) as a way of defeating social revolution in both Russia and Austria-Hungary.[26] This is the gist of three secret letters that Aehrenthal sent to Goluchowski.[27] The foreign minister, while sharing Aehrenthal's archconservative outlook and his perception of the threatening times, reacted skeptically to the ambassador's plan. Goluchowski believed that the revival of the Three Emperors' League, rather than reducing the impetus of revolutionary forces in Austria-Hungary, would intensify them to a degree that the monarchy's weak structure might not be able to withstand.[28]

In his first letter to Goluchowski near the end of July, Aehrenthal strongly recommended that the German and Austro-Hungarian emperors seek to "stiffen the spine" of the czar through meetings with him and through letters pledging adherence to conservative and monarchical principles.[29] He stressed the importance of the three imperial powers settling their Balkan and Near Eastern rivalries in the name of monarchical solidarity. After thus establishing harmony among themselves, the three emperors could turn to the task of combating revolutionary and radical currents. Aehrenthal wrote:

> The institution of the Inter-Parliamentary Conference is constantly growing in size and significance. The last meeting of this sort in London was under the influence of strongly prevailing Socialist tendencies. A permanent secretariat shall be created which shall have the task of carrying out the directives for the creation of new relations between peoples. This is to happen over the heads of monarchs and governments. This constitutes an alarm signal for them to fix their attention on the vital interests of their dynasties and in other concerns to accommodate themselves to the great principle of the unity of rulers for the purpose of preserving their position in the war against socialism and anarchism.[30]

According to Aehrenthal, the ultimate danger of the peace movement was its opposition to the ideological foundations of a conservative and monarchical order: "From the standpoint of monarchical thought the peace movement must be resolutely combatted, for in the last analysis the movement turns against heroism without which a monarchical order is unthinkable."[31]

For conservative reasons—to stave off a perceived threat of social revolution—Aehrenthal was willing to entertain the possibility of reductions in military expenditures. Such reductions, however, were to be achieved not by international conferences acting over the heads of national governments and monarchs but by the heads of state themselves, especially those of the Great Powers, in accordance with the principle of the balance of power. In his letter to Goluchowski, Aehrenthal wrote that "A powerful weapon of agitation would be wrested from the hands of Socialist demagogues if the three Emperors [of Germany, Russia and Austria-Hungary] on their own initiative broached the disarmament question and through appropriate reductions in their armies would realize savings in their military budgets."[32] Aehrenthal elaborated on this line of thought:

It would be quite a different matter for the three most powerful monarchs, through a spontaneous decision, to put off and lessen the danger of war by simultaneous reductions of their respective military budgets. A more detailed elaboration is not necessary [to show] that a revived Three Emperors' Alliance would provide greater firmness and heightened consciousness of purpose in the struggle against the threatening dictatorship of the proletariat, a dictatorship which in the end can lead only to satanic chaos. There is danger in delay and for that reason it is necessary to strengthen the dams against the flood of the materialistically inclined proletariat in which there is the absense of every divine spark. . . .[33] If Emperor Nicholas does not emerge victorious from his conflict with the Duma, which wants to reduce the emperor to the position of a Russian Dalai Lama, the next step is the formation of several republics with strong communist tendencies. The creation of such republics certainly would not stop at our frontiers.[34]

By broaching the question of arms limitation on their own, but not at the Hague conference, and by reducing their military expenditures, the three imperial powers would serve to counteract the peace movement. Aehrenthal saw such reductions as posing no danger to the ability of the three imperial governments to maintain internal order and to meet external threats. He thus wrote to Goluchowski:

For years, I have been a convinced champion of the idea of returning to smaller armies whose immediate strength would have to be relatively great. . . . The socialistic current of the time with its danger of mass-strikes makes it urgently necessary to insure that the government has at its disposal *sufficient* and *reliable* troops, two requirements which it seems to me are best met by the above mentioned small army with greater immediate effective force. In such an army, thanks to the abundantly available means, adequate provisions could be made for the recruitment, training and maintenance of a proficient non-commissioned officers corps, which would guarantee the good quality of these troops even with a shorter period of active service by the men. . . . On the other hand, the upper classes constantly would place the government in the position of intervening with decisiveness in the event of internal disturbances and finally even in case of war the value of the troops would only increase through raising the level of the non-commissioned officers.[35]

Arms reduction without any qualms about the ethos of war, a more trustworthy professional army to crush agitation for social reform or proletarian revolution, and an international conservative alliance— that was Aehrenthal's plan to preserve peace, that is, to maintain the essential foundations of the internal and external status quo.

III

After he became foreign minister in October 1906, Aehrenthal undertook the initiatives outlined in his letter to Goluchowski. He persuaded Emperor Francis Joseph to write a letter of encouragement to Czar Nicholas expressing friendship and sympathy in the struggle of monarchical authority against subversive and anarchistic elements.[36] But it was not until the beginning of 1907, after the conclusion of the decennial economic compromise between Austria and Hungary, that Aehrenthal was able to turn his attention to organizing the three imperial powers into a common front at the Hague Conference. At that time he entered into secret negotiations with Germany and Russia that lasted about four months.[37] These negotiations revolved almost exclusively around the arms limitation question and ran completely counter to a resolution that the Austrian Parliament had passed and sent to the foreign office in June 1906 urging "that the representatives of the Monarchy at the next Hague Conference be provided with instructions which call upon them to participate expeditiously in the discussion of possible proposals regarding the gradual diminution of military armaments of the various nations."[38]

In mid-February, Aehrenthal instructed Prince Karl Fürstenberg, chargé d'affaires of the Austro-Hungarian embassy at St. Petersburg, to remind the Russian foreign minister, Alexander Isvolsky, that Austria-Hungary, along with many other states, had agreed to send delegates to the conference on the basis of a program that excluded the disarmament question. Arms limitation, therefore, was an "inadmissible question" and "utterly inopportune" because of its effect on public opinion. The best thing to do was to eliminate it.[39] As an additional argument, Fürstenberg was instructed to point out to Izvolsky tactfully that a limitation of naval armaments, which England might propose, would give international sanction to Russia's defenselessness at sea since the destruction of the

Russian fleet in the war with Japan.[40] Finally, Fürstenberg was to tell Izvolsky that he (Aehrenthal) would greet a common front of the three imperial powers at the Hague Conference with even greater satisfaction because "in the tendency to limit the land and sea power of states through interparliamentary or international conferences, I [Aehrenthal] see an anti-monarchical thrust against which the chief supporters of monarchical thought in Europe—that is the three imperial courts—could not take a position soon enough and emphatically enough."[41] This ideological leitmotif is expanded in instructions to Count Leopold Berchtold, his successor as ambassador to Russia. Austro-Hungarian relations with Russia, Aehrenthal wrote, had to be evaluated from the standpoint "of the conduct of a conservative policy in Central Europe," as well as with reference to Russia's Balkan policy. Elaborating on the first consideration, Aehrenthal stressed "a close solidarity of the conservative monarchical interest" of the three imperial powers "in the common defense against the social revolutionary waves which moving from the East threaten to inundate Europe." The three imperial powers also had an imminent interest "in the integral maintenance of their territorial possessions," which meant avoiding "the unrolling of the Polish question as an international question." A similar solidarity of interest existed in the disarmament question. The three imperial powers "will have to take the edge off the British proposals by a common defensive position and, in general, form a front against the peace movement, which by emphasizing the will of the people and interparliamentary action strives to weaken monarchical prerogatives." Czar Nicholas and several of his advisers, Aehrenthal stated, "possess a correct understanding" of the community of interest of the three imperial powers. One of Berchtold's "foremost tasks" as ambassador was "to preserve and cultivate" that understanding.[42]

Fürstenberg reported back to Aehrenthal that while Izvolsky had a negative attitude toward the disarmament question, he could not reject out of hand the English and American wish to raise the issue at the conference.[43] Since Russia was the inviting power, a rejection of the Anglo-American wish would result in the "complete odium" for such a step falling on the Russian government.[44] The English might even decide not to attend the conference, thereby causing its complete failure. Russia then would become the prime target for the entire "international movement of peace fanatics."[45] As a way out of the situation, the Russian foreign minister desired rather to prepare "a first-class burial" ("un enterrement de première classe") for the disarmament question at the conference that would not offend England, with which he was seeking closer relations, or seriously impair relations with Austria-Hungary and Germany, which would bring him the disfavor of archconservative Russian court circles.[46]

Aehrenthal was not especially happy with Izvolsky's proposal because the three imperial powers would have to be the "grave diggers . . . which is in no way an especially enticing role."[47] However, from Fürstenberg's and Berchtold's reports, he concluded that while the Russian government was opposed to a discussion of the disarmament question, it was inclined to oblige England and America in some way. Hence, there was nothing left to do but go along with Izvolsky's idea of preparing "a first-class burial" for the disarmament question at the conference. There was, however, some disagreement over the funeral arrangements, and it wâs only after very detailed negotiations, during which Berlin and Vienna exerted great pressure on Izvolsky, that a common procedure for the diplomatic burial was agreed upon by the three imperial courts.[48] In brief, the procedure was as follows.[49] The Russian circular letter of April 3, 1907, formally inviting the powers to the conference, would adhere to the original Russian agenda but would mention that England reserved the right to bring up the arms limitation question and that Austria-Hungary, Russia, and Germany reserved the right not to participate in discussions that were unlikely to lead to any practical results.[50] Second, it was agreed that if a discussion of the disarmament question came up that went beyond a platonic resolution, such as the one adopted in 1899 calling upon the governments to consider seriously the desirability of limiting military expenditures, the presumptive Russian president of the conference, Alexander Nelidov, would interrupt the session in order to give the German and Austro-Hungarian delegations a chance to leave the hall.

During the course of the negotiations with Russia, in which Vienna took the lead, Austria-Hungary and Germany remained united on the point that their delegations would not participate in a discussion of the disarmament question. However, throughout these negotiations, Aehrenthal took a much more obliging and flexible attitude toward Russia than did Germany.[51] He became even more obliging when he learned that the German ambassador in Rome, Count Anton Mons, was bruiting it about that the center of resistance to a discussion of the arms limitation question lay in Vienna, not Berlin.[52] Aehrenthal showed himself to be especially conciliatory when he declared himself in agreement with the content of the Russian letter of invitation to the powers and by immediately accepting for Austria-Hungary and Germany the same reservation as Russia.[53] He stood firm against German insistence that arms limitation be mentioned specifically in the letter as one of the questions in the discussion of which the representatives of Austria-Hungary and Germany would not take part because it would lead to no practical results.[54] Aehrenthal, of course, believed that the arms limitation question was such a question, but he correctly assumed that Izvolsky never would have included such a direct reference in the letter.[55] Furthermore, he did not yield to Germany's request for a separate memorandum to the conference states announcing the agreement between Vienna and Berlin to distance themselves from a discussion of the disarmament question. Such a declaration, he feared, would become "the signal for the opening of the discussion all along the line from cabinet to cabinet as well as in the press and parliament."[56] This was precisely what he wanted to avoid. At the end of March, Aehrenthal wrote to Berchtold about Berlin's fussing over the form of the reservation: "The Privy Councillors in the Wilhelmstrasse are clever fellows but bad diplomats. . . . I may assume that Germany will follow our example. . . . I have chosen the only correct way and there the matter rests."[57] He was right. Berlin followed Austria-Hungary's example and dropped its objections to the form of the reservation. Finally, by agreeing with the Russian suggestion that the disarmament question might be settled by a *voeu* like that in 1899, Aehrenthal got Germany to back down from its uncompromising position on any mention of arms limitation at the conference.

On the other hand, Aehrenthal was as unyielding as Berlin in his insistence that Nelidov turn over the chairmanship of the conference to the vice-chairman after suspending the session in the event that a substantive discussion of the arms limitation question came up.[58] In fact, no agreement had been reached between Austria-

Hungary, Germany, and Russia on Nelidov's comportment as conference president, and Aehrenthal was wrong in later accusing Izvolsky
of contravening agreements between the three imperial powers.[59]
What had been agreed upon was to allow the delegates not to participate in discussions of the disarmament question. Since Izvolsky
was prepared to allow Nelidov to close the session if it should come
to a serious discussion of disarmament, which Izvolsky hoped to
avoid precisely by having the question referred to a commission
by Nelidov, it is not clear why Germany and Austria-Hungary pressed
Izvolsky on the issue.[60] One might have expected that Aehrenthal
would perceive that Izvolsky would not yield on the point and once
again exert pressure in Berlin. If, in this instance, Aehrenthal was
not obliging, it is still true that in the negotiations with Russia,
Austria-Hungary displayed more diplomatic skill than Germany did.
Aehrenthal succeeded in influencing Germany to modify its brusquely
negative stance on procedural matters and prevented Berlin from
being isolated before the conference opened. He was justified in
claiming that on several occasions, "I have taken a very accom-
modating position toward the Russian view and thereby contributed
not insignificantly to an almost complete reversal of the intransigent
position of the German government."[61]

In an indirect way, the disarmament question was disposed of
before the conference opened. In a speech to the German Reichstag
on April 30, Prince Bülow, the German chancellor, presented
Germany's position on arms limitation without any hostile allu-
sions to England.[62] With the Anglo-German tension somewhat re-
laxed, England and the United States agreed to bring up the disarmament question only in the form of the *voeu* of 1899, that is, in the
form of a platonic resolution again urging the governments to examine seriously the arms limitation question.[63] Thus the arrangements for the "first-class burial" proposed by Izvolsky some months
before were complete. By his obliging attitude toward Russia and
by his constraining Germany to be less intransigent, Aehrenthal had
contributed in no small way to the funeral arrangements.

IV

While the negotiations over disarmament were going on, the
Austro-Hungarian delegation to the peace conference was named.

Kajetan von Mérey, the experienced and capable chief of the political department of the Foreign Office who held the rank of ambassador, was named first delegate (head of the delegation).[64] The main lines of Austria-Hungary's position at the conference were discussed in a series of meetings of the delegation members held in April and presided over by Mérey.[65] On May 25, only two weeks before the delegation left for the Hague, a meeting was held in the Ballhausplatz under Aehrenthal's chairmanship to draw up definitive instructions. The meeting was attended by the appointed delegates, the military chiefs of staff, and the joint ministers of finance and war. No representatives of the Austrian or Hungarian governments were present.[66]

The original Russian agenda was taken up point by point. The first point concerned improvements in the existing system of international arbitration, the most important aspect of which was compulsory arbitration. Early in 1907, the German ambassador in Vienna, Count Karl von Wedel, reported that Mérey and Aehrenthal had informed him that Austria-Hungary, like Germany, rejected compulsory arbitration, specifically with regard to the neighboring Balkan states, but that a discussion of the question could not be gruffly rejected because the conference program did not exclude it.[67] Under the prodding of the delegation's legal adviser, Dr. Heinrich Lammasch, professor of international law at the University of Vienna and a well-known advocate of international arbitration, the Austro-Hungarian position on compulsory arbitration became more flexible.[68] As the two most far-reaching concessions the conferees agreed on the following. First, Austria-Hungary could approve the conclusion of a general or world compulsory arbitration treaty to replace those negotiated between individual states under two conditions: that the treaty cover only "certain limited and well defined disputes," such as legal disputes over the interpretation and application of international treaties, and that it contain a clause leaving it to each state to judge for itself if a dispute touched upon its honor or its vital interests, whereupon the treaty would be rendered inoperative. Second, the Austro-Hungarian delegation could accept a compulsory arbitration treaty in the strict sense, that is, without any reservations with regard to honor and vital interests, as long as it remained restricted to relatively harmless cases such as commercial and navigational treaties, sanitary conventions, agreements to

combat hoof and mouth disease, and agreements concerning diplomatic and consular immunity. The conferees agreed that the above
guidelines would mollify public opinion and curry international
goodwill for the monarchy.

The second, third, and fourth parts of the Russian conference
program concerned additions to the provisions of the 1899 convention regarding the conduct of war at sea and further adaptation
to maritime law of the principles of the 1864 Geneva Convention and
the Hague Convention of 1899. None of these questions dealing with
the modification and further development of the rules and regula-
tions of war was seen as seriously impairing the power and sovereignty
of the state, and details were left to be worked out at the conference. After the discussion of the official agenda items had been concluded, Aehrenthal informed the delegates of the agreements
reached between the three imperial courts on the arms limitation
question. Settling the whole matter by a "platonic *voeu*" would serve
as a sop to the "peace apostles" without any real progress in arms
limitation having been made.

V

If Austria-Hungary took the lead in the negotiations before the
opening of the conference and was able to make its wishes felt,
at the conference itself, Germany took the lead, but not immediately. A few days after the conference opened on June 15, Mérey
reported to Aehrenthal that he was struck by the "narrow-minded
and intransigent position—also with regard to details" that the
first German delegate, Baron Marschall von Bieberstein, intended
to take on arms limitation and other important points. Mérey could
not judge whether Marschall's attitude was based on his own convictions, on his instructions, or on "the too sharp dialectic" of the
second German delegate and legal adviser, Dr. Johannes Kriege.
Mérey received the impression that the German delegation wanted
to use the Austro-Hungarian delegation as a "battering-ram" in dis-
agreeable questions and to "heat us up properly for that purpose,"
that is, to induce Austria-Hungary to take equally intransigent positions as Germany did on key questions. Mérey assured Aehrenthal
that he would be on the alert and that he would strongly oppose
such a tendency if it should become manifest.[69]

In his reply, Aehrenthal stated that he thought that "the Germans wanted to take the bull by the horns [arms limitation] and send the whole thing packing." He informed Mérey that in the winter of 1907, he had pointed out to the men in the Wilhelmstrasse that their position was too intransigent. Aehrenthal referred Mérey to his instructions to Count Berchtold of June 27, 1907, in which he stated that he, like the Germans, objected to describing the disarmament question as "urgent" because it might lead to a continuation of the discussion of the question after the conference, an eventuality that Aehrenthal wanted to avoid.[70] As he told Berchtold, a mere mechanical repetition of the 1899 *voeu* was not possible, and he was not against a different wording of the *voeu* as long as the alteration did not impose on Austria-Hungary any obligations beyond those assumed in 1899. In closing, Aehrenthal instructed Mérey to work against the German effort to incite Austria-Hungary to adopt an intransigent position "and, while holding firmly to our fundamental position, to proceed *suaviter in modo* and not to quibble over details and to take upon yourself the odium attaching to that."[71]

Mérey adhered to these instructions in several minor matters, such as supporting the French proposal concerning the opening of hostilities by a declaration of war. In a letter to Baron Schonaich, the Austro-Hungarian minister of war, Aehrenthal stated that the proposal changed nothing since an attack could be launched one hour after the declaration, a position with which the minister of war agreed.[72] By and large, Mérey also adhered to these instructions in the arms limitation question. Near the end of July, England made known its intention to move the adoption of the *voeu,* a step that Nelidov would recommend to the conference for approval. After England, which altered the wording of the *voeu* at the wish of Germany, moved its adoption, it was unanimously accepted in the notable absence of the German delegation. Aehrenthal could "rejoice" that the "tiresome disarmament question" finally was interred.[73]

If Germany's attitude toward disarmament before and during the conference led to its shouldering the blame for the failure of all efforts to halt the arms race, Austria-Hungary, as Dumba notes, did not escape some of the blame. Its negative position on arms limitation before the conference did not pass unnoticed. At the conference, Austria-Hungary limited itself to supporting the formulation of a *voeu* desired by Germany and, in order to squelch any possibility of a serious discussion of arms limitation, Mérey, together with Marschall, unsuccessfully badgered Nelidov to introduce the *voeu* himself. Mérey and Marschall feared that if the English delegate moved the adoption of the *voeu,* the American delegate would then take the floor to support it and a serious discussion would ensue.[74]

Austria-Hungary's position on arms limitation alone would not have been sufficient to cast it in a bad light. That it emerged from the conference bearing with Germany the "odium for dashing pacifist hopes" for a lasting peace is attributable to Mérey's having become ensnared in details in the important question of compulsory arbitration and his surprising about-face on the issue.

After the conference had convened, Mérey informed the German delegates, Marschall and Kriege, of the Austro-Hungarian position on compulsory arbitration. Austria-Hungary itself would make no proposals but was prepared to vote for a general compulsory arbitration treaty that contained an honor and vital interests clause. Austria-Hungary was also prepared to agree to compulsory arbitration for certain juridical and technical treaties, perhaps even for trade treaties, without any reservations. According to Mérey, the German delegates, who completely rejected compulsory arbitration, were surprised by his disclosures.[75] The German ambassador at Vienna, Count Wedel, expressed his amazement to Aehrenthal that Austria-Hungary held a different position from that of Germany on compulsory arbitration. He reproached Aehrenthal for going against earlier declarations of agreement with the German position.[76] Wedel maintained that as late as April 1907, he had been led to believe that Austria-Hungary's position was in agreement with that of Germany's.[77] Aehrenthal replied by referring to the internal Austro-Hungarian discussions before the conference, which led to the conclusion that a flat rejection of the idea of a compulsory arbitration treaty "would meet with great difficulties." Austria-Hungary therefore would support a general compulsory arbitration treaty covering relatively insignificant matters.[78]

Aehrenthal reported Wedel's démarche to Mérey,[79] who responded with a long report on July 9.[80] Mérey stressed that at the time he talked with Wedel and Kriege in Vienna in winter 1907, serious internal discussions on compulsory arbitration had not yet begun, and he had pointed out then that the discussions were in the nature of first impressions. Germany and Austria-Hungary both had rejected compulsory arbitration at that time specifically because Germany feared far-reaching proposals at the conference. Only in April did the Austro-Hungarian delegates get around to serious internal discussions of concessions in the matter of arbitration. Mérey reminded his chief that at the time he had called his attention to informing Germany of the concessions, but Mérey excused the sin of omission by pointing out that the time would have been too short for the German ambassador to obtain Berlin's agreement to them. As far as Mérey was concerned, the Austro-Hungarian attitude toward compulsory arbitration was correct, and he advised Aehrenthal not to yield to the wishes of Germany. In this instance Germany would not be the "diabolus rotae" who said no to everything. Germany had showed itself obliging in a number of questions and had itself proposed the International Prize Court.[81] Therefore, it could allow itself the luxury of voting against a court of compulsory arbitration. Austria-Hungary, on the other hand, had an indifferent or negative attitude toward the majority of maritime law questions and other issues and would invite "an excessive amount of odium" if it absolutely rejected compulsory arbitration, quite apart from the fact that what Austria-Hungary was prepared to support was harmless. Mérey pointed out that since Austria-Hungary had voted for German proposals in several questions, "there existed no necessity, even with the best relations to Germany, to proceed hand in hand with Germany at the conference in everything." It would be more in accord with what Mérey called "political aesthetic" if Austria-Hungary and Germany "in one or another important matters go different ways."[82] Mérey therefore concluded that Austria-Hungary should maintain its preconference position and leave Germany to its own.

On July 18, the American delegate introduced a proposal according to which the conference states should obligate themselves to submit to the Permanent Court of Arbitration at the Hague disputes over legal questions and controversies arising out of the interpretation and application of treaties if they could not be solved by diplomacy, on the condition that these questions did not involve the

independence, honor, or vital interests of the participating states or
third parties.[83] In a speech on July 23, Marschall, the German delegate,
took a generally negative attitude toward the proposal.[84] In a dispatch to Mérey on July 25, Aehrenthal, agreeing with Mérey's point
of view in his report of July 9, instructed Mérey as follows: "From
your reports . . . I take it that the mood of the Hague Conference is
favorable to the expansion of the machinery of arbitration. . . .
Your Excellency accordingly is empowered to express your consent
not only to the conclusion of a general pseudo-obligatory convention
but to a really binding arbitration treaty covering enumerated and
minor matters as well."[85] Pursuant to his instructions, Mérey announced his agreement with the American proposal and Austria-
Hungary's willingness to go even further and examine proposals
to apply compulsory arbitration to specific matters without any
reservations.[86]

In a report to Aehrenthal of July 31, Mérey described Marschall's
speech as clever but somewhat legalistic and tactless.[87] He had tried,
unsuccessfully, to persuade the first German delegate to be more
compromising on the issue. Mérey believed that the inclination of
Austria-Hungary to vote for compulsory arbitration had produced
a feeling of isolation among the German delegates. In order to avoid
compulsory arbitration, the Germans threw their weight behind
another American proposal for a Permanent Court of Arbitral
Justice, which Mérey believed would hurt the chances of compulsory
arbitration. Mérey himself opposed the court as a "superfluous"
creation.[88] Aehrenthal, on the other hand, favored creating the
court, which he saw as separate from the question of its binding
character and as another sop for public opinion: "It can only be
agreeable to us when in this area as in that of the International Prize
Court, the Conference achieved successes which provide a certain
compensation to public opinion for so many disappointed hopes."[89]

In view of Aehrenthal's consistent support of the position on
compulsory arbitration arrived at before the conference, it must
have come as a shock to Mérey to receive instructions from Aehrenthal dated August 1 that completely reversed that position: "The
conclusion of a general compulsory arbitration treaty which, by the
inclusion of the elastic interest and honor clause is almost worthless,
is not sympathetic to me. According to your private letter of July 27

to . . . Dumba such a pseudo-obligatory world treaty, especially as a consequence of the position of Baron Marschall has retreated far into the background. By your actions, Your Excellency will consider strengthening this tendency.''[90] About a week later, after a speech by the second German delegate, Kriege, rejecting compulsory arbitration, Mérey, who had first strongly supported it, significantly moderated his support.[91] By the end of the month Mérey had retreated so far from his original position that he took over the lead in the opposition to compulsory arbitration from Marschall who had thoroughly discredited himself by his obstructive captiousness.[92]

Near the end of August, Mérey reported that the American proposal (now the Anglo-American proposal,)[93] to which had been added a list of specific cases that safely could be submitted to compulsory arbitration without any reservations, contained technical and juridical weaknesses.[94] He therefore introduced a resolution according to which the conference would express its conviction that matters at issue with regard to disputes arising out of international treaties could be submitted to international arbitration. However, since the treaties concerned very technical questions, Mérey's resolution declared that the conference was not competent to decide which treaties should be submitted. Therefore, the matter should be left to discussion among the governments after the conclusion of the conference. At a later date—perhaps January 1, 1909—the governments would inform one another through the good offices of the Hague cabinet of those treaties which they would consent to submit to compulsory arbitration.[95] From the documents it is not clear whether Mérey made the proposal on his own or whether he was influenced by the German delegation. According to Heinrich Lammasch, Mérey originally intended to refer only the question of compulsory arbitration to a later conference to which not all states would send representatives. However, he encountered sharp resistance from Marschall and changed his resolution accordingly.[96] In any case, Mérey told Aehrenthal that his resolution was intended to make it possible for Germany to avoid voting against compulsory arbitration.[97] Aehrenthal approved of Mérey's resolution and requested Mérey to take a reserved attitude toward the Court of Arbitral Justice, until, as Mérey had suggested, the matter of compulsory arbitration was decided.[98] In any event Mérey reported that there was widespread opposition to the court because of the difficulty of agreeing on a method of appointing judges. If he should join the opposition, the "odium" for its defeat "does not fall on Austria-Hungary."[99]

On October 7, the Anglo-American proposal for compulsory arbitration was introduced in a plenary session. Two weeks earlier, Mérey had advised Aehrenthal of the "hopelessness" of the definitive list of cases to be submitted to compulsory arbitration without any reservations and reminded his chief that without the list, the proposal constituted a pseudo-obligatory treaty, which he did not approve of.[100] On September 26, Aehrenthal had instructed Mérey to vote against the Anglo-American proposal and, if Germany should persist in its opposition to the pseudo-obligatory treaty, against the original American proposal as well should an attempt be made to introduce it as a compromise.[101] Thus, Austria-Hungary, which had originally favored the proposal, voted with Germany and several other states—none of them Great Powers—against it. Although a large majority voted for the proposal, it failed to obtain the unanimity insisted upon by the minority and was not adopted.[102] By its vote against the compulsory arbitration proposal, Austria-Hungary, rather than rescuing Germany from isolation as it had done before the conference, entered into self-isolation alongside Germany and acquired for itself a share of the odium for the failure of significant progress toward the elimination of war.

On October 9, the American proposal to create a Permanent Court of Arbitral Justice was adopted by unanimous acclamation with the exception of Switzerland, but only in the form of a *voeu,* that is, only in principle. Its establishment was deferred until the Powers could agree upon a method of appointing judges.[103] On October 10, Mérey's resolution, strongly opposed by England and America, was defeated despite the support of Germany, Italy, and Russia. Mérey attributed its defeat primarily to the American bloc—the United States and sixteen Latin American states.[104]

In the end the conference states did adopt a declaration recognizing the principle of compulsory arbitration and declaring that certain disputes, notably those relating to the interpretation and application of the provisions of international treaties, were susceptible to being submitted to compulsory arbitration. Although they had not yet concluded such a compulsory arbitration convention, the existing differences of opinion "have not exceeded the bounds of judicial controversy."[105] The meaningless declaration thoroughly accorded with the wishes of Germany, which was opposed to compulsory arbitration from the beginning. Mérey was satisfied with the results. He thought that there could not have been a better solution for Austria-Hungary since it had conceded much less than it originally was prepared to do: "It can only be agreeable to us if, after four months of debate on this question, the mountain brings forth such a mouse."[106]

VI

From the documents it is not possible to say conclusively why Austria-Hungary changed its position on compulsory arbitration. In his final report, Mérey sought to explain why he had departed from his original instructions, which, in a limited sense, favored compulsory arbitration, and joined Germany in opposing it. He stated that only by a thorough discussion of the question, did he acquire a fuller understanding of the matter and saw that the question was not ripe for a discussion at the conference. The German delegation, Mérey wrote, performed the service of revealing the danger of a general arbitration treaty.[107] Even if we concede that Mérey changed his position primarily because of the substantive arguments of the German delegates and not simply out of a desire to support an ally, he can be accused of having given up too soon.

Yet the responsibility was not Mérey's alone. In view of the warning to Mérey to avoid taking the odium of the conference on himself by "quibbling over details" or appearing intransigent, it is astounding that based simply on the argument that the compulsory arbitration proposal was not ripe for discussion, Vienna allowed its ambassador to change his course without reminding him of his earlier reports or instructing him to discuss the matter with Lammasch.[108] The evidence points strongly to the conclusion that Berlin exerted pressure in Vienna to which Aehrenthal yielded. If Germany did intervene in Vienna and exerted pressure on Aehrenthal as this essay assumes, it found in the Austro-Hungarian foreign minister a sympathetic party and not just a weaker ally forced to yield to the wishes of its stronger partner. Aehrenthal's sociopolitical angst had led him to conclude that the peace movement had to be fought from the standpoint of the monarchical-aristocratic principle. The original Austro-Hungarian position on compulsory arbitration reflected Lammasch's convictions, which Aehrenthal adopted for the sake of appearances. Furthermore, Aehrenthal did not wish to gain the animosity of his powerful ally whose help might be needed for the implementation of his plans to defuse the nationalities conflict within the Habsburg monarchy by a more active foreign policy.[109] Perhaps, too, the negotiations for the Anglo-Russian convention concluded on August 31, 1907, played a role in Aehrenthal's decision.

The peace conference had a low priority on Aehrenthal's list of concerns in the summer of 1907. Mérey, in a letter to his father written on August 9, the same day on which he wrote his report signaling his change of course on compulsory arbitration, harshly indicted the Austro-Hungarian Foreign Office's and Dumba's handling of the business of the peace conference:

The letters of Dumba from the [Foreign] Ministry could really demoralize someone who seeks to act according [to the instructions] of his superiors. With the exception of the disarmament question, the [Foreign] Minister appears to be completely unconcerned, the Austrian and Hungarian governments are still informed of next to nothing under the most laughable excuses, and Dumba himself, who is easy going and sloppy, does not take the trouble to read all of my reports. If, in exceptional cases, we request instructions, the latter, as a rule, do not relate to all to the specific situation reported on. At the same time, I can see from colleagues around me how intensively the other governments are concerned about the matter. All of that is not exactly encouraging.[110]

In all likelihood, Mérey's about-face on the issue of compulsory arbitration was a consequence chiefly of Aehrenthal's instructions. Mérey initially supported a position on compulsory arbitration that he believed served the interests of the Habsburg monarchy. After receiving new instructions, which departed from that position, Mérey, as his letter to his father suggests, did his best as a disciplined and conscientious official to carry them out. That he became so zealous in his opposition to compulsory arbitration might be attributed to personal motives. Perhaps he entertained a professional desire to be in the limelight at a great international conference, which he was near the end, even if that meant playing a negative role.[111] The fact that compulsory arbitration was an American proposal may have been another factor. Lammasch says that Mérey had a disdain for America as the "land of the dollar-cult" and that he engaged in sharp exchanges with some American delegates.[112] American opposition to his proposal may have sharpened Mérey's disdain and his opposition to compulsory arbitration. In the end, however, if Mérey did not argue strongly for retaining the old instructions, it was not only because of bureaucratic discipline or because he felt it useless to argue for the old instructions now that the foreign minister had changed his mind. Mérey, Like Aehrenthal, was no friend of the peace movement, and he was just as little inclined as Aehrenthal to act on his own initiative for the principle of compulsory arbitration, which did not represent his convictions. In his final report, Mérey summed up his attitude toward the peace conference in a way that reveals much about the prewar mind set:

The name "Peace Conference" so unfortunate from the beginning, is even less justified for this conference than for that of 1899. Examined closely almost all of the quite diverse, if not dazzling results of our deliberations, concerned questions relating to the laws of war. Pacificism—without regret let it be said—has not profitted at all from this conference.[113]

Aehrenthal and Mérey could be pleased with that outcome. What could have been better than a peace conference that they had subverted to a conference on the rules of war and that left the international and internal status quo intact?

Their satisfaction, however, is evidence of the lack of clarity of their aims and purposes. Austro-Hungarian diplomacy had failed to achieve its aims of avoiding the odium of blocking progress toward a lasting peace and creating a common front with Russia of imperial and conservative powers. Even more significant, Aehrenthal's and Mérey's fright of an amorphous pacifism, as well as their concern over an equally amorphous but powerful public opinion, betrays their own insecurity and their deep uncertainty over where the locus of real power lay. As a consequence of their uncertainty, the prewar mentality of Aehrenthal, Mérey, Dumba, Marschall, and their diplomatic cronies was fed by a considerable amount of sociopolitical anxiety. It may be true that they were guided by power-political considerations, but their motivation was, to a significant extent, domestic angst and not just rational chessboard-like diplomatic strategy. In any event, Aehrenthal's and Mérey's success in the summer of 1907 was short-run. In 1914, the war that the peace movement strove to prevent broke out sweeping away the status quo that the Austro-Hungarian diplomats tried to preserve by defeating the peace movement.

NOTES

1. Ballhausplatz: a reference to the Austro-Hungarian Foreign Office in the same sense as the Wilhelmstrasse for the German Foreign Office.

2. In Dumba's memoirs, as well as in the documents and literature on which this essay is based, the terms *Abrüstung* (disarmament) and *Rüstungbeschränkung* (arms limitation) are used interchangeably to refer to arms limitation, which is really what the diplomatic fuss was about in 1907. Although they are used interchangeably in this essay, it is important to keep in mind that they mean different things. *Disarmament* is the reduction of armaments to the lowest level consistent with domestic safety. *Arms limitation* is abstention from an increase in armaments. See Merze Tate, *The Disarmament Illusion: The Movement for a Limitation of Armaments to 1907* (Cambridge, 1942), ix.

3. Constantin Dumba, *Dreibund-und Entente-Politik in der Alten und Neuen Welt* (Vienna, 1931), 251-52.

4. Ibid., 252.

5. On Austria-Hungary and the 1899 conference, see F. R. Bridge, *From Sadowa to Sarajevo: The Foreign Policy of Austria-Hungary, 1866-1914* (London, 1972), 247; Richard R. Laurence, "The Problem of Peace and Austrian Society: A Study in the Cultural Origins of the First World War" (Ph.D. diss., Stanford, University, 1968), 206-14.

6. For some recent critiques of the traditional approach, see Richard Rosecrance, *Action and Reaction in World Politics: International Systems in Perspective* (Boston, 1963), 1-14, 279-306, and Arno J. Mayer. "Internal Causes and Purposes of War in Europe, 1870-1956," *Journal of Modern History* 41, no. 3 (September 1969): 291-303.

7. Elie Halevy, "The World Crisis 1914-1918: An Interpretation," in R. K. Webb, ed., *The Era of Tyranny* (Garden City, N.Y., 1965), 213-22.

8. *Diplomatische Aktenstücke zur Vorgeschichte des Krieges 1914: Ergänzungen und Nachträge zur Österreichisch-Ungarischen Rotbuch* (Vienna, 1919), III, no. 159, Mensdorff to Berchtold [Austro-Hungarian foreign minister], August 7, 1914. The quotation appears in English in Mensdorff's report.

9. Solomon Wank, introduction to Hans Wehberg, *Die Internationale Beschränkung der Rüstungen* (1919; reprint ed., New York, 1973), 5-6, 17-19.

10. Arno J. Mayer, *Wilson vs. Lenin: Political Origins of the New Diplomacy* (Cleveland, 1964), 1-22 and Mayer, "Domestic Causes of the First World War,"

in Leonard Krieger and Fritz Stern, eds., *The Responsibility of Power: Essays in Honor of Hajo Holborn* (New York, 1969), 308-24.

11. For an example of the variation, see Michael R. Gordon, "Domestic Conflict and the Origins of the First World War: The British and German Cases," *Journal of Modern History* 46, no. 2 (June 1974):191-226.

12. In diplomatic parlance before 1914, *pacifism* covered a wide range of ideas, movements, and proposals, not all of which coincided with pacifism even in the broad sense of general advocacy of peace and internationalism, let alone pacifism in the strict sense of opposition to war under any circumstances on moral and/or religious grounds. On the political beliefs of the diplomats, see part II of this essay and Paul Gordon Lauren, *Diplomats and Bureaucrats:The First Institutional Responses to Twentieth-Century Diplomacy in France and Germany* (Stanford, 1976), 215-21. On the diplomats and public opinion see ibid., 178-207.

13. On the preliminaries, especially the transfer of the initiative for calling the conference from President Theodore Roosevelt to Czar Nicholas, see J. B. Scott, *The Hague Peace Conferences of 1899 and 1907* (Baltimore, 1909), 1:90-95 and Tate, *Disarmament Illusion,* 300-03.

14. The document can be found in Scott, *Hague Peace Conferences,* 1:102.

15. Ibid., 306-07. See also A. J. A. Morris, "The English Radicals' Campaign for Disarmament and the Hague Conference of 1907," *Journal of Modern History* 43, no. 3 (September 1971):367-93.

16. Tate, *Disarmament Illusion,* 324-28, 331-332, 355.

17. For a recent example of this interpretation, see F. R. Bridge, *Great Britain and Austria-Hungary, 1906-1914* (London, 1972), 51 and Bridge, *From Sadowa to Sarajevo* (London, 1972), 284, 292-94.

18. Bridge, *Great Britain and Austria-Hungary,* 51.

19. Haus-, Hof-, und Staatsarchiv, Politisches Archiv I/475, Liasse (Fascicle) XXXII/1, Aehrenthal to Goluchowski, secret private letter, August 23, 1906 (hereafter documents from this source are cited as HHStA, PA I, followed by carton number and document citation).

20. See Solomon Wank, "Varieties of Political Despair: Three Exchanges between Aehrenthal and Goluchowski, 1898-1906," in Joseph Held and Stanley B. Winters, eds., *Intellectual and Social History in the Habsburg Empire from Maria Theresa to the First World War: Essays Dedicated to Robert A. Kann* (Boulder, Col., 1975), 203-04, 221-22.

21. For a recent summary of the decade before the war, see Leo Valiani, *The End of Austria-Hungary* (New York, 1973), 1-47. See also Solomon Wank, "Foreign Policy and the Nationality Problem in the Habsburg Monarchy, 1867-1914," *Austrian History Yearbook* 3, pt. 3 (1967):37-56.

22. HHStA, *Nachlass Mérey,* Aehrenthal to Mérey, June 22, 1905. On Mérey, see part IV of this essay. Aehrenthal's references are to the separation of Norway from Sweden in 1905 and to the conflict between Emperor Francis Joseph and Magyar political leaders over the use of Magyar language in the Austro-Hungarian Army. On the latter see Valiani, *End of Austria-Hungary,* 19-21, 25-26.

23. HHStA, *Nachlass Mérey,* Aehrenthal to Mérey, July 27, 1905.

24. For his thoughts on Russian's internal situation after 1900 and his reaction to the revolution, see the translated reports appended to Abraham Ascher, "The Coming Storm: The Austro-Hungarian Embassy on Russia's Internal Crisis, 1902-1906," *Survey,* no. 53 (October 1964):148-64.

25. Geoffrey Hoskins, *The Russian Constitutional Experiment: Government and Duma, 1907-1914* (Cambridge, Eng., 1973), 14-28, esp. 20-21.

26. On the Three Emperors' League, see William L. Langer, *European Alliances and Alignments, 1871-1890,* 2d ed. (New York, 1962), 171-212, 415-17.

27. I have incorporated the letters into a broader study of the interconnection of domestic and foreign politics in my "Varieties of Political Despair." Only those parts of the letters specifically referring to the peace movement are used here.

28. See n. 29.

29. HHStA, Pa I/475 Liasse XXXII/1, Aehrenthal to Goluchowski, secret private letter No. 1, July 20, 1906. The letter is published in Stephan Verosta, *Theorie und Realität von Bündnissen: Heinrich Lammasch, Karl Renner und der Zweibund (1897-1914)* (Vienna, 1971), 298-303. All translations from the German are my own. Goluchowski's reply of September 15 to all three of Aehrenthal's letters are in ibid., 309-12. I have used archival copies of the letters in my possession.

30. Aehrenthal to Goluchowski, July 20, 1906. The Interparliamentary Union hardly was under the control of socialists, and it is a measure of Aehrenthal's political anxiety that he should believe that to have been the case. On the Interparliamentary Union, see Tate, *Disarmament Illusion,* 85-97.

31. Aehrenthal to Goluchowski, July 20, 1906.

32. Ibid.

33. Ibid.

34. HHStA, PA I/475, Liasse XXXII/1, Aehrenthal to Goluchowski, secret private letter No. 2, July 25, 1906. This second letter was written after the Czar dissolved the Duma.

35. Aehrenthal to Goluchowski, July 20, 1906.

36. W. M. Carlgren, *Iswolsky und Aehrenthal vor der bosnischen Annexionskrise* (Uppsala, 1955), 101-10.

37. The unpublished Austro-Hungarian documents are deposited in HHStA, Administrative Registratur, Fach 60/Haag II (hereafter cited as AR 60 followed by the carton number and document citation). For the German side of the negotiations, see *Die Grösse Politik der Europäischen Kabinette 1871-1914,* ed. Johannes Lepsius et al. (Berlin, 1921-1927), 23: pt. 1 (hereafter cited as GP 23/1 followed by series number of the document).

38. AR 60/65, "Resolution der auf den 9. Juni nach Wien einberufenen Delegation des Reichrathes." Quoted in Laurence, "Problem of Peace," 220.

39. AR 60/65, Aehrenthal to Fürstenberg, telegram 13, February 13, 1907.

40. Ibid., Aehrenthal to Fürstenberg, private letter 163, very confidential, February 16, 1907.

41. Ibid.

42. HHStA, PA I/483, Liasse Geheim XXVII/b, Aehrenthal to Berchtold, instructions, no. 234, very confidential, March 6, 1907.

43. AR 60/65, Fürstenberg to Aehrenthal, telegram 16, February 14, 1907, and telegram 19, very confidential, February 20, 1907.

44. Ibid., Fürstenberg to Aehrenthal, telegram 19, very confidential, February 20, 1907.

45. Ibid.

46. Ibid., Fürstenberg to Aehrenthal, 16, February 14, 1907.

47. Ibid., Aehrenthal to Fürstenberg, private letter 163, very confidential, February 16, 1907.

48. For a detailed analysis of the negotiations between Austria-Hungary and Germany, see Silke I. Fischer, "Die Beziehungen Österreich-Ungarn zu Deutschland in den esten Jahren der Ministerschaft Aehrenthals 1906-1908" (Ph.D. diss., University of Vienna, 1959), 26-48. For brief summaries, see the works by F. R. Bridge cited in n. 15 above.

49. Aehrenthal outlined the procedure at a conference held to draw up instructions for the Austro-Hungarian delegation to the peace conference. See part IV of this essay.

50. A copy of the letter is in Scott, *Hague Peace Conferences,* 1:105-06.

51. GP 23/1, no. 7859, Wedel to Foreign Office, February 26, 1907. Count Karl von Wedel was German ambassador at Vienna.

52. AR 60/65, Lützow to Aehrenthal, telegram 25, February 22, 1907. Count Heinrich Lützow was Austro-Hungarian ambassador at Rome.

53. AR 60/66, Aehrenthal to Berchtold, telegram 31, March 28, 1907, and GP 23/1, no. 7899, Wedel to Foreign Office, March 30, 1907.

54. Ibid., Szögyeny to Aehrenthal, telegram (no number), confidential, March 29, 1907, and GP 23/1, no. 7896, Heinrich von Tschirschky (German Foreign secretary) to Ulrich von Brockdorff-Rantzau (secretary of German embassy at Vienna), March 21, 1907. Count Ladislaus von Szögyeny was Austro-Hungarian ambassador at Berlin.

55. Wilhelm Carlgren is incorrect in asserting that the reservation included a specific reference to the disarmament question. *Izwolsky und Aehrenthal vor der bosnischen Annexionskrise* (Uppsala, 1955), 57, n. 2.

56. GP 23/1, no. 7899, Wedel to Foreign Office, March 30, 1907, and AR 60/66, Szögyeny to Aehrenthal, telegram 57, April 4, 1907.

57. HHStA, *Nachless Berchtold,* March 30, 1907.

58. AR 60/66 Aehrenthal to Berchtold, despatch no. 333738/7, May 12, 1907, and GP 23/1 no. 7940, *Aide-Mémoire,* May 15, 1907.

59. AR 60/68, Aehrenthal to Berchtold, telegram 64, June 11, 1907.

60. Ibid., Berchtold to Aehrenthal, telegram 77, June 7, 1907, and GP 23/1, no. 7948 for a copy of the *Aide Mémoire* on the point that Izvolsky presented to the Austro-Hungarian and German ambassadors.

61. HHStA, PA XII/339, Liasse XXXV/10, Aehrenthal to Berchtold, despatch no. 717, very confidential, June 17, 1907.

62. Tate, *Disarmament Illusion,* 334.

63. GP 23/1, no. 7957, Metternich (German ambassador at London) to Foreign Office, June 14, 1907. See also Bridge, *Great Britain and Austria-Hungary,* 52.

64. For the names of the other Austro-Hungarian delegates see Scott, *Hague Peace Conferences,* 2:261. On Mérey see Dumba, *Dreibund,* 251.

65. The minutes of these meetings are deposited in AR 60/67.

66. AR 60/67, *Protocoll uber die am 25. Mai 1907 in Ministerium des k.u.k. Hauses und des Aeussern stattgehabte Besprechung zur Feststellung der Instruktionen für die österreichisch-ungarischen Delegierten bei der den 15. Juni nach dem Haag einberufenen II. internationalen Friedenskonferenz.*

67. GP23/1 No. 7834, Wedel to Foreign Office, January 26, 1907, and no. 7860, Wedel to Bülow, February 27, 1907.

68. Heinrich Lammasch, "Die zweiter Haager Friedenskonferenz," in Lammasch's fragmentary memoirs edited by Marga Lammasch and Hans Sperl, *Heinrich Lammasch: Seine Aufzeichningen, sein Wirken und seine Politik* (Vienna, 1922), 34. See also Verosta, *Theorie,* 15-16. The presence of Lammasch, both a respected member of the peace movement and a foreign office and government adviser who was close to Archduke Franz Ferdinand and high army officers, points out the need to differentiate carefully among various strands of the pre-1914 peace movement with regard to social composition, ideological orientation, strategy and goals. On Lammasch, see Lammasch and Sperl, *Lammasch*; Verosta, *Theorie,* 1-28, 297-316 and passim; Albert Fuchs, *Geistige Stromungen in Osterreich 1867-1918* (Vienna, 1949), 265-70; Sandi E. Cooper, "Liberal Internationalists before World War I," *Peace and Change* no. 2 (Spring 1973):11-19, and the essay by Richard R. Laurence in this volume.

69. AR 60/68, Mérey to Aehrenthal, report 2A, confidential, June 18, 1907.

70. Ibid., Aehrenthal to Berchtold, instructions 819, very confidential, June 27, 1907.

71. Ibid., Aehrenthal to Mérey, instructions 863, July 4, 1907. In the rough draft, the last part of the sentence reads "to leave to your German colleagues the odium attached to that [splitting hairs]." The sentence was crossed out in the final draft.

72. AR 60/68, Aehrenthal to Schonaich, no. 844, July 23, 1907 and Schonaich to Aehrenthal, no. 4966, July 3, 1907. This was a reversal of the position agreed upon at the conference on May 25.

73. AR 60/71, Aehrenthal to Berchtold, August 14, 1907.

74. AR 60/69, Aehrenthal to Berchtold, telegram 77, July 24, 1907.

75. Ibid., 60/68, Mérey to Aehrenthal, report 8B, confidential, July 9, 1907, and GP 23/2, no. 7988, Marschall to Foreign Office, June 18, 1907.

76. See part IVof this essay.

77. GP 23/1, no. 7929, Wedel to Bülow, April 25, 1907.

78. AR 60/68, Aehrenthal to Mérey, instructions 864, July 4, 1907.

79. Ibid.

80. AR 60/68, Mérey to Aehrenthal, report 8B, confidential, July 9, 1907.

81. This court dealt with captured property of neutrals in wartime and was not related to the issue of compulsory arbitration of international disputes to preclude the outbreak of war.

82. By "political aesthetic," Mérey seems to have meant a diplomatic tactic whereby a state might not appear to be too closely allied (or subservient) to another

state with which it really is too closely tied (or subservient). Germany, of course, was by far the stronger partner in the alliance between Vienna and Berlin, and Austria-Hungary was perceived as subservient to German wishes in all important matters. Mérey's proposed tactic is an example of the distinction between diplomacy as means and policy as ends made at the beginning of this essay. For more on "political aesthetic" see Verosta, *Theorie,* 18-19.

83. Scott, *Hague Peace Conferences,* 1:335-36.

84. Ibid., 339-40.

85. AR 60/69, Aehrenthal to Mérey, instructions 1013, July 25, 1907.

86. Lammasch, "Die zweiter Haager Friedenskonferenz," 52.

87. AR 60/70, Mérey to Aehrenthal, report 16B, July 31, 1907.

88. The word *superfluous* appears in a report to Aehrenthal of August 9 (report 21E, AR 60/70). The Permanent Court of Arbitration created in 1899 was not a court in the strict sense nor was it permanent. It consisted of a panel of arbitrators, not all of whom were trained jurists, and was in fact constituted anew for each case. Its decisions were not reached juridically but through compromise and negotiation (that is, by diplomacy). The proposed Permanent Court of Arbitral Justice would be a court in the strict sense. It would hold regular sessions at the Hague, be composed of jurists serving fixed terms, and would hand down judicial decisions. The proposed court would not replace the one created in 1899 but would exist alongside it with parties to a dispute choosing one or the other according to the nature of the dispute. See ibid., and Scott, *Hague Peace Conferences,* 1:442-45. There is no mention of the Court of Arbitral Justice in the minutes of the May 25 conference, which drew up the instructions for the Austro-Hungarian delegation.

89. AR 60/70, Aehrenthal to Mérey, instructions 1038, July 27, 1907.

90. Ibid., Aehrenthal to Mérey, instructions 1071, August 1, 1907. The new instructions moved the Austro-Hungarian position on the issue close to the German one. See Scott, *Hague Peace Conferences,* 1:339-40.

91. AR 60/70, Mérey to Aehrenthal, report 21E, August 9, 1907.

92. See Marschall's speech against compulsory arbitration in Scott, *Hague Peace Conferences,* 1:354-58. On Mérey's retreat see Lammasch, "Die zweiter Haager Friedenskonferenz," 52ff.

93. Scott, *Hague Peace Conferences,* 1:369-73.

94. AR 60/71, Mérey to Aehrenthal, report 270, August 23, 1907.

95. Ibid. For the text of Mérey's resolution see Scott, *Hague Peace Conferences,* 1:242-43.

96. Lammasch, "Die zweiter Haager Friedenskonferenz," 52.

97. AR 60/71, Mérey to Aehrenthal, report 27C, August 23, 1907.

98. Ibid., Aehrenthal to Mérey, telegram 23, August 27, 1907.

99. Ibid., Mérey to Aehrenthal, report 27C, August 23, 1907.

100. Ibid., Mérey to Aehrenthal, telegram 26, September 23, 1907. According to Lammasch, most of Mérey's objections to the proposal were inconsequential. Lammasch "Die zweiter Haagerfriedenskonferenz," 56.

101. AR 60/71, Aehrenthal to Mérey, instructions 1409, September 26, 1907.

102. Mérey informed Aehrenthal that he took the floor numerous times in opposi-

tion to the proposal. See AR 60/74, Mérey to Aehrenthal, report 47, October 18, 1907. The final vote was thirty-three for, seven against, and three abstentions.

103. Ibid., and Scott, *Hague Peace Conferences,* 1:459-60.

104. AR 60/74, Mérey to Aehrenthal, telegram 28, October 11, 1907. The final vote was fourteen for, twenty-three against, and seven abstentions.

105. See Scott, *Hague Peace Conferences,* 1:381.

106. AR 60/74, Mérey to Aehrenthal, telegram 28, October 11, 1907. See also Mérey to Aehrenthal, report 47, October 18, 1907.

107. Ibid., Mérey to Aehrenthal, report 47, October 18, 1907.

108. After speeches by Mérey on October 5 and 7 against compulsory arbitration, Lammasch submitted his resignation as the delegation's legal adviser to Mérey, who refused to accept it. Mérey did not inform Aehrenthal of the incident. Lammasch, "Die zweiter Haager Friedenskonferenz," 57.

109. Solomon Wank, "Aehrenthal and the Sanjak of Novibazar Railway Project," *Slavonic and East European Review* 42, no. 99 (June 1964):353-69.

110. HHStA, *Nachlass Mérey,* Mérey to his father, August 9, 1907. In reports to Aehrenthal shortly after the opening of the conference and near its end, Mérey complained about Austria-Hungary's inadequate preparation for the conference relative to other states. See AR 60/68, Mérey to Aehrenthal, report 8B, confidential, July 9, 1907 and AR 60/72, Mérey to Aehrenthal, report 29A, confidential, September 6, 1907.

111. See Mérey's remarks in his final report on his role during the latter part of the conference: AR 60/74, Mérey to Aehrenthal, report 47, October 18, 1907. See also Scott, *Hague Peace Conferences,* 1:157, and n.102 above.

112. Verosta, *Theorie,* 21.

113. AR 60/74, Mérey to Aehrenthal, report 47, October 18, 1907.

5

C. P. Trevelyan's Road to Resignation 1906-14: The Odyssey of an Antiwar Liberal

A. J. ANTHONY MORRIS

Charles Philips Trevelyan was born in 1870. As the eldest son in a family that had already provided two generations to serve the Liberal cause, a parliamentary career was preordained. In 1899, he was elected Liberal MP for the Elland constituency in Yorkshire, a seat he retained until 1918.

Trevelyan's advancement within the Liberal party was not as rapid as he had hoped or might reasonably have expected. Not until 1908 was he given a junior appointment. He was neither sooner nor more generously rewarded because he refused to push himself and because his blunt expression of opinions concernng domestic political issues was not calculated to endear him to those who exercised patronage.

In August 1914, Trevelyan, together with Lord Morley of Blackburn and John Burns, resigned from Asquith's administration. The two senior ministers offered no public explanation for their action. Despite his own inclination and in deference to the wishes of his colleagues, Trevelyan offered no explanation of his action to the Commons. He did, however, publish a letter to his constituents, which was suppressed by most of the national press.[1] The letter did nothing to convince many of Trevelyan's former colleagues that his action had been other than hasty and ill considered. Many supposed that he was inveigled into his association with the Union of Democratic Control[2] (the leading antiwar organization in England), as a front affording respectability to the unpatriotic designs of men like E. D. Morel, J. Ramsay MacDonald, and Norman Angell.[3] When former colleagues urged Trevelyan to acknowledge that he had made a mistake, he dismissed their claim summarily. Time strengthened his conviction that resignation had been the only honorable course. He never weakened in his belief that Britain had been wrong to go to war.

Why did Trevelyan refuse to support the government? As Arthur Ponsonby observed when writing to E. D. Morel in September 1914, before the outbreak of war Trevelyan had not been an active and overt critic of the government's foreign policy. Many Liberals who had made no secret of their distrust of Sir Edward Grey and the policies he pursued—particularly toward Germany—in August 1914 had supported the government. Why did not Trevelyan do the same?

Immediately after Grey had spoken to the Commons on the afternoon of August 3, Trevelyan retired to his room and wrote his letter of resignation to Asquith.

I am afraid that I cannot conscientiously remain any longer in the Government. . . . I have not felt justified in troubling you at such a time with an expression of my opinions. But the difference I'm afraid is fundamental and concerns our whole relations with France and Germany.[4]

Though the letter was penned hastily, for almost a week Trevelyan had thought of little else but the growing threat of war with Germany. He had talked with those whose judgment he trusted. He had listened to and weighed their advice. His letter of resignation, therefore, was not the swift response to a moment's passion. It had been calculated.

A particularly intimate friend of Trevelyan was Walter Runciman. As a minister he had been able to give Trevelyan news of the changing loyalties and stratagems that to the last had plagued the cabinet.[5] Runciman chose to remain a member of the government. He explained why in a letter to Trevelyan: "That one is miserable beyond measure is natural enough, but . . . , that is not in itself sufficient to justify us in handing over policy and control to the Tories."[6] Trevelyan was not persuaded by that argument. However, his anger was directed against neither his party nor the halting excuses of erstwhile colleagues, but the perfidy of one man.

In the past, Trevelyan had ignored advice from friends that he should not trust Sir Edward Grey. He had believed Grey implicitly when the minister had said that England was under no obligation to support France by force of arms. Now Grey, who constantly had advertised his love of peace, had committed England to an unnecessary war by his past promises and present words. It was Grey's responsibility that England had been inveigled into Armageddon instead of remaining neutral. Grey had betrayed his country, friends, and party and compounded his infamy by an appeal to the basest passions: "He gave not a single argument why we should support France. But he showed us he had all along been leading her to expect our support, and appealed to us as bound in *honour*. . . . The Tories shouted with delight."[7] The joyous Tory acclamation of Grey's speech confirmed Trevelyan's belief that his decision to resign had been the only honorable course open to him. He told his wife, Molly:

Whatever happens, I have done one thing which will at least seem to be a beacon of conduct to some of the best as well as some of the poorest and commonest of folk. It was singularly easy to do as I saw so clearly I had got to do it. The cause alone is heart rending. . . . How the world has changed! And only one week!![8]

Like most of the other Liberal MPs who returned to the Commons after the 1906 election, Charles Trevelyan was not particularly well informed about or all that interested in questions of foreign policy. His main concern was the urgent need for domestic reforms after a long period of Tory rule. He had made one reference only to foreign policy in his election address, and that was hidden away in a short paragraph emphasizing the need for economy. Britain could anticipate a long period of peace, but only "if we cultivate our present good relations with France, if we foster our growing friendliness with America, if we use our strength to enforce peace, if we recognise that the power of the dangerously aggressive bureaucracy of Russia has been crippled, probably for ever."[9] Trevelyan did not suppose it was for him to provide specific remedies for foreign policy ailments. Everything was implied by his support for free trade. He championed that policy because it emphasized the sovereign truth of the interdependence of nations.

Radical Liberals were quick to claim there was an inevitable dichotomy between Trevelyan's views on domestic issues and his loyalties as a Liberal imperialist. Trevelyan rejected their opinion. "Manchester Guardian liberals," as he dubbed his critics, undoubtedly were sincere men who meant well, but a careful examination of their theories proved them to be, as often as not, unrealistic. In the early years of the Liberal government, Trevelyan was more critical of pacifist and radical Liberals and their Labour colleagues than of the Tory leaders, Lord Lansdowne and Arthur Balfour. He admitted that some Tories undoubtedly were jingoistic, but one could not question the Tory leaders' desire for peace. Whatever they claimed to the contrary, Radicals and Socialists were "not to any real extent international. They are for peace in the main. But they have no logical or complete antimilitaristic policy. They are content at present with a policy of reduction of armaments, the encouragement of arbitration and a persistently friendly attitude towards other Powers." They impertinently supposed that Liberal imperialists were not enthusiastic supporters of peace, but they were "publicists and politicians who presume[d] a cosmopolitan knowledge that few can rightly claim." The Liberal leader, Sir Henry Campbell-Bannerman, was a Radical; the foreign secretary, Sir Edward Grey, a "Limp." Both were "men of peace": "They have behind them a party whose first demand is peace. When all rulers in all the nations of the world have as little will to quarrel as ours have now . . . wars will begin to cease."[10] During this period, Trevelyan's view of foreign policy were neither compelling nor sophisticated. He thought little about the subject and was content to leave the conduct of British affairs abroad unquestioningly in the hands of the foreign secretary and the various Foreign Office officials. Trevelyan did not doubt they could be trusted.[11]

Trevelyan hated war, but he was no pacifist—save in the sense that with many other Liberal and Labour politicians he shared a sentimental attachment to the ideal of universal peace.[12] In 1918, because of his work with the UDC, he was elected president of the

National Peace Council.[13] He never believed, however, that the traditional pacifist agencies would ever exercise a significant influence upon the conduct of nations. In private, he sometimes jested at the utopian claims of some pacifists. In November 1913, for instance, after he had spoken to an important pacifist meeting, he informed his wife in a letter that his companions had been "a funny crowd. There were even people here who thought we ought to disarm altogether."[14] Trevelyan thought himself, first and foremost, a practical politician. Idealism, nobility of intent, the highest moral aspirations were all very well, but he would never commit himself to ideas that to him seemed to be bizarre and for the most part were impractical and impossible to apply.

Trevelyan thought of himself as something of an expert on naval and military questions in general and the problem of disarmament in particular.[15] While many other Liberals affected an air of indifference or cultivated their ignorance of military matters as a supposed virtue, Trevelyan never subscribed to the Radical orthodoxy that debates on the army estimates were either a bore or a waste of time. As to Richard Haldane's tenure of the War Office, he counted that a blessing. The Radicals distrusted Haldane. They never forgave him for supporting Rosebery. Trevelyan was not only fond of Haldane, he actually claimed to understand the minister.[16] Unlike others in his party, Trevelyan did not suppose that Haldane's army reforms, which gave the lord lieutenants of the counties a more important role, were antidemocratic, reactionary, or feudal. He did not believe Haldane was intent on the militarization of British youth by encouraging the Boy Scout movement and the formation of school cadet corps. For Trevelyan, Haldane's scheme quite simply provided the best solution that had been offered the country to solve the problem of reorganizing its army. Haldane's reforms were not (as some Liberals claimed) an affront to Liberal ideals. They embodied two fundamental Liberal principles: the strengthening of the voluntary element and value for money. Radical Liberals when attacking Haldane claimed to be advertising "true Liberalism." In fact, they were merely indulging their antimilitary prejudices. Their petulant assertions that time and money wasted on the army would better be spent upon social reforms were false. Trevelyan wanted social reform as much as any Radical, but the minimal demands of national defense had to be met. The first rule of government remained salus populi suprema lex.

At the least, Trevelyan thought the Radicals should have praised Haldane for not being entirely unsuccessful in meeting the demands of the Liberal party's economists. The army estimates had been trimmed; not so those of the navy. "The main difficulty there," averred Trevelyan to his mother, "is Jacky Fisher and his sea dogs who want impossibilities and have to be thumped by the Cabinet."[17] Trevelyan certainly deprecated the ever-increasing cost of Britain's navy, but he never doubted that the cabinet did all that was possible to curb the extravagances of the sea lords. Those who were civil lords at the Admiralty (with the possible exception of Winston Churchill) were intent upon securing value for the smallest expenditure consonant with the paramount consideration that the nation's safety should never be threatened. Trevelyan believed Britain should "rule the waves." That was the best guarantee of world peace. But the price of such supremacy, though not small, could never be less than that asked of the nation and Parliament by a Liberal administration. At the height of the 1909 naval panic, when England in response to a supposed acceleration by the Germans had doubled the Dreadnought building program, Trevelyan in a speech to his constituents maintained that the Liberal government was demanding no more than was reasonable given the particular circumstances:

We must keep abreast of other nations in the newest products of military necessity. . . . I cannot say with what deep thankfullness there is not at this moment a Tory Government in power. I hardly like to think of the number of Dreadnoughts we should be building. . . . I believe this panic has been stimulated by Tory members of Parliament and Tory newspapers.

For Trevelyan there was no inconsistency between the government's asking each year for more and bigger battleships and its even more frequent protestations that its sincere desire was to reduce the expenditure on armaments. For Trevelyan there was no paradox for there had never been "a saner and more pacific Government in office," or "a saner man at the head of foreign affairs than Sir Edward Grey from whom we have never heard a single word of bravado . . . we can place our trust in the business-like men at the head of the Government."[18]

Trust was the key word in Trevelyan's speech. He trusted the Liberal government. Above everything and everyone else, he trusted Sir Edward Grey, and it is this trust for the foreign secretary that explains much of his general attitude to questions of foreign policy before 1914. Indeed, in the early years of the Liberal government, Trevelyan disagreed with Grey upon one subject only: Russia. Otherwise, he told his father, he had a "profound confidence" in Grey's "general policy and studious labours for peace."[19]

Trevelyan's concern for Russia was shared by most English Radicals and their Labour allies. The iniquities of the czar's regime struck a chord of sympathy for its victims in Trevelyan's heart quite unlike any other foreign issue. He deplored the signing of the Anglo-Russian Convention in 1907. A friend had written, "We must surely be doing something to strengthen the Russian government in exchange for the assurances she is giving us. . . . If we consider material advantages . . . , of more importance than the evil of helping the party of reaction in Russia . . . we are committing a stupendous crime."[20] Yet it could not be denied that since France, Russia's ally, had joined Britain in the entente cordiale, it made diplomatic sense for Russia and Britain to draw closer together. Grey had always declared his strong personal wish to effect a rapprochement with Russia. The foreign secretary had little sympathy for the critics of his Russian policy thinking, as did the prime minister, that demonstrations against the czar's government merely injured the cause of Russian Liberals by providing ammunition for the reactionaries. Trevelyan, however, saw the issue quite differently. Liberal championship of liberty would be hopelessly compromised if the British government associated with the czar's government, the promoters and apologists of massacre. If Grey pandered to Russian despotism, the Liberals could not hope indefinitely to preserve allegiance to vital constitutional principles at home. A diplomatic advantage should not be the price of purchase for a nation's soul. At the least, conscience dictated that Grey should be pressed to explain himself. Typically, Grey's critics formed themselves into yet another committee. The Russian Committee was hastily convened with the usual membership of MPs, academics, and journalists, and Trevelyan was elected chairman. His espousal of the anticonvention cause won him the approval of many Liberals who had suspected his soundness on the Russian issue because he was a Liberal imperialist.

George Young wrote, "You are . . . the first representative outside the Government of Liberal Imperialism, and one is glad to
know that there is no difference in spirit between that and the humanity of the free nations. . . . Honesty . . . is the best policy, and
we should pay as heavily in after years with the Russian Constitutional State for any temporary advantage we gain now by counten-
ancing the present authorities."[21]

Because it was an honestly and widely held opinion among Liberal
MPs that nothing would ever justify their government's consorting
with the czar's, when it was announced in June 1906 that the British
fleet as part of its Baltic cruise would be paying a complimentary
visit to Kronstadt, the floodgates of disaffection burst open. Trevelyan
was but one among many anxious to question Grey on what was, to
say the least, a dubious diplomatic maneuver. Grey, who hated
answering questions in the Commons, wrote to Trevelyan asking:

Could you not put off your question about the fleet? I do not think you can
realise what the effect of these questions is likely to be. I should like to
have the opportunity of explaining what I believe is the true situation to
you first. . . . You could then decide as you thought right about putting
the question.

Many, less artless than Trevelyan, were disarmed by the foreign
secretary's pleas for silence in the "national interest." Replying
to Grey, Trevelyan blustered, "Some of us care nothing for diplomatic custom where the freedom of a people is hanging in a very nice
balance. We hate the Russian Government as we have never hated
before . . . it is a case in which we cannot be silent."[22] But Trevelyan
was silent in the House, for when the foreign secretary put his finger
to his lips it was not for a Liberal MP to press for explanations.
And when Grey occasionally and reluctantly answered his critics
in the House, Trevelyan was quick to accept the proffered explanation. Sir Edward was a man of honor. He could, he must be trusted.[23]

In the long term, more significant for Trevelyan than Grey's
attitude toward Russia was the foreign secretary's handling of the
Congo question. The accident of a libel action against Trevelyan
by Sir Thomas Brooke-Hitching, a friend of King Leopold of Belgium,
led Trevelyan to ask E. D. Morel, the founder of the Congo Reform
Association, for his help. The threatened action was amicably settled,

but by then an important and lifelong friendship had been forged between Trevelyan and the man who sought at every opportunity to expose the iniquities perpetrated by the Belgians on the hapless Congolese. Edmund Dene Morel was a man of formidable energy and organizational ability. As a professional agitator, he was extraordinarily successful though inclined to be too confident and self-righteous in his judgments of men and measures. Trevelyan responded eagerly to Morel's patent enthusiasm and humanitarianism. He was soon established as one of that select band of MPs who in the Commons repeatedly advertised the scandals and iniquities of Leopold's rule in the Congo.

Morel's nature was passionate and impatient; Sir Edward Grey moved with such circumspection to solve the Congo question that it is hardly surprising his motives were suspected. Morel was heretical enough even to doubt Grey's veracity concerning the foreign secretary's frequent plaint that if the British government acted decisively in the Congo, it would most likely lead to unwanted European complications. He believed the truth was that Grey's hands were tied by a secret treaty with France. Though himself half-French, Morel had an almost pathological distrust, even hatred, of the French. He was sure that they were exerting an undue influence upon Grey and forcing the foreign secretary to adopt an anti-German stance. In the early years of their friendship Trevelyan stoutly defended Grey to Morel. In March 1908, for example, he wrote to Morel, "After seeing Grey I do not know what more can be done. . . . What else can Grey do? Are we to go to war?"[24]

For a good many Britons at the turn of the century France was still the enemy. Even more thought that the idea of an Anglo-French entente was more of a psychological paradox than a treaty between two Saxon nations (Germany and Britain). After all, the fundamental characteristics of the two nations were so similar. The *Manchester Guardian* (the daily organ by which the Liberal-Radical conscience addressed the public) in June 1909 editorially encapsulated the paradox in a question: "If our statesman had the wit to make friendship with France, and even with Russia, with both of whom our political quarrels were far older and more difficult of adjustment, then why not have Germany as a friend rather than an enemy?"[25] Trevelyan recognized the paradox, but unlike Morel and so many other Radical Liberals, he did not think that Grey deliberately intended to alienate Germany by his policies. Relations with Germany were less than amicable because an atmosphere of mutual suspicion and fear had been purposely created by yellow press vaporings. Some unscrupulous Tories, with their supporters in the establishment and the press, were prepared to manipulate popular prejudice in the hope of gaining thereby some electoral advantage. This Tory engineering of the various anti-German scares was nothing short of a national crime.[26] As far as Trevelyan was concerned, he was unconvinced by the evidence that Grey or the Liberal government in any way were responsible for the poor state of Anglo-German relations. And then came the Agadir incident.

In May 1911, the French sent a military expedition to relieve their forces in Fez after riots in Morocco. Little more than a month later the Germans despatched a gunboat, the *Panther* to Agadir, ostensibly to protect German merchants. The point at issue between the French and Germans was a request by the latter for compensation under the terms of the Algeciras Act.[27] Those few Englishmen who would have noticed these events would rightly have dismissed them as no more than another sordid example of two greedy European powers bargaining over their real estate rights in Africa. Then the situation was suddenly and dramatically changed by a speech given by David Lloyd George, chancellor of the exchequer and considered by many to be the leading pacifist in the Liberal cabinet. With the agreement of Grey, Lloyd George inserted a paragraph in an after-dinner speech to city financiers at the Mansion House that threatened Germany with what amounted to a contingent declaration of war. Because at the time British politicians were furiously engaged in the final stages of the Parliament bill, Trevelyan thought the chancellor's remarks "ill advised" as he had "already enough on his hands without taking on the German Emporer."[28] Indeed, by the time Parliament was prorogued for its summer recess on August 22, the menace of European war had so far receded as to have been dismissed as midsummer madness. Then on the last day of August Trevelyan received a letter from Walter Runciman marked "most secret." The minister's letter warned that German action in Morocco might lead to most unfortunate circumstances for Britain. Trevelyan reported to his wife, "Runciman thinks that the situation is very explosive and that we may easily become involved if Germany and France come to blows."[29]

The threat of war, however, seemed to pass as swiftly as it had emerged. Within a fortnight Runciman told Trevelyan, "The future course of events in Morocco is likely to be more tedious than dangerous, unless Germany springs an ultimatum out of the blue which I cannot believe."[30] How, then, was this "near war" episode to be explained? E. D. Morel was soon to publish an explanation, which presented a coherent, if particular, interpretation of the diplomatic antecedents to the Agadir troubles.[31] Morel claimed that Grey was so dominated by his fear of Germany that he had allowed Britain to be tied to France's chariot wheels. At Agadir Germany had a good case in law for its action; France was not the injured innocent it claimed to be; and Britain's interference with the Mansion House speech of Lloyd George was an indefensible provocation. Unwittingly, unwillingly, England was being drawn by Foreign Secretary Grey and an ally, France, into European entanglements that sooner rather than later would lead to war with Germany. Trevelyan thought Morel's whole idea exaggerated, but Morel was quick to answer that "none of the facts in my book has ever been contested."[32]

Until that long, hot summer of 1911, Trevelyan had taken little interest in foreign policy. Now there was no excuse for a lack of interest, and even less for ignorance as Radical, pacifist, and Socialist agencies in Britain demanded better Anglo-German understanding and campaigned for the democratic control of foreign policy.[33] The campaign, of which Trevelyan was no more than an interested spectator, developed into a personal attack upon Grey. The foreign secretary was charged with the unauthorized revival of the pernicious doctrine of the balance of power and converting the entente cordiale into an anti-German alliance. In November 1911, Grey, because of incessant attacks mainly from Liberal MPs, was obliged to defend himself and his policies in open debate in the Commons.

According to the prime minister, H. H. Asquith, Grey's reply to his critics torpedoed them. If that was true, then a surprising number remained both unsunk and unrepentant, and none more so than the elderly Radical Leonard Courtney. In a debate in the Lords, he launched a tremendous philippic against Grey and his handling of foreign affairs.[34] It was Trevelyan's opinion that the foreign secretary had "almost certainly" refuted the case made against him. Grey's speech had been "good." Yet there remained one nagging doubt. He did not mind admitting to his wife, "There need not have

been all that fuss there was in July. It certainly rose out of suspicion
of Germany which her ultimate action did not justify."[35] The seed
of doubt was sown. In the future Trevelyan would listen more
earnestly and with less skepticism when Radical or Labour MPs
criticized Sir Edward's conduct of the nation's diplomatic affairs.

After the excitement of the Agadir incident, there was a temporary improvement in Anglo-German relations. In February 1912,
Haldane (soon to quit the War Office for the Woolsack) went to
Berlin on a special mission. It had long been argued by the Radical
Liberals that an unprejudiced British negotiator would soon settle
the outstanding difficulties between the two nations. But the mission
did not prove the success that they had anticipated. The blame for
this they allotted in equal parts to Winston Churchill, for an imper-
tinent and intemperate speech about the German navy, and Edward
Grey, for his less than enthusiastic support for his friend's mission.
Whoever was to blame, there was little to encourage men of goodwill in either country who were anxious to repair relations and soothe
away suspicion and jealousy. One such man, the pacifist editor of
Nord und Süd, Ludwig Stein, following the Agadir crisis turned
his journal into the single most important forum for the discussion
of international tensions. When Stein visited England in July 1912,
Trevelyan invited him to stay at their London home. Trevelyan
told his wife how "very good" Stein's work was and how he wished
to do something to help, but "it is not easy to see what to say as a
member of the Government."[36] In this admission lies the key to
understanding why Trevelyan was so reluctant to avow openly his
discontent with Grey. Above all other considerations, Trevelyan
was convinced of his duty to support the government. Possibly
the memory of how he had been passed over for junior office until
1908 exaggerated his concern to be seen by the leaders of his party
as a loyal and responsible supporter. More likely in terms of practical
political priorities, Trevelyan recognized that it would be little short
of idiotic to put at hazard the future of the Liberal administration
for the sake of a conscience troubled by mere suspicion when there
was the certainty that a Tory government would be overtly jingoistic,
extravagant in demands for armament expenditure, and unsym-
pathetic toward social reform. The Liberal leaders were well aware
of the dilemma of conscience suffered by their more Radical sup-

porters, and they worked assiduously to undermine any resolve to rebellion by raising the convenient specter of a Tory government. So it was that Trevelyan, with great reluctance, was prepared to admit, even to those closest to him, only that he was concerned about the direction British foreign policy was taking under Grey. He wrote to his mother in late July 1912: "The home situation is wonderfully improved since the beginning of the Session. What is serious is the foreign one. All that can be said in regard to that is that an opinion is being formed to take foreign politics seriously instead of leaving it to the diplomatists."[37] He still found it almost impossible to bring himself overtly to express his doubts about or censure the Liberal foreign secretary. A meeting with Professor Edward Granville Browne in October, however, was to change that.

E. G. Browne was a leading opponent of the Anglo-Russian Convention. He was vice-chairman of the Persian Committee, a group of Radical politicians and academics that constantly attacked Grey. Browne's thesis was simple, and it was an even more devastating critique of Grey than Morel's. The professor maintained that Sir Edward had destroyed Morocco to please France. To please Russia he was prepared to destroy Persia. His unceasing feud with Germany had given rise to perpetual war scares and constantly increasing expenditure upon armaments. The foreign secretary was impatient of parliamentary criticism and contemptuous of public opinion. Browne concluded his catalog of Grey's sins by insisting that he could pursue his "contemptible course" only so long as he could "count upon the support of the official Liberals as well as the great majority of the Unionists." Trevelyan did not enjoy hearing this indictment, which implicated supporters of the government who took the same line as himself. But Browne's vigorous advocacy roused him to admit to his wife that he was

becoming more and more definitely opposed to Grey and his whole outlook and policy, his reticence and his sympathies. However, there is nothing sufficiently tangible to quarrel with openly. But I have practically made up my mind that if we begin verging towards war, or seriously quarreling to uphold either the Russian or the French alliance, I will not be party to it.[38]

Trevelyan's conscience was troubled, and to salve it he turned from Sir Edward Grey and made a slashing attack upon Lord "Bobs"

Roberts and the National Service League with its campaign for conscription. Sir George and Lady Caroline congratulated their son for his attack. "Detestable . . . the most wicked thing I almost ever remember," wrote Sir George, almost managing to equate conscription with original sin. "It was right you spoke out," affirmed Lady Caroline, "and you have performed a good service to Liberalism in doing so."[39] But parental satisfaction apart, few took any notice, even though Trevelyan's censures had been complemented by a speech by Runciman from the same platform concerning peace and the need to improve Anglo-German relations.

In the late spring of 1912, Trevelyan had paid a short visit to Germany to talk with German labor leaders, editors, and members of the Reichstag about the mutual suspicions that haunted relations between their two countries. For a few weeks after his return, Trevelyan spoke and wrote frequently of his concern for Anglo-German relations, especially as there seemed not a little justification for the German fear that although France and Russia stood armed and hostile upon its borders, it was Britain who encouraged the entente powers in the policy of encirclement. "I am more and more troubled about Germany," he wrote to his wife. But he offered neither counsel of hope nor action. "All one can do is preach peace and appeal to the general sense of men." But it had been a difficult parliamentary session. Trevelyan was exhausted by it all: "I am weary of London; I am weary of Germany; I am weary of the Navy."[40] The Great Powers constantly repeated their desire for peace and as constantly continued to arm, increasing the cost and the tempo. When Winston Churchill announced his dubious scheme to cut naval expenditure by a "naval holiday," Trevelyan, once more upon his German travels, was making it his particular business to advertise British friendship to any person prepared to listen.[41] Yet again he visited the Reichstag and conversed with leading German politicians, but even in Socialist circles it was clear there was a widespread distrust of Britain. All Trevelyan could do was relay this pessimistic intelligence to Runciman. To Trevelyan's amazement, Runciman seemed not unduly worried.[42]

Rather than exacerbating the already strained relations between Germany and Britain, the outbreak of war in the Balkans allowed for cooperation between the foreign offices of the two nations. Thus the spring of 1913 promised not only the mending of Anglo-German relations but also recantation by Grey's most vociferous critics who had so frequently accused him of "Germanophobia." The threat of a European war arising from the Balkan imbroglio had been averted by the efforts of the kaiser and Sir Edward Grey—at least, that is what the publicists in Germany and England told the public. And with ministers talking of each other's countries in considerate and conciliatory tones, rapprochement at last seemed a practical possibility. In this somewhat euphoric atmosphere, Asquith, in a debate in the House in March 1913 where he had been extolling the cooperative efforts made for peace by the Great Powers, silenced a difficult Tory critic by asserting categorically that Britain had no military obligations toward France, official or otherwise. There was the unequivocal statement that all Radicals had so long demanded: a guarantee from the prime minister that Britain retained a "free hand" in diplomatic affairs.[43] The Germans could safely forget ideas about Britain's conspiring with France against them, and Asquith's repetition of the guarantee a fortnight later should have quelled any remaining doubts. It was not only the Germans who could discard their doubts: Trevelyan was both delighted and relieved that Grey's critics had been wrong and that he could abandon his own uncomfortable suspicions. He was pleased to learn from letters he received from Germany that the prime minister's assurances had made a splendid impression.[44] Morel, among Trevelyan's friends Grey's sternest and certainly most constant critic, sent a copy of an article he had written for the *Daily News* that declared unreservedly that Anglo-German relations were better than they had been for a decade. But then came a warning for Trevelyan: those who wished to retain this happy state of affairs should recognize that there were powerful influences in both France and England who were intent upon wrecking the new-found accord between Germany and Britain. In France the chauvinists, unforgiving and unforgetting of the humiliation of 1870 and intent upon revanche, were known, and their tactics to involve Britain in their designs were obvious. But in Britain the danger, though no less insidious, was not so obvious. Morel quoted as an example the remarkable growth in the propaganda for conscription. There could be no worthier object of attack by a Liberal MP than Lord Robert's National Service League. Trevelyan had written to Morel stating his determination "to enter upon a vigorous *private* campaign" to refute Tory claims that were responsible for "keeping the Germans from the best relations with us."[45] He had also written to Norman Angell asking for "suggestions for a practical parliamentary platform for pacifism."[46] Of course, as a junior minister he would have to be discreet and serve the cause of peace without embarrassing the government. Now in Morel's letter lay the perfect solution: Trevelyan determined he would prepare a new statement of the anticonscriptionist case.

With typical energy, Trevelyan set about his task. He wrote to, among others, Edouard Bernstein, the German Socialist leader. Trevelyan described conscription for Britain as "entirely unnecessary . . . from any point of view," but Bernstein replied that "conscription is necessary in our country."[47] German Socialists had always coupled the reference of international dispute to arbitration with "the training for universal capacity to bear arms." For them this was no more paradoxical than for British Radicals to profess their love of peace coupled with the pride and determination to maintain British world naval supremacy.[48] In both Germany and France, it was difficult to recruit evidence against the case for conscription. One of Trevelyan's research aides, Leonard Reid, wrote that people were "afraid to write or speak their real opinions on a subject of this kind. So I fear I am not able to assist you to anything really useful."[49] Despite this, and similar doleful intelligence from his other helper, Geoffrey Marchand, the pamphlet was eventually written but was published only when Trevelyan agreed to bear the cost. The first issue was soon sold, and there were requests for a reprint. In English Liberal circles the pamphlet met with general approval, and Runciman went so far as to describe it as "quite the best statement of the Liberal view yet written."[50]

In the autumn of 1913, the Liberal disarmament group was more active and noisier than usual. It was known that Winston Churchill was preparing yet another extravagant set of estimates for the navy, and their worst suspicions were confirmed when the prime mininster, addressing the National Liberal Federation meeting at Leeds in November, stated that he saw no hope of any substantial relief in the armaments' burden for the future. Then on New Year's

Day, 1914, an interview with Lloyd George was published in the *Daily Chronicle* that reviewed the "organised insanity" of "the overwhelming extravagance of our expenditure on armaments." Despite the moral overtones, the Welsh Wizard obviously was engaged in a struggle with his erstwhile ally in economy, Winston Churchill, and was appealing over the head of a divided cabinet for support from the public to strengthen his hand in negotiation and bargaining. Trevelyan for one was not slow to respond to the appeal. He wrote, "How glad I am to see that you have declared yourself against the huge armament increases."[51] But the "fratch between the two competitors for the Liberal leadership," as Trevelyan described Lloyd George and Churchill's dispute over naval costs, was overtaken by events, and "delicate" consciences conceded to harsh political actuality.[52] Churchill's increased estimates were accepted because they were measured against the imperative need to maintain party unity, not in the scales of morality. Under the circumstances, many who deplored Churchill's success hid their anger and impotence by claiming they had acceded to the first lord's estimates because of the Ulster troubles. But no one was deceived for a moment by this excuse. "We understand well the difficulties of our friends in the Commons," wrote the editor of the pacifist monthly *Concord;* then he added wearily, "Yet we cannot but think that they might have done something more to bring home to the country and the Cabinet, the monstrous character of the Admiralty programme."[53] At the beginning of February Trevelyan wrote to his mother that "everywhere Liberals seem generally cheerful." If they had beaten their breasts in vain over the naval estimates, at least the party was "very much against conscription." Perhaps even more important in what counted for a practical political consideration, the Tory party was in hopeless disarray: "Their fortunes have actually gone back since 1910 elections."[54]

Once the furor stirred by the naval estimates had been settled, the attitude of the Liberal party (and in this Trevelyan was typical) was complacent toward questions concerning foreign policy. Domestic issues dominated politics, but there were indications and opportunities enough for those who had previously expressed concern about Grey's conduct of affairs and the general European diplomatic scene to probe and question. Instead they gave every impression of satisfaction. When Lloyd George spoke at the Guildhall in July 1914 of relations between Germany and Britain, he maintained that they were better than ever. He did not seem to consider the Sarajevo murders as significant. The day after the chancellor's speech, Austria delivered an ultimatum to Serbia. Trevelyan certainly agreed with Lloyd George's estimate. It was not until a week before his resignation from the government that Trevelyan, in a letter to his wife, first mentioned the European scene: "As to Europe, I think there will be a great war. But I do not think that we will be drawn in. At any rate, all my energies will have to be devoted to urging my Cabinet friends not to let ourselves be involved in the smallest degree."[55]

The sudden crisis promoted a furious exchange between the Radical and the Tory press. The *Manchester Guardian* and the *Daily News* insisted the government's duty was to proclaim Britain's neutrality: The *Times* countered that Britain was obliged by the terms of the Anglo-French entente to join with France against Germany. Trevelyan was not unduly concerned by this last claim, pinning his faith in "the real peace party within the Cabinet." He considered it "most unlikely we shall allow ourselves to be dragged in even if there is Armageddon."[56] When his parents suggested that perhaps the Tories had made a deal with Asquith over home rule as the price for entering a European war, Trevelyan, who was always prepared to believe the worst of the Tories, insisted that things could not be "quite as bad as that."[57] There was a terrifying sense of helplessness, subject as Liberal MP's were to the exchange of claims and rumors and effectively reduced to being able to do little more than trust in the government's often repeated past assurances that they were determined to maintain the peace. But would Grey prove to be strong enough in these difficult and dangerous circumstances? When Trevelyan had met Grey by accident in the lobby of the Commons, he had thought the foreign secretary "coldly angry" with him for presuming that Britain would remain neutral. Trevelyan wrote of this encounter to his wife: "A man is not to be trusted who does not at least say *to himself,* whatever others do we cannot go to war. . . . If Russia goes to war, if then Germany goes to war with her, it will be our duty to say that we will on no account take part in the struggle."[58] If nothing else, this letter revealed that Trevelyan had already decided who should be cast as the villains in the tragedy now playing out its final scene upon the European stage. Russia was the only nation anxious to fight. If Britain should enter the war, then the fault would be Grey's, for the foreign secretary would "not see the utter wickedness of our being drawn in under any conditions, and therefore we may get dragged along by circumstances." Trevelyan did not believe that Grey wanted war. The trouble was that "he will not say we won't go to war."[59]

Trevelyan was not the sort of man who could readily stand by and wait upon events. There was little, he knew, that the individual could do, but that did not stop him from censuring "the inactivity of the mass of people who do not want war." He decided he would stay in London and do what he could to support and manufacture protest for British neutrality: "a curious case of nothing ever being done unless you do it yourself."[60] He still believed that Britain could avoid war, and the news from Runciman that the cabinet had decided that the Expeditionary Force would not be despatched to France seemed to confirm that belief. But events moved so swiftly in those final days of peace that in the space of twelve hours Trevelyan was obliged to take a far less optimistic view of Britain's remaining neutral. In a second letter he wrote on August 2, Trevelyan admitted to Molly:

Everything is as bad as can be, except that our Government are trying to keep out of war if they can. . . . The single great point of danger is Belgium. Germany is almost certain to violate Belgian neutrality by passing through Belgium to attack France. She may do more and try to conquer Belgium. In the second case it would be a position of unparalleled difficulty for a British Government however anxious to avoid a collision.[61]

There were many Liberals as anxious as Trevelyan that Britain should remain neutral. For most, Belgium proved the stumbling block. Richard Holt, a friend of Trevelyan, recorded in his diary that much as he personally desired peace, "when Germany decided upon an unprovoked attack upon Belgium . . . , it seemed impossible for us to stand by."[62] Why did not Trevelyan adopt the same attitude? On Monday morning, August 3, his mind was made up only so far as to affirm that "unless the Prime Minister gives a satisfactory account of what they are doing, I shall have to resign." There was no point in discussing the matter further for "everything is the decision of an hour . . . we shall know nothing until this afternoon."[63]

When Grey rose to address a crowded, excited, and expectant Commons in the afternoon of August 3, 1914, everyone present knew that the decisive moment of the crisis, as far as Britain's fortunes were concerned, had arrived. Grey's appeal won the acclamation of all but a handful of his audience.[64] After Grey's speech there was no longer any hope of Britain's remaining neutral. Grey had spoken of honor (that "hateful mediaeval survival," in Trevelyan's words) and of England's "interests." He spoke as well of obligations owed to France, those very obligations that on previous occasions he as well as the prime minister had publicly and expressly denied. Now the reason England was committed to war with Germany was all too patent. "I was never more clear in all my life," Trevelyan told his wife. "We have gone to war from a sentimental attachment to the French and hatred of Germany."[65] If Trevelyan's logic was somewhat wayward, his resolution could not be faulted. He knew he must resign. He was not to be shaken in that determination even by the passing years.

There is a virtue as well as attraction in simple explanations of human conduct, but the truth of a matter is seldom easily and neatly encapsulated. Those who thought like Trevelyan claimed they had been duped, and more—that Liberalism itself had been betrayed by Grey and Asquith's duplicity and the conspiracies of diplomatists. It was not so easy to admit that perhaps they had been as much confounded by the contradictions in their own thinking as by the perfidy of those they had chosen to or had cause to trust. The almost inescapable conclusion is that Radicals like Trevelyan (who were, after all, to become the founding fathers of Labour's foreign policy after the Great War) did not seek too avidly for the truth lest they should discover it. They would on occasion criticize Grey, but they were even more eager, given the excuse, to applaud and defend him. They censured the notion of the balance of power, yet they assented to its practice in the name of the Concert of Europe. But, if history requires the allotment of blame, then the greatest burden must be borne by those nominal Radicals (so swift to censure Grey after August 1914) who were privy to the secrets of the cabinet. Loreburn, Morley, and Burns are more guilty of confusion arising from self-delusion than Grey and Asquith of the deceit and collusion with which they were subsequently charged. In the last year of peace, Grey had reminded his colleagues in the clearest manner of the entente policy's inherent naval and military obligations. Grey had sought and received approval from his erstwhile critics even though he had acknowledged that Anglo-French military arrangements were concerned with "hopes of assistance." No one had thought to ask Grey in what exact circumstances Britain would side with France in a war against Germany.

NOTES

1. Trevelyan considered his letter important as, "a public record of some of the reasons against this miserable business." C. P. Trevelyan to Lady Caroline Trevelyan, August 4, 1914, Sir George Otto Trevelyan mss. (hereafter cited as GOT), box 67. Local newspapers in Elland apart, the *Manchester Guardian* carried the full text, and A. G. Gardiner's *Daily News* offered an abbreviated version. As was to be expected in the circumstances, the *Nation* commented favorably, and the *New Statesman* offered qualified approval. The rest of the press, for the moment, was silent.

2. Trevelyan wrote a brief account of the organization, *The Union of Democratic Control: Its History and Its Policy* (London, 1919). H. M. Swanwick provided a more lengthy account in *Builders of Peace: Being Ten Years' History of the Union of Democratic Control* (London, 1924). All earlier accounts of the UDC have been superseded by Marvin Swartz's detailed account, *The Union of Democratic Control in British Politics during the First World War* (Oxford, 1971). For an account that concentrates on Trevelyan's role in the UDC, see A. J. A. Morris, *C. P. Trevelyan, 1870-1958: Portrait of a Radical* (Belfast, 1977).

3. See *New Witness,* September 17, 1914; *John Bull,* November 14, 1914.

4. C. P. Trevelyan to H. H. Asquith, August 3, 1914 (draft), C. P. Trevelyan Mss. (hereafter cited as CPT), ex. 106.

Note: The Sir George Otto Trevelyan papers, together with those of his son Charles, are held in the Library of the University of Newcastle upon Tyne. The Walter Runciman papers are also held at Newcastle. The E. D. Morel Papers and the Courtney Papers are held by the British Library of Economic and Political Science, London. The Lloyd George Papers, part of the Beaverbrook Archive, are now in the House of Lords Record Office. The Richard Holt Papers are in Liverpool City Library. I want to express my sincere gratitude to Pauline Dower, daughter of Charles Trevelyan, for giving me access to the private family papers and to Alistair Elliot, keeper of manuscripts at the University Library of Newcastle upon Tyne, for his generous help.

5. The best account of these ministerial negotiations is in Cameron Hazlehurst, *Politicians at War, July 1914 to May 1915* (London, 1971), pt. I.

6. Walter Runciman to C. P. Trevelyan, August 4, 1914, CPT, 17.

7. "CPT's Personal Record of the Days That Led up to the War of 1914," typescript, n.d., CPT, 5.

8. C. P. Trevelyan to M. K. Trevelyan, August 4, 1914, CPT, ex. 106.

9. See "G. P. Trevelyan's 1906 Election Address," CPT, 50.

10. "England & Peace," draft typescript, n.d., CPT, 42.

11. Immediately after the outbreak of the war, Trevelyan adopted an entirely different attitude. See, for example, C. P. Trevelyan to M. K. Trevelyan, September 8, 1914, CPT, ex. 107: "During dinner Willy Tyrrell came in and sat next but one to me. I studiously avoided looking his way. I hate him (the loathsome, lying little creeping Catholic) more than anyone else in the world. Poor silly child-like Grey has, I believe, been his puppet all these years." Tyrrell had been Grey's private secretary from 1907.

12. For a discussion of the problems associated with the notion of "pacifist," see A. J. A. Morris, *Radicalism Against War, 1906-14: The Advocacy of Peace and Retrenchment* (London, 1972), pp. 198ff. See also Keith Robbins, *The Abolition of War* (Cardiff, 1976), passim.

13. Swartz, *Union of Democratic Control,* pp. 11-12, citing A. C. F. Beales, *The History of Peace* (London, 1931), states that Trevelyan was a co-founder of the National Peace Council. I have found no evidence to support this, either in the Trevelyan family papers or the papers of the NPC.

14. C. P. Trevelyan to M. K. Trevelyan, November 29, 1913, CPT, ex. 105.

15. Trevelyan's interest in military matters was used against him by the "patriotic" press during the war. On the Trevelyans's "war game," see G. M. Trevelyan, *Autobiography and Other Essays* (London, 1947), p. 12.

16. Trevelyan, parliamentary diary, n.d., CPT, ex. 71.

17. C. P. Trevelyan to Lady Caroline Trevelyan, December 18, 1907, GOT, 60.

18. Newspaper cutting of speech made in Elland, March 24, 1909, CPT, 54.

19. See C. P. Trevelyan to G. O. Trevelyan, October 19, 1908, GOT, 61.

20. A. D. Sanger to C. P. Trevelyan, June 2, 1907, CPT, 7.

21. George Young to C. P. Trevelyan, June 25, 1906, CPT, 6.

22. Grey to C. P. Trevelyan, June 22, 1906, and C. P. Trevelyan to Grey, n.d., CPT, 6. Grey's decision concerning the fleet's visit was an overhasty initiative that was welcomed neither by the czar nor by Isvolsky. See J. Lepsius, A. Mendelssohn-Bartholdy, and F. Timme, eds., *Die Grosse Politik der Europaischen Kabinette, 1871-1914* (Berlin, 1922-27), xxv.i, 8512-15.

23. On the trust placed in Grey by even his most vocal critics in the Commons, see Howard Weinroth's brilliant article, "The British Radicals and the Balance of Power," *The Historical Journal* 13 (1970):653-82.

24. C. P. Trevelyan to E. D. Morel, March 31, 1908, Morel Mss., F.8.

25. *Manchester Guardian,* June 7, 1909.

26. See G. O. Trevelyan to C. P. Trevelyan, December 21, 1909, CPT, Ex.52.

27. The Algeciras Act, signed between Germany and France in 1906, was intended

to delineate the rights and spheres of influence of the two powers in North Africa.

28. C. P. Trevelyan to Lady Caroline Trevelyan, July 28, 1911, CPT, Ex.66.

29. C. P. Trevelyan to M. K. Trevelyan, August 31, 1911, CPT, Ex.16.

30. Walter Runciman to C. P. Trevelyan, September 18, 1911, CPT, Ex.65.

31. E. D. Morel, *Morocco in Diplomacy* (London, 1912).

32. E. D. Morel to C. P. Trevelyan, September 8, 1913, CPT, Ex.35.

33. On the Radical Liberal foreign policy committees, see Morris, *Radicalism Against War,* pp. 265ff.

34. For the debate in the Commons, see, *Hansard,* vol. 32, cols. 60ff. For an account of Courtney's speech and the comments of contemporaries, see G. P. Gooch, *Life of Lord Courtney* (London, 1920), pp. 568-70.

35. C. P. Trevelyan to M. K. Trevelyan, November 28, 1911, CPT, ex. 16.

36. Ibid., July 16, 1912, CPT, ex.68.

37. C. P. Trevelyan to Lady Caroline Trevelyan, July 26, 1912, CPT,220.

38. C. P. Trevelyan to M. K. Trevelyan, October 22, 1912, CPT, ex.99.

39. G. O. and Lady Caroline Trevelyan to C. P. Trevelyan, October 27, 1912, CPT, ex.67.

40. C. P. Trevelyan to M. K. Trevelyan, July 22, 1912, CPT, ex.68.

41. Despite Churchill's annual declaration when he introduced the naval estimates that next year "things would be different," the cost of the navy continued to soar. The essence of Winston's naval holiday proposal was the promise that if Germany built no Dreadnoughts for a year, then Britain would respond in the same manner. The scheme was riddled with faults, ambiguities, and suspicions. No one, with the possible exception of Churchill, took the proposition seriously.

42. See Runciman to C. P. Trevelyan, February 28, 1913, CPT, ex.35.

43. Much the best general account of the effects of the Anglo-French military conversations upon Britain's freedom to act independently in matters of foreign policy is contained in S. R. Williamson, Jr., *The Politics of Grand Strategy: Britain and France Prepare for War, 1904-14* (Cambridge, Mass., 1969).

44. See Hecksher to C. P. Trevelyan, March 17, 1913, and Dudley Ward to C. P. Trevelyan, March 16, 1913, CPT,26.

45. C. P. Trevelyan to E. D. Morel, February 20, 1913, Morel Mss, F.8.

46. See Norman Angell to C. P. Trevelyan, April 18, 1913, CPT, 26.

47. C. P. Trevelyan to Edouard Bernstein, May 28, 1913, and Bernstein to Trevelyan, June 4, 1913, CPT,26. By 1913, Germans of all political parties recognized that their country's future existence in an armed Europe depended upon the maintenance of her armies at peak strength and efficiency. A weltpolitik based upon a huge navy intended to challenge British naval supremacy was no longer realistic. Thus, there was now in Germany a much more favorable climate for détente with Britain. This, however, did not imply any lessening of intent to maintain Germany's armies by conscription.

48. British Radicals would have argued that the British navy was a "defensive" and not an "offensive" force.

49. L. J. Reid to C. P. Trevelyan, February 21, 1913, CPT,26.

50. Walter Runciman to C. P. Trevelyan, January 4, 1914, CPT,17.

51. C. P. Trevelyan to D. Lloyd George, January 6, 1914, Lloyd George Mss., c/4/12/4.

52. C. P. Trevelyan to Runciman, January 5, 1914, Runciman Mss., R1/17/1-22.

53. *Concord,* April 1914, p. 3.

54. C. P. Trevelyan to Lady Caroline Trevelyan, February 1, 1914, GOT,67.

55. C. P. Trevelyan to M. K. Trevelyan, July 27, 1914, CPT,ex.106.

56. Ibid., July 28, 1914, CPT,ex.106.

57. C. P. Trevelyan to Lady Caroline Trevelyan, August 2, 1914, CPT,ex. 69.

58. C. P. Trevelyan to M. K. Trevelyan, August 1, 1914, CPT,ex.106.

59. Ibid., August 2, 1914, CPT,ex.106.

60. Ibid., August 1, 1914, CPT,ex.106.

61. Ibid., August 2, 1914, CPT, Ex.106. For the tribulations of the Radical Liberals during the last days of peace, see M. Swartz, "A Study in Futility," in A. J. A. Morris, ed. *Edwardian Radicalism, 1900-1914* (London, 1974), pp. 246-61.

62. Richard Holt, diary, August 9, 1914, Holt Mss.

63. C. P. Trevelyan to M. K. Trevelyan, August 3, 1914, CPT,ex.106.

64. See for the debate, *Hansard,* vol. 65, cols. 1809ff.

65. C. P. Trevelyan to M. K. Trevelyan, August 4, 1914 (1st letter), CPT,ex.106.

6
Opponents of War Preparedness in France, 1913-14

DAVID E. SUMLER

The passage of the three-years' law on military service (to lengthen the period of service of a conscripted soldier from two years to three) by the French National Assembly in the summer of 1913 has been generally interpreted as the culmination of a nationalist revival and as evidence of a national consensus on issues of foreign affairs and national defense. The parliamentary opposition to the military bill has been narrowly defined and identified with the Socialist party (SFIO) alone, although historians usually also make reference to a noisy but insignificant protest by the General Confederation of Labor (CGT); and the motivations of these two groups are often considered to have been similar.[1]

This interpretation needs revision, for, in fact, far from there being a consensus on foreign affairs and national defense, France was severely polarized from the summer of 1913 until the outbreak of war. The nationalist revival was the product and the preserve of partisan political groupings on the center right and the right and never extended beyond those groups.[2] Furthermore, the opposition to increased war preparedness was much broader than has been recognized; it extended from the CGT on the extreme left through the SFIO to include a majority of the Radical party and certain liberal internationalists on the center right. The groups that combined to form this heterogeneous opposition and later were an effective political bloc capable of toppling a government in December 1913 and of winning the national legislative election of April-May 1914 were motivated by different, sometimes irreconcilable, ideologies. It will also be a purpose here to identify the components of this opposition to war preparedness, to analyze their motives, and to attempt to measure the effectiveness of their campaign.

Premier Aristide Briand asked the Chamber of Deputies on March 6, 1913, to lengthen the period of service of a conscripted soldier from two years to three. While premier in an earlier cabinet (1909-10), Briand had initiated a conservative resurgence built around his program of "national union" to be achieved through a lessening of political tensions—a code word for the postponement of divisive social reforms. His program, which had originated within a purely domestic context, had been applied to foreign affairs by Raymond Poincaré, who had been premier throughout 1912. In January 1913 Poincaré was elected president of the Republic, clearing the way for Briand's return to power.[3] Almost immediately Briand met with French military leaders, his relevant cabinet members, and Poincaré and decided to call for an increase in the size of France's standing army through an extension of compulsory military service. Since one class of conscripts was drafted each year, it was estimated that this measure would add approximately 180,000 soldiers to the standing army, which numbered 531,000 under the two-years' law of 1905. Briand's cabinet contended this increase was necessitated by similar changes in the German military system in 1912, which had raised the number of Germans in arms to 850,000.

The proposed military reform, however, was considered an insult by the Radicals and Radical-Socialists who sat on the center left of the Chamber's hemicycle. The Radicals had enacted the two-years' law as a symbol of their victory over the reactionary forces in the military responsible for the Dreyfus affair. Briand's policy of national union since 1909 had been aimed specifically at blocking reforms desired by the left wing of the Radical party; and now the left Radicals felt he was trying to go further by repealing reforms made in the past. To counter this move, the Radicals managed to mobilize enough votes to topple Briand on an issue of favoritism to church schools.[4]

Briand's successor, Louis Barthou, was also determined to pass the three-years' law. To ensure the support of the right for his ministry, Barthou asked a Progressist, Joseph Thierry, to join his cabinet.

This invitation was significant, for no Progressist had sat in a cabinet since the Dreyfus affair. The parliamentary debate on the three-years' law which began on July 2, raged for seven weeks, and public opinion in France became extremely polarized. Both opponents and proponents of the bill vilified the opposition as either *patriotes d'affaires* and *réacctionnaires* or as antipatriots, anarchists, and traitors. There was no middle ground.[5] The most crucial vote on the three-years' law passed the Chamber relatively easily, 339-223, and established the principle of three years of service. Only left Radicals, Independent Socialists, and the SFIO parliamentary group voted against it; the majority included right Radicals, moderates of the center right groups, Progressists, and reactionaries. After the final passage on July 19, the struggle against war preparedness was conducted outside parliament and by mass rallies, propaganda distribution, and quiet political maneuvering until the fall legislative session opened. This continuing agitation was aimed at either repealing the bill or making it an issue in the 1914 national legislative election.

The most prominent spokesman for the coalition against the three-years' law was Jean Jaurès, the dominant figure in the SFIO. As editor of and frequent contributor to *l'Humanité,* he was the universally recognized voice of the majority of the Socialist party, although strong minority factions challenged his dominance at every party congress. The dominant Socialist conception of international affairs was based upon an acceptance of the inevitability of the nation-state and a class analysis of politics within the national community. Only one small faction of the SFIO rejected the nation-state as the natural form of political organization—the followers of the antipatriot Gustave Hervé—and its influence on the SFIO was negligible. Both the revisionist Juarès and the orthodox Marxian Jules Guesde agreed on the finality of the nation-state.[6] In each nation-state politics was a class struggle between the property-owning bourgeoisie and the working classes. War was not a struggle between nations but was an instrument of the ruling bourgeoisie within each nation. War, then was an expression of the international competition among the capitalist classes of the various states. Guesde concluded from this that Socialists should ignore foreign policy and concentrate on seizing power within each state. Juarès and the so-

cialist majority, however, concluded that the socialist task was to
prevent war so as to save the lives of the workers who would otherwise be sacrificed to the greed of competing capitalists.[7]

This concept of the international system led Socialists to reject
chauvinist nationalism and militarism as self-serving expressions
of bourgeois interests. Colonial expansion, although occasionally
supported by Socialists in the name of humanitarian extension of
civilization, was usually denounced as a rapacious search for capitalist profits. For these reasons, the Socialist parliamentary group op-
osed virtually every expansion of the armed services and regularly
voted against the military expenditures in the national budget. Yet
Juarès and the SFIO were not antinationalist or antipatriotic. Assuming the continued existence of nation-states, the French Socialists
resolved to defend the French nation if it were ever attacked[8] and
embodied this position in motions adopted at their party congresses
from 1906 to 1914. They based their resolution on the formula that
the proletariat should defend the nation from unprovoked attacks
but that the SFIO would use "parliamentary action, public agitation,
popular protest meetings, even the general strike and insurrection"
to prevent the French government from launching a war of aggression.[9]
There was an obvious dilemma inherent in this position: the difficulty
of distinguishing between a defensive and an offensive war.

The French Socialists, however, did not intend to wait until the
beginning of hostilities to take action against war. They made efforts
to decrease the possibility of war. One way was to fight against militarism in France. A second was their activity in the Second International to coordinate the peace efforts of the international socialist
movement. Juarès was one of the foremost believers in the efficacy
of international socialist activities. He believed that, in accordance
with a resolution adopted by the Stuttgart Congress of the Second
International, all socialist parties would attempt to prevent their
own governments from launching a war of aggression. In the existing
international situation, this meant that he placed his ultimate faith in
the willingness and the ability of the German Social Democrats to
prevent the German government from invading France. His almost
blind faith in the Germans was often expressed.[10] He believed that
if the socialists came to power in France or Germany, the danger of
war would disappear.

Another means by which the Socialists hoped to avoid war was through the encouragement of international arbitration and the eventual establishment of a European federation in which the nation-states would be bound by international law. In this, Jaurès and the SFIO shared the vision of certain liberal internationalists. According to this optimistic view, the rival alliance systems were actually the building blocks of a united Europe. Juarès felt that individual states were insecure enough and free enough to resort to reckless international adventures. When a state entered into a formal alliance, it surrendered some of its freedom but gained in security, making irresponsible policies less likely. With all of the Great Powers organized into alliance systems, rationality in foreign policy would be correspondingly increased. If the two alliance systems could increase cultural contacts, trade, and arbitration agreements on limited issues, they might evolve into a European federation based on a mutual interest in orderly international relations.[11] This vision placed Juarès in the seemingly contradictory position of praising the European alliance system as it had developed since 1894 while denouncing the military establishments that accompanied the system.

Juarès never considered leaving France defenseless; he was an antimilitarist, not an antipatriot. In fact, he devoted much energy from 1906 to 1914 in devising and propagandizing military reforms that he felt would guarantee France's survival in case of an attack but would avoid the dangers of militarism. He published his proposals in a book, *L'Armée nouvelle,* in 1910. The new army was to be a universal, civilian reserve force, including all ablebodied men: "Every boy from age of ten to twenty years would be trained in gymnastic exercises, rifle practice, and emulative sports. This training would be followed by six months at the school for recruits, after which the recruit, although returning to his civil occupation would become a part of the army. The army would include all men from twenty to thirty-four years of age, organized by locality and brought together periodically for maneuvers. . . .Each man would keep his arms at home, and mobilization would be facilitated by an extensive system of railroads and major transport."[12] The officer corps would would be one-third professional military and two-thirds reservists. The reserve officer corps would have to meet exacting educational standards and take part in regular training sessions.

Such an army, Juarès was sure, would only be effective fighting a defensive war; but, in such a war, it would be invincible. It would prevent an aggressive or reckless foreign policy because the reservists would not be willing to leave their homes to fight an expansionist war. It would also avoid the dangers to democracy and to peace inherent in the creation of a large military establishment, such as the inculcation of antidemocratic ideas into conscripts during their period of service, which they would then take back to civilian society.[13]

These, then, were the ideas that inspired Juarès in his battle against the three-years' law in 1913. In the many speeches he made attacking Barthou's measure, he never denied the necessity of ensuring the national defense. Rather, he contended that the extra year of service might weaken that defense by diverting funds and efforts from building up the reserves, increasing the border fortifications, and producing badly needed artillery. The cost to the nation would be enormous in terms of increased military expenditure—an estimated 300 million francs to support the extra year in the barracks—and in terms of productivity lost to the French economy, when 180,000 young males were withdrawn from the labor force. And what would be gained? According to Juarès, very little. In a parliamentary speech, he argued that of the 180,000, only 20,000 would be available on the front lines on the frontier in case of attack since 60,000 would be exempted from active duty because they helped support their families;70,00 would not be on the frontiers but stationed elsewhere in France; 20,000 of those at the frontier would be based at second-line stations; and 10,000 of the remaining 30,000 would be on leave at any one time. Thus, in return for the vast drain on the nation's resources, France would gain only 20,000 effective front line troops.[14] On the other hand, if the military would concentrate on developing the reserves in the eastern departments, it would be possible to mobilize 100,000 on short notice to defend the frontier.

Juarès did not limit his activity to speeches. The SFIO organized rallies throughout France and instructed its local branches to agitate against the military law. Pamphlets were prepared and distributed, and Socialists circulated petitions, which were sent to politicians or published in Socialist papers.[15] The SFIO also campaigned against the three-years' law in the August 1913 local elections. Finally, the Socialists formed a parliamentary bloc with the Radicals to overthrow Barthou in December 1913, and they continued this coalition by adopting an electoral program almost identical to the Radical electoral program during the 1914 legislative electoral campaign.[16]

The CGT was allied to the SFIO in many of these activities, but the motives of the CGT leadership were very different from those of Jaurès. Whereas he was patriotic, the CGT was officially anti-patriotic. Whereas Juarès was antimilitarist because standing armies contributed to international tension and threatened parliamentary government, the CGT was antimilitarist for reasons of domestic concern and cared little for the preservation of parliamentary democracy. Whereas Juarès advocated gradual reforms to eliminate the causes of chauvinism and militarism and to encourage international arbitration to settle disputes among states, the CGT was prepared to launch a revolutionary general strike to prevent war. These two branches of the French labor movement were very unlikely partners.

It is perhaps misleading to speak of "the CGT leadership" in 1913, for the CGT was undergoing a change in leadership and in doctrine that was to shape the future of the French labor movement. The transition was from a revolutionary, apolitical, confrontation-oriented leadership dominated by Victor Griffuelhes and Georges Yvetot to a reformist, technocratic leadership dominated first by Alphonse Merrheim and then by Léon Jouhaux.[17] The factions that adhered to the ideas of these leaders and theoreticians approached the issues of foreign affairs differently, but they all shared a common syndicalist heritage, and they all opposed the three-years' law.

The revolutionary bloc in the CGT had completely dominated the organization during the tenure of Victor Griffuelhes as national secretary (1902-09). Griffuelhes's radicalism was supported most effectively by Georges Yvetot, secretary of the *Fédération des Bourses du travail.* The three pillars of this bloc's political stance were anti-parliamentarianism, antipatriotism, and antimilitarism. The bloc was convinced that parliamentary institutions were expressions of the bourgeois control of society. They considered direct confrontation with both employers and the government on wages, conditions of work, length of the workday, and other bread-and-butter issues the only realistic way to improve the position of France's workers.

They scorned Socialist attempts at legislating social reforms and called any prolabor bill passed by the French parliament an obvious fraud.

As antipatriots, the revolutionary syndicalists rejected Jaurès's argument concerning the inevitability of the nation-state. For them the state was a bourgeois institution to aid in the control of the working classes. Social classes knew no territorial boundaries; German workers and French workers were both at war with the same capitalist rulers. They expressed this idea in several ways. Griffuelhes put it bluntly: "The fatherland of the worker is his stomach." Gustave Hervé, a maverick Socialist who was close to the revolutionary syndicalists, used a different phrase: "Our nation can only be our class."[18] The logical conclusion was that the working class had no interest in bourgeois wars; therefore, French workers should not fight to defend their rulers' property.

The problem of what to do if war were declared was solved at the CGT Congress at Amiens in 1906 and reaffirmed at the Marseilles Congress two years later: "The Congress declares that, from an international point of view, it is necessary to educate the workers so that in case of war among the powers the workers will respond to the declaration of the revolutionary general strike."[19] The general strike, a universal cessation of work by all members of the French working class, would lead to the collapse of the bourgeois economy and political system and usher in a socialist society. Griffuelhes, Yvetot, and other revolutionary leaders realized that such a strike was not possible in 1906 or 1908, but they hoped to educate the workers through the tactics of confrontation over purely economic issues.

The antimilitarism of the revolutionary syndicalists was even more virulent than their antipatriotism, and this sentiment was shared by the reformist faction as well. This hatred of the army was a response to the French government's repeated use of the army to break strikes. Very often this method led to clashes between troops and workers, and casualties among the workers were not unusual. As Léon Jouhaux, a reformist leader, said, "Antimilitarism was born the day when the government violated its neutrality and led the army into strikes to protect capitalist interests."[20] The cruelest part for the trade unionists was that the soldiers who fired upon strikers were themselves sons of the working class, conscripted for only two or three years to serve their bourgeois masters. Therefore, the syndicalists considered the army to be not the military arm of the French but the oppressive instrument of the French bourgeoisie. It taught workers authoritarianism, class betrayal, and obedience to the bourgeois state; furthermore, it exposed them, while in the barracks, to alcoholism, venereal disease, and immorality.

The major weapon of the CGT in its battle against the military was the *Sou du soldat,* the term applied to many practices used by union locals and by *bourses du travail* to maintain contact with workers conscripted into the army. At regular intervals the labor organizations would send soldiers a small sum of money (the *sou,*) which would be accompanied by antimilitarist propaganda urging soldiers to disobey orders if their unit were used to break a strike. More serious from the government's viewpoint was the request contained in the same propaganda that the soldier participate in the general strike if war were declared. After 1902 the *Manuel du soldat,* a pamphlet Yvetot wrote, was given to soldiers receiving the *sou.* This inflammatory tract labeled belief in fatherland an "idiotic religion" and denounced military service as "an apprenticeship of brutality and baseness," a "school of crime, vice, laziness, hypocrisy, and cowardice," and urged either desertion or antimilitarist and revolutionary agitation within the army for those who did not desert.[21] The antimilitarist campaign seems to have had an effect: the number of *insoumis* (draft dodgers) and deserters increased annually from 1900 to 1914.[22] Various French cabinets attempted to stop this trafficking in subversion, including Joseph Caillaux's Radical-dominated cabinet in August 1911, but all such efforts failed.

The revolutionary tactics and rhetoric of Griffuelhes and Yvetot were challenged during the years 1911 to 1913 by a second generation of syndicalist leaders. There are many complex reasons for the appearance of this challenge and for the ultimate victory of a moderate, reformist leadership. The wave of labor unrest that had swept France from 1906 to 1911 had begun to subside, and membership in the CGT declined alarmingly from 1910 to 1914. Griffuelhes resigned his post in 1909, making way for younger men. A general strike called for December 16, 1912, to prevent French intervention in the Balkan war was a dismal failure and provided the opportunity

for repressive measures by the government. These various events dis-
illusioned many syndicalists in revolutionary doctrines and led to a
reorientation of the theoretical bases of the labor movement.

Alphonse Merrheim, secretary of the *Fédération des métaux,*
supplied the intellectual framework for this reorientation, and
Léon Jouhaux, the new national secretary of the CGT, extended
Merrheim's ideas and converted them into policies and administrative
realities. Merrheim was impressed by the strength of the *patronat,*
the employers, in France and deplored the weakness, ignorance, and
lack of organization of the working class. He admired the centralization and efficiency of the *Comité des forges,* an organization for
the coordination of the policies of the various companies in the iron
and steel industry. He suggested a similar national coordinating body
for the labor movement, basing his ideal on the highly professional,
well-disciplined national unions of Great Britain. Therefore, he
advocated the fusion of syndicates into one powerful national
federation. In order to achieve this goal, he desired a greater concentration of French industrial ownership and productive capacity,
which, he felt, would make the organization of the working class far
easier. Although he rejected the revolutionary tactics of Griffuelhes,
he also rejected the parliamentary methods of Jaurès. Politics were,
he argued, irrelevant; real power lay in economic organizations.
Therefore, he urged the CGT to devote all its efforts to organizational matters: increased centralization, better discipline, increased
membership.[23]

Although Merrheim greatly influenced many of the rising cadres
of the CGT, it was Léon Jouhaux who did the most to apply Merrheim's theory. No mere echo, however, Jouhaux developed his
own conception of the relationship between peace and the labor
movement. He felt that a strong labor movement required a strong
economy, and the French economy could prosper only in peace.
Because military expenditures sapped French industry of badly
needed investment capital, and military consription reduced the size
of the labor force, the CGT must fight militarism if it were to build
a strong labor force.[24] The logic of this argument gradually forced
Jouhaux into a position best described as "economic patriotism."
He felt that France was locked in an economic competition with
Germany, and to a great extent the fate of the French working class

depended upon French economic supremacy. Therefore, he wanted the CGT to take the lead in furthering the rationalization, modernization, and concentration of French industry. Jouhaux rejected the radical tactics and antipatriotism of the revolutionary syndicalists in favor of a technocratic vision of an expanding economy directed by a coalition of experts drawn from labor and capitalist circles.[25]

Both the revolutionaries and the reformers of the CGT opposed the Briand-Barthou three-years' law, but, in keeping with their theoretical positions, they did so for different reasons and used differing tactics. Georges Yvetot, one of the declining number of revolutionaries still in important positions in the labor movement, continued to use the antipatriotic rhetoric of the Amiens Congress and the *Manuel du soldat.* He continued to advocate the general strike and disobedience among the soldiers.[26] He was more than an embarrassment to Jouhaux and the reformers; such activities gave the *Sûreté,* the political police, an excuse to carry out nationwide raids of CGT offices and *bourse du travail* headquarters in May 1913 and then to arrest several prominent CGT organizers, including Yvetot, in July 1913. The activities of the *Sou du soldat* were forbidden by the Barthou government.[27]

The CGT reformers opposed the three-years' law for two principal reasons. First, their profound antimilitarism made them natural opponents of any law that placed more workers in the army's barracks for longer periods of indoctrination and corruption. Second, convinced that the real source of French strength was its industrial capacity, not its military forces, the reformers argued that increased military spending would only weaken France vis-à-vis Germany and would distract the nation from its real task of modernizing and expanding industrial production.[28]

Although the CGT reformist leaders coordinated their opposition to the three-years' law with the SFIO, the gulf between their interpretation of the situation and that of Jaurès was immense. The syndicalist critique of Jaurès was set forth most clearly by Françis Delaisi, who often collaborated with Merrheim (for instance, they had co-authored *La Métallurgie,* a study of the iron and steel industry). Delaisi denounced Jaurès's *armée nouvelle* as a betrayal of the working class and a surrender to reactionary nationalism. He charged that the militarization of the primary schools, which Jaurès recom-

mended, would inevitably lead to an authoritarian society, placing
the education of the working class in the hands of their enemies.
Furthermore, Delaisi held that Jaurès's army would have an exclusively bourgeois officer corps because no worker would be able
to meet the educational requirements Jaurès had established. Finally,
Delaisi attacked Jaurès's acceptance of increased military strength
as a guarantee of peace. Just the opposite was true, wrote Delaisi.
Only a weak French army could prevent the French government
from undertaking adventurous and hazardous foreign policies. The
real conflict between France and Germany, Delaisi concluded, was
an economic and commercial rivalry in which armies would play
no part.[29]

Still, the clash of factions within the CGT and the antagonism between the CGT and the SFIO did not prevent these two organizations from cooperating in the struggle against the three-years' law.
The national offices of both organizations requested their local
affiliates to organize protests against the military law. That the
local agitation was vigorous and involved large numbers of people
throughout France is indicated by the numerous rallies, demonstrations, and protests reported by the political police in only one department: Nord. The departmental archives of Nord contain police
reports on thirty-seven separate meetings, rallies, and even protests
by municipal councils in Nord from April 16 to August 10, 1913.
Most of these were probably merely the regularly scheduled meetings
of SFIO sections or of trade unions. Yet some of them were rallies
called for a special purpose. Such rallies were not unique to Nord,
a department known for its strong socialist and trade union organizations; police reports of similar events are also to be found in the
departmental archives of Loir-et-Cher. (Nord and Loir-et-Cher are
noted because each was, in different ways, a microcosm of French
politics. Populous Nord had twenty-three deputies in the Chamber
representing all political viewpoints. Loir-et-Cher, represented by
only four deputies of the center right and center left, was typical of
rural and Radical France. Research in other departments would
most certainly give further evidence of this agitation, for comments
in the Parisian press suggest that the protest was indeed national
in scope.) In addition, both the CGT and SFIO staged mass rallies
in the Paris area. The SFIO meeting on June 1 drew an estimated
100,000 (police estimate)[30] to 150,000 (*L'Humanité* estimate).[31] A

CGT rally on July 13 was less successful, drawing only 20,000.

Liberal internationalists were less dramatic in their opposition to war preparedness than were the Socialists and the syndicalists. Placing their hopes for peace on the gradual acceptance of international law and arbitration by the political leaders of European states, the liberal internationalists did not engage in the same mass propaganda as did the working-class movements. Indeed, once again, they were very unlikely allies for the leftists. As liberals, they were often openly antisocialist. A constant theme in their speeches and literature was the fear that a general European war would inevitably lead to social upheaval, which was, of course, exactly what the CGT was promising.[32]

The liberals rejected the socialist class analysis of international relations; instead, they considered each nation-state as an individual actor. Their view is captured in the following comments of a British activist in the 1892: "As long as an individual lives in a community, he is necessarily subject to the law, for his rights . . . can be determined only . . . in relation to the rights of all. . . . The place of a nation in its relations with others is analogous, and when this analogy is recognized . . . international rights and responsibilities will be simple."[33] It was this liberal vision—an international community of free and equal states analogous to the national community of free and equal citizens—that determined the liberal internationalists' proposals for preventing war: arbitration treaties; international tribunals such as the Hague Tribunal; binding international law; general agreements for the limitation of armaments; international exchanges of parliamentarians, students, businessmen, and cultural leaders; and free travel and free trade among all nations.[34] And these goals determined their means: propaganda aimed at and personal influence exerted upon elites. Liberal internationalism was an elitist movement, staffed by professionals, businessmen, and intellectuals, that spoke to the political decision makers rather than the general public.[35]

The foremost French spokesman for the liberal internationalist cause in 1913 was Baron Paul Henri d'Estournelles de Constant, a member of the French Senate, chairman of the *Groupe parlementaire pour l'arbitrage,* and a winner of the Noble Peace Prize. He was a vocal critic of the three-years' law as one more step in the disastrous arms race that endangered peace rather than secured it. Furthermore, he argued that the measure was based on a misreading of German policy. He was certain that the leaders of Germany were not so blind as to launch a war that would only destroy its economy, lead to social revolution, and would lead to no gains.[36] Germany, he warned, would not be deterred from aggression by a larger French army but, to the contrary, would feel even more threatened and embattled. So the three-years's law would increase the bellicosity of Germany, not diminish it. Therefore, d'Estournelles endorsed Jaurès's proposal for a defensive army composed of reservists. This would prove to Germany that the French government had no plans for aggression.[37] Both d'Estournelles and Jaurès attended a meeting of French and German parliamentarians at Berne in May 1913 at the height of the three-years' law controversy. They led a delegation of 150 French legislators who discussed disarmament and international arbitration with 70 German politicians.[38]

The activities of the liberal internationalists had less impact on the French public than did the rallies, demonstrations, editorials, and pamphlets of the SFIO and the unions, but this measure should not be used to indicate their influence. Most of the liberal internationalists as socially prominent members of prestigious professions were more likely to have an impact on the middle and upper classes and on the centrists in the National Assembly than were leftists, such as Jaurès and Jouhaux. Nor were they alone in appealing to these strata. Their message was echoed by the intellectual luminaries of the *Ligue des droits de l'homme,* such as the novelists Anatole France and Romain Rolland and the historians Charles Seignobos and Alphonse Aulard.[39]

Complementing the elitist propaganda of the internationalists and the mass agitation of the leftists, the left Radicals, led by Joseph Caillaux and Félix Chautemps, waged a more pragmatic, less ideological, and increasingly partisan political campaign against not only the three-years' law but also the full range of Briand-Poincaré-Barthou policies. By far the largest party in the Chamber, the Radicals were unable before 1913 to combat the conservative resurgence Briand and Poincaré had fostered because of a lack of party unity and discipline.[40] They achieved unity in 1913 and ultimately ousted the Barthou government because they saw the issue of military reform not in the context of Franco-German relations but as a conservative plot to repeal the domestic reforms the Radicals had enacted in the aftermath of the Dreyfus affair. This theme was repeated again and again by Caillaux, Chautemps, Jean Augagneur, Adolph Messimy, and others in parliamentary debate.[41] And *le Radical,* the party newspaper, leveled the same charges in its editorials.[42]

In their attitudes toward international affairs, the Radicals were closer to Briand and Poincaré than they were to Jaurès and Jouhaux. They endorsed the idea of a strong traditional national defense rejecting Jaurès's reserve army as impractical. They were nationalists and even imperialists, vehemently rejecting a class analysis of foreign policy and arguing that nations must expand—especially economically—to be great. They supported—indeed, they had largely created—the alliances with Russia and Great Britain as necessary to restrain an ambitious Germany. Commercial cooperation between France and Germany might decrease the tensions between the two nations, but, in the meantime, France must maintain a strong defensive posture.[43]

The only common ground the Radicals shared with the Socialists, syndicalists, and liberal internationalists was a strong antimilitarism. They thus rejected the "nationalists revival" of Poincaré, the "national union" of Briand, and the three-years' law of Barthou. It was, in fact, solely on grounds of domestic policy that the Radicals joined the coalition against war preparedness. Yet, for the same reason Caillaux was able to extend the battle beyond the issue of military reforms because he was able to create a lasting political coalition out of these disparate elements.

During 1913 the left Radicals had gained control of the Radical party machinery; as their leader, Caillaux tried to forge a new *Bloc des gauches* with the SFIO to counter the centrist-Progressist-nationalist coalition built by Briand, Poincaré, and Barthou. Even before the debate on the three-years' law began, Caillaux had laid the foundations for a second battle to follow the debate on miltary reform. He demanded a tax reform, based on a progressive income tax, to pay for the increase in military spending that the expansion of the army would require. If compulsory military service was a "blood tax," he said, it was a retrogressive tax, weighing most heavily on the poor; therefore, the proponents of extended military service should be the first to accept a progressive income tax to equalize the burden of national defense.[44] Jaurès praised this position and realized its potential as a weapon against the government.[45]

124   DAVID E. SUMLER

The final assault on the Barthou ministry was opened by Caillaux
in a dinner speech to Radical notables on November 30. His major
theme was not his opposition to the three-years' law but rather the
enervating effect Briand's policy of national union was having on
the nation.[46] Two days after he delivered this speech, Caillaux led
an attack in the Chamber against Barthou's proposal that the new
military expenses be covered by a bond issue, with the interest derived
from the bonds being tax free.[47] This extremely regressive fiscal ex-
pedient was the perfect target for the now unified left. After Caillaux's verbal assault, the Chamber voted "no confidence" in the
ministry, 290-262. A breakdown of this roll call by parliamentary
groups reveals that the polarization of the Chamber was absolute.
The advocates of war preparedness had been ousted from office on
the issue of financing military expenditures, and the opponents
of the three-years' law formed the next government. Caillaux became minister of finance in the new cabinet, which was headed by
Gaston Doumergue. This cabinet, backed by left Radicals, the SFIO,
and independent Socialists, governed France until the 1914 elections,
which allowed the electorate to prounounce a judgment on the three-
years' law. That judgment appears to have been negative. Parties
of the center and right lost fifty-three.

None of the four groups discussed here was essentially pacifist.
None rejected violence in all situations. Only three of them were
antiwar—the Socialists, syndicalists, and liberal internationalists.
But all of them shared antimilitary sentiments, and their antimilitarism was more an expression of their hopes for a certain type of French
society rather than their concerns for the international order. The
liberal internationalists might be an exception, although they too
disparaged militarism as a breeder of chauvinism and international
tensions. On balance, then, the opposition to increased war preparedness must, after all, be seen as another aspect of French domestic
politics.

NOTES

1. Georges Bonnefous, *Histoire politique de laTroisième République* (Paris:
Presses universitaires de France, 1956), 1:334-39; Jacques Chastenet, *Histoire de la
Troisième République* (Paris: Librairie Hachette, 1957), 4:116-19; George Michon,
La Préparation de la guerre: la Loi de trois ans (Paris: M. Rivière, 1935), pp. 137-
94; Richard D. Challener, *The French Theory of the Nation in Arms, 1866-1939* (New
York: Columbia University Press, 1955), pp. 66-90; Eugen Weber, *The Nationalist*

Revival in France, 1905-1914 (1959; reprint ed., Berkeley: University of California Press, 1968), pp. 120-28.

2. David E. Sumler, "Domestic Influences on the Nationalist Revival in France, 1909-1914," *French Historical Studies* 4, no. 4 (Fall 1970):517-37.

3. Briand had been premier from June 1909 to March 1911. For an account of Poincaré's policies as premier, see ibid.

4. *L'Humanité,* March 19, 1913; *Le Bulletin de l'Alliance républicaine démocratique,* March 30, 1913; and Georges Saurez, *Briand: sa vie—son oeuvre* (Paris: Librairie Plon, 1938), 2:428-29.

5. An excellent study of the polarization on the local level is supplied by Bernard Machut, "La Presse régionale et la loi militaire de 1913" (Diplome d'étude superieur, Faculté des lettres, Université de Lille, 1962). See also David E. Sumler, "Polarization in French Politics, 1909-1914" (Ph.D. diss., Princeton University, 1968).

6. Harvey Goldberg, *The Life of Jean Jaurès* (Madison: University of Wisconsin Press, 1968), pp. 351-52, 378-79; Harold R. Weinstein, *Jean Jaurès: A Study of Patriotism in the French Socialist Movement* (New York: Columbia University Press, 1936), pp. 132-33.

7. *Goldberg, Jaurès,* p. 378.

8. Weinstein, *Jaurès,* pp. 133-34.

9. Goldberg, *Jaurès,* p. 379.

10. James Joll, *The Second International, 1889-1914* (New York: Harper & Row, 1966), p. 143; Goldberg, *Jaurès,* pp. 435-36; Weinstein, *Jaurès,* p. 260.

11. Goldberg, *Jaurès,* p. 304.

12. Weinstein, *Jaurès,* pp. 136-37.

13. A Fryar Calhoun, "The Politics of Internal Order: The French Government and Revolutionary Labor, 1898-1914" (Ph.D. diss., Princeton University, 1973), pp. 515-16.

14. Michon, *Trois ans,* p. 150; Goldberg, *Juarès,* p. 441.

15. For many examples of socialist activity and the government's reaction to it, see Calhoun, "Internal Order," pp. 565-77, and Geoffrey Chapman, "Decision for War: The Domestic Political Context of French Diplomacy, 1911-1914" (Ph.D. diss., Princeton University, 1971), pp. 99-107, 228-30. Much evidence of the widespread agitation against the law can be found in police reports in departmental archives: see Archives départementales, Loir-et-Cher, M., *Police généerale, 1891-1914: Loi des trois ans* (hereafter cited as AD Loir-et-Cher), and Archives départementales, Nord, M 154/232, *Police générale. Manifestations contre les trois ans* (hereafter cited as AD Nord).

16. Sumler, "Polarization," chap. 6.

17. Michael S. DeLucia, "The Remaking of French Syndicalism, 1911-1918: The Growth of the Reformist Philosophy" (Ph.D. diss., Brown University, 1971).

18. Goldberg, *Jaurès,* pp. 351, 378.

19. Cited by Calhoun, "Internal Order," p. 530.

20. Ibid., p. 516.

21. Ibid., pp. 517-18.

22. "From 1890 to 1900 Ministry of War figures showed a total of 1900 deserters and 4000 draft dodgers ("insoumis"); for 1902-04 the numbers were 2000 and 5000

respectively; for 1909-11, 2600 and 10,000. By 1911 a total of nearly 80,000 individuals were being sought by the army and the police for default of their military obligations." (Ibid., p. 533. See also, *Le Temps,* February 15, 1910.)

23. DeLucia, "Remaking of French Syndicalsim," pp. 1-6, 10-31, 70-71, 80-81, 85-86, 93.

24. Ibid., pp. 110-11.

25. Ibid., pp. 116-18.

26. Ibid., p. 114.

27. AD Loir-et-Cher, M., *Police générale, 1891-1914: Loi des trois ans;* AD Nord, M 154/232, *Police générale. Manifestations contre les trois ans.*

28. DeLucia, "Remaking of French Syndicalism," pp. 111-12.

29. Ibid., pp. 100-02.

30. Chapman, "Decision," p. 100.

31. *L'Humanité,* June 1-2, 1913.

32. Sandi E. Cooper, "Liberal Internationalists Before World War I," *Peace and Change* 2 (1973):11-19. For a fuller treatment, see Cooper, "Peace and Internationalism: European Ideological Movements Behind the Two Hague Conferences (1899 and 1907)" (Ph.D. diss., New York University, 1967).

33. From a speech by Hodgson Pratt at the Universal Peace Congress, Berne, 1892, cited by Cooper, "Peace and Internationalsim," p. 120.

34. From Baron Paul d'Estournelles de Constant, *La Conciliation internationale,* pp. 6-7, cited by Cooper, "Peace and Internationalsim," p. 220.

35. Cooper, "Liberal Internationalists," pp. 14, 16.

36. D'Estournelles de Constant made speeches in the Senate giving these arguments on February 6, 1912, and August 1, 1913, and at the Berne Interparliamentary Congress, May 11-18, 1913.

37. Michon, *Trois ans,* p. 172.

38. Chapman, "Decision for War," pp. 93-94.

39. Carter Jefferson, *Anatole France: The Politics of Skepticism* (New Brunswick, N.J.: Rutgers University Press, 1965), pp. 181-82, 188-89; Chapman, "Decision for War," pp. 98-99, 227.

40. See Sumler, "Domestic Influences."

41. Speeches by Caillaux, Chautemps, and Amadée Thalamas, respectively, in France, Chambre des députés, *Journal officiel, Débats,* July 19, 1913, p. 2813, June 2, 1913, pp. 1653-54, June 5, 1913, p. 1746 (hereafter cited as *JOC Débats*).

42. *Le Radical,* February 24, May 3, 19, 1913.

43. John C. Cairns, "Politics and Foreign Policy: The French Parliament, 1911-1914," *Canadian Historical Review* 34 (1953):250-54; Michon, *Trois ans,* pp. 154-67.

44. *JOC Débats,* May 29, 1913, p. 1608.

45. *L'Humanité,* May 30, 1913; Caillaux, *Mes Mémoires* (Paris: Librairie Plon, 1942), 3:61; cf. also Charles Paix-Séailles, *Jaurès et Caillaux* (Paris, n.d.), pp. 86-89.

46. *Le Radical,* December 1, 1913.

47. *JOC Débats,* December 2, 1913, pp. 3,714-19.

7
Can the Peace Movement Prevent War? The U.S.-Mexican Crisis of April 1914

MICHAEL A. LUTZKER

The United States and Mexico barely escaped confronting each other in a major war when on April 21, 1914, American Marines met armed resistance shortly after they landed at Veracruz. As reports of sizable casualties flashed across both countries, a wave of national resentment swept the various factions engaged in Mexico's civil war, the embattled Mexican government broke diplomatic relations with the United States, and the American press overwhelmingly assumed that the bloodshed meant war. Although neither nation had been intent on armed conflict, it seemed for a time that events had gone beyond the power of leaders to control them. Ultimately war was averted, but there is disagreement among historians as to what factors were crucial. In our own age of recurring confrontation, we would do well to examine and reconsider the means by which nations in the past have pulled back from the brink of war. This essay focuses primarily upon the American peace movement, a significant influence in the pre-1914 period, to assess its role in preventing war with Mexico. At the same time, one cannot avoid considering the importance of such elusive concepts as patriotism and national honor, as well as the role of leadership in a time of crisis.

By any conventional standards, the peace movement as of 1914 was better organized, had more influential supporters, and had more funds than at any other time since its inception a century

earlier. The formation in 1910 of both the $10 million Carnegie
Endowment for International Peace, and the $1 million World
Peace Foundation, plus the growth of the older American Peace
Society, served to underscore developments that had taken place
during the preceding decade.[1] Stimulated in part by the first and
second Hague Peace Conferences in 1899 and 1907, encouraged
by Theodore Roosevelt's successful mediation of the Russo-Japanese
War of 1905, world peace, international arbitration of disputes, and
proposals for a world court became the goals of internationalists.
These ideas attracted substantial numbers of lawyers, business
leaders, clergymen, journalists, and former diplomats, who lent
their presence to international peace congresses, served as leaders
of peace societies, and encouraged greater American participation
in world affairs.[2]

The movement grew significantly in those innocent years before
1914, when Americans were relatively free from what have since
become known as world responsibilities. The two oceans then offered
substantial protection from the other Great Powers. In the absence
of a credible threat from abroad, the United States had no large
peacetime military establishment. Peace advocates did not incur
the risk of being denounced as subservient to a foreign ideology. On
the contrary, peace became the most respectable of reforms. For
most it meant a stable, ordered world. The ideas of a world court
and of arbitration as a substitute for war were attractive to the conservative minded who feared war not only as a threat to commerce
but as a breeder of upheaval and socialism. On the positive side
they envisioned the United States as exercising a leading role in the
search for world peace. The movement directed its efforts to edu-
cating the public to internationalist ideas; but in attempting to influence national policy, its leaders were inclined to prefer informal
access to those in power rather than the organization of mass pressure. The elite bias of the movement is illustrated by the 1914 report
to the membership committee of the New York Peace Society, which
recommended that "quality rather than quantity should be sought in
the enrollment, the judgment being that too large a number of names
would not add to the political effectiveness of the organization . . .
while it would make the process of using [the list] an expensive one."[3]
Executive committees of peace societies often met in the quiet, taste-

ful rooms of prestigious metropolitan clubs. Banquets at well-appointed hotels, with distinguished visitors from abroad as guests of honor, were popular gatherings for the membership. In the cordial atmosphere of good food and drink, toasts were offered to international friendship.

An impressive number of peace leaders had served at the top levels of government; in cabinet posts or as ministers abroad.[4] Others were leaders in the business and financial communities.[5] The educators among them headed prestigious universities though their influence ranged far beyond their own institutions.[6]

This, then, was the peace movement that attempted to respond to events in Mexico.

II

Beginning in 1911, Mexico underwent a series of upheavals and protracted civil conflicts that were to last more than a decade. In the process U.S.-Mexican relations approached a state of conflict on more than one occasion.[7]

Porfirio Díaz, whose authoritarian rule had stood as the very symbol of order in Latin America for thirty years, was toppled from power in 1911 by a reformer, Francisco Madero. The new regime attempted to undermine the authority of the landed aristocracy, the Catholic church, and the army. These elements proved too powerful for the reformers. In February 1913, the government was overthrown by supporters of the army commander, General Victoriano Huerta. Madero and his vice-president were murdered as Huerta ruthlessly consolidated his power. Despite the repression, Huerta's regime was soon recognized by the major European powers. In so doing they followed the traditional practice of making no moral judgments but based recognition on a government's presumed ability to preserve public order and protect foreign investments.

The forces of change set in motion by Madero's administration were not easily suppressed. Followers of the martyred leader withdrew to the mountainous northern states of Mexico and raised the standard of rebellion. Their leader was Venustiano Carranza, the governor of Coahula. Designating themselves Constitutionalists, they pledged to destroy Huerta's regime.

These dramatic events, beginning with the overthrow of Díaz by
Madero, had been followed with great interest in the United States,
for American investments in Mexico equaled the combined total of
all U.S. holdings in the West Indies and the rest of Latin America.[8]
President William Howard Taft had accorded recognition to the
Madero government. When incidents of violence threatened American lives and property in Mexico, Taft acted promptly to inform
the Madero administration of its responsibilities to preserve order.
By discretionary use of an arms embargo, and by stationing American troops near, but not on, the U.S.-Mexican border, Taft succeeded in neutralizing cries for intervention.[9] He was less successful
in controlling the actions of the American ambassador in Mexico,
Henry Lane Wilson, who, as a bitter critic of Madero, played a
substantial behind-the-scenes role in ousting the Mexican leader.
Following the coup considerable international pressure was put on
General Huerta to guarantee the safety of the deposed leaders, the
principle of sanctuary being strong in Latin American tradition.
Ambassador Wilson, however, declined to use his substantial influence with the new regime. The news of Madero's murder shocked
foreign observers, it destroyed the credibility of the American
ambassador in Mexico, and it deeply affected the course of U.S.-
Mexican relations.

Taft's policy of relative restraint served as a contrasting model for
many peace leaders as they watched the evolution of Woodrow
Wilson's relations with Mexico during the years that followed.
President Wilson took office in March 1913, just one month after
Huerta's coup. The 1912 election campaign represented a high tide
for the Progressive reform movement in America. The crusades
to end corruption in government and enact legislation to curb mono-
polistic practices, child labor, and the use of alcohol were all characterized by a heavy moral tone. Wilson's early presidential pronouncements indicated a strong desire to apply to foreign relations
the high moral standards he sought in domestic affairs.

Wilson was appalled by the assassinations that accompanied
Huerta's coup. Moreover, he was impressed by reports from U.S.
consuls in the north of Mexico that indicated strong support for the
rebel Constitutionalists. Equally important were clear indications
that Ambassador Wilson had been involved in the plot against Madero.

The combined weight of these factors led to President Wilson's refusal to recognize the Huerta regime.[10] His actions, though defensible on moral grounds, were not in accord with traditional diplomacy. What President Wilson wanted was an elected government that would be broadly representative of the Mexican people. The problem was that if each side trusted the other enough to engage in an election, they would not have been fighting a civil war. However, in the process of trying to help Mexico achieve representative government, Wilson became convinced that a way had to be found to force Huerta's resignation. His strong belief led him to an ever-deepening involvement in Mexico's internal affairs.

Soon peace leaders began to view President Wilson's policy with growing concern. They had applauded Taft's reluctance to become enmeshed in Mexican affairs. Most urged Wilson to recognize the Huerta regime as the best alternative to continued instability that might lead ultimately to U.S. intervention. David Starr Jordan, head of the World Peace Foundation, cautioned Wilson that any armed intrusion would result in a general massacre of Americans in Mexico and would poison U.S. relations with all of Latin America for a century.[11]

Underlying the concern of some for restraint, however, was an assumption of national (if not racial) superiority. Andrew Carnegie, for example, wrote to the president that he shared Wilson's desire to encourage a peaceful election but added that Mexico was not up to that standard. Nicholas Murray Butler, a leader of the Carnegie peace endowment, was less subtle. Butler confided to his friend, Lord Morley, that Wilson's Mexican policy was "absurd in the highest degree," but the endowment's leaders had refrained from saying so publicly "for fear of making new trouble." The Mexicans, Butler believed, were "no more ready for representative democratic institutions than a tribe of wild bushmen would be. What they really need is another fifty years of enlightened dictatorship like that of the older Diaz."[12]

Among those associated with the peace movement, none followed the Mexican situation more closely than the men with substantial investments in that country. They had been among the strongest supporters of Taft's cautious policy, and their objections to intervention had a practical as well as a philosophical basis. They were convinced that nothing would unite the fiercely nationalist Mexicans more quickly than an invading Yankee army. In the process of resisting any such alien force, the infuriated people would confiscate or destroy any American holdings. Thus they bombarded the Wilson administration with advice to recognize Huerta or any other leader who was able to restore order.[13]

Arthur B. Farquhar, one-time president of the National Association of Manufacturers and a vice-president of the American Peace Society, urged immediate recognition of Huerta. He wrote to the State Department: "I have been familiar with Mexico for a great many years, have been a guest of [ex] President Porfirio Diaz at his palace . . . and I know that it took him a number of years to restore order in Mexico, and he pursued a good deal the same method as that followed by Huerta." Farquhar believed it would be of "immense service to the business interests of this country . . . to have the United States acknowledge the Huerta government. . . . America has a thousand million dollars invested in Mexico. Its loss would bring vast suffering upon our community, with a corresponding [sic] lower standard of living."[14] As the civil war became prolonged and exacerbated, peace advocates found themselves in an increasingly difficult position. Their commitment to stability and order came into conflict with their belief in nonintervention.

In July 1913, Ambassador Wilson was recalled from his post in Mexico without being officially replaced. This move, coupled with increased fighting in regions near the U.S.-Mexican border, led the Hearst chain of newspapers and the *Washington Post* to issue renewed cries for intervention.

Leaders of the Carnegie peace endowment, alert to the increased danger of war, embarked upon at least two private initiatives designed to mediate between the two warring factions in Mexico.[15] Both were intended to utilize the influential contacts enjoyed by the endowment leaders, and the evidence suggests that they were independent of one another.

The most ambitious plan was projected by Nicholas Murray Butler. After clearing the idea with the State Department, the endowment set aside the not inconsiderable sum of $20,000 to be used for the project. Preparations had apparently been under way beforehand, for four days later Butler dispatched Francis Loomis, former assistant

secretary of state, to Paris to act as a representative of the endowment and to confer with influential Mexican diplomats and former
cabinet officials.

The plan was to set up a commission composed of government
representatives from Holland and Switzerland, plus a person desig-
nated by the endowment. This commission would suggest to a carefully chosen list of influential Mexicans that they form "an advisory
council to a provisional president, and devote themselves to the task
of forming and establishing a provisional government."[16] The
advisory group was to consist of three men from the ousted dictator
Díaz's cabinet, three who had served in the Madero cabinet, and
five others characterized as independent. They would urge an armistice,
to be followed immediately by a conference to arrange the finances
of a new government, and also to ensure the safeguarding of life and
property (that is, foreign holdings). They hoped that a republican
form of government would come about through the use of "moral
pressure backed by the public opinion of the world." Loomis was
advised in Paris that Huerta would be likely to consider their proposals favorably. In the case of Carranza the reliance was, again,
on the force of public opinion, and the same was true for President
Wilson. The documentation is not available regarding the informal
discussions, but it is clear that the plan was not successful. In retrospect
it would seem that despite the numerical balance, the plan favored
the Huerta forces.[17] Probably the key man in the proposed advisory
council was José Limantour, former treasury secretary and the most
powerful individual in the old Díaz cabinet.

Meanwhile, Oscar Straus, a Carnegie Endowment trustee but
apparently not privy to the executive committee's efforts, publicly
proposed a mediation commission, which he hoped Wilson would
name. In advancing his proposal Straus was aware that such a government-sponsored commission was unthinkable without advance
assurance that one or both of the Mexican factions would receive it.
Thereupon the former diplomat embarked upon some extraordinary
efforts to demonstrate to Wilson that his plan was sound. First
he arranged to have a vice-president of the New York Life Insurance Company contact that firm's agent in Mexico City to sound
out leading figures on how such a commission would be received.
This enterprising gentleman went one step better and secured a

private interview with General Huerta himself, who seemed pleased with the plan and gave assurances that such a commission would be received and accorded every protection.

When advised of this development, Straus arranged to have lunch with William F. McCombs, chairman of the Democratic National Committee, and presenting him with the confidential telegrams, convinced McCombs to place the matter before President Wilson and request an interview with Straus. The president was, to put it mildly, not at all appreciative of this bit of private diplomacy. He had long since decided that the United States would conduct no negotiations with Huerta and was interested only in ways of forcing the general from power.[18]

In pursuit of his aim Wilson employed a variety of tactics, including unofficial promises to aid those around Huerta if they would depose him. When this meddling failed, the president turned to dealing with the Constitutionalists. Here again he met with frustration, for Carranza was fully as inflexible as Wilson himself. The Constitutionalist chief rejected the assumption underlying all of Wilson's actions—that Americans knew better than Mexicans the kind of government its people should have.[19]

Relations between the two nations reached an acute stage of tension over the famous "affair of honor."[20] Despite the civil war a large number of Americans remained in the Mexican port of Tampico where most were connected with the oil refineries. Tampico was held by the Huerta forces, but in April 1914 it came under siege by the constitutionalists. In the waters off Tampico was an American battle squadron "showing the flag." The ships could be used to evacuate the Americans if necessary. Tensions ran high in the city. On April 10, 1914, the paymaster and crew members of the U.S.S. *Dolphin* were arrested by a Huertista colonel when they landed without permission. As soon as the Mexican commander, General Morelos Zaragosa, learned of the incident he immediately ordered the men released and extended a personal apology to Admiral Henry T. Mayo, the American commander. The incident should, of course, have ended there. But the apology was not sufficient for Admiral Mayo, who demanded a twenty-one gun salute to the American flag by the Mexicans. To the consternation of those who regarded Wilson as a friend of peace, the president backed the admiral's demand because he saw an opportunity to humiliate Huerta and force his resignation. When the demand for the salute was refused, Wilson treated it as a deliberate affront to the national honor of the United States. He issued an ultimatum to Huerta to salute the American flag or risk the consequences. The U.S. fleets off Mexico were put on battle alert, and war plans were drawn in Washington. Newspaper headlines around the nation screamed that war threatened.

Meanwhile, Huerta caught the humor, if not the danger, of the situation and agreed to fire the salute, provided an American warship returned it volley for volley. Such an action would have implied recognition of the Huerta government and Wilson abruptly rejected it. The whole situation resembled a political opera bouffe, confided Nicholas Murray Butler to a friend but, he added, "it would be exceedingly amusing if it were not so appalling."[21]

However elevated Wilson's ultimate objectives may have been and however limited his intentions, by invoking the honor of the United States he risked loosing a tide of popular emotion that could have swept the nation into war.[22] For months the sensationalist press and at least one wing of the Republican party had been in full cry for intervention. Wilson had resisted such agitation. Now he appeared ready to outdo the war hawks with his insistence upon a point so trivial that by comparison it seemed to make the historic incident of Jenkins' ear a genuine casus belli.

Wilson had tapped that vein of national sentiment that has no use for reason. It was enough for Americans to be told that the flag had been insulted. Conditioned by a lifetime of ceremonies in tribute to that sacred symbol, the blood of every patriot quickened as the president declared that the honor and dignity of the United States had to be upheld, no matter what the cost. Americans might be divided on the question of intervention, but here was an issue unsoiled by economics, property interests, and the like. Americans were peace loving as always. However, as one typical telegram to Wilson put it, "Even the scourge of war is preferable to continued insults."

In the face of the appeal to national honor, the peace movement divided sharply as to how to respond. Many of its adherents had been attracted to the movement in the placid years of Hague Conferences and carefully hedged arbitration treaties. Most had no wish to swim against anything that might become a tidal wave of public sentiment. Some, like Andrew Carnegie, retained a steadfast faith in Wilson. He wrote to the president that he could not imagine that Wilson could be moved by "such a trifling thing as whether the flag salute takes place simultaneously or a few seconds after each other." Although the steelmaster told of receiving numerous telegrams calling for protest meetings, his advice to all was to wait. As president of the New York Peace Society and an important backer of other peace groups, Carnegie was in a position to discourage public protests. Throughout the crisis he bombarded the president with private advice, but he continued to oppose any public criticism of Wilson.[23]

In Massachusetts, the historic center of the peace movement, the World Peace Foundation under Edwin D. Mead's leadership issued statements by prominent men calling on the nation's leaders to act with deliberation. The precipitous nature of the crisis, declared Mead, "must not be allowed to betray our people into irremediable mistake or wrong."[24] The American Peace and Arbitration League took a different view, urging that all stand behind the president because "politics must stop at the water's edge."[25] A strong public statement came from the Commission on Peace and Arbitration of the Federal Council of Churches whose ministers asserted that "the voices clamoring for war do not represent the sentiment of the sane and substantial people of the Republic." They denounced the newspapers, which were clamoring for extreme measures, as the voices of "mischief makers and of certain vested interests whose aggrandisement is furthered by war."[26] However, the pleas of the ministers and other appeals to reason missed their mark. The danger of war came less from the "mischief makers" than from the fact that most Americans were ready to follow the president wherever he might lead, and at that point Wilson seemed determined to intervene.

On April 20 the president went before Congress and asked for consent to use the armed forces to gain the "fullest recognition of the rights and dignity of the United States." If war should come, Wilson asserted, it would be only against General Huerta and his supporters, not against the Mexican people. The president had been assured of support for any emergency action by congressional leaders of both parties. After a two and one half hour debate the House voted 337-37 to support Wilson's position.[27]

In the Senate the debate was more extended. Henry Cabot Lodge and some fellow Republicans countered with their own resolution supporting intervention, but on the broader grounds of protecting American lives and property in Mexico. Administration supporters defended Wilson's resolution by arguing that he was not asking for a declaration of war. He only wanted congressional backing for an authority he already possessed: the use of the armed forces to stop aggression on the U.S. flag and its honor. Lodge's resolution was denounced as a declaration of war.

Then Elihu Root took the Senate floor. As a former secretary of state he was, together with Lodge, the Senate's most knowledgeable spokesman on foreign affairs. He was also president of the Carnegie Endowment for International Peace. His words received a respectful hearing. Root took little time in coming to the point: "It is intervention, technically, but it is war in its essence that we are to vote to justify tonight." He deplored a move that would sacrifice lives over a quarrel concerning the manner of rendering a salute to the flag. He then ascended to higher ground. In back of the flag incident, he found a history of violence and anarchy in Mexico, with a disregard for American lives and property. Since diplomacy had failed to obtain redress, he insisted, "The real object to be obtained by the course we are asked to approve [intervention] is not the gratification of personal pride, it is not the satisfaction of an admiral or a Government. It is the preservation of the power of the United States to protect its citizens under these conditions."[28] Therefore, Root favored Lodge's substitute resolution justifying intervention on the basis of protecting American lives and property. If Wilson's proposals brought the United States to the brink of war, the Republicans' contribution (by broadening the basis for intervention) seem designed to ensure the headlong plunge. An added irony is that privately Root had deplored Wilson's policy of interference in Mexico. According to Root's able biographer, Philip Jessup, the crisis arising over the flag salute caused the senator deep personal anguish.[29]

The debate in the Senate went on into the night. John Sharp Williams of Mississippi, another leader identified with the cause of peace and international arbitration, insisted that the power of an unleashed patriotism had effectively left Wilson with no choice. If the president had passed by the insult to the flag, "there would

MICHAEL A. LUTZKER

have gone up from every hilltop and every valley in the United States resounding denunciations of his 'cowardice', his 'pusillanimity', his lack of 'patriotism.' . . . With humanity as it is . . . semi-civilized, no nation has ever yet failed to resent an insult to its flag and to its uniform."[30] The applause from the galleries was such that the presiding officer ordered them cleared. Senator Williams declared his support for Wilson's intervention directed against Huerta.

Senators who wished to spare the country war over the flag insult were offered a resolution by John Works, a maverick Republican of California. Works urged that the president accept Huerta's apology. The resolution (which Works conceded had no chance of passage) never came to a vote, for in the meantime Wilson had acted without waiting for the senators to complete their debate.[31]

Anxious to intercept a German munitions ship destined for Huerta's forces, the president gave the order to seize the port of Veracruz. By the evening of April 21, the news was flashed across both countries that a bloody battle had taken place costing the lives of four Americans with several wounded and scores of casualties on the Mexican side.[32] At the end of the day 3,000 American marines held Veracruz. Mexico immediately broke diplomatic relations with the United States. For the next few days most newspaper accounts and statements of public figures assumed that the two nations were at war. The U.S. press rallied to the president. A meeting of the American Newspaper Publishers Association closed ranks declaring, "We are not furnishing advice to the President of the United States; we are supporting him." The *Boston Globe,* the *New York Evening Sun,* the *Washington Post,* the *Philadelphia Press,* the *Louisville Courier-Journal,* the *Worcester Telegram,* and the *New York Evening Journal* all gave enthusiastic support to efforts for a quick military victory. Other newspapers that favored strong action included the *Cincinnati Commercial Tribune,* the *Cincinnati Enquirer,* and the New *Orleans Times-Picayune.* Even the *New York Evening Post,* whose editors believed the United States had acted as the aggressor, conceded that "the drumming of the guns is now the only oratory that counts." Most of the London press agreed that war was at hand.[33] A number of congressmen told Wilson they were ready to serve in the military. Governors offered their state's militia. Ordinary citizens wrote to the president volunteering to fight.[34]

Despite widespread evidence that the country would rally to the president's side, it is clear that Wilson was deeply affected by the bloodshed at Veracruz. Wrote one correspondent, "I remember how preternaturally pale, almost parchmenty, Mr. Wilson looked when he stood up there and answered the questions of the newspaper men. The death of American sailors and marines owing to an order of his seemed to affect him like an ailment. He was positively shaken."[35]

In retrospect it seems almost incredible that Wilson could have accepted the assurances of those who said there would be no forcible opposition to American seizure of the port. Yet an examination of the reports he was receiving and Wilson's own certainty as to his high purpose and limited objectives makes it possible to understand why he acted. In the crucial hours following the landing, Wilson declined to take any of the follow-up actions urged upon him by Secretary of War Lindley Garrison and others—actions that would certainly have led to open hostilities. He replied to letters and telegrams from those Americans offering to serve in the military by expressing the hope that war might be averted.[36] Despite his restraint, events seemed for a time to slip beyond his power to control them.[37] What convinced Wilson to hold back and ultimately to exert his power to prevent war? A significant factor, according to Arthur Link, was an outpouring of peace sentiment that "profoundly influenced" the president.[38] It is this contention that I would like to examine.

IV

In the days surrounding the Veracruz landing, as the nation hovered on the edge of war, sentiment in the peace movement remained equivocal. The American Peace Society's organ, the *Advocate of Peace,* published several resolutions from peace groups under the heading "Protests Against War With Mexico."[39] The Washington D.C. Peace Society conveyed to the president "the assurances of deep sympathy and appreciation of his . . . efforts to avert war" and expressed the hope that the two governments could adjust their differences "with honor."[40] The president could have read such a message as supporting his actions in Veracruz since there was no criticism of the landing.

The Buffalo Peace and Arbitration Society expressed its confidence in the president and noted with "much approval" his statement that "no further invasion or aggression against Mexico will be permitted *unless rendered necessary* [emphasis added]." However, if further intervention should be necessary, the Buffalo peace advocates urged that it be a joint action to include Great Britain, France, Germany, and Spain, other nations with large interests in Mexico. They reasoned that while "the Mexicans are very hostile to . . . the United States and will fight any invasion by our soldiers . . . there will be an entirely different feeling in the case of the proposed joint action."[41] Equating peace with stability and order (imposed if necessary), these peace advocates had concluded that intervention in a country weakened by civil war was a positive step, provided it was undertaken by a concert of powers. (One can only wonder what their view would have been toward intervention in the American Civil War by the major European powers.)

An altogether different note was struck by Edwin Mead, who insisted that another war with Mexico would be a "crime against humanity." The activity of Mead and his Boston colleagues is evident in a number of telegrams from that area calling upon Wilson to prevent war. Mead telegraphed his fellow peace workers in Philadelphia to preach against war at that critical moment, but the messages reaching Wilson from the Philadelphia area were less numerous.[42]

Meanwhile Oswald Garrison Villard, a peace leader and editor of the *New York Evening Post,* was taking his own protest directly to Washington. Seeking out members of Wilson's cabinet, he found Commerce Secretary William Redfield, who had been touring the Midwest, convinced that the American people were overwhelmingly behind the president. Treasury Secretary William McAdoo insisted (to Villard's disgust) that the flag had been insulted and the honor of the nation had to be upheld. He found a more somber attitude from Franklin Roosevelt of the Navy Department, who had just returned from the Pacific Coast. Roosevelt told Villard that people there felt the president had made a mistake but that the country would have to go into Mexico anyhow and "make the best of a bad job."[43]

To his surprise Villard found the army leaders to be less than enthusiastic about a Mexican campaign. They foresaw an enormously difficult and drawn-out conflict with no glory for anyone. In this instance he considered them friends of peace. But Villard was less certain about the New York Peace Society, which, as he complained to Carnegie, seemed woefully lacking in leadership and energy. Villard wanted a dynamic organizer at work for the society: "A thousand telegrams a day should be going . . . to the members of the Cabinet."[44]

The New York Peace Society's quiescence seems fairly typical. There is little evidence that the other affiliates of the American Peace Society reacted strongly to the crisis. The reports of the society's field secretaries around the country show no concerted effort to mobilize public sentiment. The elderly secretary of the Chicago group wrote that the "Mexican situation has kept me sitting on the edge of the telephone wire almost constantly," but his report to the national secretary contains no recital of actions taken. There was a similar dearth of activity in the South Atlantic and West Coast regions. In all, only a handful of petitions regarding Mexico appear in the *Congressional Record* (there were ten times as many favoring prohibition), and a modest number of protests were sent directly to the president. The biographer of a leading peace advocate concludes that despite "a case of aggression by the strong against the weak about as flagrant as any that had occurred in recent history . . . pacifists were generally silent."[45]

If the organized peace movement failed to mobilize substantial opposition to the impending conflict, was antiwar sentiment manifest in other quarters? Ironically, the largest public protests came from auspices other than peace groups. An overflow meeting at Cooper Union in New York was organized on two days' notice by a committee of women. One of the effects of the crisis was to bring together both suffragette leaders and women who had refused to join the suffrage movement. The suffragettes, in particular, were more accustomed to controversy than were many peace advocates, and this is reflected in the unequivocal character of their resolutions: "Since time began [it said in part] women have been devoting their best efforts to the saving of human life. It is eminently fitting that at this crucial time in our history we should protest in burning words against the tragic folly of involving this country in war with Mexico."[46] The women called upon Wilson to "put the noble words he has uttered in the past into deeds . . . and immediately withdraw our troops from Mexico, and thus, with true courage and the finest sense of honor, repair the harm already done."[47]

Even more outspoken were the socialists, who almost overnight displaced the peace movement as the center of war opposition. Bill Haywood, the leader of the Industrial Workers of the World and head of the Western Federation of Miners, reflected the militant attitude of some other labor leaders during this period of violent strikes. A war against Mexico, declared Haywood to a Carnegie Hall rally, would be the signal for a general strike led by the nation's mine workers "who will simply fold their arms and when they fold their arms there will be no war." The *New York Times* denounced his statement as seditious.[48]

Rallies organized by the socialists and statements from labor leaders stressed that war would spill the blood of workers, not capitalists. There were sarcastic calls for Hearst to lead the first regiment into Mexico. One socialist orator made clear to his audience the price of protest: "We must go from this hall ready to brand war as murder. The jail will come but that is to be expected."[49]

Most labor leaders were far more cautious. The Chicago Federation of Labor commended Wilson for his efforts to "restrain the greed of commercial interests and to protect the American people from the horrors of war" and called upon the president and Congress to exhaust every possible means to prevent U.S. involvement in war.[50]

There is a considerable amount of conflicting evidence on whether public opinion favored or opposed war during the hectic days of the crisis. At Yale University 2,000 students paraded, sang patriotic songs, and cheered Huerta's refusal to salute the flag. However, at Stanford University a professor informed his colleague abroad that "the Mexican War or the prospect of it was certainly not popular with anyone here except Hearst." Henry L. Stimson wrote to Elihu Root that opinion in New York "among all classes of men that I have talked to" was in accord with Root's speech calling for full-scale intervention to protect Americans in Mexico. Yet the day before, a Wall Street broker advised the White House that he had personally canvassed members of the various securities exchanges and found "an entire lack of sympathy with the action of the President and his advisors in the Mexican matter."[51]

Any attempt to assess the public temper should bear in mind that observers who saw little evidence of war hysteria were comparing it with an earlier example that remained in their minds: the frenzy on the eve of the Spanish-American War. Tried by that test, enthusiasm fell short of 1898.[52] But the spirit of nationalism, the readiness to rally round the flag, hovered near the surface of popular emotion and required little to touch it off. The day after the Veracruz landing, a small group of anarchists took to the streets to denounce war with Mexico before a large lunchtime crowd in downtown New York City. They were attacked and pelted by the office workers, and only police intervention saved them from serious injury.[53] Perhaps the clearest indication of popular response came from a socialist who wrote plaintively to the *New York Call,* "War mania has hypnotized the people. Members of the working class are storming the recruiting offices clamoring for the right to be shot." He urged his fellow socialists to put aside their factional strife and begin a nationwide antiwar agitation.[54]

When all the protests, the militant speeches, and the sober critiques of the president's action are carefully assessed, they do not sustain Link's contention that their cumulative effect represented one of the critical elements in Wilson's decision making. Says Link,

during the week following the Vera Cruz action, petitions begging the President not to permit the incident to develop into full scale hostilities poured into the White House from church councils, peace and anti-imperialist societies labor and socialist groups, and from leaders in all walks of life. As he was always keenly sensitive to public opinion, the President could not have failed to be profoundly influenced by this outpouring.[55]

A close examination of the messages reaching Wilson shows three distinct patterns. First, there were those who urged him to refrain from waging war. Second, there were those urging him to intervene; "Sooner Mexico City taken, less lives to mourn. Act Quickly," read a typical telegram.[56] Finally, there was a larger group than either of these two that backed the president completely: they backed him when he was (as they saw it) upholding the honor of the United States, they pledged their support following the bloodshed at Veracruz, and they hailed his later announcement that defused the situation (his statement that he would accept mediation from Argentina, Brazil, and Chile).

From the *Provo* (Utah) *Herald* came the message: "Utah endorses your Mexican policy since the beginning and to this day. Flags flying here" (Twenty signed; after the bloodshed but before mediation). A mass meeting of the citizens of Effingham County, Georgia, unanimously endorsed Wilson's policy "in showing the Mexicans that these United States must be respected" (sent April 23, after the bloodshed but before mediation).[57] Another substantial source of support was recent immigrants, many of whom equated patriotism with unquestioning obedience. Thus the editor of the *Daily Slovak American* managed to cover every possible contingency: "The Slovak people of this country feel that it is an opportune time to assure your excellency of their undivided support and approval for everything you have done and may do in the future for the welfare of this nation."[58]

By far the largest number of messages gave the president a blank check to do what he considered right. Those sent before the Veracruz landing could be read as support for intervention; those sent after the landing could be taken as support either for prosecuting the war (which most people assumed was on) or for efforts to hold it back, provided those efforts were honorable.

Professor Link argues further:

it was difficult to find a responsible spokesman among any group or class in the United States who thought Wilson had acted wisely. There was no demand for war from the financial leaders who had a large material stake in Mexico. Republican spokesmen, generally, were outraged by what they regarded as Wilson's diplomatic bungling and his desire to make political capital out of the Mexican crisis.[59]

One can agree with each of these statements, yet it should be added that none of them made any significant difference in the decision for war or peace. A lack of belief in the wisdom of Wilson's actions did not necessarily translate into opposition to those actions. The financial leaders did not demand war, but they were far from demanding peace. Republican spokesmen were indeed outraged at Wilson, but if they had their way most would have gone to war on the broad principle (as they saw it) of protecting American lives and property.

Two factors are critical in explaining Wilson's pullback from war. First was his recognition that full-scale military intervention would not provide a solution. He had made this unmistakably clear two months earlier in a revealing private interview with Thomas B. Hohler, first secretary of the British legation in Mexico City.[60] However strongly Wilson felt about deposing Huerta and however ready he had been to apply pressure and the threat of intervention, the actual decision to occupy Veracruz was made on assurances from the U.S. consul on the scene that the landing would be unopposed. That explains why Wilson was so shaken by reports of the casualties.[61] In fact, the Huerta forces had withdrawn from the city. Resistance had come unexpectedly from youthful naval cadets and armed civilians. The second vital factor in staying Wilson's hand was the reaction of both sides in Mexico's civil war. Nothing seems to have aided the politically bankrupt Huerta regime as much as the invasion at Veracruz. It allowed the general to assume the mantle of defender of Mexico from Yankee aggression. A British correspondent reported from Mexico City on the effects of the landing:

Three years of fratricidal war was forgotten in a day. The Mexican revolution ceased and the nation was blended into a unity which seems formidable. The utmost enthusiasm and devotion for President Huerta was displayed in all classes today, and President Wilson's name was greeted with howls of "Death to the Americans." Patriotic demonstrations are unceasing. The Indian masses whom the revolution was driving into anarchy are now offering themselves as volunteers . . . [the] statue of George Washington was toppled from its pedestal.[62]

To make matters worse, Carranza, whose cause Wilson believed he was aiding, denounced the intervention in strong terms: "the permanency of your forces in . . . Vera Cruz are a violation of the rights that constitute our existence as a free and independent sovereignty and will drag us into an unequal war . . . which until today we desired to avoid."[63] The Constitutionalist leader's insistence that he would fight both Huerta and the United States, if necessary, received the support of all his generals with the exception of Francisco Villa. In the south, Zapata declared that he too would defend the Republic from an American invasion but would not unite with Huerta to do so.[64]

Outraged Mexicans stoned American residences and consulates in several Mexican cities. In Monterrey people stormed the consulate, burned American flags, and, led by Huertista officers, arrested the American consul.[65] Despite these affronts to the dignity of the United States (each of which was more serious than the original indignity), Wilson was no longer interested in pursuing this tack. To the violence against Americans in Mexico were added anti-American riots and fierce denunciations of Yankee imperialism throughout Latin America. In addition, the European press had considerable to say about Wilsonian hypocrisy.[66]

Recognizing that his policy of interference in Mexico was a shambles, aware that instead of forcing Huerta from power he had unleashed a Mexican nationalism that threatened to produce precisely the opposite of what he had intended, Wilson abruptly changed the whole course and tone of his policy. From that moment his determined leadership became the crucial factor. As long as events did not slip beyond his control, he was able to draw strength from the sentiments of those who had rallied to his side in the heat of the crisis and utilize their support to check the impending conflict. He halted the efforts of his cabinet members who were anxious to begin the march to Mexico City. He thrust aside plans for further military campaigns, issued orders to the American forces in Veracruz to make no further advance, and was careful to avoid further provocation. When mediation was offered by the envoys of Argentina, Brazil, and Chile, Wilson quickly accepted it, as did Huerta.[67] Arthur Walworth, one of Wilson's biographers, has characterized the mediation offer as an act of "Providence."[68] One need not be a cynic to suggest that once Wilson had determined upon a course other than war, he could have found a way to encourage mediation.

In conclusion, it is difficult to share Link's view that an outpouring of public sentiment for peace materially shaped Wilson's decision. True, there was no overwhelming enthusiasm for going to war, but that is not to say a determined leader could not have aroused it. Then too, as we have seen in our own time, enthusiasm is not a necessary ingredient to waging war in someone else's country. Nothing is clearer from this study than the support it gives to those students of the presidency who assert that, particularly in the area of foreign policy, the president by his actions creates public opinion.

Peace leaders had not been slow to recognize the dangers of Wilson's provocative actions, but most were too wedded to the political norms, too respectful of authority, to challenge him openly. The strong statements of the socialists and others were perhaps more frightening to them than the prospect of war. Some doubtless felt that protests were useless. Over the years their elitism had isolated them from potential allies. Attempts at private initiatives were more their style. Yet their mediation efforts had been unacceptable to the principals involved.

It remains a disturbing fact that had Wilson determined war was necessary, he could have found support for it in the statements of a number of peace groups. In earlier years, peace advocates had wrestled with the difficult question of defending one's country against invasion. In 1914 that point was not at issue, for Mexicans were too busy fighting each other to represent a threat to the United States.

Despite its prestige, the movement counted for little once Wilson decided to commit an act of war on such a flimsy basis. It is worth noting that peace organizations were not the victim of a government intent on stifling opposition. Yet they spoke with divided voice, or spoke not at all. For many it was enough that Wilson's heart was pure. They would have followed him, misgivings and all, to war.

NOTES

1. Similar groups formed during the decade prior to 1914 include the American Association for International Conciliation, the American School Peace League, the American Group of the Interparliamentary Union, the American Peace and Arbitration League, the International Peace Forum, the German-American Peace Society, the Intercollegiate Peace Association, the Cosmopolitan Clubs, and in 1914, the Church Peace Union. See Julius Moritzen, *The Peace Movement of America* (New York, 1912).

2. After having witnessed in our own time a decade of resistance to the Vietnam war, it is difficult to convey the essential qualities of the pre-1914 peace groups. The two movements could hardly have differed more in character. The anti-Vietnam war effort was forged as a direct challenge to wartime government policies. In the face of a hostile government and substantial public resentment, it sought to mobilize mass pressure to put an end to American involvement in the Vietnam conflict.

Two able studies of the early twentieth-century peace movement are C. Roland Marchand, *The American Peace Movement and Social Reform* (Princeton, 1972), and David S. Patterson, *Toward a Warless World* (Bloomington, 1976). The early years of the Carnegie Endowment are analyzed in Michael Lutzker, "The Formation of the Carnegie Endowment for International Peace; 1910-1914: A Study of the Establishment-Centered Peace Movement," in Jerry Israel, ed., *Building the Organizational Society* (New York, 1972).

3. Committee report, March 1914 in folder Committees' New York Peace Society Papers, Swarthmore College Peace Collection.

4. These included, for example, Elihu Root, Oscar Straus, Joseph Choate, and John W. Foster.

5. Andrew Carnegie, James J. Speyer, John Hays Hammond, Arthur B. Farquhar, and George Foster Peabody, among others.

6. Nicholas Murray Butler of Columbia, Charles W. Eliot, president Emeritus of Harvard, and David Starr Jordan of Stanford. Peace advocates could also count upon the support of influential publications through editors who were associated with their organizations. Among the best known were Lyman Abbott of the *Outlook,* Hamilton Holt of *The Independent,* Oswald Garrison Villard of the *Nation* and the *New York Evening Post,* and Robert U. Johnson of the *Century.*

7. I have drawn mainly on the following works: Charles C. Cumberland, *Mexican Revolution: The Constitutionalist Years* (Austin, Texas, 1972); Howard F. Cline, *The United States and Mexico,* rev. ed. (Cambridge, 1967); Arthur Link, *Woodrow Wilson: The New Freedom* (Princeton, 1956); P. Edward Haley, *Revolution and Intervention: The Diplomacy of Taft and Wilson with Mexico, 1910-1917,* (Cambridge, 1970); Robert Quirk, *An Affair of Honor* (New York, 1962); and Stanley R. Ross, *Francisco I. Madero: Apostle of Mexican Democracy* (New York, 1955).

8. Harold U. Faulkner, *The Decline of Laissez Faire, 1897-1917* (New York, 1951), 78.

9. P. Edward Haley argues that had Taft's presidency extended into the period of greater instability during the Huerta regime, he might well have intervened. He characterizes Taft and others like him as representing the "party of order," citing the term used by Arno J. Mayer. The reaction of men like Elihu Root and others tends to support Haley's analysis. It should be noted that holding a leadership position in a peace organization in this period does not preclude identification with the "party of order." See Haley, *Revolution,* 260-261ff.

10. There is a careful discussion of the factors influencing President Wilson's decision in Cumberland, *Mexican Revolution,* chap. 4. See also, Ross, *Madero,* 333-335.

11. Jordan to Wilson, March 8, 1913, Wilson Papers, Library of Congress, series 4, case file 196. This letter shows remarkable foresight for most events as they later developed.

12. Carnegie to Wilson, November 3, 1913, Wilson Papers, series 4, case file 95A. Butler to Morley (copy), September 13, 1913, correspondence, Nicholas Murray Butler Papers, Columbia University, Special Collections. See also Oscar Straus to Wilson (copy), February 17, 1913, Straus correspondence, Straus Papers, Library of congress.

13. Elihu Root to Taft, February 17, 1912, Taft Papers, Library of Congress, series 2, case file 95C; Rep. James Slayden to Taft, September 8, 1912, ibid.; Charles

D. Hilles to Knox, December 18, 1912, ibid., case file 95B; William Vernon Backus
to Taft, October 21, 1912, ibid., case file 95C; Rep. William Kent to Joseph Tumulty
(personal), Memo re: certain Americans and interests (received August 12, 1913),
Woodrow Wilson Papers, series 4, case file 95A; Carnegie to Wilson, March 14,
16, 1914, Andrew Carnegie Papers, Library of Congress. Carnegie Correspondence,
vol. 222; George Foster Peabody to Rep. F. H. Gillett, January 6, 1914, cited by
Louise Ware, *George Foster Peabody; Banker, Philanthropist, Publicist* (Athens, Ga.,
1951), 172-173.

14. Farquhar to John Bassett Moore, June 17, 1913, box 20, John Bassett Moore
Papers, Library of Congress. Moore was counselor for the Department of State.
See also Farquhar to Moore, November 20, 1913, ibid. James Speyer of Speyer
and Company and the New York Peace Society also urged recognition of Huerta.
Speyer and Company held treasury notes of the Mexican government to the amount
of $10 million. Some were coming due, and the Huerta regime was having trouble
refinancing them since it had been denied recognition by the United States. Speyer
argued that financial default by the Huerta government could lead to chaos and
possible intervention by the United States. See memo by J. B. Moore of his conversation with Speyer, May 3, 1913, Moore Papers, box 92.

15. There were apparently a number of behind the scenes efforts by Americans
to influence the course of the Mexican Revolution. Two of these are suggested in
letters to Andrew Carnegie requesting funds, but they are a far cry from the ordinary
pleas for money that one finds by the score in the Carnegie Papers. One request
was to pay for the departure into exile of those friends of Huerta and thereby prevent
an uprising in Mexico City. Another unofficial effort was aimed at "retard[ing]
the progress of the revolutionists by loosening the bonds between Carranza and
Villa." See William S. Bennet to Carnegie, May 20, July 8, 1914, Carnegie Correspondence, Carnegie Papers. At this time Bennet was a partner in the Wall Street
law firm of Bennet and Cooley.

16. There is much in the way of informal discussion or confidential messages
that I have not found in any written record. Butler may have been urged by his
friends in British political circles to have the endowment make the effort, but the
evidence is not clear on this point. Butler cleared the idea with the State Department. Butler to J. B. Moore (personal and confidential), February 10, 1914; Moore to
Butler (personal and confidential), February 12, 1914; Butler to Moore (personal
and confidential), February 13, 1914; Moore to Butler (personal and confidential),
February 17, 1914: Moore Correspondence, Moore Papers, box 25. Mediation was
discussed in vague terms, though both men agreed that the question of land tenure
was a central issue. Butler also indicated that he had been in contact with representatives of both Mexican factions. It should be noted that in clearing the project with
Moore, Butler was dealing with a former member of his faculty at Columbia University.

17. Loomis to Butler (copy) confidential, March 10, 1914, Carnegie Endowment Archives, Division of Intercourse and Education, 1914 volume, documents
1634-1650, Columbia University, Special Collections. The members of the projected
advisory council were Manuel Calero, Ernesto Madero, and Pedro Lascurain,
all from Madero's cabinet; José Limantour, Olegario Molina, and Emilio Rabasa,

from the Díaz cabinet; and the following independents: Luis Mendez, Sebastian Mier, General Jacinto B. Trevino, Francisco S. Carvajal, and Louis Perez Verdia. It is noteworthy that the three men from Madero's former cabinet were among its most conservative members. (Stanley R. Ross characterizes them as "obstructionist.") Indeed Manuel Calero had denounced the Madero government from the floor of the Mexican Senate. These men were in no way representative of the Madero regime. See Ross, *Madero,* 220-222. The three from the Díaz cabinet were, of course, strongly conservative and identified with the old regime. The men described as independents may not have fit that description. General Jacinto Trevino, for example, was one of the few initial signers of Carranza's "plan of Guadalupe," the first public statement calling for rebellion against the Huerta regime. If General Trevino was a supporter of Carranza, Francisco Carvajal, chief justic of the supreme court, was an equally strong supporter of Huerta. That the proposed advisory council was acceptable to the Carnegie Endowment prompts two comments. The endowment's orientation was staunchly conservative and indicates a strong preference for a Díaz type regime or else it betrays a considerable ignorance of Mexican politics.

18. Thomas Buckner to Albert Baird (tele-confidential), March 11, 1914, Baird to Buckner, March 12, Buckner to Baird, March 13, Baird to Buckner, March 18, McCombs to Wilson, March 20, Wilson to Bryan, March 21: Wilson Papers, series 2. See also Straus to Carnegie, March 14, 18, Carnegie to Wilson (copy), March 16: Carnegie Correspondence, Carnegie Papers. There is a brief account in Ray Stannard Baker, *Woodrow Wilson: Life and Letters,* 8 Vols. (Garden City, N.Y., 1927-39), 4:311. I have found no indication that there was any connection between the Straus initiative and the Carnegie Endowment's efforts. I am indebted to Professor P. Edward Haley for much of this material.

19. See John Bassett Moore's memo of his converation with Cecil Spring Rice, February 22, 1914, box 93, Moore Papers; Quirk, *Affair of Honor.*

20. See the excellent account in Quirk, *Affair of Honor.*

21. Butler to John Morley (copy), May 8, 1914, Butler correspondence, Butler Papers. This letter was written after the landing in Veracruz and after the offer of mediation from Argentina, Brazil, and Chile, but Butler still thought war a likely possibility.

22. Arthur Walworth, *Woodrow Wilson* (New York, 1965), 1:374.

23. Carnegie to Wilson (copy), April 21, 1914, Carnegie Correspondence, Carnegie Papers; Carnegie to John A. Stewart (copy), May 8, 1914, ibid.

24. Printed statement of World Peace Foundation, Boston, April 23, 1914, in Wilson Papers, series 2, case file 95C.

25. American Peace and Arbitration League to Wilson, April 22, 1914, Wilson Papers, series 2, case file 95A. See also, *Springfield Republican,* April 23, 1914.

26. Federal Council of Churches to Wilson, April 21, 1914, Wilson Papers, series 2, case file 95F.

27. Cited by Cline, *United States and Mexico,* 158; *Baltimore Sun,* April 21, 1914.

28. Quoted in Philip C. Jessup, *Elihu Root,* 2 Vols., (New York, 1938), 2:258-260.

29. Root's position was supported by Reverend Lyman Abbott, a leader of the American Peace Society and the American Association for International Concilia-

tion. Ibid. Nicholas Murray Butler also approved of Root's speech, Butler to Root (copy) personal, April 23, 1913, Butler Papers.

30. *Congressional Record,* 63d Cong., 2d sess., 51, 6969-6970. Senator Williams was a trustee of the Carnegie Endowment for International Peace.

31. *Baltimore Sun,* April 22, 1914.

32. Ibid. This was the initial casualty report. But with each subsequent report the total rose. In all 19 Americans were killed and 71 wounded, while 126 Mexicans died and 195 were wounded. Josephus Daniels, *The Wilson Era: Years of Peace, 1910-1917* (Chapel Hill, 1944), 197-98.

33. See the summaries of editorial opinion from a wide range of newspapers in the *Baltimore Sun,* April 23, 1914, *Springfield Republican,* April 24, 1914, and *New York Times,* April 23, 26, 1914.

34. See, for example, Wilson's replies to the following: Govenor George W. Hays, April 22, 1914; Senators Morris Shepard and Albert B. Fall, April 23, 1914; Governors John F. A. Strong, John Gary Evans, and William T. Haines, and Congressman Willis J. Hulings and Joseph B. Thompson, all April 24, 1914. These and other acknowledgments of offers to volunteer are in Wilson Letterbooks, series 3, vol. 12 (microfilm reel 137), Wilson Papers.

35. H. J. Forman to Ray Stannard Baker, quoted in Baker, *Wilson,* 4:330.

36. See, for example, Wilson to Governor George W. Hays of Arkansas: "I still hope and pray there will be no necessity to call for volunteers." April 22, 1914, Wilson Letterbooks, series 3, vol. 12, Wilson Papers.

37. Ibid., 331; Walworth, *Wilson,* 1:374; Link, *Wilson: New Freedom,* 400.

38. Link, *Wilson: New Freedom,* 403-04.

39. *Advocate of Peace* 76 (May 1914):112.

40. Ibid.

41. Ibid.; Frank F. Williams, secretary of the Peace and Arbitration Society of Buffalo, N.Y., to Elihu Root, April 28, 1914, General Correspondence, "W" folder, Root Papers, Library of Congress.

42. *The Independent* 78 (May 4, 1914):193; for peace groups telegrams from the Massachusetts area, see H. Boyd Edwards et al. to Wilson, Wilson Papers, series 2, case file 95E; and Alice Debney et al. to Wilson, ibid., case file 95D; also Mead to William I. Hull, telegram, April 25, 1914, Mead to Hull, April 26, 1914, both in Hull Papers, box 2, Swarthmore College Peace Collection.

43. Villard to Carnegie (copy), April 28, 1914, Villard Correspondence, Villard Papers, Houghton Library, Harvard University.

44. Ibid. I have found no record of a public protest by the New York Peace Society. Although Carnegie, its president, opposed public criticism of Wilson, he continued to protest privately. See Carnegie to Joseph Tumulty (Wilson's secretary): "I wish to be candid: There is scarcely a friend—indeed I do not know of one—who justifies the President's interference in Mexican affairs; Root, (Joseph) Coate, (Henry) White, and others, all state this first, and then extol the President's character, with this critical deduction. It takes a great man to acknowledge his mistake but such a man I credit the President with being." May 7, 1914 (copy), Carnegie Correspondence, Carnegie Papers.

45. See "Correspondence," April-May 1914, box 8, American Peace Society

Papers, Swarthmore College Peace Collection; *Congressional Record,* 63d Cong., 2d sess., vol. 51, pt. 7, 7116-7181; Woodrow Wilson Papers, series 2 (chronological file), and series 4, case files 95A-Z; Edward McNall Burns, *David Starr Jordan* (Stanford, 1953), 24.

46. *New York Times,* April 24, 1914; *Advocate of Peace* 76 (May 1914):112. Leaders of the women's meeting included Mrs. Henry Bruere, Mrs. Henry Villard, Charlotte Perkins Gilman, and Florence Kelley.

47. *New York Times,* April 24, 1914.

48. Ibid., April 20, 1914. In addition Max Kasimirsky, general organizer of the United Hebrew Trades, called for a turnout of 150,000 workers on May Day to protest war with Mexico. He said there was a greater need for intervention in the Colorado miners' strike (where more than a dozen women and children had been killed by state militia) than there was in Mexico.

49. *New York Call,* April 20-24, 1914; Noble Dawson to Rudolph Foster, April 25, 1914, Wilson Papers, series 2, case file 95D, including a copy of a labor newspaper, the *San Francisco Bulletin,* April 25, 1914.

50. *New York Call,* April 22, 1914. The New York Central Labor Federation seemed most concerned with establishing its patriotic credentials. It approved a resolution preserving "the honor of the American flag and the dignity of the U.S. Government." See ibid.

51. *Springfield Republican,* April 20, 1914; Edward B. Krehbiel to David Starr Jordan, May 1, 1914, Jordan Papers, Hoover Institution, Stanford University; Stimson to Root, April 23, 1914, General Correspondence, Root Papers; Herbert Falk to Joseph Tumulty (private and confidential), April 22, 1914, series 2, Wilson Papers.

52. See, for example, Ellen Maury Slayden, *Washington Wife: The Journal of Ellen Maury Slayden,* ed. Walter Prescott Webb (New York, 1963), 235-236; also Nicholas Murray Butler to John Morley (copy), May 8, 1914, Butler correspondence, Butler Papers.

53. *New York Call,* April 23, 1914.

54. Max Sherover, letter to editor, *New York Call,* April 23, 1914. See also dispatch from Chicago ("Many Recruits in Chicago") *New York Times,* April 25, 1914. A recent study supports this view; see Karl Schmitt, *Mexico and the United States, 1821-1973: Conflict and Coexistence* (New York, 1974), 141.

55. Link, *Wilson: The New Freedom,* 404-405. See also Link, *Woodrow Wilson and the Progressive Era* (New York, 1954), 123-126.

56. Frank Annis to Wilson, April 23, 1914, Wilson Papers, series 4, case file 95A.

57. See Wilson Papers, series 4, case file 95, series 2, case files 95A-Z.

58. Rev. Christopher L. Orbach to Wilson, April 22, 1914, Wilson Papers, series 2, case file 95D.

59. Link, *Wilson: The New Freedom,* 404.

60. Hohler's account of the meeting is in a memo dated February 11, 1914, in Cecil Spring Rice to Edward Grey, with enclosures, Foreign Office document 371/2025, No. 8667, Public Record Office. This document is forthcoming in volume 29 of *The Papers of Woodrow Wilson,* ed. Arthur S. Link et al. I am grateful to Professor Link for this and other material.

61. W. W. Canada to William Jennings Bryan, April 20, 1914, enclosure I with Bryan to Wilson, April 21, 1914, forthcoming in ibid. See also Wilson to George C. Carothers, April 21, 1914, State Department Records, RG 59, 812.00/11608a, National Archives.

62. Quoted in the *Baltimore Sun,* April 25, 1914; see also *New York Times,* April 25, 1914. It should be noted that this point forms an important part of Professor Link's analysis, though he appears to accord it equal weight with that of American peace sentiment.

63. *Springfield Republican* April 23, 1914.

64. John Womack, Jr., *Zapata and the Mexican Revolution* (New York, 1969), 185-186. Womack says that both the Mexican and American governments believed war to be "unlikely." He cites no evidence. I believe he tends to underestimate the dangers during the crisis.

65. Quirk, *Affair of Honor,* 109-110.

66. Link, *Wilson:The New Freedom,* 405.

67. Carranza did not oppose mediation but continued to insist that Wilson evacuate Veracruz and that no nation had a right to intercede in Mexico's internal affairs. He sent observers to Niagara Falls, where the mediators met, but never formally participated in their efforts. The difference between Carranza's position and that of Wilson was one of degree. The American president sent delegates to the mediation conferences, but his instructions to them were to find a way to eliminate Huerta from power. Wilson had decided against intervention as a tactic, but his goal remained unchanged.

68. Walworth, *Wilson,* 1:374.

8
The Consulta and the Italian Peace Movement, 1914-18

JAMES A. YOUNG

I

The Italian peace movement developed during World War I amid circumstances more advantageous than those in most other belligerent countries. Unlike those countries that were swept into the war in July and August, Italy experienced an extended period of neutrality, during which arguments for and against intervention in the conflict could be debated. Further, unlike other latecomers into the war—Bulgaria, Rumania, Greece, and the United States—Italy contained both a strong socialist party, the Partito Socialista Italiano (PSI), and the Vatican, each of which maintained a straightforward antiwar position. Moreover, the liberal bourgeois element of the peace movement, which had existed in Italy for over forty years, was supplemented by the pragmatic neutralism of Giovanni Giolitti and his followers, who had led the country to war against the Turks in 1911. Yet because of the very breadth of these forces, the peace movement failed to fuse into a coherent, coordinated movement. The obstacle that the peace movement might pose if the Italian Foreign Office (the Consulta) decided for war was more apparent than real.

Initially, the government of Antonio Salandra showed little indication that it could muster the resources for forging a new and vigorous path in foreign affairs. Salandra's cabinet, which was formed after Giolitti's resignation in April 1914, was expected to be merely an interim government. It was commonly assumed that Giolitti, the hegemonic figure in the Italian parliament, would return to power at a suitable moment, as he had done on several other occasions in the past. Until such time, Giolitti could influence foreign policy, it seemed, through the Marchese San Giuliano, who had headed the Consulta for four years under Giolitti and who had striven to improve Italy's ties with Austria.[1] However, three incidents—the eruption of Red Week in June, the outbreak of hostilities in July, and the death of San Giuliano in October—gave Salandra and other rightists a chance to create a new base of power, which had long been Salandra's aim.[2]

The general strike in June strengthened Salandra's position and contained implications for the future peace movement. Despite the widespread nature of the strikes, which had arisen in protest of the reintroduction of military conscription, the workers failed to rally support outside of their own ranks, and the Red Week movement was quashed within two weeks. For his handling of Red Week, Salandra won high marks from much of the bourgeoisie, who had become restless over the years with what they viewed as a permissive posture toward workers by Giolittian cabinets.[3] The support thus gained became important to Salandra during the crisis over intervention. Moreover, the isolation of the workers presaged the divisions within and between groups that would plague the peace movement.

The outbreak of the war delayed Giolitti's return. San Giuliano's subsequent death denied the Giolittians any direct influence in the formulation of foreign policy and opened the way for the appointment in November of Baron Sidney Sonnino as head of the Consulta.

The Consulta, under both San Giuliano and Sonnino, received pressure from the peace movement and also utilized such pressure when it was convenient to do so. San Giuliano, for example, justified Italy's neutralist posture to the German ambassador by citing the unanimous hostility of the Italian public toward the dual monarchy.[4] Sonnino, who had been one of the few to urge Italian support of the Central Powers during the opening days of the war, similarly used the peace movement to justify policies that he intended to pursue in any case, especially after Italy's intervention.[5] Yet neither the peace movement nor any other popular force was to exercise much influence on foreign policy while Sonnino remained at the Consulta.

The attitude of Sonnino and Salandra toward popular movements was clear: insofar as they exerted any influence, they constituted a hindrance to rational policy making. In his celebrated
article "Torniamo allo Statuto" (1897), Sonnino had even argued
that, as in 1848, premiers should be responsible only to the king so
that the king could rule as a prince-dictator.[6] Parliaments, pressure
groups, and popular forces only posed complications for leaders
like Sonnino, who suffered from what Antonio Gramsci later labled
"Cadornism" (after the Italian chief of staff, Luigi Cadorna):
"The conviction that a thing will be done because the leader con-
siders it to be just and reasonable that it should be done."[7]

So imbued with the prerogatives of leadership were Sonnino and
Salandra that in 1915 they sought to repress even those who supported their policies, if that support were expressed too vehemently.
Only a short time before his decision that Italy should switch alliances
and make war upon the Central Powers, Sonnino paused to inquire
of Salandra about measures that might be taken against the interventionist deputy Arturo Labriola, who had attacked the German
and Austrian monarchs in the pages of *Il Roma*.[8] Salandra showed
little more tolerance. Throughout the spring of 1915, Salandra's
instructions to his prefects made it clear that he trusted progovernment and prowar demonsrators no more than he trusted antiwar
marchers.[9] As the two men prepared to lead Italians into the unprecedented violence of World War I, they insisted that the path-
way be orderly.

II

The peace movement was spearheaded by the PSI and its sympathizers, although most socialists were not, properly speaking,
pacifists. Many argued, in familiar Marxian terms, that wars between bourgeois governments are not in the interest of workers
and that only class war against such governments is justifiable.
Hence, as hostilities began in July 1914 the PSI, joined by the socialist
trade unions (the Confederazione General del Lavoro or CGL) and
cooperatives (the Lega Nazionale delle Cooperative or LNC), proved
to be "the happy exception," as V. I. Lenin noted, to the tendency
of parties of the Second International to support their governments'
decisions to wage war.[10]

The socialists' failure even to obstruct the war against the Turks had served to radicalize the PSI further and to steel its members' determination to thwart another such venture.[11] As the guns opened fire along the Austro-Serbian front and often thereafter, the PSI warned the government that any attempt to involve Italy in the war would be met with a general strike.[12] Such early threats, however, probably had little influence at the Consulta because San Giuliano had decided already upon his course. It is also unlikely that Sonnino felt much concern over such assertions. In the first place, Sonnino had noted in 1911 that the Turks were counting upon the antiwar efforts of Italian socialists, but the efforts failed.[13] Moreover, if Sonnino and Salandra feared a serious challenge to their leadership, they viewed the interventionists with even greater apprehension than they did the neutralists. As early as September 1914 the two leaders agreed that if the war were to end without Italy's acquisition of its Austrian-ruled irredenta and the guarantee of Italian interests in the Adriatic and the eastern 'Mediterranean, "Public opinion would revolt vigorously against the government . . . and perhaps also against the monarchy."[14] Nevertheless, the PSI could not be discounted, and many in its ranks prepared to oppose actively Italian intervention.

The PSI was better equipped than the other groups of the peace movement to launch a sustained antiwar effort. It published a major national newspaper, *Avanti!* as well as many lesser papers. Moreover, the party was linked directly to the CGL and to LNC. In addition, every town of any size boasted its own Chamber of Labor where Socialists could reach nonparty workers. Finally, as the Italo-Swiss meeting at Lugano on September 27, 1914, showed, certain international socialist communications remained open, including those with Lenin, who argued that revolution could be made from the war.[15]

The Socialist element of the peace movement did suffer the drawback of isolation from nonsocialists. In 1914 and 1915, this resulted largely from the policy prevalent in some areas of refusing to cooperate with nonsocialists and from the bitterness and suspicion directed at the Socialists because of Red Week.[16] In addition, Socialist leadership was divided over the posture to be taken should the government decide to go to war; and some working-class leaders, such as Benito Mussolini, even defected to interventionism. Mussolini was

joined by a large segment of the Syndicalist movement, led by Filippo
Corridoni and by anarchists of the Labriola stripe. Before long, the
largely Syndicalist labor movement in Parma would openly advocate
war.[17] The "official Socialists," then, were isolated even from some
of their fellow socialists.

III

Throughout the war the Vatican repeatedly called upon the belligerents to end hostilities. Yet its efforts were tainted by pro-Austrian
partisanship, at least in the early years, and were hampered from
arousing a mass movement in Italy because of the Holy See's deep-
seated assumptions of hierarchical order and its conservative, diplomatic approach to the problem.

From the outset Italian clericals favored neutrality. Filippo Meda,
leader of the Catholics in the Chamber, echoed the Vatican's position in August 1914 in demanding the regime's absolute neutrality.
Similarly, the Association of Catholic Youth called upon its members
to "refrain from all such manifestations which anywhere could be
presumed to be the cause of Catholicism adhering to one or another
of the belligerent parties."[18] Count Dalle Torre, head of the powerful Unione Popolare, placed organized Catholicism, along with the
Unione's seven national and many local publications, behind the
peace movement. Unlike 1911, then, when many Catholics defied
the pope and supported war against the Turks as a modern crusade,
1914 found Italian Catholic forces solidly neutralist.[19]

Contributing to both the strength and the weakness of the Catholic segment of the peace movement was the role played by Benedict
XV, who was elected pope following the death of Pius X in August.
In his encyclical *Ad Beatissimi* of November 1914, Benedict stressed
the pacifistic theme with which he would be closely associated throughout the war. Yet, the papacy aroused suspicion on at least two issues:
Austrophilism and the papal desire to recover temporal power over
Rome. The latter question was raised on the very day Benedict
delivered *Ad Beatissimi* by the intransigently neutralist organ *Unità
cattolica,* which also warned that, if called to war, Italian Catholics
would respond without enthusiasm, "only as victims to the slaughter-
house."[20]

The charge of papal Austrophilism won wide acceptance in Europe,
and Italian clericals were sensitive to the allegation. Men of diverse

backgrounds and views agreed that Pius and Benedict were fearful
about the fate of the multinational empire and about the threat of
Orthodox Russia's penetration into Central and Southern Europe.[21]
Moreover, conservative and reactionary clericals supported neutrality because of their open affinity for Austria's aristocratic system. And it was commonly assumed that the *Corriere d'Italia* and
other clerical papers received German subsidies.[22] Nevertheless,
moderate and democratic Catholics supported the Vatican for other
reasons, even though the prevailing medieval concept of the just
war left them little moral basis from which to oppose a government
that had decided to go to war. Two Catholic deputies of the left,
Giulio Padulli (Cantu) and Adamo Degli Occhi (Affori), went so
far as to join in October 1914 a predominantly Giolittian group that
opposed Italy's being pushed into the war.[23] Finally, Catholics
associated with Guido Miglioli's radical Po Valley peasants' union
stood firm against intervention on grounds similar to those of the
PSI.[24]

Like the PSI, the Catholics suffered defections to interventionism
and suffered further from an inability to mount a truly militant
antiwar campaign through the full use of its multiple resources.
For Benedict and his Vatican advisers, "politics" meant primarily
the use of diplomacy within the context of a social status quo. Therefore, with few exceptions, the bulk of Italian Catholics—which
included almost the entire peasantry—failed to adhere to any other
antiwar groups or to undertake on their own the practice of mass
action. For them to have done so might have threatened the Vatican's
position vis-à-vis the Italian government, might have caused Vienna
to feel that it would not have diplomatic difficulties maintaining
Italy's neutrality, thus increasing the likelihood of war, and would
in any case have run contrary to the time-honored principles and
procedures that encrusted the Vatican bureaucracy.[25] The pope
reiterated his public posture of "absolute neutrality" in his allocu-
tion to the cardinals on January 22, 1915, but made no move to
mobilize the Catholic masses. Meanwhile, in France he became
known as "Papa Bosch."[26]

IV

Bourgeois pacifist and quasi-pacifist groups had existed in Italy
in some numbers since the establishment of a branch of Frederic

Passy's League of Peace in 1868.[27] By the time of the crisis over Italian intervention, however, such groups were in need of the support they were to receive from the pragmatic Giolittians, for they were neither so pacifistic nor so unified as they had hoped to be.

In the opening weeks of the war the bourgeois pacifists supported wholeheartedly the government's neutralist stance. Displaying international solidarity, Countess Teresita Pasini, head of the Lombard Committee for Female Suffrage, associated herself with the International Women Suffrage Alliance's exhortation for "putting an end to human horrors never heard of before in all the civilized world."[28] Similarly, the Italian branch of Conciliation Internationale, led by Edoardo Giretti, supported neutrality, even while condemning the German invasion of Belgium. Most bourgeois pacifist arguments were reinforced by the church and by the Giolittian liberals, with whom the efforts of the pacifists and quasi-pacifists often merged. As with other segments of the peace movement, this faction also suffered defections, including eventually Giretti and the Conciliation Internationale.[29]

Among the nonclerical bourgeois opponents of intervention, Giolittians provided the rallying point. Bourgeois pacifists, Radicals and moderates, and even many Catholics looked to the powerful Giolittians to keep the peace. Correspondingly, when a group was formed to prevent Italy's being thrust into the war, a majority of these "respectable citizens" were Giolittians, with a few Catholics of the Left, a Radical, two Moderate Liberals, and a Liberal of the Left. Within a short time the group expanded and took the name the Committee for the Protection of the National Interest.[30]

Both the theme and the method of the Giolittian peace advocacy were characterized by what may be termed the "parecchio" mentality. "Parecchio" became a popular symbol as the result of the publication of a letter from Giolitti to the deputy Camillo Peano in February 1915. The letter explained Giolitti's stance concerning the war.[31] In the original version, Giolitti stated that Italy could obtain a great deal ("molto") in concessions from Vienna in return for remaining neutral. Yet, the version of the letter published in *La Tribuna* substituted "parecchio" ("quite a bit") for "molto." The softening of terminology, which Giolitti effected out of regard for the diplomatic situation, points up a weakness in the Giolittians as a force for peace, for they were tied to the interests of the state, its values and procedures. Consequently, Giolitti weakened his antiwar position among Italians rather than weaken the Italian position vis-à-vis Austria by leading Vienna to think that Giolittians expected such gains (molto) from negotiations that they would never countenance the government's resorting to war. Conversely, Giolittians dared not antagonize Vienna and thus jeopardize the talks by seeming to claim much too much. Although Sonnino himself pursued a "parecchio" course until March, the concept was not a very imaginative instrument to use upon undecided Italians. Moreover, the term provided the interventionists with a weapon with which to bludgeon the Giolittians and all other segments of the peace movement. After all, the neutralists would betray Italy's "national mission" for a "little concession of earth."[32]

Giolittians, then, suffered something of the same disability in opposing the policies of the Consulta as did the church and the bourgeois pacifists: they recognized the legitimacy of the state and its aims. Consequently, each held back from launching the kind of massive attack of which the Giolittians and the church were capable and to which traditional liberal peace groups could have contributed. The Giolittians feared the repercussions should the talks with Vienna founder; the church worried about its position in relation to the state and about the maintenance of order; the bourgeois pacifists and quasi-pacifists respected the ends, if not the means, of the interventionists.[33] As a result, the various bourgeois neutralists' arguments fell upon Italian ears with the flat, clanking sound of mechanically calculated material interests: Italy is prospering as a neutral; the war will be long and hard and will demand greater sacrifices than can be compensated; Italy simply cannot afford the expense of a major military effort; the country can achieve "parecchio" without going to war.[34] In view of the rather uninspiring pragmatism of the bourgeoisie and the equivocal pacifism of the church, the mantle for action fell to the Socialists and to individuals.

V

Many individual peace advocates attempted to stave off Italian intervention. One of the first prominent figures to place himself

and his office squarely in opposition to the initial move toward
intervention—a military buildup—was Salandra's Minister of the
Treasury, Giulio Rubini. Rubini, a man of the traditional right,
opposed intervention for purely fiscal reasons. The country, he
argued, simply could not afford higher military spending. He also
opposed mobilization in the absence of an attack upon Italy. When
it became clear, with the dismissal of War Minister Domenico
Grandi and the death of San Giuliano, that Salandra would be free
to pursue his interventionist leanings, Rubini resigned and thereby provoked a cabinet crisis. But instead of opening Salandra's rearmament policy to a tough debate in the Chamber, Rubini's move
only paved the way for the creation of a new cabinet, which was
more interventionist than the last one.[35] Bound as they were to the
assumptions of Salandra about the state, the group best able to force
debate in the Chamber—the Giolittians—actually supported Salandra over Rubini on military spending. It was at this point, too,
that Sonnino took over at the Consulta.

Other incidents of peace advocacy dot the path to Italian intervention. In February 1915 Raffaele Capelli, vice-president of the
Chamber, discussed with German Catholic Center leader Matthias
Erzberger the terms under which Italy would agree to remain neutral.
Capelli's reward for his efforts—about which he informed the Consulta—was a dressing down by Sonnino, who recorded that Capelli
had ruined the basis of the Foreign Ministry's talks with the German
representative, Prince Bernhard von Bülow. When, on the next
day, the Prince di Camporeale, Bülow's brother-in-law, tried to
follow up on the Capelli-Erzberger talk, Sonnino rebuffed him.[36]

Of the numerous individual efforts to preserve the peace during
the final weeks of Italian neutrality, those of Roberto Prezioso
and Alfredo Frassati exemplify the frustration of the liberal bourgeoisie and provide an insight into the Consulta's strategy during the
period.[37] Prezioso, a journalist from Trieste, had established contact
with Vienna in autumn 1914 through Baron Leopold von Chlumecky.
He also made contact with Frassati, a Giolittian senator and publisher of *La Stampa* of Turin, and by April 1915, the two of them
were being used by the Austrians to convey proposals and information to the Giolittian camp, a situation about which Frassati informed Sonnino. It was through this channel that the Austrians

revealed their intention to offer Sonnino new, enlarged concessions during the first week of May and through which Giolitti then
conveyed to Sonnino his willingness to support the government in
the Chamber if the Consulta would accept the latest proposal from
Vienna. For some time Sonnino played along with the Prezioso-
Frassati connection, only to assert in the end that Vienna should
have followed diplomatic procedures with the offer and to close the
door on the proposal.[38] Sonnino, with some apparent justification,
doubted the sincerity of the offers coming from Austria at the last
minute. But his behavior in this matter seems to indicate also that
he was following the strategy first proposed by his secretary-general,
Giacomo De Martino, some months earlier: if the government
decided to go to war, the Consulta should nevertheless continue
talking with Vienna until the "decisive moment."[39] If peace advocates could be used in this duplicitous exercise, so much the better.

VI

The immediate crisis over Italy's intervention—the "radiant days
of May"—followed the announcement of the Salandra cabinet's
resignation on May 13. The crisis illustrated the renewed strength
of the right, which supported Salandra and Sonnino, as well as
the fragmented and irresolute nature of the peace movement.

As it became clear that Salandra was in trouble because of his
lack of support in the Giolittian-dominated Chamber, and the government then resigned, progovernment interventionist demonstrations erupted, even in the heretofore quiescent south. Bari went
up on May 12 and 5,000 marched in Catania on May 14. With much
more emphasis upon backing the regime than upon war, support
came forth from Sicily, Abruzzi, Campania, and Puglia—largely
from traditional ruling and leading classes who supported Salandra's
anti-Giolittian social "solution" and war.[40] Unlike the north, where
interventionists regularly met with counterdemonstrations, the south—
where the church was strong and the PSI weak—produced no opposition to the wave of bourgeois support of Salandra and Sonnino.
The north also witnessed the defection of some peace advocates
to the interventionists. Bourgeois liberals could be won over by the
example of Bonaldo Stringher, head of the Banca d'Italia, who

emphasized Dalmatia's importance, or by the prospect of ameliorating the class struggle with a "short, successful war."[41] Moreover, led by interventionist Giuseppe Donati, some Catholics also began to break ranks.[42]

Socialists were united in their opposition to the war but divided over the means to be employed against it. On May 12, as 300 deputies left calling cards at Giolitti's Rome residence in a display of support, 15,000 Turinese factory workers struck spontaneously to show their opposition to intervention.[43] In Milan, where Giacinto Serrati long had been leading neutralists in street clashes, a general strike hit on May 15, following the death of a young Socialist in a clash with interventionists. Florence, Genoa, and Bologna also experienced bloodshed and many arrests.[44] But it remained for Turin—"Red Turin Against the War," as the title of a postwar book described the city—to stand in contradistinction to Rome, where interventionists were allowed to run rampant and physically intimidate neutralists.[45]

Like interventionist Rome, neutralist Turin was not a typical city. It had lost most of its petit bourgeoisie when the capital moved to Florence. Its later development coincided with that of the heavy engineering industry and had resulted in the creation of a "compact proletarian mass which gives the city its . . . character, perhaps unique in all Europe."[46] Moreover, much of the bourgeoisie was Giolittian and neutralist. Therefore, while neutralists were attacked in Rome and appeared impotent in the South, cries for open rebellion were heard in Turin.[47] However, a national labor-PSI conference on May 16 showed so little unity that it was decided that local organizations should each determine what its response would be if war threatened. In Turin a general strike erupted on the next day, and over 80,000 demonstrated against the war. Barricades soon went up, and for three days workers battled police and troops, leaving one dead and dozens wounded. At Salandra's request, the deputies Oddino Morgari and Giulio Casalini, schooled as they were in Engels's observation that "If the troops fight, resistance is madness,"[48] returned to Turin to convince their Socialist constituents to stop fighting.[48] Order was restored on May 19.

The events in Turin were not likely to influence the Consulta. Symptomatic of the peace movement's fragmentation, local PSI and Chamber of Labor leaders had rejected a united front with clericals and conservatives for preserving the peace.[49] Moreover, even the limited success of the Turinese workers remained the exception. In Milan the general strike failed completely, and no other city fared better. Everywhere but in Turin the interventionist minority gave the impression of superior force.[50] At a time when almost all clericals, Giolittians, and bourgeois pacifists passively submitted to intervention, little more perhaps could be expected from a workers' movement for which collective bargaining still "rarely reached beyond provincial boundaries."[51] Yet proletarian resistance continued to glow as Italy entered the war.

VII

Italy entered the war on May 24, despite the widespread recognition that the majority of Italians remained neutralists. Victor Emmanuel III even suggested that if new elections were held, the majority of neutralist deputies would be increased.[52] Giolitti, aware that his replacement of Salandra would be interpreted as an end to the threat of war and might, thus, result in Vienna's withdrawal of any significant concessions to Italy, declined to form a new cabinet. Once more the Giolittian attachment to the values and methods of the state served to frustrate the realization of their aims.[53] When on May 20 emergency powers were considered by the Chamber, only the PSI's parliamentary leader, Filippo Turati, spoke against the measure, which then passed, 407-74. In the Senate, which in January had mustered sixty votes against seating the interventionist publisher Luigi Albertini, a handful of abstentions served as a token disapproval of war.[54]

The outbreak of hostilities did not result in much of a change in the relationship between the Consulta and the peace movement. As in the spring of 1915, the Giolittians remained basically loyal to the state, although they criticized and grumbled. Nor despite their highly touted strength in the Chamber, did Giolittians overturn a cabinet of their own accord. The fall of both Salandra in June 1916 and of Paolo Boselli in October 1917 resulted from their failure to retain the support of some interventionists, as well as that of the Giolittians and the PSI. Moreover, Sonnino, who became the symbol of intervention and resistance to a compromise peace, stayed

at the Consulta through each change, despite the opposition of
neutralists and—by 1918—of some interventionists.

For his part, Sonnino continued to deal with the peace movement
much in the same way as he had in the past. He tolerated the movement's existence because of its strength and because he found such
opponents useful in countering the pressures of Italy's allies. Particularly in meeting Allied pressure for a declaration of war on Germany
and in deflecting England's Prime Minister David Lloyd George's
projects for enticing Vienna into a separate peace (to the unavoid-
able detriment of Italian ambitions), Sonnino utilized the well-
known lack of Italian support of the war—invariably described in
hushed tones as "the internal situation"—to reinforce his diplomatic position.[55] Meanwhile Sonnino continued to view the movement with deep suspicion.

Despite Allied pressure on the German question, only in February 1916 did the government forbid trade with Germany (in a decree
that went unenforced for over a year). Also, Sonnino, who worried
about Italy's German-Swiss credit sources, staved off on repudiating
the Italo-German commercial treaty until mid-1916, when Rome's
exclusion from Allied talks on Ottoman spoils forced moves against
Berlin, including a declaration of war.[56] Until then, Sonnino successfully raised the specter of the internal opposition that would
be activated by such a step.[57]

The Consulta's deft use of the peace movement also dampened
the hope of drawing Austria into a separate peace. Such a peace
would have nullified at least some of the promises made to Italy in
the Pact of London. Lloyd George and French Premier Alexander
Ribot went so far as to discuss Italy's receiving Cicilia instead of
the Trentino in an accord with Austria.[58] Sonnino firmly opposed
such a separate peace and once more employed the known Italian
opposition to the war to his advantage. When confronted at St. Jean
de Maurienne with Habsburg Emperor Charles I's peace overtures,
Sonnino informed Lloyd George that Italians might well not continue in the war following a peace agreement with their primary
enemy. Two months later Sonnino reiterated his position, and in
September—after the Turinese insurrection—he cited the dangers
of internal instability in opposing the King's accepting an invitation to meet with George V and President Poincaré when Sonnino

was actually concerned only that Victor Emmanuel might be per-suaded to approve talks with Vienna.[59] The peace movement could serve the Consulta's interests.

VIII

Until after the August 1917 rebellion in Turin and the subsequent military disaster at Caporetto in October, the peace movement car-ried on in a somewhat curtailed form. Following intervention, Giolitti called for unified support of the war effort, and Count Dalle Torre provided Catholics with the slogan, "All our duty, but no respon-sibility for the war." Moreover, the position of the PSI—"Neither support nor sabotage"—presented no threat to the interventionists in the Consulta. And, union leader Bruno Buozzi even led the Italian Federation of Metallurgical Workers (FIOM) in participating in government-sponsored citizen committees for the war effort.[60] While it is untrue that after intervention there was virtually no Italian peace movement, Italy was calm for a while.[61]

The PSI met with Swiss socialists at Lugano in September 1914 to prepare the way for international socialist action against the war. Similarly, Italians were represented at conferences of socialist antiwar women and of youth in the spring of 1915 and played a leading role in organizing the Zimmerwald Conference of Septem-ber 1915. The Zimmerwald Conference reinvigorated antiwar so-cialists in Italy. The conference denounced war-makers for lying to their people about the war and for "burying the liberty of their own nations together with the independence of other peoples." It ended with the adoption—with Italian support—of a compromise on or-ganization: the creation of an antiwar International Socialist Com-mittee instead of the formation of a new International, as Lenin urged. Moreover, two of the four members of the ISC, Balabanoff and Morgari, belonged to the PSI.[62]

Zimmerwald had considerable impact in Italy, despite the censor-ship. In October Serrati managed to print the Swiss socialists' call to the conference in *Avanti!* At about the same time 100,000 Zim-merwaldian leaflets were printed in Milan, and their arrival in Turin created a sensation and lifted the sense of isolation that had permeated the Socialists there since May.[63] The close, hard-fought victories of the intransigents—Francesco Barberis, Morgari, Pietro Rabezzana,

Elvira Zocca, and others—over the conciliarists suddenly seemed worthwhile.[64] Perhaps there was still hope of ending the war.

By the end of 1915 it was apparent that the war would not be won soon, and "a sort of undercurrent" of criticism emerged that accused the cabinet of having "misread the signs."[65] By late winter the Salandra regime's support was waning because of both interventionist and neutralist dissatisfaction—with the course of the war, with the rigid censorship, and with an attempt to prorogue parliament and rule by decree. Further, both Salandra and Sonnino resisted any broadening of the cabinet.[66]

In June this discontent resulted in Salandra's fall. Giolittians, Socialists, and antiwar Catholics joined interventionists in toppling this last of Italy's traditional liberal regimes. The subsequent cabinet of Boselli did include Filippo Meda, a recent Catholic convert to intervention, as well as Leonidza Bissolati, the leading democratic interventionist. But these short steps could not defuse smoldering antiwar sentiment.

The year 1916 witnessed the continued growth of "a strong spirit of hostility to the war, accompanied by a growing aversion to the bourgeoisie" that developed in both countryside and cities. Peasants were overburdened, and real wages were down 15 percent from 1913, as compulsory arbitration favored industrial interests.[67] To express their anger, CGL leaders abruptly repudiated a commitment they had made in May to attend a conference of Allied Socialists at Leeds in July.[68] Meanwhile, a second Zimmerwaldian conference had been held in Switzerland and continued the leftward trend set at the first. The resulting manifesto argued forcefully the defeatist view: *"Neither victors, nor vanquished. Rather, all vanquished."* The church and bourgeois pacifists, as well as social patriots, war profiteers, and the "mercenary press," were reviled, and the manifesto demanded immediate peace without annexations, a position that was gaining popularity.

The real watershed for the Italian peace movement was 1917. Even before the German and American peace initiatives of December 1916 unsettled the Boselli government, the British ambassador in Rome complained that the clerical *Corriere d'Italia* and *Avanti!* were "singing the same tune," while other antiwar papers harmed the war effort by attacking British profiteering at Italy's expense.[69] The peace movement seemed to have gained popular support following the peace initiatives. The PSI demanded that the cabinet respond with a proposal of its own, and reports circulated that the papal Secretary of State, Cardinal Gasparri, had met with Joseph Caillaux, the French peace advocate. In a Christmas address Benedict XV repeated Clement of Rome's description of war as "self-murder and madness." But just then, as the cabinet seemed to be in jeopardy, Sonnino counterattacked. He pressed for a crackdown on the Socialists and took a hard line on the need to continue the war. Before December's end, Sonnino had clearly checked his opponents.[70]

Sonnino's parliamentary victory in December brought only temporary relief to the Consulta. The March 1917 revolution in Russia suddenly gave credence among Socialists to the assertion of the Kienthal Manifesto: "Power could be yours if you so wished." Soon the PSI's reformists published their demands for postwar Italy: a republic, disarmament, universal suffrage, abolition of the Senate, and social reforms. Intransigents such as Amadeo Bordiga replied by demanding a break with the reformists and called for revolution. A conference in Rome on February 25 had already asked Socialists to "cut decisively all bridges with the bourgeoisie" and withdraw from all citizens' committees. This extreme position failed to carry the day, but the PSI did refuse to attend the Conference of Allied Socialists in Paris.[71] Meanwhile, uprisings occurred in the countryside and in Milan; and, some girls in Tuscany assured an American visitor that Sonnino, the "bad man who made the war," dared not show his face there in his home town.[72]

Sonnino replied to renewed agitation by seizing the socialists' passports in order to prevent them from attending the Stockholm Conference scheduled for the summer. Further, he made clear his wish that the touring Russian prowar socialists, including the ex-Bolshevik Josef Goldenberg, not visit Italy. Orlando, however, prevailed in the latter case, and the Russians were invited to Italy.[73]

With or without the Russian social patriots, sufficient evidence of combustibility existed to give caution to the wary. Real wages fell again in 1917. The previously prudent *La Stampa* had been dropping ominous hints since the end of 1916; and, in June the Giolittian mayor of Turin, Teofilo Rossi, scandalized political circles with the pointed assertion that "Giolitti is more than ever in the hearts of Italians." Giolitti himself joined the fray on August 13 with a speech emphasizing the unequal sacrifices brought on by the war. Mean-

while the Russian Revolution moved "from popularity to revolutionary symbol." Although the "rigid" intransigents fared poorly
in elections for the Turinese PSI executive committee, the annual
May Day demonstration was very impressive; and Socialists' "private
meetings" commonly drew from 800 to 2,000 persons to hear Serrati
and other antiwar figures. Barberis reminded one audience that
the factories were full of explosives that could be used in a revolt.
Yet, flaming rhetoric aside, the "rigids" made no effort to organize
for insurrection, and Serrati's proposal to provide coordination of
such activities in various cities was defeated at a national conference in Milan.[74]

While Socialists moved toward violence and Giolittians grew
restive, the pope formulated his well-known peace proposal of
August 1, 1917. Benedict feared that prolonged hostilities would
provoke social revolution in the warring states, and he was encouraged by both Central Powers' monarchs to break the Socialists'
near-monopoly on peace advocacy.[75] Having offered what aid it
could to Austria's proposals during the initial Anglo-Austrian discussions in the spring, the Vatican then undertook its own initiative.[76]

As Sonnino suspected, the pontifical note was the product in
part of Vatican-German discussions, through Monsignor Pacelli,
the apostolic nuncio for Bavaria. The note, which was published
on August 15, called upon the belligerents to end the "useless carnage"
on the basis of the status quo ante. Sonnino's reaction was predict-
able: "With all respect for the person and the good intentions of the
Holy Father," he told the Dutch ambassador, "his intervention
could not have come at a more inopportune time." The replies of
the other governments were not substantially better than that of the
Consulta, and by October the matter was dead.[77]

It was within the context, then, of spreading antiwar sentiment,
of the constant example of the Russian Revolution, and of a major
peace pronouncement by the pope that events in Turin assumed
truly insurrectionary proportions. The details need not concern us
here, but it may be important to note that the uprising began spontaneously and caught the "rigids" unprepared.[78] Moreover, as in 1915,
the action of Turinese workers failed to embolden opponents of
the war in other cities or in other clases. The rising did serve to keep
alive the specter of revolutionary violence that Sonnino tried to use
to extort concessions from Woodrow Wilson in 1918-19. Most

importantly, the deeds of Turin illustrated the deep divisions within the peace movement and the fragmented, leaderless condition of the PSI, which reappeared during the postwar uprisings and in the feeble efforts to check the rise of fascism.[79]

If the failure of the Turin revolt could not consolidate the position of the Consulta, the threat of military defeat could serve that end. The Boselli government staggered into the fall of 1917 under fire from all sides and fell on October 25, on the eve of the disaster of Caporetto.[80] Initially, the Austro-German breakthrough seemed to threaten Italy's very ability to stay in the war. The losses of men and materiel were enormous, and the army was driven back behind the Piave River, a distance of over seventy miles in some areas. Cadorna immediately attributed the defeat to the "cravenly" conduct of units of the Second Army and to the internal enemy who had inspired such behavior. Yet, responsibility for Caporetto, according to Marshal Ferdinand Foch, stemmed from the fact that there was "practically no High Command" in the Italian army.[81]

Recriminations aside, the general response to Caporetto was to rally to the *patria*. The remnants of the peace movement drowned in a sea of patriotism and redoubled efforts, including prosecutions, against peace advocates. Even the upper clergy preached the Catholics' duty to defend the *patria,* a stance echoed by the *Osservatore Romano,* Giolitti, and Turati.[82] Opponents of the new Orlando cabinet and/or of the war had one final card to play, however: the demand, made through a new organization, the Parliamentary Union, for the creation of parliamentary committees of control, which were to review cabinet policies and which seemed to be aimed largely at Sonnino.

In opposing the move, Sonnino pointed to the French and British examples, in which executive authority had been concentrated in even fewer hands than before. As in the struggle a year earlier, Sonnino, after having been pummeled, bounced off the ropes and won out.[83] The "bad man who made the war" remained the symbol of the determination to carry on.

IX

The Italian peace movement was spent by 1918. The now-famous Turinese Socialist section led a semiclandestine life after August, and many of its leaders were in prison. Similarly, Serrati and party secretary Constantino Lazzari were soon to be imprisoned for the duration of the war. Most of the remaining Socialists, with the exception of Bordiga, Gramsci, Giovanni Germanetto, and a few other intransigents who lacked even a paper insurrectionary committee, either remained silent or joined the parliamentary reformists in praising the liberal bourgeois war aims set forth in January 1918 by Wilson and Lloyd George. Much the same was also true of the Giolittians and other bourgeois liberals, whose counterpart to the Frenchman Caillaux, Filippo Cavallini, was arrested on November 20. Edoardo Giretti had even convinced himself by this time that Sonnino had become a Wilsonian, and Catholics fell into line as Benedict congratulated Wilson on his Fourteen Points and prayed for a seat at the postwar peace conference. Even the once-fiery Miglioli had almost nothing to say during the December debates on foreign policy and committees of control.[84] The alternatives of revolt and parliamentary maneuvering had both failed to dislodge the hold of Sonnino on the Consulta and the grip of the Consulta on the nation.

For his part, Sonnino continued in much the same manner as before. In January 1918 he refused passports to those who wished to attend a new socialist conference in Stockholm, because to do so, he argued, would result in the "complete triumph of Germanic insidiousness and the exaltation of the Bolsheviks, . . . of socialist, of anarchist, and ultra-pacifist, with all the international and internal consequences that would accrue to us."[85] That done, the aging foreign minister now turned to face that as-yet unvanquished enemy, the anti-imperialist democratic interventionists, such as Bissolati.

NOTES

1. Riccardo Bollati and Giuseppe d'Avarna-Gualtieri, *Il carteggio Avarna-Bollati, luglio 1914-maggio 1915,* ed. Carlo Avarna di Gualtieri (Naples: Edizioni scientifiche italiane, 1953), 2-5. See also T. N. Page to W. J. Bryan, June 3, 1914, in U.S., Department of State, Records of the Department of State Relating to Internal Affairs of Italy, 1910-29, microcopy 527, roll 4, Archives of the United States.

2. On Salandra's "national policy," see Raffaele Colapietra's review essay on *Salandra inedita* in *Rassegna storica del Risorgimento,* 61, no. 3 (July-Sept. 1974): 477-80.

3. Even the moderate leftist Gaetano Salvemini had kind words for Salandra's handling of Red Week. See G. B. Gifuni, "Salvemini e Salandra," *Nuova antologia* 508 (Jan.-April 1970): 37-42. T. N. Page to Bryan, June 13 and 17, 1914, Internal Affairs of Italy, M. 527, roll 4.

4. San Giuliano's circular, July 16, 1914, *Sonnino Papers,* reel 47 (Ann Arbor:

University Microfilms, 1968-69). See also San Giuliano to Bollati, August 7, 1914, in Italy, Ministry of Foreign Affairs, *Documenti diplomatici italiani* (Series 5; Rome: Instituto poligrafico dello Stato, 1954-56), 1:55-56.

5. Antonio Salandra and Sidney Sonnino, "Carteggio tra Salandra e Sonnino nella prima fase della neutralità italiana (agosto-dicembre 1914)," *Nuova antologia* 377 (January-February 1935):484. Sidney Sonnino, *Diario 1914/1916,* vol. 2: *Opera omnia di Sidney Sonnino,* ed. B. Brown and P. Pastorelli (Bari: Laterza, 1972), 8.

6. Un Deputato, "Torniamo allo Statuto," *Nuova antologia,* 151 (January-February 1897):9-28.

7. Antonio Gramsci, *Selections from the Prison Notebooks,* trans. Quinton Hoare and Geoffrey Smith (New York: International Publishers, 1971), 145.

8. Salandra to Sonnino, January 23, 1915, *Sonnino Papers,* reel 47.

9. Brunello Vigezzi, "Le 'Radiose giornate' del maggio 1915 nei rapporti dei Prefetti," *Nuova revista storica* 43 (September-December 1959):313-44, cites extensively telegrams sent by Salandra to his prefects, February to May.

10. Quoted in Paolo Spriano, *Torino operaia nella grande guerra (1914-1918)* (Turin: Einaudi, 1960), 79.

11. Leonardo Saviano, "Il Partito Socialista Italiano e la guerra di Libia (1911-1912)," *Aevum* 48 (May 1974):288-307; Luigi Salvatorelli, *The Risorgimento in Thought and Action,* trans. Mario Domandi (New York: Harper and Row, 1970), 184. Angelica Balabanoff, *My Life as a Rebel* (New York: Greenwood, 1968), 95-96. See also George Haupt, *Socialism and the Great War* (Oxford: Clarendon, 1972), 63-66.

12. Haupt, *Socialism,* 201, quotes Oddino Morgari's statement before the International Socialist Bureau in late July. On other early Socialist antiwar efforts, see Balabanoff, *Life,* 118-20; Spriano, *Torino operaia,* 79-80; *Avanti!,* July 20, 26, 30, August 16, 1914.

13. Sonnino, *Diario 1870/1914,* 1:505, entry of November 26, 1911.

14. Fears of the interventionists' "War or Revolution!" threat are expressed in *ibid.,* 2:16-19; Ferdinando Martini, *Diario, 1914-1918* (Milan: Mondadori, 1966), 98-101; Giacomo De Martino (secretary-general of the Consulta) to Sonnino, November 30, 1914, Sonnino Papers, 47.

15. Balabanoff, *Life,* 123, notes that Mussolini begged off on the basis of illness. Helmut Gruber, *International Communism in the Era of Lenin: A Documentary History* (Ithaca, N.Y.: Cornell University Press, 1967), 53.

16. Earlene Craver, "The Rediscovery of Amadeo Bordiga," *Survey,* 91/92, no. 2/3 (Spring-Summer 1974):160, notes Bordiga's success in antibloc efforts in Naples, 1911-14. Turinese Socialists also rejected a united front against the war. For the effect of Red Week upon the PSI's ability to gain nonproletarian support, see Spriano, *Torino operaia,* 67-69, and Page to Bryan, June 17, 1914.

17. Arrigo Serpieri, *La guerra e la classi rurali italiane,* in *Storia economica e sociale della guerra mondiale,* ed. James T. Shotwell, Italian Series (Bari: Laterza, 1930), 35. Leonida Bissolati's Reformed Socialists also supported the war, while Errico Malatesta, the anarchist leader, remained neutralist.

18. Ernesto Vercesi, *Il movimento cattolico in Italia (1870-1922)* (Florence: Società Anonima Editrice "La Voce," 1923), 139. On Meda, see Ivone Bonomi, *La politica italiana da Porta Pia a Vittorio Veneto* (Turin: Einaudi, 1946), 360.

19. Vercesi, *Movimento cattolico,* 131; Bonomi, *Politica italiana,* 359-61. On Catholics and the 1911 war, see A. William Salomone, *Italian Democracy in the Making* (Philadelphia: University of Pennsylvania Press, 1945), 99.

20. Vercesi, *Movimento cattolico,* 141

21. Henry Howard (Vatican) to Grey, April 7, 1915, in Great Britain, Public Record Office, Foreign Office file 371, folio 2372; Martini, *Diario,* 433. On Pius X's Russophobia, see John P. McKnight, *The Papacy: A New Appraisal* (London: McGraw-Hill, 1953), 243.

22. Gino C. Speranza, *The Diary of Gino Speranza,* ed. Florence C. Speranza (New York: AMS Press, 1940), 1:163-64, 2:156. See also Martini, *Diario,* 433; Howard to Grey, March 16, 1915, Foreign Office file 371, folio 2375.

23. Italy, Parlemento, Camera dei Deputati, *Comitati segreti sulla condotta della guerra* (Rome: Archivo storico, 1967), 47. On just war doctrine, see Luigi Sturzo, *Church and State,* trans. Barbara B. Carter (Notre Dame, Ind.: University of Notre Dame Press, 1939), 471.

24. Serpieri, *La guerra,* 34, 88; Vercesi, *Movimento cattolico,* 140-41.

25. Howard to Grey, January 11, 1915, Foreign Office file 371, folio 2371.

26. McKnight, *Papacy,* 247.

27. A. C. F. Beales, *The History of Peace* (1931; reprint ed., New York: Garland), 121.

28. Countess Pasini to Rosika Schwimmer, September 16, 1914, in U.S. Department of State, Records of the Department of State Relating to World War I and Its Termination, microcopy 367, roll 12, 763.72119/15, Enclosure, Archives of the United States.

29. Conciliation Internationale, *L'Action de la Conciliation Internationale pendent l'anée 1917: Rapports de nos secrétairés généraux* (Paris: Delagrave, 1918), 13.

30. Olindo Malagodi, *Conversazioni della guerra, 1914-1919* (Milan: Riccardo Riccardi, 1960), 1:41n. Also, Italy, *Comitati segreti,* 47.

31. Giovanni Giolitti, *Memoirs of My Life,* trans. Edward Storer (London: Chapman and Dodd, 1923), 390-91.

32. Raffaele Colapietra, *Leonida Bissolati* (Milan: Feltrinelli, 1958), 219. See also Vittorio E. Orlando, *Memorie (1915-1919),* ed. R. Mosca (Milan: Rizzoli, 1960), 31-32. Sonnino said that he agreed in principle with Giolitti: Malagodi, *Conversazioni,* 1:42-43.

33. A. C. Jemolo, *Church and State in Italy, 1850-1950,* trans. D. Moore (Philadelphia: Dufour, 1961), 163.

34. Luigi Mondini, "Neutralità ed Intervento," *Rassegna storica del Risorgimento,* 60, no. 1 (January 1973): 95. See also Luigi Salvatorelli, *Storia del Novecento* (Milan: Mondadori, 1957), 450.

35. Salandra to Sonnino, October 22 and 27, 1914, in Salandra and Sonnino, "Carteggio," 496-98; Salandra, 142-43; Rodd to Grey, October 31, 1914, Foreign Office file 371, folio 2007; Page to Bryan, November 3, 1914, 'Internal Affairs of Italy, roll 5, 865.00/18.

36. Sonnino, *Diario,* 2:92-94.

37. Corrado De Biase, ed. "Il 'Diario' del ministro Vincenzo Riccio (1915)," *Nuova antologia* 455 (December 1955):527-46, cites many notable persons who wrote or called upon Riccio in May in efforts to turn him against intervention. See also

Senator Riccardo Carafe to Sonnino, no date, Sonnino Papers, 53.

38. Prezioso to Frassati, May 5, 1915, in Sonnino, *Diario,* 2:357-60; *ibid.,* 129, 144. Prezioso to Sonnino, August 14, and enclosure, *Sonnino Papers,* 47. See also Sonnino's entries in mid-May, *Diario,* 2:144-48, 149-50, 152-55.

39. De Martino to Sonnino, November 30, 1914, *Sonnino Papers,* 47.

40. Vigezzi, "Le 'Radiose giornate'," 54-56. Such notables commonly monopolized political activity in the South.

41. A Caracciolo, "La crisi politica italiana del 1914-1915," *Società* (October 1954): 1012. See also Ernesto Galli Della Loggia, "Problemi di sviluppo industriale e nuovi equilibri politica alla viglia della prima guerra mondiale: La fondazione delle Banca Di Sconto," *Rivista Storica Italia* 82, no. 4, 824-86. On Stringher, see Deputy Roberto [indecipherable] to Sonnino, November 18, 1914, *Sonnino Papers,* 47. In July 1915 it was reported that Stringher was ready to help found an Anglo-Italian bank, which would aid in the battle against German capital in Italy. See Martini, *Diario,* 489-92.

42. Mondini, "Neutralità ed Intervento," 94. Orlando, *Memorie,* 47, notes the valuable interventionist support from some conservative Catholics.

43. Spriano, *Torino operaia,* 102.

44. Vigezzi, "Le 'Radiose giornate'," 87ff.

45. Spriano, *Torino operaia,* 103; Giolitti, *Memoirs,* 400; *Comitati segreti,* 148. See also Alberto Monticone, *Nitti e la grande guerra (1914-1918)* (Milan: Giuffré, 1961), 16.

46. Antonio Gramsci, "The Programme of Ordine Nuovo," *The Modern Prince and Other Writings* (New York: International Publishers, 1957), 26.

47. Spriano, *Torino operaia,* 104-12, provides most of the following account of events of May 16-20. See also John M. Cammett, *Antonio Gramsci and the Origins of Italian Communism* (Stanford: Stanford University Press, 1967), 14-38.

48. Quoted in Martin Berger, "Engels' Theory of the Vanishing Army: A Key to the Development of Marxist Revolutionary Tactics," *Historian* 37, no. 3 (May 1975), 426, from a letter to Paul Lafargue.

49. Spriano, *Torino operaia,* 122, 138 (n. 4).

50. Vigezzi, "Le 'Radiose giornate'," 87-92. In Austrian-ruled Trieste, Italian and Slavic workers rejected nationalist appeals: Ennio Maserati, *Il movimento operaio a Trieste dalle origini alla prima guerra mondiale* (Milan: Giuffré, 1973), 206.

51. Maurice Neufeld, "The Inevitability of Political Unionism in Underdeveloped Countries: Italy the Exemplar," *Industrial and Labor Relations Review* 13, no. 3 (April 1960): 366.

52. For the King's comment, see Rodd to Grey, May 22, 1915, Foreign Office file 371, folio 2377. See also De Biase, " 'Diario'," 538-39; Salandra, *Italy,* 313-14. Vigezzi also concluded that a majority were neutralist.

53. Malagodi, *Conversazioni,* 1:56-64. See also Macchio (Rome) to Burian (Vienna), May 11, 1915 (intercepted and deciphered), *Sonnino Papers,* 52, on Giolitto's refusal to overturn Salandra. Giolitti, *Memoirs,* 394, 400.

54. Salandra, *Italy,* 200-01.

55. Italy had declared only against Austria. Declarations followed against Turkey (August) and Bulgaria (October), but it was August 28, 1916, before Germany was added to the list.

56. On May 4, 1915, Salandra had assured Bülow that no Italians wanted war

with Germany: Macchio to Burian (intercepted and deciphered), May 5, 1915, Sonnino Papers, 47. For Sonnino on credit sources, see "1915," *ibid.* See also Francois Charles-Roux, *Souvenirs diplomatiques* (Paris: Fayard, 1958), 112-13; Martini, *Diario,* 689.

57. Sonnino told Rodd that because of opposition from Giolittians and the upper classes, he was reluctant to proceed further: Rodd to Grey, September 10, 1915, Foreign Office file 371, folio 2379.

58. David Lloyd George, *War Memoirs* (London: Odham's Press, 1938), 2:1175, 1187.

59. Memorandum on the Anglo-French-Italian Conference, April 19, 1917, in Great Britain, Cabinet, Public Record Office, Cabinet Minutes, folio 28, document 2, Allied Conference Series. The procés-verbal is in Sonnino Papers, 47. See also Sonnino, *Diario,* 3:154-55, 395. Luigi Aldrovandi-Marescotti, *Guerra diplomatica: Ricordi e frammenti di diorio* (Milan: Mondadori, 1936), 126.

60. On these initial stances, see Giolitti, *Memoirs,* 401-02; Gabriele De Rosa, *Storia politica dell'Azione Cattolica in Italia* (Bari: Laterza, 1953-54), 2:423; Spriano, *Torino operaia,* 123.

61. As suggested in Beales, *History of Peace,* 301.

62. Balabanoff, *Life,* 123, 131-37, and Alberto Malatesta, *I sociolisti italiani durante la guerra* (Milan: Mondadori, 1926), 86-87. Gruber, *International Communism,* 44-47, 53-57.

63. The Italian censorship was one of the strictest: Orlando, *Memorie,* 514-15.

64. The top intransigent candidates for the local PSI executive committee won by only ten and seven votes, respectively, in July. Elections in August provided the intransigents with a wider lead: Spriano, *Torino Operaia,* 126-29.

65. Page to Lansing, December 4, 1915, in U.S., Department of State, *Papers Relating to the Foreign Relations of the United States: The Lansing Papers* (Washington: U.S. Government Printing Office, 1942), 1:730-32.

66. Martini, *Diario,* entries of March 1-20, 1916. See also U.S. Embassy in Rome to Lansing, March 6, 1916, Internal Affairs of Italy, roll 4, 865.00/22.

67. Serpieri, *La guerra,* 37-39. Antonio Fossati, *Lavoro e produzione in Italia dalla metà del secolo XVIII alla seconda guerra mondiale* (Turin: Giapichelli, 1951), 630-34.

68. Maurice Neufeld, *Italy: School for Awakening Countries* (Ithaca, N.Y.: Cayuga Press, 1961), 364.

69. Rodd to Grey, November 11 and December 9, 1916, Foreign Office file 371, folio 2687. Howard to Grey, October 8, 1916, *ibid.,* and H. G. Wells, *Italy, France and Britain at War* (New York: Macmillan, 1918), 70-71.

70. Serpieri, *La guerra,* 88. Orlando to Sonnino, December 21, 1916, Sonnino Papers, 52, in which Gasparri's denial is repeated. Franziskus Stratmann, *The Church and War* (New York: Garland, 1928), 84, on the speech.

71. For the manifesto, see Gruber, *International Communism,* 65-69; Jules Humbert-Droz, *L'origine de l'Internationale Communiste* (Neuchatel: Baconnière, 1968), 190-98. For the reformist program, see *Avanti!,* May 3, 1917. See also Craver, "Rediscovery," 162; Filippo Turati, *Discorsi parlementari* (Rome: Tipografia della

Camera dei Deputati, 1950), 3:1468. Rodd to Balfour, May 3, 1917, Foreign Office file 371, folio 2946.

72. Speranza, *Diary,* 2:42. See also Giovanni Pirolini's speech, *Comitati segreti,* 14.

73. Spriano, *Torino operaia,* 226, notes Orlando's approval. See also Sonnino, *Diario,* 3:160-61.

74. Real wages fell in 1917 to 73.1 percent of their 1913 level: Fossati, *Lavoro e produzione,* 567-69. Spriano, *Torino operaia,* 208-20. Alberto Monticone, "Il socialismo torinese e il fatti del agosto 1917," *Rassegna storica del Risorgimento* 45, no. 1, 58, argues that the "rigids' " lossess in PSI elections freed them to agitate and propagate revolutionary sentiments. See also Luigi Albertini, *Venti anni di vita politica* (Bologna: Zanichelli, 1950-53), 4:517, and Louis Hautecoeur, *L'Italie sous la ministère Orlando, 1917-1919* (Paris: Bossard, 1919), 42-43.

75. Pacelli to Gasparri, (2) June 30, 1917 (intercepted and deciphered), Sonnino Papers, 48.

76. Gasparri to Valfré (Vienna), April 10, 1917 (intercepted and deciphered), ibid.

77. Pacelli to Gasparri, June 20 and July 27, 1917, and Gasparri to Pacelli, June 20, 1917, ibid. Sonnino, *Diario,* 3:181-82; Aldrovandi, *Guerra diplomatica,* 123. Ragonesi to Gasparri, August 18, 1917, confirms the response of the Allies: Sonnino Papers, 48. See also *Giornale d'Italia,* September 22, 1917.

78. Spriano, *Torino operaia,* 221.

79. Ibid., 236-61. Domenico Zucaro, "La Rivolta di Torino del 1917 nella sentenza del Tribunale militare territoriale," *Rivista storica del socialismo* 3, no. 10 (May 1960): 437-69. John E. Haven (Turin) to Lansing, September 5, 1917, Enclosure, Internal Affairs of Italy, roll 4, 865.00/30.

80. Sonnino made a long presentation to the Chamber shortly before Boselli fell by a 96-314 vote. See Bonnino, *Diario,* 3:200.

81. Minutes of the Anglo-French meeting at Rapallo, November 5, 1917, Britain,, Cab. 28/2. See also Malagodi, *Conversazioni,* 1:179, 184, 193-94; Orlando, *Memorie,* 181, 227-32, 239-41. Italy, Ministry for War, Committee of Inquiry, *Le cause e le responsibilità degli avvenimenti,* vol. 2 of *Relazione della Commissione di inchiesta* (Rome: Stabilimento tipografico per l'amministrazione della Guerra, 1919).

82. Giovanni Giolitti, *Discorsi parlamentari* (Rome: Tipografia della Camera dei Deputati, 1953-56), 3:1698-99. Malagodi, *Conversazioni,* 1:188-90. On Turati's support of the government, see Orlando, *Memorie,* 555. See also Spriano, *Torino operaia,* 275, and Turati, *Discorsi,* 3:1557.

83. *Comitati segreti,* 107-218, contains the debates of December 13-18. See also Sonnino, *Diario,* 3:213-15, 223-39, 241-44; and J. C. Powell, "Neutralist Tactics in Italy," *New Europe* 6, no. 66 (January 17, 1918):21-24.

84. Spriano, *Torino operaia,* 269, 275-76, 281-85. Zucaro, "La Rivolta." Hautecoeur, *L'Italie,* 78. *Comitati segreti,* 205, contains Miglioli's one brief statement. Edoardo Giretti, "Exposé de l'état des esprits en Italie en cours de l'anée 1917," in *Conciliation Internationale, 1917,* 33-39.

85. Sonnino to London and Paris embassies, January 3, 1918, Sonnino Papers, 42.

9

The Dilemma of British Socialists during the Great War: Revolutionary Peace or Pacifist Reconstruction

HOWARD WEINROTH

The temper of the masses in favour of peace often expresses the beginning of protest, anger and a realisation of the reactionary nature of the war. It is the duty of Social-Democrats to utilize that temper. They will take a most ardent part in any movement . . . motivated by that sentiment, but they will not deceive the people with admitting the idea that a peace without annexations, without oppression of nations, without plunder . . . is possible in the absence of a revolutionary movement. . . . whoever wants a lasting and democratic peace must stand for Civil war against the governments and bourgeoisie. (V. I. Lenin)[1]

Lenin's advice to socialists about establishing a "democratic peace" through revolutionary struggle and the overthrow of bourgeois regimes, if generally valid, hardly was tenable in Britain during World War I. What was not wholly unrealistic, however, was the possibility of creating a militant peace movement that might force the government's hand to the point where it would be obliged to negotiate with the enemy. This, in fact, was the stated aim of most British socialists whose deep commitment to an antiwar philosophy had its roots both in the domestic environment and the internationalist ideas assimilated from continental colleagues. As Europe sank into a state of near-military exhaustion, as social distress and popular disillusion with the war spread throughout Britain, the prospects of achieving this aim brightened. It is somewhat puzzling, therefore, that socialist efforts for an early cessation to hostilities had little, if any, effect upon the government and no more than a marginal influence on the working class. Any examination of why this was so cannot dwell simply upon the numerical insignificance of socialist groups or the general climate of opinion, which seemingly discouraged "unpatriotic" appeals for a "peace without victory." Account must also be taken of the socialists' ideological conceptions, their response to specific issues, and, most pertinently, their relationship with the working class.

For the period preceding 1914 and even to the dramatic reawakening of Labour militancy in 1916, it is customary to view the socialist position on war as polarized in two (at the most four) nationwide organizations. According to this neat division, the Independent Labour party (ILP) stood on one side. Towering above all other socialist bodies in Britain in terms of sheer numbers and by virtue of its unique contribution to Labour politics, it was staunchly anti-militarist, blending in its program for world amity a curious mixture of ethical-emotional pacifism, a Radical criticism of foreign policy, and proletarian distrust of "capitalist intrigues" in international affairs.[2] On the other side was the Marxist Social-Democratic Federation which, after several secessions and organizational revisions, in 1912 became the British Socialist party (BSP). Dominated by the personality of Henry Hyndman and a clique of lesser figures who ran the party weekly, *Justice,* it had veered in a jingoist direction ever since the rise of Anglo-German naval rivalry. Hyndman and his supporters tended to encourage suspicion of German imperialism while competing with the Tories in demanding a more substantial policy of national defense. The BSP's loyalty to the socialist pledge of maintaining international peace was thus rather questionable even before the outbreak of the war. Among the smaller socialist bodies were the Fabian Society, whose pro-imperialist, pro-establishment prejudices are repeatedly cited in every historical text, and the Socialist Labour party (SLP), an adjunct of De Leonite Marxism, which advocated antimilitarist agitation and insurrection but otherwise was unconcerned with the international scene.[3]

Without denying the helpfulness of organizational distinctions, it is worth stressing that differences in attitude toward war and national defense were far more complex all along the socialist spectrum, frequently cutting across party lines. The BSP, for instance, was irreparably split over such questions when the Hyndman faction began flaunting the slogans of "citizen army" and unchallenged naval supremacy. Opposition to this leadership crystallized around John Maclean of Pollockshaws and several London-based Russian-Jewish Marxists. Firmly internationalist in their views, they narrowly missed overturning the party's policy on imperialism and defense in 1911. A compromise was effected, though, allowing free expression on such matters.[4] Nor did the ILP, despite the impression it conveyed, have an unblemished record in fighting chauvinist tendencies. Peace rhetoric sometimes concealed a strain of "defensism" to which several of its political pundits were addicted. Ramsay MacDonald's revealing statement during the Agadir crisis suggests as much. He hoped "that no European nation will assume for a single moment that party divisions in this country will weaken the national spirit or national unity."[5] So does the 1914 defection of J. R. Clynes and James Parker to the prowar camp, as well as the ambivalent statements issued by the ILP executive on recruiting and British commitments to intervene in the European conflict.[6] What is more, rank-and-file sympathies did not always correspond with those of their leadership; in many cases, the rank and file, though lacking in sophistication, were considerably more principled in upholding the program of socialist antimilitarism.[7]

Of greater relevance were the influences fashioning socialist thinking on the international order and the dangers of impending catastrophe because of imperialist tensions: the Kautskyian notion of the decreasing inevitability of war because of the "cartelization" of capitalist industries on a world scale and the mounting strength of social democracy, and Norman Angell's well-publicized argument that the universal interdependence of credit and finance would reduce the danger of armed strife. Both influences contributed to a pacifist atmosphere in socialist circles.[8] Kautsky's subtle analyses of capitalism and war, printed in *Justice* as well as in the German press, left their mark on left-wing theorists in Britain, most notably H. N. Brailsford, but also Zelda Kahan and Theodore Rothstein of the BSP. Certainly they can be traced in Brailsford's constant reference to the European conflict that would never go beyond a bloodless duel, *"a war of steel and gold,"* though they are also detectable in

BSP criticism of the left Zimmerwaldians in 1916.[9] Strange to say, but a radical Marxist like Rothstein, only weeks before the Bolshevik revolution, still echoed the Kautskyian thesis that "finance must become internationalised, and then the quarrels will disappear."[10] Norman Angell's doctrine had a more pervasive effect because it reached a broader audience. Ever since the appearance of his book, *The Great Illusion,* the ILP had waxed enthusiastic over his ideas: several of its London-based branches became engrossed in debating their validity.[11] Although left-wing members of the party might challenge what they regarded as "his false conceptions," they were not immune to the pacifist spirit emanating from them. Typical was J. T. Walton Newbold, a future communist MP who treated contemptuously what he considered Angell's "shallow" approach to problems—his lack of concern for facts—but unwittingly accepted the central argument of this "bourgeois pacifist" that the "financial interests" of the "City" would never allow the government to go to war.[12]

As a result of the growing belief in the possibility of preserving the international order from self-destruction, socialists concentrated their energies on publicizing the technical means designed to promote world stability. Like the dissenting "bourgeois Radicals" who harassed the government on foreign and defense policies, they pressed for the establishment of a system of international arbitration and the reduction of armaments and democratic diplomacy, insisting that by carrying forward such a program and imposing it on governments the threats to world peace could be lessened.[13] The fortunate resolution of the Agadir crisis and the localization of the Balkan struggles reinforced this optimism. But one area, perhaps the quintessential element in the success of any antiwar movement—the role of the working class—was generally neglected. True, it was supposed that the workers would at some point in time, nonviolently or otherwise, overturn the government and thereby usher in the socialist millennium from which international harmony would automatically ensue. But until then, they were assigned the modest task of supplying the backbone of support for political pressure exercised by socialists; at most, their energies were to be channelled into vast antiwar demonstrations similar to those that occurred at the end of 1912.[14] Keir Hardie's panacea—the general strike against war—did not seriously qualify this stance, for the strike was conceived as a partial stoppage, a kind of limited deterrent to check government plans for mobilization.[15] Certainly its ILP sponsors were not interested in using it to foment mass insurrection. Industrial stoppages bent upon achieving such a purpose were contemplated solely by the SLP and syndicalists. Thus, in a sense, British socialists, despite their attempts to distinguish themselves from "bourgeois pacifists," adopted the strategy of the latter in dealing with the peace question. They were not, as Rothstein aptly remarked, "an independent force capable of counteracting the vile machinations and the supreme folly of our rulers."[16] Much worse, they were gradually becoming convinced they would never have to face the prospect of a European conflagration.

This is not the place to recount in detail the response of British socialists to the fateful days of July-August 1914: their confusion, bewilderment and final resignation; the sudden about-face of the Labour party (an affiliate of the Second International) from condemning Sir Edward Grey's interventionist policy to a promise of unswerving loyalty to the national cause; the disarray of the BSP, hopelessly divided between the animated jingoist section under Hyndman and the critical internationalists; the compassionate "pacifism" of the ILP, which helped it withstand the general surge of patriotism but placed it in political limbo.[17] Attention will instead be focused on the less familiar though highly problematic theme of socialist reorganization for a peace offensive in the very midst of war, the stages through which this offensive passed, and the character it eventually assumed.

That socialists were verbally, if not emotionally, committed to availing themselves of every weapon possible to hasten the advent of peace was meaningless during the first weeks following British military intervention on the continent. The general indecisiveness of all groups dissenting from the policy of involvement in Europe's insanity, an indecisiveness with its roots in the fear of confronting a hostile public at a moment when the scales of war weighed against the Allied cause, precluded dramatic action.[18] In truth, this temporary paralysis of dissent permitted at most a reaffirmation of the socialist faith, the establishment of contact with sympathetic elements, and refusal to participate in the parliamentary recruiting campaign. At worst, it induced organizational introspection and excessive caution. The ILP, in the van of dissent, struck the characteristic note:

As the weeks go by and the horrors of war increase, both on the scene of conflict and in the homes of the people, we believe a great wave of revulsion will sweep the country. The I.L.P. must, in the meantime, husband its resources and maintain its organisation intact. Protest meetings will at the moment serve to arouse Jingo feeling rather than suppress it. The N.A.C. [National Administrative Councl] has decided to postpone arrangements for the special autumn campaign.[19]

Instead of open protest on the issue of the day, the ILP executive encouraged, as did its BSP counterpart (the internal leadership struggle notwithstanding), concern for socioeconomic matters. From the inception of the War Emergency Workers National Committee, a body embracing the multifarious sections of Labour, socialist leaders figured prominently in its battle to defend the workers' standard of living. They directed their own rank and file to take part in citizen committees in order to channel "their efforts into the immediate problems of poverty, unemployment, sickness, and destitution," urging them to secure measures on food, rent control, adequate pensions, and so forth.[20] While such concern underscored the antiwar socialists' close identification with their opponents inside the Labour movement, it disguised fundamental ideological-political cleavages arising out of the war. It also produced an inversion of priorities among many of these socialists, diverting their energies from vigorous peace propaganda to agitation for "equality of sacrifice," the "conscription of riches," and the increasing nationalization of industry. Symptomatic of this economist trend, later taking the form of programs for social reconstruction, was the reluctance of socialists to promote the peace theme during the food and pension conferences held in the early months of the war.[21]

Nevertheless, despite an overwhelming preoccupation with domestic issues, pacifist, though not revolutionary, dissidence emerged. As early as the winter of 1914-15, articles appeared in the socialist and Radical press suggesting that Germany might be ready for talks if only "the Allied Powers declared a willingness to state their terms." Simultaneously, in several urban centers (including London and

Glasgow) antiwar organizations sprang up, demonstrations were staged, and resolutions were passed, calling upon the government to define its reasons for fighting and the kind of settlement it would accept.[22] Here was the first trickle of peace dissent. And though scarcely audible in controversy-ridden BSP circles, it was afforded an ample airing at the Easter conference of the ILP. At Norwich ILP delegates stepped beyond their executive's rather ambivalent attitude about "seeing the war through." They not only revised the party's official explanations on several points, specifically the origins of international strife, but also critically scrutinized every sign of weakness or compromise in NAC policy. Successive speakers reiterated the need for a widespread movement in favor of compelling the government to state its peace terms. Indeed, close to half those present veered behind Dr. Alfred Salter's pacifist motion, which stated that it was the duty of socialists to defy every war entered into by capitalist governments.[23] The spirit that prevailed seemed to verge on out-and-out resistance to the government; and some of the younger rebels, impatient with the expository methods of the Radical-dominated Union of Democratic Control and ILP parliamentarians, hinted at the desirability of starting a stop-the-war movement.[24] But the keynote of the conference, as that of the succeeding months, was the more moderate demand to mount an aggressive campaign for negotiating with the enemy.

The failure to sustain and broaden this campaign has frequently been attributed to the virtual isolation politically of the ILP and other internationalists. Undoubtedly the 1915 Trade Union Congress was unreceptive to socialist-inspired appeals for a balanced view of the world situation. In trade union ranks, patriotic fervor was now at its peak.[25] But it is also true that the pacifically inclined socialist leadership vacillated and curbed the momentum of the peace rebels. In the BSP, the Fairchild-Fineberg combination, reflecting the rising fortunes of Marxist "centrism," pursued an inconsistent, if not totally contradictory, course.[26] E. C. Fairchild, for example, while recognizing that the continuation of the war imperiled socialism, warned that all action calculated to endanger national defense should be rigorously avoided: the "only hope for a satisfactory settlement [lies] in the united demand of the international working class for the conclusion of a peace which will restore Belgium," and "the necessary

preliminary to the formation of that demand" was the reconstruction of the International. J. Fineberg, on the other hand, was dis-
turbed by the thought of a "victory for German militarism": it
would signify universal disaster, and whether it could "be averted
by a fight to the finish or not . . . is a matter of opinion which I am
prepared to argue."[27] Similarly, the ILP's National Council, having
succumbed to the pressure for "negotiated-peace" agitation, studiously refrained from galvanizing the rank-and-file membership for
this object: the "peace-by-negotiations" theme was given a low
profile by NAC lecturers, and little was done to coordinate branch
activity. Preference was shown instead for "rescue work" and calm,
persuasive propaganda: in Chairman Fred Jowett's words, that
which "would assuage the feeling of hatred and spread the philosophy of pacifism."[28]

Nor was this all. If the NAC equivocated about launching the
peace campaign, it was no more daring in handling the vexatious
question of international socialism. At the February 1915 Conference of Allied Socialists, its representatives compromised the party's
position by approving a resolution that singled out Germany as the
aggressor and spoke of the inflexible resolve "to fight until victory."
In the summer of the same year it tried to rally the British section of
the International Socialist Bureau in support of the German Social-
Democratic party's peace manifesto, but in the absence of unanimity
it chose not to issue its own statement.[29] Meanwhile, in concert with
the centrist leaders of the BSP, the NAC insisted that the bureau's
officials summon a full meeting of its constituents so that a special
world congress might be arranged. There was hope that once the
prewar system of socialist contact was revived, differences between
and within parties would be ironed out, a common program would
be formulated, and the celebrated Stuttgart resolution would be
implemented. Even though the special congress was never held, the
socialist left in Britain continued to cling to the fiction of resurrect-
ing the International. They might welcome the initiative of the
Zimmerwald Commission in gathering together the revolutionary
opponents of war, but they refused to see it as a replacement for the
defunct bureau; nor would they join in the Zimmerwaldian attacks
upon "social chauvinists"—the *majoritaires* of the European socialist
movement.[30] In their minds, the bureau remained the sole legitimate

authority of the movement, in which agreement could be reached by its diverse sections, prowar and antiwar, if a tolerant attitude was adopted.

This latitudinarian approach on the international level had its parallel in the NAC's unrepentant defense of ILP parliamentarians who sided with the government, its unbending allegiance to the Labour party, and its recurrent decision not to vote against the war credits.[31] At bottom, what motivated the NAC (both on the domestic and international scene) was the desire to live in harmony despite dissent, so appropriately expressed by J. S. Middleton, a recent convert to the ILP and secretary of the War Emergency Workers National Committee: disunity because of "violent differences on War policy . . . will be fatal to the whole future of Labour."[32] The Marxist centrists of the BSP, in full accord with Middleton, persuaded themselves that it was essential to subsume their disagreements with prowar Labour under the banner of unity.

But the strategy of accommodation, carefully fostered by socialist leaders in the NAC and the centrist wing of the BSP, provoked discontent among left-wing rebels. By the late spring of 1915, many of them discerned that the peace initiative was passing into the hands of the Union of Democratic Control. Firebrands like Fenner Brockway, Clifford Allen, and Ellen Wilkinson, irritated because the ILP executive was dragging its feet (waiting "for some popular response before taking a bold move"), asserted that the party would "cease to count if it is going to postpone" its peace offensive "until everyone else is also disposed to do the same."[33] In spite of the perpetual threat of police raids against socialist organizations, confiscation of antiwar literature, and arrests conducted against party activists, the indecisiveness of socialist policy drove the left-wing rebels into the open. Within the BSP John Maclean began publishing the revolutionary journal *Vanguard,* which called for purifying the party ranks while underlining the incompatibility of supporting *pari passu* the Zimmerwald manifesto and the reactionary leaders of "social chauvinism."[34] Maclean's emergence as a critic on the left, signaling as it did the beginning of the BSP's organizational split in 1916, promised a more determined opposition to the war. Less dramatic, though equally significant, was the increasing influence of ILP advocates of a militant peace platform. After unsuccessful attempts to get the NAC to abandon its anomalous, if statesmen-like, position on a score of issues, they managed at the 1916 conference to carry the controversial Bermondsey (or pacifist) resolution by an over-whelming vote. Although the ILP was not as deeply imbued with the philosophy of nonresistance as the vote suggested, rank-and-file elements were at least afforded the opportunity of venting frustrated feelings.[35]

It is improbable, however, that the socialist "rebels" were instru-mental in revitalizing the campaign for a negotiated settlement. Factors of a more general nature seem to have impelled dissenters of various political colors to brush aside their reservations and adopt an unequivocal stance in favor of shortening the war. In the back-ground was the horrific stalemate on the Western Front and the unhappy demise of the Dardanelles expedition, which caused war weariness at home. Domestically there were growing restrictions on civil liberties, the hounding of the left-wing press, and, most omin-ous of all, the introduction of conscription, which, as the dissenters saw it, threatened the rise of the militarist state. Doubtless also rumors of peace moves by neutral statesmen, compounded with the left-wing challenge in the socialist movement, reinforced the belief that the time for action was rapidly approaching. Thus toward the end of October 1915, the dissenting left, and specifically the UDC Radicals (E. D. Morel, Charles Trevelyan, Arthur Ponsonby, J. A. Hobson, and C. R. Buxton) and Lords Courtney and Loreburn, opened a debate in the press and Parliament, stressing the futility of continuing the European slaughter and the timeliness of considering terms of settlement.

Three months later they launched a full-scale discussion of the negotiation theme: Philip Snowden expounded the underlying rationale for terminating hostilities before either side of the belligerent powers achieved victory.[36] By April 1916 the ILP, in collaboration with the UDC, the No-Conscription Fellowship, diverse pacifist societies, and Sylvia Pankhurst's Workers' Suffrage Federation, inaugurated the Peace Negotiations Committee.[37] Liberated from Hyndmanite obstruction, the BSP also joined the newly formed pacifist alliance. Indeed, its centrist executive in the persons of Fairchild and Fineberg was all aglow with praise for the committee and the Peace Memorial it sponsored to put pressure on the government to seek peace negotiations immediately. This was "the real test of strength of the peace forces in the country. . . . It must be the immediate and special work of the British Socialist Party to secure signatures to the Memorial amongst the masses of wage-earners."[38]

There is ample reason to believe that the peace memorial campaign had some impact upon popular consciousness even in 1916. The leading organizers, of whom C. R. Buxton, Herbert Dunnico, and E. P. Wake were the most prominent, stumped the country in an effort to sway public opinion and found a sympathetic response in working-class communities. Buxton, citing personal experience, spoke of eager and sober audiences ranging from 50 to 800 people at the meetings he addressed.[39] He was not exaggerating: the reports of ILP branches indicated its rallies were numerically encouraging; large numbers of signatures were appended to the peace memorial (more than 150,000 individuals plus trade union bodies, representing 75,000 members, signed); there was an increasing tendency of local Labour parties and trades councils to record their support; and most significantly, substantial minorities of the engineers, the miners, and textile workers favored a negotiated peace.[40]

In the spring of 1917 the peace mood seems to have gained considerable momentum, in part because of the February revolution in Russia but also because of the accumulating domestic burdens and disillusion with the progress of the war. Certainly the May Day marches, unprecedented in scope and highlighted by slogans of peace and international working-class solidarity, reflected this trend.[41] Buxton, whose assessment in the previous year had been rather reserved, now wrote elatedly:

My last three nights' meetings have been marvellous. I really don't know "where unto this will grow". Resolutions carried by vast crowds in open market places demanding "peace without annexations and indemnities". Last night the only interrupter (a very mild one at that) [was] nearly mobbed by the crowd—and escorted away by the police.[42]

A curious, if not paradoxical, development marked this burgeoning peace crusade. Although it was fed by the same discontent and restlessness that sparked demonstrations against soaring food prices and industrial disturbances, there was no apparent connection between them. For example, in the Sheffield engineering strike (November 1916) against "combing out" a skilled worker for military service or in the massive wave of engineering stoppages that unexpectedly hit the country in May 1917, antiwar sentiment was not in evidence. Stranger still, both government sources and militant shop stewards like J. T. Murphy have argued that even though the strikes were led by "stop-the-war" individuals, any suggestion that they be used for a political purpose such as ending the war would have been met with a negative reaction from the rank and file.[43] The same held true with respect to mounting protest over the food situation. While trades and labour councils organized demonstrations of angry workers and set up vigilance committees to exercise pressure on local authorities, working-class consciousness was limited to the issues at hand: high prices, the threat of shortages, the callousness of government, and the inadequacy of the system of distribution. At most there was a sense of class injustice, but the peace theme failed to register.[44]

This dichotomy in the working-class mind, in which the problem of peace was set in one compartment and social-industrial matters in another, can be explained partly by Theodore Rothstein's observations on the socialists' inability to confront the historical tasks before them:

Have we already done the initial thing which the German [socialist] minority began doing long ago—that is, organising our views in "fields, factories and workshops"? So far we have been proclaiming them to the outside world at public meetings [but have not] attempted to organise the sympathetic section of the working class in their favour. . . . Is it not time to pass to the next stage where real historical action begins? It is only by such action that Acheron will be moved and the mass of our own body will be increased.[45]

The distinction here is crucial: although antiwar propaganda was trumpeted from the pages of socialist journals and at public gatherings, it was hardly voiced within the workshops and in local Labour organizations. Revolutionary shop stewards who often took their cue from the Socialist Labour party were either too absorbed in conducting the rank-and-file rebellion against trade union officials to devote themselves to the politics of world strife or were guided

by the notion that industrial activity took precedence over everything else.[46]

On the other hand, by its very nature, peace propaganda could
not be expected to evoke more than passive assent from the workers.
Borrowed from the armory of Liberal dissent and formulated by a
coterie of UDC Radicals, Quakers, and social pacifists who ran the
Peace Negotiations Committee and who definitely were not socialist
rebels, it was designed mainly to attract a middle-class audience.
Men of the stature of E. D. Morel, Charles Trevelyan, Arthur Ponsonby, and C. R. Buxton, however indefatigable they were in spreading the spirit of internationalism, had little understanding of working-
class concerns. They spoke of the secret engagements Britain had
undertaken with its Allies, thus hindering compromise with the Central Powers; they harped on the danger of "an economic war after
the war," as signified by government statements and the Allied
Economic Conference in 1916; they insisted that now was the time
for "the right kind of peace"—not a "peace at any price," but one
that was moderate and reasonable if only the government would
negotiate.[47] Although such arguments were probably assimilated by
politically conscious working men, it is difficult to see how they
alone (devoid of class content) could have stirred Labour's rank and
file into action. Nor did socialist spokesmen come forth with anything more moving. Ramsay MacDonald, Snowden, Fairchild, and
W. C. Anderson, to cite but a few, periodically dressed their popular
appeals in revolutionary phraseology, emphasizing the need for
working-class solidarity and a broader political perspective.[48] But
they were caught in the circle of Radical argumentation: the conditions for a negotiated settlement were ripe; the workers had only to
demand it, and "every effort must be exerted to make it clear to them
that the fratricidal struggle can be brought to an end when they *will*
it."[49]

Even so, deeds, not words, were the vital element that escaped the
peace movement. The early-formed stop-the-war committees, if less
than marginal in the context of political opposition, vaguely grasped
this point. Perhaps that is why many of their leading figures, together
with ILP rebels, instinctively, but also for lack of other alternatives,
opted for absolute conscientious objection; it provided some form
of challenge to the capitalist-military state.[50] But it was precisely the

active mass challenge that socialist luminaries—from MacDonald on the right to Fairchild and George Lansbury on the left—would not countenance. Averse to industrial action in a period of national emergency, they preferred to dissociate their program for a negotiated settlement from working-class militancy.[51] It is surely noteworthy that the socialist journals, excluding the organ of the Socialist Labour party, gave restricted coverage to the May strikes and omitted mentioning their significance for stepping up the peace campaign. Just as revealing was the utter silence at the 1917 conferences of the ILP and BSP about the virtues of linking the pacifist and industrial movements. Delegates at the ILP conference, though enthused about the Russian Revolution and the brightening prospects for a termination of hostilities, were, noted Sylvia Pankhurst, "conspicuously lacking in constructive energy"; they confined themselves to upbraiding the NAC for its moderate behavior but proposed nothing new for the peace offensive. At the BSP convention, the chairman, Sam Farrow, despite a rousing appeal to the BSP to "voice all growing discontents" (becoming "the lion's mouth of Labour") and never relax its internationalist ardour, condemned "hunger revolts which will lead to the transformation of our towns and cities into bloody shambles" and "industrial violence, the delight of *mouchards* and secret agents."[52]

Socialist leaders were disinclined to exploit social-industrial tremors to further the crusade for a negotiated settlement. This is not to say, however, that they abandoned the mobilization of antiwar forces. In June, under the auspices of the United Socialist Council (the product of ILP-BSP collaboration), they assembled the bulk of the antiwar movement at Leeds. While the Leeds conference, impressive in its galaxy of delegates from socialist bodies, local Labour parties, trades councils, and unions, has often been described as filled with "wild talk about the imminence of revolution," historically it marked a turning point in the fortunes of the peace offensive.[53] In the first place, the already crystallizing differences between the social reconstructionists (those who advocated preparing the groundwork for postwar social reconstruction while espousing the case for a negotiated settlement) and the revolutionary opponents of war became more sharply defined. At Leeds and thereafter, the reconstructionists, or "social pacifists," made it clear that they would not depart from the path of constitutionalism; if they would have workers' and soldiers' councils, then these were "not intended to be subversive of military responsibilities." At the same time, some of them betrayed second thoughts about the feasibility of negotiating with Germany should it reject the Allied Socialists' war aims or seek a "patched-up peace" with revolutionary Russia.[54] Against this tendency to backslide, the left-wing rebels underwent a process of radicalization, mirrored in the writings of Tom Quelch, Walton Newbold, and Sylvia Pankhurst. Their thoughts were no longer upon conferences, resolutions, and pacifist proposals but on workers' power, heightening class consciousness, and implementing a dictatorship of the proletariat. They now constituted a revolutionary stream in the peace movement but one that was as politically and organizationally ineffectual as it was ideologically disoriented about wedding peace and revolution.[55]

Second, and most important, the antiwar campaign, sustained through the early summer of 1917, ground swiftly to a halt. The reconstructionists who had conducted it, having stood aside from the industrial troubles while persisting in an unrewarding strategy of exhortations, were in August outflanked by Labour officials in the realm of international politics. The determination of Arthur Henderson to lead Labour to the international meeting of socialists at Stockholm placed British socialists in the shadows. Lamented one rebel: "The I.L.P. section (backed by the B.S.P.), previously defiant and aggressive," had begun to combine "the wisdom of the serpent with the harmlessness of the dove" and was hardly distinguishable in the ranks of Labour.[56] Henderson's action, though it corresponded with what the social reconstructionists had been preaching, had not come about because of their persuasion. Rather, Labour and trade union officials reached the conclusion that it was absolutely essential to shore up the moderate revolutionary regime in Russia committed, as it was, to supporting the Soviets' insistence on attending the conference. Further, they might have seen participation in such a gathering as a means of heading off a more militant pacifism in Britain.[57] Labour's approval of the Stockholm meeting, moreover, did not signal, as several historians contend, its conversion to an internationalist foreign policy.[58] Nor did the war aims memorandum, which the Labour party and the TUC executives subsequently adopted, mean more than a slight shift in favor of a more equitable peace settlement. It was, as both Snowden and Fairchild recongized, a document formulated from "the British rather than the internationalist point of view" and unlikely to lay the foundations for a "people's peace."[59] Nevertheless, socialist leaders, even blossoming revolutionaries, deluded themselves into imagining that there was a "turning of the tide." In their bid for a broad Socialist-Labour unity they interpreted minor revisions in Labour's policy as proof that they had altered its mind on the most fundamental issues: "the indefinite pursuit of a war inherent with aims of imperialist capitalism, and the participation of Labour in Governments formed for the conduct of the war."[60]

Ironically, while the social reconstructionists became obsessed with examining the virtues and defects of Labour's documents on a peace settlement, sections of organized workers commenced their first and only mass agitation to halt the European conflict, an agitation that verged on revolutionary resistance to the government. In the winter of 1917-18 several factors, of which food shortages and additional manpower for the army were the most significant, combined to stoke up widespread discontent and arouse serious distrust of the government's wartime policies. The food shortages that appeared in November and were a major domestic worry by Christmas, produced waves of public unrest. By mid-January there were queues of mammoth proportions, agitated crowds stormed shopping centers, and organized workers laid down tools sporadically as a protest against the mishandling of food distrubution.[61] In the midst of this explosive atmosphere, observed with grave anxiety by local authorities, Sir Auckland Geddes introduced a new military service bill. This was the signal for an outburst of working-class anger. In the forefront, the militant engineers threatened direct action unless the government started peace negotiations: the manpower bill was to be opposed until a pledge was given that an armistice would be arranged. At Liverpool, on the Clyde, in Barrow-in-Furness, in Sheffield, and in the Midlands, Geddes's plea for calm understanding was rebuffed. In London, 10,000 engineers swarmed into an unofficial delegates' meeting in Albert Hall, determined to resist the comb-out of men from the workshops. Nor were they alone. Similar views were expressed by railwaymen and the

miners of South Lanarkshire. Even groups of less-skilled operatives—
in the Workers' Union—urged the government to follow the "Russian democrats" and negotiate with the enemy.[62]

For one brief moment, the peace offensive was raised to a new
level as antiwar consciousness fused with industrial militancy. The
reports of the National Union of Railwaymen's locals, the majority
of which rejected the government's invitation to send delegates on
a tour of the Western Front, are an excellent index of this development.[63] But by the beginning of February the tide was ebbing. Dr.
Hinton has detailed the sudden decline of the revolutionary impulse
among the engineers;[64] a careful study of the miners would probably
reveal a similar result. Yet the explanation is still shrouded in mystery.
Did the fault lie with the skilled engineers, untrustworthy vanguard-
ists because their gaze was always fastened on securing special priv-
ileges for their own craft? Was it rather because of the shop steward
militants who believed they sensed a narrow craft objective behind
their followers' outcry against the comb-out and fearing this would
antagonize other sections of Labour, chose not to lead the rank and
file? Or was there in general a deep-seated patriotism, which contained rebelliousness within the workshop as well as the community?
As J. T. Murphy claimed and Walton Newbold hinted at somewhat
earlier: "There is a great distance to travel before the war weariness
and "fed-up feeling" develops into outspoken and hostile activity."[65]

Any reply to these questions must be tentative because of the scant
information available on rank-and-file consciousness. Still, it would
seem that, leaving aside objective conditions (the relative improvement of the food situation by the end of February 1918 and the impending German offensive), the socialist leaders were chiefly responsible for the dissipation of antiwar fervor. On a theoretical level,
they had never clarified in their own minds what stages a peace
crusade would have to pass through to be effective or what it implied in terms of working-class action. Unwilling to face the fact
that a detemined popular effort to impose the negotiated-settlement
formula would at some point require mass resistance bordering on
"revolutionary defeatism," they sowed the illusion that a "peace
without victory" would be attained through a political miracle: the
belligerent powers would be enjoined to open talks because of increasing pressure, *exerted simultaneously,* by the different national

sections of the European working class. This left the antiwar elements of the working class, to the extent they had accepted this view, in a quandary. How far should they press their own militancy? *Solidarity,* the organ of syndicalism, put the dilemma quite poignantly: "A general strike in the big key industries of Europe would put an end to the war in less than a week. . . . If we could only be certain that the German workers would follow suit we should have no hesitation in calling for an immediate policy of down-tools and damn the consequences."[66] Obviously there could be no certainty, and this is perhaps why the engineers delayed their decision to initiate a strike against the manpower bill until the International Allied Socialist Conference had met at the end of February.[67] In a sense, they were waiting for a higher authority to resolve the dilemma, recognizing at the same time the overriding importance of political direction.

On a more practical level, the socialist leaders, both the "social reconstructionists" and many who stood to the left of them, either held aloof from industrial-social movements or discouraged them. At the 1918 Labour party conference, during the height of the antiwar groundswell, W. C. Anderson, reflecting NAC opinion, was horrified lest "a terrific industrial upheaval at the present moment might be dangerous from the standpoint of securing a People's Peace." For Anderson, as for MacDonald, Jowett, and others, such upheavals spelt "economic and social chaos," the antithesis of their evolutionary reconstructionist approach.[68] Even if certain ILP branches featured prominently in food demonstrations and here and there individual members had a hand in the industrial turmoil, the hostility of their leaders to militancy put a damper on these activities. By contrast, the BSP, en route to becoming the nucleus of a communist party, had dynamic shop stewards like Willie Gallagher, George Peet, and William McLaine who had begun to estimate correctly "that the Man-Power Bill and the difficulties with the food supply were bringing about a temporary revolt which was the only kind of class consciousness we had the right to look for." Or, in McLaine's words, there was "a movement of revolution from below . . . fighting industrially and politically also, forcing the Government to withdraw [or modify] political measures when the opportunity came along."[69] Yet they, too, were restrained by an executive psychologically bent on resolutions, not revolutions, an executive that felt the British were "accustomed to move much more slowly . . . than the people of some other countries" and that, incidentally, did not discuss industrial strategy with its workshop representatives but continued to reiterate the slogan of the International Socialist Conference" as the only means by which a really democratic and lasting peace can be established."[70] It is no wonder that the shop-steward militants, detecting a recession in antiwar sentiment, yielded to the deeply imbedded syndicalist philosophy of rank-and-file decision making and abdicated their own leadership responsibilities. Caught between the wavering attitude of the men in the workshops and the socialist pundits who almost consistently divorced politics from industrial action, there was no other option but resignation.[71] While it is true that the shop stewards and the more politically minded workers had reached a high pitch of antiwar consciousness, they had only done so by way of precedent—the Bolshevik revolution. Their appeal for peace by negotiations was, in fact, stimulated by that revolution and the publication of the secret treaties. As yet, however, there were no Bolsheviks in Britain to whom they could turn for further instruction.[72]

It would be unreasonable to argue that British socialists could have profoundly transformed the political situation in 1918 by harnessing the workers to a widespread campaign for a negotiated peace. The government, apparently determined not to budge from its war policies, handled the domestic unrest with remarkable firmness. The workers, if mentally ready for strike action, were organizationally unprepared to apply the kind of pressure necessary for any momentous change. But it is indicative of the socialist movement's character that its leaders, having taken no measures to "utilize the temper of the masses" for terminating the military conflict since the spring of 1917, found themselves incapable of seizing the most appropriate occasion for promoting their own objectives. Bound on the one hand by a pacifist outlook and habits of mind that did not countenance proletarian "revolt" and indisposed, on the other, "to adopt a critical attitude" because of the German offensive on the Western Front, they refrained from directly challenging the state. Instead, they chose to pursue the phantom of a reconstituted Socialist International or, as in the case of the ILP executive, to cast about for a Radical-Socialist alliance under the directorship of Lord Lansdowne.[73] This may have been part of their larger vision of reconstructing society, as well as ensuring Labour unity, through collaboration and compromise, but it inevitably undercut the crusade for an immediate peace.

NOTES

1. V. I. Lenin, *Collected Works* (Moscow, 1974), 21:315-316.

2. See its political organ, the *Labour Leader* (see, e.g., F. W. Jowett's attack on secret diplomacy, April 21, 1911) and the ILP annual conference reports from 1911 to 1913.

3. A. M. McBriar, *Fabian Socialism and English Politics, 1884-1918* (Cambridge, 1966), pp. 124-126, 135-140. Of course, there was always a strong minority among the Fabians who, as McBriar himself points out, dissented from the predominant views of the society. As for the SLP, see Walter Kendall, *The Revolutionary Movement in Britain, 1900-1921* (London, 1969), pp. 75, 111.

4. Kendall, *Revolutionary Movement*, pp. 50-61.

5. *Hansard Parliamentary Debates,* Commons, 5th series (27 July 1911), 26:1830-31. See A. J. Morris, *Radicalism Against War, 1906-1914* (London, 1972), p. 251, for an explanation of socialist vacillation on questions of peace and internationalism.

6. ILP, *Report of the Annual Conference* (Norwich, 1915), pp. 80-82; see also Ralph Miliband, *Parliamentary Socialism* (London, 1964), p. 44.

7. It is interesting to note that at the outbreak of the Great War, several ILP branches, like that of Hebden Bridge in Yorkshire, spontaneously called for a "stop-the-war" movement.

8. The term *pacifist,* as used in this essay, covers a broad spectrum of Radicals, socialists, and religious nonconformists who believed that peace was not only a practical and vital interest of the civilized world but that it was actually attainable in their time (A. J. P. Taylor in the *Trouble Makers* [London, 1957], p. 47, n. 1 defines the term in approximately the same way). During the Great War, however, the pacificists became what I later refer to as social reconstructionists—advocates of laying the foundations of peace while calling for a negotiated settlement.

9. See the translation of Kautsky's speeches in *Justice,* April 20, 1911, and June 1, 1912; cf. Zelda Kahan-Coates' criticism of the left "impossibilists" at Zimmerwald (*Call,* June 22, 1916) and Theodore Rothstein, under the pseudonym of John Bryan, on "Technicals of a Durable Peace" (*Call,* June 29, 1916). Brailsford's acceptance of Kautskyian views on imperialism are in evidence in his *War of Steel and Gold* (London, 1914).

10. *Call,* October 4, 1917.

11. ILP Papers, British Library of Political and Economic Science, No. 6 Divisional Council Minute Books of the ILP, October 10, 1912.

12. J. T. Walton Newbold Papers, Manchester University (hereafter cited as WNP: autobiographical notes).

13. This position was characteristic of most British socialists who in the pre-1914 period struggled to preserve world peace.

14. *Justice,* November 23, December 21, 1914, and ILP, *Report of the Annual*

Conference, 1913, p. 104; also George Haupt, *Socialism and the Great War* (Oxford, 1972), p. 93.

15. W. C. Anderson, *Labour Leader,* June 23, 1911. Anderson contended that a "few sections of industry refusing to aid warlike operations" would be sufficient to deter the government from acts of aggression. Besides, the partial strike was conditional on socialists in other countries taking similar action simultaneously.

16. Theodore Rothstein, "The War Crisis and Its Lesson," *Justice,* August 5, 1911.

17. Carl Brand, *British Labour's Rise to Power* (Stanford, 1941), pp. 29-34; G. D. H. Cole, *A History of the Labour Party from 1914* (London, 1948), pp. 17-22.

18. Marvin Swartz, *The Union of Democratic Control* (Oxford, 1971), pp. 29-37; also see the "Morrow of the War," UDC pamphlet, E. D. Morel Papers, British Library of Political and Economics Science; Bertrand Russell to Charles Trevelyan, October 2, 1914, in Trevelyan Papers, University of Newcastle-on-Tyne, and National Peace Council Minutes, January 6, 1915.

19. *Labour Leader,* August 13, 1914.

20. ILP Papers, City of London ILP Correspondence, circular letter to ILP membership, August 12, 1914, ILP, IIb.

21. Ibid., "Circular for High Prices on Food and Fuel," February 13, 1915, ILP, IIb, items 181-2. There is no mention of peace in ILP circulars of this kind.

22. Articles by Fenner Brockway, George Lansbury, Gerald Gould, and Clifford Allen in the *Labour Leader* and *Herald* for the early months of 1915. For a Radical's views, see A. C. Pigou's letter to the *Nation,* February 6, 1915. Two militant anti-war organizations founded at the local level were the Women's International Peace Crusade and the East London Peace Association.

23. ILP, *Report of the Annual Conference* (Norwich, 1915), pp. 88-93, 109-12. Dr. Salter's motion (originally presented as a refusal "to support any war entered into by *Capitalist* Governments," but subsequently amended to read "all governments"—emphasis added) was defeated by 121 to 120 votes.

24. WNP, autobiographical notes.

25. TUC, *Annual Report* (1915), pp. 317-30.

26. E. C. Fairchild and J. Fineberg rose to prominence in the BSP executive soon after the war broke out. They, together with H. Alexander, represented a position among British Marxists akin to that of Hasse and Kautsky in Germany.

27. *Justice,* April 29, 1915; see also Kendall, *Revolutionary Movement,* pp. 92, 97.

28. *Labour Leader,* July 15, 1915. The ILP executive, the NAC, also decided against including peace terms in its manifesto (ILP, Minutes of National Administrative Council, hereafter cited as NAC, April 16, 1915) and was severely reproached by rank-and-file elements for "trying to suppress the 'Peace Manifesto'." See ILP Papers, City of London Branch ILP, May 23, 1915; ILP II,a2.

29. ILP, *Report of the Annual Conference* (Norwich, 1915), p. 11. Initially, the NAC refused to recognize the Zimmerwald initiative (NAC minutes, July 27-28, 1915). On the other hand, the centrists in the BSP, even though they were more sympathetic to the Zimmerwaldians, continued to be critical of its demand "to investigate the faults of various socialist parties." *Call,* May 31, 1917.

31. For Jowett's explanation of why it was inappropriate for ILP parliamentarians to vote against the war credits, see *Labour Leader,* March 16, 1916.

32. War Emergency Workers National Committee Papers (Labour Party Library, Transport House), J. S. Middleton to J. R. Clynes, August 1, 1917: WNC 12/205.

33. Clifford Allen, *Labour Leader,* May 27, 1915; cf. correspondence in ibid., June 3, 1915.

34. Kendall, *Revolutionary Movement,* pp. 95-6.

35. ILP, *Report of the Annual Conference* (Newcastle-on-Tyne, 1916), pp. 82-99. It is quite likely that there were several delegates at the conference who were unhappy about passing pious resolutions (see Neil Maclean's speech on p. 88) but nonetheless supported this one. In any event, the Bermondsey resolution, a symbolic gesture of ultra opposition to war, was meaningless in terms of hastening the peace, and it undoubtedly deluded many of the rank and file into believing that they had fulfilled their socialist commitments.

36. See speeches of Lords Courtney and Loreburn, *Hansard Parliamentary Debates,* Lords, 5th series, (November 15, 1915), 20:1450-9, 1558-62, and Philip Snowden in his defense of the concept of "peace without victory." Ibid., Commons, 5th series, (February 23, 1916), 80:715-20; see also C. R. Buxton, "Why Not Find Out," *The U.D.C.,* November 1915.

37. See the "Minutes of a Special Meeting to Consider . . .Petition to His Majesty's Government to Seek Peace Negotiations," April 28, 1916, in the Norman Angell Papers, Ball State University, AP, C-86-9.

38. *Call,* June 8, 1916.

39. C. R. Buxton Papers (I am indebted to the Buxton family for permitting me to inspect these papers), C. R. Buxton to Reginald McKenna, H. W. Massingham, W. Runciman et al., October 9, 1916.

40. Figures on the number of signatories to the Peace Memorial are cited in the *Labour Leader,* October 12, 1916, and in other journals. The final count was over a million. As for peace sentiment in trade unions, there are no precise estimates; but a member of the National Union of General Workers contended that at the Labour Party Conference in January 1917 at least a third of his union was opposed to the "fight to the finish" stand of its executive while 60,000 engineers also dissented from the official position of the Amalgamated Society of Engineers. See ibid., February 1, 1917.

41. Ibid., May 10, 1917; *Call,* May 10, 1917.

42. C. R. Buxton Papers, C. R. Buxton to Dorothy Buxton, June 8, 1917.

43. J. T. Murphy, *New Horizons* (London, 1942), p. 44. In *Preparing for Power* Murphy mentions antiwar propaganda being disseminated by shop stewards during the Sheffield strike, but it is unclear to what extent and in what manner. J. T. Murphy, *Preparing for Power,* (London, 1934), p. 132. An inspection of government documents in the Public Record Office and the Beveridge Papers (British Library of Political and Economic Science) disclosed nothing on antiwar activity during these strikes.

44. The War Emergency Workers National Committee Papers (WNC 9-13) provide an abundance of correspondence on the protest movement over food prices, yet

none of the correspondents ever urged that the peace slogan should be raised as the solution to inflation and intolerable conditons.

45. *Call,* September 28, 1917.

46. The shop stewards, in revolt against trade union officialdom and strongly influenced by James Connoly's vision of the industrial republic, had little faith in politics (see Kendall, *Revolutionary Movements,* pp. 161-61). John Maclean, very much aware of this, ridiculed the idea of placing industrial unity on a higher level than socialist unity (*Call,* July 19, 1917).

47. E. D. Morel, "Editorial," *The U.D.C.* (December 1916); C. R. Buxton, "Peace This Winter," *The U.D.C.* (September 1916); J. A. Hobson, "The Open Door," *The U.D.C.* (December 1916); C. R. Buxton, "The Situation" (typewritten manuscript), September 16, 1916, in Buxton Papers.

48. See, for example, the speech by J. R. MacDonald at Coventry, cited in *Labour Leader,* February 1, 1917; see also Colin Cross, *Philip Snowden* (London, 1966), p. 158.

49. *Call,* June 29, 1916 (emphasis added). Cf. statement on "British Socialist Party and Allied War Aims" (*Call,* February 25, 1917). Apparently, BSP leaders felt it was sufficient for the workers to demand peace or express their will for peace and the government would automatically yield to their wishes.

50. Although absolute conscientious objection was considered by many socialists as the highest expression of opposition to the military state, it actually led them from the main theater of political struggle to the path of moralistic martyrdom. See Walton Newbold's criticism of this trend. WNP: "autobiographical notes."

51. Philip Snowden, "Review of the Week," *Labour Leader,* May 17, 1917; see also George Lansbury in *Herald,* May 27, 1916.

52. Sylvia Pankhurst, "A Conscientious Objectors' Conference," *Women's Dreadnought,* April 21, 1917; and BSP, *Report of the Annual Conference* (Manchester, 1917), p. 9.

53. D. Lloyd George, *War Memoirs* (London, 1938), p. 1154; see also Cole, *History,* p. 33, and James Hinton, *The First Shop Stewards' Movement* (London, 1973), p. 239.

54. *Herald,* June 9, 1917. On the equivocation of Fred Jowett and Robert Smillie concerning negotiations with Germany, see *Women's Dreadnought,* June 23, 1917, and *Call,* August 23, 1917.

55. The *Call* is replete with articles by Quelch and Newbold on such subjects as workers' power, revolution, and dictatorship of the proletariat from May to September 1917. But it is noteworthy that Newbold at this time had become schizoid about working for peace and revolution simultaneously (ibid., May 3, 1917).

56. Cedar Paul, "The Turning of the Tide," *Workers' Dreadnought* (previously *Women's Dreadnought*) (August 18, 1917).

57. J. M. Winter, *Socialism and the Challenge of War* (London, 1974), pp. 253-58. The Labour party executive had in any event made it amply clear that it would attend the Stockholm conference only on a consultative basis. Even then the executive felt that there had to be agreement among the Allied Socialists before setting out for such a conference. See Labour Party, Minutes of the Executive Committee (Transport House), August 9, 14, September 6, 1917.

58. Ibid., pp. 256-59; see also Swartz, *Union,* pp. 166-69.

59. Snowden, "Review of the Week," *Labour Leader,* January 3, 1918; see also Fairchild, "The Labour Party and a People's Peace," *Call,* December 28, 1917.

60. See "The Labour Party Conference" in *Call,* January 31, 1918.

61. Sir William Beveridge, *British Food Control* (London, 1928), pp. 195-205. More detailed accounts can be found in the daily press (*Times, Manchester Guardian, Daily Despatch,* and so forth).

62. *Herald,* February 2, March 2, 1918; *Co-operative News,* February 2, 1918; *Labour Leader,* January 24, February 7, 1918; *Workers' Dreadnought,* January 12, 1918.

63. See Minutes and Proceedings of the National Union of Railwaymen, Annual General Meeting, June 17-21, 1918, p. 15 and the branch reports of the NUR in the *Railway Review* for January-February 1918.

64. Hinton, *First Shop Stewards' Movement,* pp. 261-67.

65. Ibid., pp. 262-63. Hinton is convinced that the failure of the antiwar struggle stemmed from the last-minute loss of confidence of the skilled engineers who abandoned the general attack on the military service bill and reverted to the parochial tactics of protecting the ASE men. The left-wing newspapers, *Call* and the *Herald,* convey a different impression. Walton Newbold's explanation for the antipacifist sentiments in the South Wales' coal mines is to be found in *Plebs* 9, no. 17 (December 1917):247.

66. *Solidarity,* February 1918 (emphasis added.)

67. *Call,* February 14, 1918. The leader writer of *Call,* in chiding the engineers for delaying their decision to strike until the Allied Socialist Conference had met, apparently forgot they were abiding by the strategy laid down by socialist leaders.

68. Labour Party, *Report of the Annual Conference* (Nottingham, 1918), p. 129; W. C. Anderson, "A Letter to the Editor," *Nation,* December 8, 1917.

69. BSP, *Report of the 7th Annual Conference* (Leeds, 1918), pp. 18, 21.

70. Ibid., p. 6. On the BSP's neglect to offer guidance to the shop stewards, see Murphy, *Preparing for Power,* p. 134.

71. ILP, *Report of the Annual Conference* (Newcastle, 1916). P. J. Dollan's reply to a delegate's stress on industrial action for ending the war—"until the workers got control of the political machinery of this country they could not prevent war"—typifies the artificial separation that many British socialists made between politics and economic power. Ibid., pp. 88-89.

72. Doubtless there were several revolutionary socialists, especially in the BSP, who were gravitating toward the Bolshevik position, but they formed no coherent group. John Maclean has frequently been cited as identified with the Leninist advocacy of "revolutionary defeatism." Yet, despite his relentless efforts to educate Scottish workers, Maclean failed to sway the BSP leadership in arguing the Leninist approach; nor did he present theoretical formulations to counter the centrist influence in his party.

ILP, *Report of the Annual Conference* (Leeds, 1918), p. 44. The proposal for such an alliance, uttered by Snowden and other members of the executive, evoked criticism from many socialists to the left of the NAC. It portended, in their eyes, a withdrawal from the concept of socialist unity.

10

The American Peace Movement and the State Department in the Era of Locarno

CHARLES DeBENEDETTI

Between the conclusion of the Locarno treaties in December 1925 and the ratification of the Kellogg-Briand Pact in July 1929, the United States enjoyed a position of international preeminence that great powers seldom know. Militarily, no threat existed to American security. Economically, American business enterprise overseas sped ahead with breathtaking momentum, expanding by 1929 to a level two and one-half times what it had been a decade earlier. Politically, relations among the Great Powers were unusually harmonious. Or at least the Locarno treaties made them seem so. When Britain and Italy underwrote at that idyllic Swiss village the mutual pledges of nonaggression and arbitration already concluded among France, Belgium, and Germany, they not only eased France's rancorous fears of renewed German aggression but they also helped to isolate the Soviet Union by drawing Germany's friendly attentions toward the West. On both counts Washington was pleased.

Yet the American government was also highly sensitive to the tensions and problems that remained impervious to the glow of Locarno. Some, like the question of war debts and reparations and Italian fascism, stemmed directly from the Great War and its aftermath. Others, like the revolutions in Mexico and China and the recurring instability in Latin America and the Near East, reflected long-term changes in the relationship between Western colonialism

and the underdeveloped world. Still others, such as the future direction of a dynamic Germany, the prospects for arms control agreements, and the growing strain of Anglo-American economic competition, signaled major alterations in the constellation of Great
Powers. For all these problems the U.S. government felt deep concern and interest. And in facing them it confronted through its
State Department an active new front of citizen peace workers,
dedicated groups of men and women who had learned during the
world war that peace was too important to be left to politicians.

The relationship between the State Department and the peace movement during the Locarno years moved along a continuum that stretched
from easy cooperation to undisguised contempt. It all depended on
which peace workers were pressuring for what kind of peace. Department leaders worked comfortably with Republican foreign policy
elders like Elihu Root and Charles Evans Hughes, whose conservative legalist conception of peace dominated the work of the Carnegie
Endowment for International Peace, the American Society of International Law, and the American Peace Society. But with others,
they felt less easy. They maintained a polite distance from liberal
internationalists in the Foreign Policy Association and the League
of Nations Non-Partisan Association, which stood for American
accession to the League of Nations and fuller U.S. cooperation in
the international organization of peace. And they discretely ignored
the many church groups, women's organizations, and pacifist cadres
that pressed for the demilitarization and "Christianization" of
American foreign policy.

In practice, the relationship between the State Department and
American peace seekers played itself out through a dynamic that
was at once personal, institutional, and functional. Personally,
State Department officers felt little sympathy with the reform-
minded activism of most peace workers, who acted out of a creed
of liberal humanism that had little in common with Coolidge Re-
publicanism. Furthermore, the pride felt by department leaders in
their institutional professionalism induced them to comprehend
peace as the expression of national power and not—as peace leaders
would have it—as an end in itself. If the war had shown that peace
was too fragile to be left to the politicians, the diplomatists maintained, it proved equally that peace was too volatile to be left to the

people. Peace was a job for professionals. Institutionally, peace was their province.

Functionally, State Department policy makers realized that their premises were quite alien to the aspirations of the country's peace leaders. Department officers well knew that it was their responsibility to superintend the unilateral defense of American material interests overseas for the sake of prosperity and social stability both at home and abroad: peace prevailed with the extension of the American will. Top activists in the American peace movement understandably saw things otherwise. Although divided by several programmatic differences, they generally agreed that their purpose was to move the American people into cooperative action with peoples abroad in the multilateral realization of a world order based on justice and security under the auspices of international and transnational agencies. The State Department could be helpful, hostile, or irrelevant in this endeavor. They hoped that it would be helpful.

Usually, however, the State Department chose to be irrelevant. During the late 1920s, peace workers used traditional techniques of pamphleteering, lobbying, and petitioning to stimulate impressive levels of public support for broader arbitration treaties, fuller disarmament, and the revision of American neutrality in line with the collective work of the League of Nations. Yet the State Department remained powerfully resistant to these expressions of popular pressure and remained committed to its official policy preferences. The department's resilient but unyielding posture drew form from several sources, but it gained operating power mainly as those personal, institutional, and functional factors intersected at two working points: the political cautiousness of the cantankerous secretary of state, Frank B. Kellogg, and the conservative commitment among State Department career officers to the professionalization of American diplomacy.

Kellogg's caution was by far the more significant. A wealthy St. Paul lawyer with Wall Street connections, the sixty-eight-year-old Kellogg was inaugurated secretary of state in March 1925, after serving one undistinguished term (1916-22) as U.S. senator from Minnesota and a three-year term as ambassador to Great Britain. His sharp temper and profanity were the subjects of wide comment. His talents were not. The influential Senator William E. Borah, chairman of the Senate Foreign Relations Committee, dismissed him as a "boob!" Others thought he was "a time-server," a gnarled figurehead installed by President Coolidge to bridge the tense division within the GOP between conservative eastern internationalists and progressive western isolationists.[1]

Certainly Kellogg had no desire to aggravate the party's foreign policy division. Although he consistently looked to eastern leaders like Root and Hughes for policy direction, he deferred with equal obeisance to Idaho's Senator Borah and other western isolationists. The frail secretary of state stood for no new ideas. He proposed no fresh policy initiatives. Indeed, he seemed desperately anxious not to disturb the placid presidency of Calvin Coolidge, the last president within memory to confess that "there were some times when I wondered what I was going to do next."[2]

The effect of Kellogg's caution in weakening the impact of peace reformers in Washington was aggravated by the need felt in the 1920s by some of the nation's most highly regarded career diplomats for the professionalization of American diplomatic practices. Overseas this concern was espoused by such effective diplomatists as Joseph Grew, Hugh Gibson, and Lewis Einstein. In Washington it was personified in William R. Castle, Jr.[3]

Brusque and acerbic, Castle was a man of independent wealth and Ivy-League training who aimed to refine the State Department into an elite center of informed policy making. Heir to a Hawaiian shipping and planting fortune, the former Harvard College administrator joined the department in 1921 at the age of forty-three as director of the prestigious Division of Western European Affairs. Six years later he rose during a controversial departmental shakeup to the position of assistant secretary, a post that he retained until Franklin Roosevelt's accession to power in 1933.

Almost from the start of his tenure at State, Castle became absorbed in the complex intragovernmental politicking that resulted by 1924 in the Foreign Service Act. Known more popularly by its progenitor, Massachusetts Congressman John Jacob Rogers, the Foreign Service Act joined the diplomatic and consular services together for the first time in American history in a new Foreign Service that through competitive examinations, higher pay scales, and better retirement benefits was designed to attract a broader

cross-section of the nation's population into overseas service. With
the other brahmin careermen in the department, Castle feared that
the egalitarian implications of the Rogers Act would militate against
the development of a more professional American diplomacy. Yet
neither they nor he knew how to resist those egalitarian implications
except by flaunting their superior professional credentials.

From this concern, Castle led the attempt to convert the department into a more businesslike operation. He established more orderly
and efficient lines of administrative authority. He cooperated closely
with Secretary of Commerce Herbert Hoover's efforts to expand
governmental support for American business enterprise overseas.
And he insisted upon less partisan and more objective analyses of
developments abroad. In theory, the concern shared by Castle and
other department careermen for professionalization represented a
sensible attempt to convert State from its clumsy nineteenth-century
practices into a more efficient instrument for confronting the problems of modern industrial interdependence. In practice, however, the
drive for professionalization operated under conservative premises
that worked almost as well as Kellogg's caution in blunting the influence of peace activists in postwar Washington.

Castle seldom concealed those conservative premises. Blasting the
"sickly internationalism" of peace sentimentalists, he charged that
the peace movement incorrectly emphasized the settlement of disputes that might lead to war, while State Department professionals
rightly sought to quash the root causes of those disputes. "There,"
Castle held, "is where diplomacy comes in." Extolling the virtues
of a professional foreign service of peace-minded career officers,
he insisted that "earnest and energetic support of the President in
building up such a foreign service, the main purpose of which is to
prevent disputes rather than compose disputes, will do more for
world peace than membership in all the outlawry of war and arbitration leagues in the country." Diplomats constituted "truly an advance guard of peace," Castle declaimed. They moved with the
Republican State Department to build "no exposition peace palace
of stucco and electric lights, but a permanent granite monument to
the ideals of America." Anything but ostentatious, the new diplomacy was stolidly commonsensical and briskly businesslike.[4]

Interacting with Kellogg's caution, the conservative assumptions
of the professionalizing diplomatic corps led State Department leaders

to perceive themselves in the 1920s as aloof middlemen in the country's ongoing domestic struggle between the militant right and organzed peace reformers. Profound and bitter, that struggle first arose during the 1916 preparedness controversy, persisted through the bloody implementation of wartime patriotism, and continued into the postwar red scare. In the 1920s, the struggle took on new form as the right gained fresh power through the formation of the American Legion and the reinvigoration of the Ku Klux Klan and the Daughters of the American Revolution. Together these groups made no secret of their dedication to native ways, their contempt for social progressives, and their commitment to the fuller militarization of a unilateral foreign policy.

Standing implacably for property and order, rightists lashed out with particular vehemence at pacifists and progressives who challenged the antilibertarian dangers of a more militarized society and who spoke sympathetically of the Soviet experiment. Shoved to the defensive, peace seekers meanwhile pleaded for a fuller national accounting to international institutions and agencies, even as they battled in defense of First Amendment freedoms to gain access to schools and churches closed to them by local right-wing elements.[5] And all the while the State Department pretended to steer a middle course. It chastized "realists" on the right for exaggerating fears that might inhibit the administration's work for "moderate preparedness." And it disparaged the "muddled thinking" of peace workers who believed that peace could exist without the assertion of American influence.[6]

Posing as the honest broker of a commonsensical national policy, the State Department cooperated most consistently with those peace leaders connected with Elihu Root and Charles Evans Hughes in the Carnegie Endowment for International Peace, the American Society of International Law, and the American Peace Society. Upholding the tenets of order through law, these conservative legalists envisioned peace as the end result of a long evolutionary process that occurred as the ruling elites of the advanced industrial states agreed to respect the judgments of an international judicial system in resolving their disputes.

Socially, conservative legalists represented a composite of the corporate boardrooms and legal professions of the metropolitan East. Politically, they were mostly old-guard Republicans who aimed to extend the work of the prewar Hague system, their lasting achievement in the organization of peace. Temperamentally, they expressed great fear over the expansion of mass democracy in the wake of the Great War. Determined to protect the State Department as a policymaking preserve free from the reach of an untutored democracy, conservative legalists promised to bring peace through the gradual internationalization of that same courtroom justice by which American lawyers had organized the country's dynamic social order. Peace inched forward through juridical processes, and courts were its main defense.

Linked by these common sentiments, the State Department and conservative legalists shared mutually satisfying working arrangements. Kellogg not only looked dutifully to Root and Hughes for guidance on major policy questions. He also deployed them and their chief lieutenants as top-echelon troubleshooters. Hughes served as head of the American delegation to the Havana Conference of 1928, where he made a stirring defense of the administration's intervention in Nicaragua and its querulous policy toward Mexico. Root journeyed to Europe in 1929 at the age of eighty-four in an attempt to unsnarl the tangled World Court question, while his aide, James Brown Scott, worked for the department between 1923 and 1928 on inter-American legal questions within the Pan-American Union.[7]

Conservative legalist peace organizations returned State's attention with deep praise. The venerable American Peace Society (APS), the parent organization of the peace movement in America, hailed the department as "our greatest peace society." "It deals directly, continually, and almost always effectively with definite international situations," APS leaders exclaimed; and its success was "directly attributable to the wisdom with which it handles realities."[8] Conservative peace leaders shared State's resentment of more ambitious peace seekers. All too many American peace workers, one APS officer complained, were nothing more than "un-American propagandists" who refused to see that peace would most surely be a reality when others emulated America's juridical achievements.[9]

The Carnegie Endowment for International Peace (CEIP) and the American Society of International Law were equally aware of their responsibility to seek peace by assisting the State Department. Both provided State with detailed studies of international legal practices and opportunities. Both organized appreciative audiences for Washington policy pronouncements. And both maintained a ready reservoir of manpower talent for departmental needs. Early in 1925, for instance, CEIP trustee Robert E. Olds, a member of the influential New York law firm of Sullivan and Cromwell and Kellogg's former law partner, quietly gravitated into assistant secretary of state in Kellogg's new regime. Another CEIP trustee professed embarrassment over the ease with which Olds slipped from peace leadership into the government. But former endowment president Root was unmoved: "I don't know why the relations between the State Department and the Carnegie Endowment should be embarrassing," he said curtly. "The Endowment has been almost a division of the State Department, working in harmony constantly. I don't see any reason for embarrassment."[10]

Relations between the department and advocates of American attachment to the League of Nations were more complicated, mostly because of State's confusion over the internationalists' political influence and power. And there was good reason for that confusion. Organized in voluntary organizations like the Foreign Policy Association and the League of Nations Non-Partisan Association, pro-League activists were able to generate much noise but little real power in the Republican 1920s. Some were veteran Republican stalwarts like the New York lawyer (and former attorney-general in the Taft administration) George Wickersham. But more were independents like the Columbia historian and CEIP officer James T. Shotwell and the Harvard law professor Manley O. Hudson. Most were acknowledged Wilsonian Democrats—former Supreme Court Justice John Hessin Clarke, the Cleveland attorney and former War Department secretary Newton D. Baker, and New York lawyers Raymond B. Fosdick and Norman Davis, who together maintained a base in, but not control of, the postwar Democratic party. Lacking solid party support, pro-League leaders were incapable of building a national political constituency in the 1920s. Yet they managed to appear through their reputation, connections, and commitment as the foreign policy arm of the Democratic government-in-exile.

Certainly Kellogg's State Department treated them in this way. Though opposed to membership in the League, the department joined internationalists in seeking American accession to the World Court, despite the opposition of western Republican isolationists. Kellogg also drafted pro-League leaders for specific diplomatic as-

signments. In 1925 he named Wickersham to head the American
delegation to a League-affiliated commission on the codification
of international law. Early the next year, he asked Shotwell to head
an advisory group that would assist Allen Dulles, who was known
(with his brother John Foster) to harbor pro-League sympathies,
in his work as head of theAmerican delegation to the League Pre-
paratory Commission for a world disarmament conference. In addition, Kellogg tolerated an extraordinary amount of private diplomacy
that pro-League Americans practiced overseas. Periodically, however, he chafed at their meddlesomeness and yearned for "the auto-
cratic power to increase passport fees on the thousands of these
Americans who go over to tell Europe what to do."[11]

Impatience was far more typical of Kellogg's attitude toward the
feminist, church, and pacifist organizations that pressed the department for more cooperative policies overseas. Along with State's
professional diplomatic corps, Kellogg felt the antiwar activism of
these largely religious peace seekers to be emotional at best and
traitorous at worst. He and Castle consistently condemned the
political fatuity of members of the Women's International League
for Peace and Freedom, the Federal Council of Churches of Christ
in America, the National Council for Prevention of War, and the
Fellowship of Reconciliation, all of which worked for disarmament
and the cooperative realization of peace through social justice. Department leaders scorned the guiding ideals of peace reformers and
bristled at the unusually effective opposition that the reformers
raised in the early winter of 1927 against Washington's intervention in Nicaragua and its menacing attitude toward Mexico. Stung
by the political effectiveness of the peace resistance, Kellogg stepped
back from a confrontation with the Mexican government, com-
plaining of "these societies which are like blowholes for whales"
and "*never* in favor of their own country."[12]

This confrontation over Latin American policy strengthened
department leaders in their conviction that most peace societies
existed to subvert the policies of the American government. One
unidentified special agent advised Kellogg's secretary, William Beck,
of "the fact that all radicals at this time support Peace Societies
because by doing so they help to cripple the U.S." Castle in the meantime labeled the pacifists Jane Addams, Oswald Garrison Villard,
and their colleagues in the American Civil Liberties Union as "con-

stitutional troublemakers." Out of this concern, Castle also ordered that the vocal antiwar activist, Brent Dow Allison, be placed under surveillance during a European trip because he was connected with "the International Youth Movement in its less attractive phases and is a man of pretty bad reputation, being mixed up in all sorts of radical activities."[13] Secretary Kellogg also took a leading role in denying visas to radical European republicans like the Countess Karolyi and hampering the attempts by the revolutionary pacifist, Rosika Schwimmer, to gain naturalized citizenship. One newspaper felt that it required uniquely "Kelloggical" thinking to bar foreign radical republicans from the United States on the grounds that they would subvert good republican Americans.[14] But the "know-nothing" implications of his policies did not trouble Kellogg. Tacitly but effectively, he and the department provided support in the late 1920s to conservative groups that attacked pacifists and radical clerics who spoke boldly of peace as a spiritual force that transcended American power.

Progressive peace seekers lashed back at State's hostility with sharp criticism. The irrepressible Oswald Garrison Villard, the pacifist editor of *The Nation,* maintained that "blundering" was the chief feature of Kellogg's diplomacy. *The New Republic* described the doddering Minnesotan as a spineless politician who invariably deferred to the advice of bellicose department officials. The Reverend John Haynes Holmes, a reform leader who was pastor of the Community Church of New York and one of Gandhi's principal disciples in America, dismissed Kellogg as "the worst secretary of state that this country has ever had."[15]

Yet the reformers' criticisms no more altered the substance of Republican diplomacy than did their petitions and prayers. Partly their weakness resulted from their lack of raw political power, the one attribute that department officials most sincerely respected. Even more, the progressives' struggle to realize their peace ambitions through the State Department was hampered by their own nationalist sentiments. Like their adversaries in official Washington, progressive peace leaders felt sure that America was "the key to world peace" as "the one nation able to prevent another world war."[16] Peace would prevail when the American people awakened to the need to increase their moral hegemony. In a related way, peace reformers were weakened in their relations with the State

Department because of their paradoxical determination to establish an alternative world order both through and beyond the American political order. They certainly wanted to help Washington in its conservative desire to "stabilize the world," but they envisioned that stability in an alternative world order that secured peace through justice, not gunbarrels.[17] Perversely, they sought to establish through the State Department a supranational order that would effectively displace the department and the condition of order that it existed to maintain.

State Department leaders knew better than to believe that their own conception of peace coincided with that of progressive peace seekers. The peace that official America sought was a "voluntary peace" that drew nations individually to stand by a legal order that statesmen chose freely to respect out of a sense of national honor. It was a peace shaped by shared economic well-being and national self-respect and shorn of political commitments, military obligations, and formal legal constraints. As William Borah expressed it in words approved by the administration, "The highest hope of a world governed by law instead of by force is a strong, free, independent, untrammeled, uncontracted America."[18] Out of this vision, department leaders rejected not only formal ties with the League of Nations and other entangling connections in European politics but also resisted proposals for an international inspection of disarmament agreements and international checks upon the world's arms traffic, to which the United States was a most active contributor. Washington wanted in no way to be constrained in its unencumbered pursuit of the American national interest, for through that would come peace.

The crowning irony of the department's commitment to peace through unilateral action was that it produced an official concern for peace that was much vaguer than the "muddled thinking" that it attributed to citizen peace activists. Postwar peace workers advanced a great number of prescriptions for peace, but basically their proposals were precise: the League of Nations, the World Court, a third Hague Conference, continuing disarmament, renunciation by churches and schools of war, and individual resistance to war. Peace seekers might have been excessively sanguine as to the popular American interest in peace, yet they never failed to demonstrate their determination to construct alternative structures through which peaceful political processes could be maintained in an on-going manner.

The State Department was much fuzzier in its description of how peace was to be realized in those places where American power could not be made manifest. Castle spoke in one confusing breath of how peace would come through "the growth of character," a spreading willingness "to let others live their own lives as they see fit so long as their choice does not interfere with the happiness of the rest of the world," and "a consistent and unselfish support of national rights." Kellogg promised that peace would appear through the glacial development of a common will to peace. President Coolidge characteristically thought that it would come through "hard work and self-denial."[19]

Significantly, State Department officials were much more enthusiastic than peace leaders were with the peace achievement most usually associated with the Coolidge administration—the Kellogg-Briand Pact of 1928. In terms shaped by Kellogg, sixty-two nations pledged not to use war as an instrument of national policy and to seek only pacific means in resolving their disputes. Kellogg fondled the pact as his one piece of "personal glory," and anxiously hoped that it would bring him the Nobel Prize, as it did in 1929. Castle believed that the treaty was a "master stroke" that helped the United States to take the lead in the peace cause without entrapment in European politics. Coolidge praised the pact as the crown jewel in the Republican foreign policy tiara of "preparation, [arms] limitation, and renunciation."[20]

American peace workers were hardly as impressed. Except for a handful who dreamed that the pact would begin to end war through its outlawry, most peace activists treated the document as a diversion from more pressing issues. Women and church organizations argued that the pact disguised the administration's failure to effect necessary naval disarmament. Pro-League supporters saw it as a distraction from their attempts to tie the nation more closely to Geneva through the revision of American neutrality in the League's favor. Pacifists viewed it as a cloak over Kellogg's continuing intervention in Nicaragua, where he was busily trying "to run an election" while organizing governments against war.[21] As Dorothy Detzer of the Women's International League for Peace and Freedom summarized sentiment among serious peace seekers, it was "almost

impossible for the Peace Movement to go on with great and wide
enthusiasm when Kellogg continues his policy in Nicaragua and
says that it [the pact] should not at all interfere with a big Navy. I
think we should force him on this, but it is awfully hard to get people
to accept his sincerity."[22]

It actually mattered little to Kellogg and the State Department
whether peace reformers took their diplomatic triumphs seriously,
for they knew the difference between political theory and official
practice in democratic America. In theory the object of popular
pressures, department leaders well knew that it was they who decided
to which pressures they would accede and which they would resist.[23]
They consequently responded to the demands of peace leaders in
several ways, ranging from the gravest respect for Elihu Root to
the plainest contempt for Brent Dow Alllison. Peace leaders, conversely, sought to move the department with whatever levers they
found effective, ranging from appeals to the White House and the
Congress to attempts to mobilize public opinion in their own behalf.
But they never could be more than voluntary citizen appellants, a
fact that was seldom overlooked at State. Flowing from that mixture of personal, institutional, and functional factors, the relationship between the two therefore played itself out according to the
very asymmetry of purposes and the very imbalance of political
power that existed between them.

State Department officials worked to apply America's massive
power to preserve world conditions essentially as they were in those
most satisfying of times. And that they called peace. Contrarily,
peace workers sought to stir and organize concerned citizens into
moving official Washington toward the realization of a more just and
adaptable world order that could absorb inevitable international
change without collapsing into new war and violence. Put another
way, the State Department wanted in the era of Locarno to keep the
peace. Peace seekers aimed to make it. With the conflict at this basic
level, there was little doubt in the American 1920s as to which force
was to triumph. But that is no reason to stop reflecting on what
might have been.

What might have happened instead was the advance of the movement for international reform. Locarno offered American diplomatists their best modern opportunity to build a working peace. Yet
government professionals not only failed to build peace; they even

proved incapable of preventing new war. Grotesquely, however, the diplomatists succeeded in one thing in the 1930s: they managed to shift the blame for their failures to the very peace activists who protested their blunderings. The consequences were critical. Confused by the twin threats of Hitlerism and communism, U.S. policy shapers completely mishandled the diplomatic crises of the 1930s, gave way to military strategists during World War II, and then used diplomacy's prewar failures throughout the Cold War to justify the armed prosecution of unilateral national security policies devoid of international constraints. American diplomatists devoted most of the half-century after Locarno to *waging* peace. They dismissed internationalists as naive and pacifists as utopian. Anticipating struggle, they organized a national security apparatus designed to contain international change through Great Power deterrence and counterrevolutionary violence. They excelled—at least until the late 1960s—in managing conflict. But they could not and cannot make peace break out. For that work we might reconsider the forgotten alternative of international reform.

NOTES

1. Robert James Maddox, *William E. Borah and American Foreign Policy* (Baton Rouge, 1969), 179 n. 81; Raymond Fosdick to Arthur Bullard, January 29, 1925, Raymond B. Fosdick Papers, Princeton University.

2. Transcript of interview with Claude Feuss, 78, Oral History Research Office, Columbia University.

3. Waldo H. Heinrichs, Jr., *American Ambassador: Joseph C. Grew and the Development of the United States Diplomatic Tradition* (Boston, 1966), 95-108; Heinrichs, "Bureaucracy and Professionalism in the Development of American Career Diplomacy," in John Braeman et al., eds., *Twentieth-Century American Foreign Policy* (Columbus, 1971), 167-171; Jerry Israel, "A Diplomatic Machine: Scientific Management in the Department of State, 1906-1924," in Israel, ed., *Building the Organizational Society: Essays on Associational Activities in Modern America* (New York, 1972), 187-88, 192, and Robert D. Schulzinger, *The Making of the Diplomatic Mind: The Training, Outlook, and Style of United States Foreign Service Officers, 1908-1931* (Middletown, Conn., 1975), 4-11.

4. Transcripts of Castle speeches in California, September 29, October 31, 1925, box 18, William R. Castle, Jr., Papers, Herbert Hoover Presidential Library, West Branch, Iowa. For an excellent analysis of the self-styled realism of the professionalizing diplomatic corps, see Schulzinger, *Making of the Diplomatic Mind,* 8-11, 90-100 passim.

5. J. Stanley Lemons, *The Woman Citizen: Social Feminism in the 1920's* (Urbana, 1973), 210-11, 225; Paul L. Murphy, *The Meaning of Freedom of Speech: First Amendment Freedoms from Wilson to FDR* (Westport, Conn., 1972), 198-200.

6. Castle's speeches, quoted in *New York Times,* January 16, February 3, 1928.

7. George Finch, "History of the Carnegie Endowment for International Peace, 1910-1946," 1:295-97, James Shotwell Library, Carnegie Endowment for International Peace, New York.

8. "Our Country's Greatest Peace Society," *The Advocate of Peace Through Justice* 90, no. 2 (February 1928):78, 80.

9. Lacey Zapf to Anna Garlin Spencer, November 11, 1927, box 1, Anna Garlin Spencer Papers, Swarthmore College Peace Collection.

10. Minutes of the board of trustees meeting, December 5, 1925, p. 61, #1244, Records of the Carnegie Endowment for International Peace, Butler Library, Columbia University.

11. Kellogg to Hugh Gibson, November 2, 1926, box 17, Frank B. Kellogg Papers, Minnesota State Historical Society, St. Paul.

12. Kellogg to William Hard, August 17, 1927, William Hard Papers, in the possession of Eleanor Hard Lake, New Canaan, Conn.

13. N.E.B. to William Beck, October 27, 1927, box 27, Kellogg Papers; Castle to Alanson Houghton, December 2, 1925, box 2, Castle Papers; Castle to Sheldon Whitehouse, August 10, 1927, box 3, Castle Papers.

14. Editorial clipping from *Cincinnati Post,* November 13, 1925, Kellogg Scrapbooks, Kellogg Papers.

15. "Kellogg Must Go," *The Nation* 124, no. 3217 (March 2, 1927):224; "Watch the State Department," *The New Republic* 50, no. 640 (March 9, 1927):60; *Unity* 98, no. 21 (January 24, 1927):323.

16. Frederick Libby, "The American Peace Movement—An Interpretation," National Council for Prevention of War *News Bulletin* 7, no. 6 (June 1, 1928):3; and Libby, "Why an American Peace Movement?" ibid., no. 7 (July 1, 1928):1.

17. Libby, "Why an American Peace Movement?" 1.

18. David Jayne Hill, "The Multilateral Treaty for the Renunciation of War," *American Journal of International Law* 22, no. 4 (October 1928):825. Borah quoted in *Washington Herald,* April 5, 1925, reel 1, microfilm copy of William E. Borah Scrapbooks, Manuscript Division, Library of Congress.

19. Castle in *New York Times,* January 15, 1928; Kellogg memorandum in David Bryn-Jones, *Frank B. Kellogg: A Biography* (New York 1937), 239; Coolidge's message to the Congress, December 3, 1924, *Papers Relating to the Foreign Relations of the United States, 1924* (Washington, D.C., 1939), 1:xx.

20. Castle to Hugh Gibson, April 17, 1928, box 1, Castle Papers; Castle to David Reed, December 19, 1928, box 3, Castle Papers; *New York Times,* November 12, 1928. Cf. Schulzinger, *Making of the Diplomatic Mind,* 139.

21. Kellogg to Alanson Houghton, April 14, 1928, box 28, Kellogg Papers.

22. Detzer to Emily Greene Balch, January 23, 1928, box 5, Records of the Women's International League for Peace and Freedom, U.S. Section, Swarthmore College Peace Collection.

23. Cf. Dexter Perkins, "The Department of State and American Public Opinion," in Gordon A. Craig and Felix Gilbert, eds., *The Diplomats 1919-1939* (New York, 1965), 1:282-83, 308.

11

"Peace in Our Time": The Personal Diplomacy of Lord Allen of Hurtwood, 1933-38

THOMAS C. KENNEDY

In January 1935 Sir Eric Phipps, the British ambassador in Berlin, wrote to Sir Robert Vansittart, permanent head of the Foreign Office, noting

that one of the odd features of a very odd situation is the anxiety of Hitler's political opponents in all countries to interview and negotiate with him. . . . The more German pacifists he throws into his concentration camps the more of that ilk arrive from abroad to see him.[1]

Phipps's bemused comment was inspired by a conversation with Lord Allen of Hurtwood (Clifford Allen) who was soon to be ushered into the presence of the führer. The picture of the saintly looking Allen—"frail, Shelley-like" the *Manchester Guardian* called him—contesting wills with Hitler seems even more ludicrous in our own time than it did to Phipps forty years ago.[2] What hope could inspire, what vanity could delude men like Allen to set for themselves the task of calming, by gentleness and reason, the raging beast of ascendant nazism?

Clifford Allen was convinced that he could reason with Hitler and by so doing help guide the world along the road to "peace in our time" and for all time. His herculean personal crusade, however, reveals the tragic dilemma of the rational, "constructive" peace lover confronted by political ideologies and human depravities far beyond the ken of his nineteenth-century liberal imagination. Among the dramatis personae of the appeasement era, Clifford Allen is generally listed as a supporting player, though descriptions of his role are often drastically different. To some observers he is a minor, if particularly egregious, villain—one of those "illusionists" or "busy romantics" who visited Nazi leaders, beguiled ignorant cabinet ministers, and gained unlimited access to the correspondence columns of the *Times* until, finally, their "intimate, insidious, bigotedly certain" counsel prevailed. For others Allen is an enlightened internationalist whose speeches and writings inspire a feeling of "absolute rightness."[3] One historian attacks him both as "the consumptive fanatic of pacifism" and as a supporter of military sanctions by the League of Nations; another confers upon him a "palm for moral courage" for his "single-minded devotion to pacifism."[4]

All of these characterizations are inaccurate or incomplete. The idea that men such as Allen were to blame for the policies pursued by the national government is absurd.[5] Furthermore, Allen was no fanatic nor was his pacifism single-minded, else he could not have accepted the principle of armed collective security. But, however inspiring his brand of enlightened internationalism, the outbreak of World War II demonstrated its ultimate failure. Still, there was much about Allen that is fine and worthy of admiration. He was a soldier of peace, an apostle of reason, a champion of democracy, and, above all, a man of conscience who attempted to translate the sufferings, sorrows, and disappointments of a lifelong quest for peace into a philosophy of universal application.

The message Lord Allen preached was the product of a decade and a half of careful, sometimes bitter, reflection on his experiences in the Great War. As a conscientious objector and chairman of the No-Conscription Fellowship (NCF), an organization that united over 10,000 men of military age in a pledge not to aid in the prosecution of the war, Allen had served eighteen months in prison. From the time of his release, because of an advanced case of tuberculosis, which made him a semi-invalid for the rest of his life, Allen had become increasingly convinced that the NCF's struggle against compulsion and violence, however edifying for the individual pacifist, had served no socially or politically constructive purpose. It had failed to shorten the war and generally alienated public opinion. Later Allen recalled how too many war resisters had acted with "a certain arrogance that stiffened opposition to us and engendered really bitter hatred. . . . We seemed to wrap ourselves in coil after coil of finely spun logic, to raise our pedestal upon a mountain of phrases and formulas and to be unresponsive to the altered mood of those whose opinions we sought to change."[6]

By the early 1930s, memories of the Great War and the fear of another had created a large and receptive audience for peace advocates. Allen was afraid that this new-found sympathy might be estranged by the same sort of negative, elitist war resistance that had proved so inadequate during the last war.

In contrast to what he considered the narrow self-righteousness of "pacifist" activities such as the Oxford Union's sensational resolution never "to fight for King and County," Allen preached the gospel of "constructive" pacifism.[7] In scores of speeches, articles, and letters to the press, he emphasized that pacifists had to broaden their vision and their appeal if they expected to establish meaningful contact with the majority.

It is fatally easy for the pacifist to hunt for spiritual luxury for himself and to lose touch with the heart and mind of an anxious public who want to know how to achieve peace now, and not many generations ahead. War resistance only rings true when it is a personal testimony of the individual soul. It should never be diverted to a deliberate political instrument. It is most dangerous to recruit war-resistance out of war-weariness. Exploited in that way, it will break the heart of the war-resister when the test comes; and will put a barrier of angry emotion between his message and the public, which has never been more eager to listen.[8]

Allen was convinced that public opinion could be mobilized behind an internationalist and ultimately even a pacifist foreign policy if such a policy were presented on its own merits, free from the sort of militant rhetoric that alienated ordinary citizens. Peace, Allen believed, should be sought peaceably and not through "certain forms of passionate and negative advocacy. . . . There is," he said, "only one kind of passion which is relevant . . . the passion of steel-like intellectual precision."[9] Fundamental to Allen's campaign was his faith in the efficacy of reason, to which he clung with a tenacity that astonished the staunchest fellow peace workers. "Do you really believe," asked

Carl Heath, general secretary of the Friends Service Council, "that the human spirit is primarily controlled by reason?" "Yes," Allen replied, "I do definitely pin my faith to the belief that at last in the 20th century an appeal can be made to reason."[10] Not even the apparent triumph of unreason and despotism in Italy, Germany, and elsewhere could shake Allen's confidence:

The man who claims to be a pacifist will . . . be undeterred by the momentary revival of violence and dictatorship; he will certainly avoid permitting that revival to affect his own outlook. He will be tolerant, fearless and filled with hope. . . . He will above all things feel it more important to prove an idea right than a man . . . wrong.[11]

Allen's long-range plan was to use constructive pacifism and a rational, open approach to mobilize public opinion—and eventually government policy—behind two fundamental goals. The first of these was to ensure Britain's strong and unrelenting support for the principle of armed collective security as embodied in the League of Nations. For him, the League, imperfect and incomplete as it was, represented an indispensable step in civilizing the world as it progressed "through the various stages from anarchic war to pacifism." If there was to be security for the weak during the transitional period, only the League could provide it. So long as the majority of the populace was nonpacifist and the states of the world remained armed, the collective force of the League acting on behalf of international justice was preferable "to the old fashioned use of force . . . by the self-judged right of each nation."[12] Allen's unequivocal support of collective security seemed an odd stance for one who claimed to be an absolute pacifist. And in response to the indignant protests of some pacifist colleagues, Allen admitted that he was playing a role that exposed him "to the charge of inconsistency," but he was prepared to accept this "provided I can help my fellow citizens along the road to peace."[13]

The essence of Allen's second objective was the removal of a formidable obstacle along that same road: an angry, frustrated, humiliated German nation suddenly won over by a man and an ideology promising to remove, by any means necessary, the causes of the nation's resentment. It was to deal with this obstacle that

Clifford Allen set out upon his journeys for peace. Armed with a secure belief in the efficacy of collective security and a stalwart faith in the superiority of reason and democracy, Allen confidently committed his frail body and fertile mind to the task of appeasing a capricious, misguided but, he believed, ultimately redeemable Germany.

Allen's advocacy of the German cause during the 1930s was simply a continuation of a long-standing view. From 1914 when he had written a pamphlet, *Is Germany Right and Britain Wrong?,* Allen had insisted that Germany was not solely, or even primarily, responsible for causing the war.[14] After 1919 he accepted the Keynesian view of the settlement and consistently advocated drastic revisions to the "wicked" Versailles Treaty so that Germany might be released from the unjust burdens imposed upon it. The installation of the Nazi regime, though personally abhorrent to Allen, did not alter his view about the wrongs done to Germany at Versailles.[15] He could no more deny the legitimacy of complaints from a Nazi government whose actions he despised than he could place the welfare of a much beloved Britain before the interests of world peace. Therefore, Allen unhesitantly enlisted his personal resources and political influence in a campaign for the satisfaction of Germany's just grievances.

A decisive step in implementing Allen's program of reconciliation was the formation, late in 1933, of the Anglo-German Group[16] whose goal was the reduction of tensions between Britain and Germany "by a comprehensive instruction of British public opinion and . . . by the exercise of influence on the British Government."[17] Acting through the aegis of this informal gathering of politicians, journalists, Quakers, and academicians, Allen hoped to establish liaison with important Nazi officials. His intermediary was Dr. Fritz Berber, an expert in international law connected with the semiofficial Institute für Aussenpolitische Forschung in Berlin, who had developed close friendships in British Quaker circles. Berber has been called "one of Ribbentrop's most effective propagandists," though British friends who knew and trusted him have insisted that he was an anti-Nazi who, at grave personal risk, worked unceasingly for peace.[18]

Whatever his motives, Berber did make several visits to London to consult with the Anglo-German Group and also sought to impress contacts in the German Foreign Ministry with the importance of garnering sympathy in Britain. Despite the disastrous effects on British public opinion of the Roehm purges and the Dollfuss murder during 1934, the group would not be deterred from its aim of securing peace. As Allen told the German ambassador, "I have both in my speeches . . . and my letters to the press done all I could to steady British public opinion with regard to the German situation."[19] By the end of 1934, Allen's strategy and the Berber connection finally began to pay dividends. Berber convinced officials in the Foreign Ministry that Allen should be received in Berlin by the highest-ranking Nazi leaders, including, if possible, Hitler himself. When the Foreign Ministry wrote to the German embassy in London about the proposal and asked for information on Allen, the embassy responded by calling attention to recent public statements in which Allen had stead-fastly supported German demands for equality of status and revisions of the Versailles settlement.[20]

In the Foreign Ministry, a glowing account of Allen's "loyal atti-tude toward Germany" was circulated with a note from State Secre-tary Bülow describing him as "a representative of British Labour circles . . . , a personal friend of MacDonald's and . . . a man of integrity and impartiality" who was actively promoting Anglo-Ger-man understanding. Bülow felt that since the Labour party was grow-ing in strength, Allen's influence (which he greatly overestimated) should be utilized if at all possible.[21] Thus the German view of Allen's visit was purely exploitive, springing from a desire to penetrate and possibly influence hostile Labour circles.

Allen had a rather more exalted vision of his mission. First, it would provide him with the opportunity to meet influential Germans and to convince them of the widespread desire in Britain for a just resolution of Germany's grievances. Second, Allen hoped to use his contacts as an opening wedge for a discussion of the treatment of political prisoners and minority groups in Germany. He and his associates were convinced that mitigation of political and racial persecution was not only a humanitarian but a political necessity. Nazi atrocities were, in their view, the one insuperable barrier to the British public's acceptance of a new and fruitful direction in Anglo-German relations. Finally, and most significantly, Allen believed that interviews with the highest-ranking Nazis would allow him to place before them his own comprehensive plan for a European settlement.[22]

After he arrived in Berlin, Allen revealed his scheme to the British ambassador, Sir Eric Phipps, who was appalled by its "revolutionary character." Because Allen was convinced that German ill manners arose largely from their obsession with *gleichberechtigung* (equality of status), he proposed to offer them a plan for complete equality of armaments with France and Britain contingent upon a supplementary agreement committing the signatories to joint military action against any party violating the pact. When Phipps pointed out that no British cabinet was likely to approve of such a plan, Allen "showed some impatience with criticism and evidently has the deepest faith in the efficacy and reasonableness of his proposals. He most emphatically rejected the suggestion that the British electorate might jib at such extensive commitments." The ambassador concluded by noting that, while Allen seemed a charming man, his visit could "only do harm," especially since "Lord Allen spoke as though he were entrusted with a definite mission and I cannot help thinking that the German Government will take the same view of his overtures."[23] Vansittart responded to the Phipps report with a mixture of outrage and condescension. "Lord Allen," he said, "has evidently been behaving as an unwise busybody."[24]

Though Allen had no official status, a remarkable number of doors were opened to him in Berlin. During his stay he talked with von Neurath and other officials of the Foreign Ministry, spent many hours as von Ribbentrop's special guest, interviewed Frick, Goering, Goebbels, and Hess, and, on January 25, as the capstone of his visit, engaged in a two-hour conversation with Hitler. Allen saw the führer as a very different man from the volatile bully portrayed in the British press:

With me he was quiet, restrained, but nonetheless ruthless. Sincere to his finger-tips, with a fanaticism somewhat resembling I should imagine that of Oliver Cromwell. . . . This man looks upon politics as a kind of religion, and, as history records over and over again, he too will persecute for his religion, kill for it and die for it. But nonetheless he believes it with an honesty and determination which it is folly either to disguise or caricature.

As for their discussion, Allen viewed himself as approaching Hitler on terms of complete equality and mutual respect, giving as good as he got:

We discussed the whole European situation in technical detail. We estimated
alternative lines of foreign policy. We examined the motives and intentions
of all the major countries in Europe. . . . The argument was precise, the
sequence quick and logical; nor was the conversation one-sided.[25]

The official German record of the interview gives a rather different view. Hitler *did* seem to dominate the conversation, emphasizing
his desire for peace, stopping to batter away at Versailles, then returning to Germany's willingness to conclude armaments agreements. Allen's own pet project of an arms convention backed by a
mutual assistance pact was immediately quashed by Hitler's comment "that there could in no circumstances be any question of this."
Nor would Hitler commit himself to a statement of how Germany
would behave once it was granted equality of rights. Because he
could be totally flexible in his pronouncements, Hitler scored all
the important points. When Allen's initiatives were brushed aside,
he had nothing left to do but offer the chancellor repeated assurances of British goodwill.[26]

Though officials of the German Foreign Ministry had the impression that Allen seemed entirely satisfied to see and hear whatever
they made available to him, there is no record of any personal reference to him by Hitler.[27] One wonders what the German führer did
think of people like Allen and of the even more pliant Lord Lothian
who visited him a few days after Allen's departure.[28] Did such well-
intentioned men simply reinforce his view of England as a "timid,
apprehensive . . . feebly well-meaning" nation filled with the sort
of "effeminates and cranks" that he took care to lock up in Germany?[29] Did the ease with which he handled Allen and subsequent
messengers of peace nourish his megalomania and his sense of the
inevitability of triumph in any test of wills?

If Hitler did think these men foolish and deluded, so by and large
did officials of their own government and Foreign Office—at least
until 1938. Just after the Allen and Lothian visits, there was un-
warranted speculation that they had made a significant contribution
to the Franco-British Agreement of February 2, 1935.[30] Twenty-five
years later one of Britain's finest diplomatic historians still believed
that the reports Allen and Lothian submitted to the Foreign Office
"must have played a large part in persuading Simon into undertaking his visit . . . to Berlin in March 1935," which planted the

seeds for the Anglo-German Naval Agreement.[31] The now-opened record reveals that no one at the Foreign Office seems to have been impressed by the Allen-Lothian reports. They were indeed carefully perused by Ralph Wigram, the head of the Central Department, for an indication of what the Nazis would try to "put over" on the secretary of state when he traveled to Berlin. But Wigram's subsequent memorandum called them "a marche des dupes," which recalled "the similar methods of duplicity . . . that Germany practiced towards us before the War."[32] Simon agreed with Wigram's "interesting analysis," pointing out that reports from Berlin indicated "the extent to which Lords Lothian and Allen were duped. . . . Germany doesn't want equality. . . . She means to have dominance."[33] These were hardly the words of a man persuaded of Germany's good intentions by the idealistic optimism of unofficial ambassadors of peace.

Lord Allen himself had returned from Germany convinced, as he told the *Daily Telegraph,* that Hitler "genuinely desires peace," but he also cautioned that the price of peace would be providing Germany with equality of status by releasing it from the discriminatory disarmament provisions of Versailles.[34] Of course, Allen was not satisfied simply to report his optimistic impressions to the press and Foreign Office. He saw the publicity arising from his and Lord Lothian's visits as the opening round of a new and intensified peace campaign based upon two vital principles: the appeasement of Germany and real collective security through the League.

Allen hoped that the means for mobilizing public opinion behind his campaign could be provided by the Next Five Years Group (NFYG). Broader in scope and more prestigious than the narrowly based Anglo-German Group, the NFYG had its genesis during the spring of 1934 in two manifestoes on "Liberty and Democratic Leadership," which, largely through Allen's initiative, had been signed by over 150 "leaders of opinion" and published in national newspapers. The public response to these manifestoes had been so favorable that Allen, in collaboration with Harold Macmillan, Sir Arthur Salter, and others, planned and helped to write a collective book setting out a comprehensive plan for both foreign and domestic affairs, which could be implemented during the life of one parliament—hence *The Next Five Years.*[35]

Although the major emphasis of the book was on domestic reform, the section on international relations was chiefly concerned with Allen's consistent message that peace could be preserved only by the "widespread and loyal acceptance of collective security to prevent, and in the last resort to restrain, a state from resorting to war." But although the authors believed that the League alone offered meaningful security, they also emphasized that it could not be fully effective until Germany had rejoined the collective peace system on terms of complete equality. The collective system, they said, might be made to work even without the Germans but only at the risk of a preventive war between the League powers and a Germany driven to national suicide by frustration, isolation, and fear. The world could be spared such a tragedy if the League, while remaining strong, could develop machinery "for the solution of the outstanding problems concerning peaceful change in the *status quo.*" Only when these difficulties were resolved could the world begin to take steps toward effective disarmament.[36]

Published in July 1935, *The Next Five Years* was so widely and favorably reviewed that one can scarcely blame Allen for believing that the book was helping to create a groundswell of opinion that would force the government to give its unequivocal pledge on behalf of collective security. When Italian designs on Abyssinia seemed about to put Britain to the test, Sir Samuel Hoare, the new foreign secretary, made his famous pronouncement that Britain stood with the League "for the *collective* maintenance of the Covenant . . . and *collective* resistance to all acts of unprovoked aggression." Allen believed that his hopes for the League had been fulfilled.[37] Within the month these hopes were dashed by the tanks, bombers, and poisonous gas of Mussolini's new Roman legions. And the British government responded not with meaningful sanctions but with the Hoare-Laval Pact, which would have handed the aggressor two-thirds of Abyssinian territory as the price of peace.

Even these dismal events did not destroy Lord Allen's confident faith, for in the public's rejection of Hoare-Laval and Baldwin's expeditious banishment of Sir Samuel Hoare, Allen saw the sort of democratic wisdom that could yet raise the League to the exhalted status it required. Arnold Toynbee said that Allen summed up "the prevailing opinion of the 'vast majority of the nation' " in a letter to the *Times* (December 28). The British public, Allen said, believe that the risks of continuing to honour and develop the collective system are far less than those which follow surrender to the aggressor. To pay off the lawbreaker would not only encourage other aggressors but would leave every nation without any alternative, except a race in modern armaments in a desperate and unsuccessful search for safety.[38]

They were brave words, and probably true. But they have a hollow ring when compared with those of Allen's next published letter to the *Times* (March 10, 1936) in which he spoke of the Nazi militarization of the Rhineland as a "new and hopeful chance . . . for acting along the whole peace front." Why the disparity? How was the spokesman for international justice transformed into an apologist for Hitler's naked violation of Locarno and Versailles? For Allen the difference was obvious. Mussolini had committed an unprovoked act of aggression on a weak and primitive neighbor, thereby threatening world security; Germany, provoked for fifteen years by a malevolent treaty and intransigent neighbors, had reoccupied its own strategic frontier in the face of a Franco-Russian treaty of encirclement. The move was unfortunate and no doubt dangerous, but logically Allen could not protest. In his view the essential requirement was not to ensure that Germany adhered to outmoded treaties but to bring Germany back into the League as an equal member.[39]

Surely there was a deeper, more personal cause for Allen's patience with the Nazis. He must have feared that one ill-placed word or ill-considered action would sweep away the bridge of goodwill he had so carefully constructed. In any case, Allen continued to present a sympathetic view of Germany's position, "notwithstanding all her unreliability and evil conduct," and to offer his services—as he did to Ribbentrop in July—in helping to bring about a "very genuine understanding."[40] He got his reward. In late July Ribbentrop asked Allen to be his guest at the Olympic games in early August, noting that "contacts . . . between you and myself are always useful in the interests of our two countries."[41] Ribbentrop's invitation was precisely what Allen had been hoping for, but upon receiving it he was suddenly overwhelmed by doubt. Would his visit be exploited by the press? Would the atmosphere of the Olympic games be conducive to serious diplomatic discussions?[42] So grave was Allen's anxiety that he overcame it only when Ribbentrop put off the time

228 THOMAS C. KENNEDY

of the visit until the September *Parteitag* in Nuremberg and Hitler added his own personal invitation.[43]

At Nuremberg Allen was rushed about from one spectacle to another; he returned to England impressed, and somewhat alarmed, by the examples of mass discipline and violent rhetoric to which he had been exposed. His reports were more guarded than before, and he took care to note that he had not been "hoodwinked" nor "overturned with blind enthusiasm."[44] Still, he saw reason to be hopeful. He was, for example, extremely sanguine about Ribbentrop's appointment as ambassador to London because he believed that if the correct psychological approach were used, Ribbentrop might become much more pliant in the company of these English gentlemen he so envied and admired.[45] Furthermore, Allen was convinced that he might establish a special relationship with Ribbentrop through the influence of Fritz Berber, who supposedly was coming to London as Ribbentrop's unofficial adviser.[46]

A second cause for optimism was Allen's belief that at Nuremberg he had finally succeeded in his attempts "to bring home to the German Government the profound distress which almost every British man and woman feels at the severity meted out to Jews and other minorities."[47] Allen's continued harping on this point not only made him unique among specially invited guests to Nazi Germany but may also explain why Hitler did not see him at Nuremberg. The führer did not like the topic brought up, especially by foreigners. Whenever Allen spoke or wrote to Ribbentrop or Hitler or some other high-ranking Nazi about political or racial persecution, he would acknowledge the delicacy of his intervention in domestic affairs, but again and again he broached the subject, reminding the Germans that this question more than any other hindered those who sought to create a climate of goodwill.[48]

The Nazis either ignored him or used his petitions, as Ribbentrop did in 1935, to illustrate how badly foreign democrats misunderstood the National Socialist revolution.[49] Even in England Allen's efforts were sometimes ridiculed, but he never ceased to believe that protests on behalf of political prisoners were a necessary and proper part of his mission.[50] Unfortunately, these endeavors were largely in vain. Indeed, their ultimate futility was starkly underscored in 1938 when Sir Neville Henderson, ambassador in Berlin, told Lord Halifax that the protestations of Allen and other well-meaning persons were actually increasing the suffering of Nazi victims.[51]

In any event, all of Allen's hopes arising from Nuremberg proved barren. Political and racial persecution continued apace; Berber stayed in Berlin; and Ribbentrop, when he deigned to answer Allen's letters, did so in a vain and peremptory fashion. By early 1937 even Allen was beginning to show some signs of irritation. In February when Lord Londonderry refused to speak to Ribbentrop about political prisoners because he feared it might diminish his influence with the Nazis, Allen impatiently told him, "We do not strengthen our influence unless we show quite frankly our distress. . . . The Germans are always trying to carry us along as their sponsors without actually doing any of the things we ask."[52]

Nor did matters augur well in Allen's home front campaign to mobilize public opinion on behalf of collective security. With Britain leading the way, the League seemed to have surrended the last vestiges of honor to Italy. As the League evaporated, Allen's own proud creation, the Next Five Years Group, rent by internal dissension, drifted toward oblivion. Allen fought back with all the weapons at his disposal—speeches, letters to the editor, and, perhaps most effectively, the published version of his address in June 1936 to the National Peace Congress, *Peace in Our Time,* which purported to offer new proposals for the autumn meeting of the League assembly but was actually a restatement of the case for constructive pacifism through the collective system.[53] Eloquent, powerful, and at times deeply moving, *Peace in Our Times* is a ringing testimony of Allen's faith in the efficacy of his ideals and the rationality of his fellow men. But a study of some of the reactions to it can also serve as a distressing illustration of how Allen had isolated himself from the absolute pacifists who had been his closest friends and allies.

Supporters of the League of Nations who read *Peace in Our Time* found much to compliment in what Arnold Toynbee called a "self-consistent plan" for uniting armed collectivists and pacifists in common cause, but most influential pacifists were having none of it.[54] In rejecting Allen's ideas Canon Dick Sheppard of the Peace Pledge Union told him, "No one ever blazed the trail for peace more nobly than you, but I wish to dickens we had you still in our extreme camp." Aldous Huxley wrote to say that he could not support the League: "I simply cannot believe that an organization prepared to drop thermite . . . on open towns . . . can be an effective instrument for peace." Another old pacifist colleague warned, "No plan for guaranteeing peace by threatening war will ever bring peace."[55]

All this, the jibes of old allies, and the now apparent failure of his entire scheme must have taken a terrible toll on Allen. But he was not prepared to capitulate. With the Next Five Years Group defunct, the League a hopeless ruin, and the Nazis increasingly aggressive, he embarked upon a new, infinitely more dangerous, course.

The first hint of the change in Allen's approach appeared in July 1937 when he asked readers of the *Contemporary Review* whether League supporters who still clung to sanctions were not shirking from "that most formidable of all disciplines: a willingness to adopt the practical expression of our ultimate ideals . . . to meet an ever-changing position."[56] He had already shown his own willingness to modify his technique by submitting an article to the British-baiting *Berliner Tageblatt* (July 11, 1937). In this piece Allen presented himself as "an unofficial interpreter of English public opinion" who was certain that his countrymen regretted Versailles as a "betrayal of . . . President Wilson's fourteen points," humiliating to Germany, and harmful to Britain. Englishmen, Allen continued, were "ashamed" of the failure of British governments to take the initiative in treaty revision or to respond to Hitler's frequent calls for negotiations. England had behaved badly again and again, he said, but now he was convinced that the nation preferred to arbitrate differences, even if the decision should go against its interests.[57]

Heady stuff, especially for the Nazi propaganda mill; and this point was not lost upon the indignant Foreign Office officials who passed this "deplorable article" to the foreign secretary. Understandably, Eden was outraged: "This is very harmful to peace," he scribbled atop the report and later expressed a desire "to show up Lord Allen to his countrymen. . . . I shall not forget this article when next this individual is telling me how to conduct this country's foreign policy."[58] While Allen's article infuriated the foreign secretary and provoked a stinging attack from the *Birmingham Post* (July 19)—inspired no doubt by the Foreign Office—it fell on deaf ears in Germany; no prisoners were released; no new peace initiatives were announced.[59] Still, the *Berliner Tageblatt* episode pointed the way in which Allen was moving away from collective security into the mire of direct appeasement.

By the end of 1937 Allen could with fairness be described as one of Chamberlain's retinue, trying, as he told Lord Halifax, "to be as helpful as I possibly can."[60] In all his public and private communications, Allen played down collective security and, especially after Eden's resignation as Foreign Secretary, urged restraint upon critics of government policy.[61] This new Allen was certainly more useful to the government than the old, but at the same time he was becoming a vexing enigma to those supporters of the collective system who had been his last important allies.

One long-time admirer troubled by Allen's apparent shift was Arnold Toynbee. In the spring of 1938, Toynbee asked how Allen could support the Chamberlain government in preference to collective security. Allen's troubled reply was both a tragic admission of failure and a last desperate cry of forlorn hope:

I am prepared to back international law by force . . . but unless the force is overwhelming, I think one then has to choose between two evils—the evil of a catastrophe in trying to uphold the law, and the evil of allowing temporary casualties in morality. It is for that reason I am willing to take risks with morality during the transitional period with the hope—perhaps a vain one— that events will play into our hands.[62]

Such a tortured faith could not satisfy those who believed that the democratic states might not survive another retreat from fascist aggression. During the early days of the Czech crisis in March 1938, Lord Robert Cecil, who had worked closely with him in the League of Nations Union, bluntly rejected the line Allen intended to pursue:

Fundamentally, I am afraid you and I do disagree because you believe that it is advantageous to negotiate with and try to placate the dictators. I am, unfortunately, convinced that a policy of that kind merely increases their prestige without making it materially less probable that they will adopt an aggressive attitude. . . . We ought to make a great effort to revive the league and give up this rather hopeless policy of putting salt on dictators' tails.[63]

Just as Allen had previously isolated himself from the extreme pacifists, he was now suspect in the eyes of those who still supported collective security. But because he had retained, however tenuously, his German contacts and had now gained the ear of Lord Halifax, Allen was confident that he might yet make some decisive personal intervention to halt the slide toward disaster in Central Europe. One who encouraged Allen in this view was a Quaker colleague from the days of the No-Conscription Fellowship, T. C. P. Catchpool. If the twentieth century has produced any saints, Corder Catchpool is one of them. During World War I he was both decorated for service as a volunteer ambulance worker and jailed as a conscientious objector. Between the wars Catchpool spent most of his time in Germany and later in the Sudeten area of Czechoslovakia doing relief work among the poor and persecuted, all for the sake of spreading love and the spirit of reconciliation. Indeed, it was with this spirit that Catchpool had introduced Fritz Berber to the Anglo-German Group.[64]

In early June 1938 Catchpool and Allen made plans for a journey to Berlin and Prague. The idea they developed was that Allen, with Catchpool acting as his aide and interpreter, would offer his services to the German government as a knowledgeable but disinterested third party who might mediate a settlement between the Czechs and Sudeten Germans. Pressure on the two parties from Berlin—Allen naturally believed that the Germans wanted a peaceful solution—might allow Allen to assume such a role and thus preserve the peace.[65] To prepare the way for this initiative, Allen planned to submit a letter to the *Times,* signed by a number of distinguished persons, asking the Czechs and Sudeten party to accept the judgment of a third party.[66]

A madly pretentious design? Perhaps. It was, of course, precisely the scheme proposed by Chamberlain when he sent Lord Runciman off on his ultimately futile mission of appeasement. By the time the Runciman mission was announced (July 26), Allen's plans were nearly completed, though the *Times* letter had not been published. After an interview with Lord Halifax, Allen scrapped the letter as irrelevant but persisted, apparently with Halifax's approval, in his private journey for peace.[67] At this stage probably nothing could have turned Allen aside. Certainly, he was undeterred by his doctor's advice not to aggravate his advanced tubercular condition by flying above 5,000 feet in a nonpressurized airplane.

In early August Clifford Allen set off on a last pilgrimage of appeasement. As his plane climbed to 10,000 feet and he gasped to bring oxygen to his diseased lungs, the mood throughout Europe was already one of grim despair. Gilbert Murray caught it well in a letter to Lord Cecil: "I got the impression from talking to people of all sorts and nationalities that every nation in Europe is preoccupied by terror of Germany, almost cowering in silence like small birds when there is a hawk in the air."[68] Some, of course, were not cowering, but the odds seemed stacked against them as well. Corder Catchpool later recalled those August days in Berlin and Prague: "Allen struggled courageously through a programme of ceaseless interviews, in spite of a heat wave which added enormously to his breathing difficulties. The distressing cough became persistent."[69]

Allen emerged from his talks with Ribbentrop and others in Berlin convinced that if Lord Runciman failed to find a satisfactory solution to the Sudeten problem, the only remaining choices would be war or a conference of the four great Western European powers.[70] In all his discussions in Prague, Allen stressed the necessity of either making the Runciman mission a success or accepting the principle of a four-power conference. A Sudeten German representative at one session between Allen and Sudeten party leaders was obviously impressed:

From last night's conversations with Lord Allen . . . one might almost get the impression that he was the second envoy sent by the British Government who, now that Lord Runciman's Mission is regarded in London with the greatest pessimism and skepticism, has been sent to prepare . . . the new step, namely, the four-power conference.[71]

Some have subscribed to the view that Allen was the original architect of Munich.[72] It is certainly true that upon returning to England, Allen reported to Lord Halifax; it may be of significance that in a letter to the *Times* (September 19) a fortnight before the Munich conference, Allen prescribed a "dual remedy" of self-determination for the Sudeten Germans and an international guarantee for the remainder of Czechosovakia.[73] What is unquestionably true is that one of the few remaining consolations of Allen's life was his belief "that the actual formula for the Four-Power Conference, which we worked out and put to Ribbentrop when we were in Berlin, should have been the instrument which saved the peace of the world."[74]

When he wrote these words to Mrs. Corder Catchpool the week after Munich, Allen was a dying man. Almost as soon as he left his interview with Lord Halifax, Allen took to his bed and never rose again. As Lady Allen told a friend, "His ugly enemy has got . . . hold of him."[75] But depressed though he was by the vicious attacks upon him in the wake of Munich, he never ceased to believe that what he had done was right. So long as he had strength to read and write, he defended Chamberlain's surrender at Munich as "the lesser of two catastrophes."[76]

Finally, too weak to sit up, he was carried in December to a Swiss sanitorium where he died on March 3, 1939, two months before his fiftieth birthday and twelve days before Hitler's troops marched into Prague. Both Halifax and Ribbentrop sent their condolences to the stricken widow.[77] It was the least they could have done; both had used him (he so earnestly wished to be used) and thus helped to hasten his departure. There was also a letter from Allen's personal physician, Dr. Thomas Hoader, who had warned him not to risk the journey that eventually killed him. The message was sincere and heartfelt: "My dear! Was it not well that he left us on the eve of this chaos he would have so hated and was powerless to avert? But his message remains, forever."[78]

But does it? Certainly an awareness of men like Allen would seem to strip the irony from A. J. P. Taylor's comment that Munich was "a triumph for all that was best and most enlightened in British life."[79] But in the truest sense, Munich was a triumph only for the swaggering malevolence of Hitlerian Germany. How could the civilized, humane, selfless ideas of men like Allen lead them inexorably to support such a total debasement of justice? Perhaps there was a hint of what went wrong in the words of the Quaker leader Carl Heath. "It always seems to me," he told Allen in 1933, "that the rational faculty is an absolutely essential part of the make-up of the intelligent pacifist; but if he is not to be swept away again and again by unreason, he must be an integral pacifist not merely a rational one."[80] Allen could not accept such an admonition. He wanted peace as earnestly as Heath did but differed from him in believing that reason was the ultimate weapon in achieving their mutual goal. Indeed, Allen was a nearly perfect prototype of Kierkegaard's ethical man. His enlightened mind could not grasp the horror that rational men might see the good and prefer evil. Reason drove him to abandon absolute pacifism for collective security and collective security for peace without honor. But if reason failed, Allen, unlike

Heath, had no religious faith to fall back on. When the weapons he brought to bear against nazism proved to woefully weak, Allen could only lean on the most elusive prop of all: hope. He hoped too much and believed too long. In the end what Allen lacked was not courage or humanity but a sense of evil. In attempting to do battle on these terms with the transcendent irrationality of Nazi Germany, he could end only as an inspiring failure.

NOTES

1. Phipps to Van[sittart], January 22, 1935, PRO, C857 in FO371/18876/9210.

2. *Manchester Guardian,* January 2, 1932.

3. See A. L. Rowse, *Appeasement: A Study in Political Decline, 1933-39* (New York, 1963), 11; Correlli Barnett, *The Collapse of British Power* (New York, 1972), 240; and Arthur Marwick, *Clifford Allen: The Open Conspirator* (Edinburgh, 1964), 199.

4. Barnett, *Collapse of British Power,* 64, 351, and Arnold Toynbee and Frank t. Ashton-Gwatkin, eds., *Survey of International Affairs: The World in March 1939* (London, 1952), 36.

5. On this point see Donald Birn's excellent essay, "A Peace Movement Divided: Pacifism and Internationalism in Interwar Britain," *Peace and Change* 1(Spring 1973): 20-24.

6. Quotations from *Tribunal,* November 20, 1919, and Allen's unpublished manuscript on conscription and war reistance, Chap. 1: 9, 12, Clifford Allen Papers, McKissick Memorial Library, University of South Carolina, Columbia, S.C. For the general topic, see Thomas C. Kennedy, "Public Opinion and the Conscientious Objector, 1915-1919," *Journal of British Studies* 12 (May 1973): 105-19.

7. Lord Allen to *Manchester Guardian,* February 22, 1933.

8. *Manchester Guardian,* November 16, 1936. Also see Allen's articles "The Sure Way to Disarmament," *Everyman* (July 22, 1933):113 and "Leadership Through Democracy: A Challenge to Violence in Politics," *The Cambridge Review* (October 26, 1934): 45-46.

9. From a speech to the National Peace Congress, June 1936, reprinted as *Peace in Our Time* (London, 1936), 8-9.

10. Carl Heath to Allen, July 27, 1933, and Allen to Heath, August 3, 1933, Allen Papers.

11. Allen, "Sure Way to Disarmament," 113.

12. Allen to Harrison Barrow, April 29, 1936, and to Helena Swanwick, December 22, 1936, Allen Papers.

13. Allen to Charles Tritton, January 20, 1938, Allen Papers. See also Lord Allen of Hurtwood, "The Politics of Courage: Reason Versus Violence," *The Cambridge Review* (May 26, 1933):428 and *Peace in Our Time,* 20-21.

14. Reprinted in a piece of German propaganda, *England on the Witness Stand* (New York, 1915), 63-71.

15. In 1934 Allen told Ellen Wilkerson: "Like yourself, I am terribly concerned over the horrors and dangers of German Nazism and am determined to go to any length to help in preventing the extension of Facism over here, . . . [but] I incline to think it would be a mistake to seem to be on the side of France about the secret rearming of Germany under the Versailles Treaty. To do that means . . . that we appear to re-endorse that wicked Treaty." April 30, 1934, Allen Papers. Also see Allen to *Manchester Guardian,* May 18, 1922, and "The Politics of Courage," 428-29.

16. Lists of important members are provided by Marwick,*Clifford Allen,* 159-60, and D. C. Watt, *Personalities and Policies* (South Bend, 1965), 125. The Anglo-German Group should not be confused with the Anglo-German Fellowship, which was much more overtly pro-German; for details see C 2168/1697/18 in FO 371/18878/9289.

17. Dr. Fritz Berber to Dr. Lammers, January 12, 1934, 1506/371242-6, *German Reichs Chancellery Records,* Foreign and Commonwealth Office Library (FCO), London. Also see Marwick, *Clifford Allen,* 160.

18. William R. Hughes, *Indomitable Friend:Corder Catchpool, 1883-1952* (London, 1964), 117-19. Cf. Watt, *Personalities and Policies,* 125.

19. Allen to Leopold von Hoesch, June 11, 1934, Allen Papers.

20. Dieckhoff to Bismarck, December 10, 1934, 5740/HO31832, and Marschall to Dieckhoff, December 14, 1934, 5740/HO31833, *German Foreign Ministry Records,* FCO. The embassy referred to Allen's letter to the *Times* (December 5, 1934) and to a speech at Gainsborough on December 9 reported in the *Times* the next day.

21. Bülow to Meissner, January 10, 1935, 5740/HO31841-43, FCO. This letter is also printed in *Documents on German Foreign Policy* (Washington, D.C., 1956), series C, III, no. 422, 798-99 (hereafter cited as DGFP). Also see memorandum on Lord Allen, January 7, 1935, 5740/HO31844-6, FCO.

22. Corder Catchpool to Allen, December 21, 1934, Allen to W. O. Arnold-Forster, January 9, 1935, also see Dorothy F. Buxton to Allen, January 16, 1935, Allen Papers.

23. Phipps to Van[sittart], January 22, 1935, C857, in FO 371/18876/9210.

24. Memorandum by Perowne and minute by Vansittart, January 24, 1935, C856/856/18 in FO 371/18876/9210. Also see Vansittart to Phipps, February 1, 1935, ibid.

25. From an unpublished manuscript in the Allen Papers. Also extensively reprinted in Marwick, *Clifford Allen,* 160-62, and Martin Gilbert, ed., *Plough My Own Furrow* (London, 1965), 357-58.

26. "Record of the Conversation between the Führer and Chancellor and Lord Allen of Hurtwood on January 25, 1935," Reich Chancellery to the Foreign Minister, January 29, 1935, 5740/HO31890-5, FCO. Also printed in DGFP, C, III, no. 463, 873-76.

27. Memorandum to Bismarck, January 22, 1935, 5704/HO31880-2, FCO.

28. For Lord Lothian's visit, see copies of his interview with Hitler, which he sent to Simon, Baldwin, and MacDonald, January 30, 1935, Lothian Papers, 201, Scottish Record Office, Edinburgh. Also reprinted in J. R. M. Butler, *Lord Lothian* (London, 1960), 330-36.

29. Barnett, *Collapse of British Power,* 403, and A. L. Kennedy, *Britain Faces Germany* (New York, 1937), 174-75.

30. This proposal indicated the lines on which a general settlement between Germany and the other powers could be negotiated, with the idea of superseding the disarmament provisions of Versailles and also urging the prompt negotiation of a Western air pact. Also see C860/856/18 in FO 371/18876/9210.

31. D. C. Watt, "Christian Essay in Appeasement," *Weiner Library Bulletin* 14, no. 2 (1960): 30-31, and "The Anglo-German Naval Agreement of 1935: an Interim Judgment," *Journal of Modern History* 28 (July 1956): 155-75. On the general topic, also see Keith Middlemas, *Diplomacy of Illusion* (London, 1972), 95-96.

32. Memorandum by Wigram, March 9, 1935, C2518/55/18 in FO 371/18832.

33. Minute by Simon in ibid.

34. See Allen's report to Eden, March 1, 1935, Allen Papers and C1926/856/18 in FO 371/18876/9210. Also see article on Allen's visit to Germany in *Daily Telegraph,* January 28, 1935.

35. For the Next Five Years Group, see Arthur Marwick, "Middle Opinion in the Thirties: Planning, Progress and Political Agreement," *English Historical Review* 79 (1964): 285-98, and Thomas C. Kennedy, "The Next Five Years Group and the Failure of the Politics of Agreement in Britain," *Canadian Journal of History* 9 (April 1974): 45-68.

36. Allen, *The Next Five Years: An Essay in Political Agreement* (London, 1935), 216-92 passim.

37. See Allen's letters to the *Times,* September 17, 1935 and to *The New Statesman and Nation* 10 (October 12, 1935), 479-80. For an excellent analysis of Hoare's speech, see Arnold Toynbee, *Survey of International Affairs, 1935* (London, 1936), 2:187-89.

38. See ibid., 69.

39. See Allen to Lord Cecil and to L. G. Montifiore, March 10, 1936, Allen Papers.

40. Allen to L. G. Montifiore, March 10, 1936, and to Ribbentrop, July 15, 1936, ibid.

41. Ribbentrop to Allen, July 28, 1936, ibid.

42. Allen to W. Arnold-Forster, July 31, 1936, ibid.

43. Count R. Durckheim to Allen, August 4, 1936, and Allen to Arnold-Forster, September 8, 1936, ibid.

44. Allen to Lady Allen, September 11, 1936, and to Gore-Booth, September 23, 1936, ibid. Also see Allen "The Meaning of Nuremberg," *The Spectator* 157 (September 25, 1936): 487-88, and "My Impression of Germany," *The Contemporary Review* 150 (November 1936): 521-25.

45. Allen to Eden, October 19, 1936, C7613/4/18 in FO 371/19914. Also see Halifax to Allen, October 20, 1936, Allen Papers.

46. Corder Catchpool to Allen, September 4, 1936, and Allen to Arnold Toynbee, October 16, 1936, ibid.

47. Allen, "Meaning of Nuremberg," 487.

48. Allen's work on behalf of German prisoners and especially the lawyer Hans

Litten has been recounted in detail by Marwick, *Clifford Allen*, 166-74, and Gilbert, *Plough My Own Furrow*, 358-95 passim. The Allen Papers contain extensive material on Allen's attempts to help German political prisoners and refugees.

49. See Allen to Hitler, October 31, 1935, C7912/1821/18 in FO 371/18878, and Ribbentrop to Allen, December 8, 1935, C8369/1821/18 in ibid. Both letters are reprinted by Gilbert, *Plough My Own Furrow*, 368-71.

50. F. A. Voigt, *Manchester Guardian* correspondent in Germany, sent the following postcard to Allen: " 'Friendly remonstrance' à la Hurtwood has about as much chance of stopping the Nazis from committing atrocities as it would of stopping the Danakils from castrating Mussolini if they catch him." July 30, 1935, Allen Papers.

51. See Neville Henderson to Halifax, March 10, 1938, Halifax to Allen, March 12, 1938, and Allen to Halifax, March 14, 1938, Allen Papers. Also reprinted in Gilbert, *Plough My Own Furrow*, 393-95.

52. Allen to Londonderry, February 8, 1937, Allen Papers.

53. Allen, *Peace in Our Own Time.*

54. Toynbee to Allen, August 7, 1936, Allen Papers. Also see Lord Lytton to Allen, August 2, 1936, ibid.

55. Sheppard to Allen, July 18, 1936, and August 6, 1936, Huxley to Allen, October 3, 1936, and Helena Swanwick to Allen, August 4, 1936, ibid. For the difficulties between absolute pacifists and peace advocates who supported an armed League of Nations, see Birn, "Peace Movement Divided," 21-24.

56. Lord Allen of Hurtwood, "Constructive Peace Policy," *Contemporary Review* 152 (July 1937): 11.

57. A translation of Allen's article is contained in C5080/270/18 in FO 371/20736.

58. Minutes by Eden, July 12, 16, 1937 and minute by W. Strang, July 14, 1937, ibid.

59. A copy of the *Birmingham Post* article is in ibid.

60. Allen to Halifax, November 10, 1937, Allen Papers. Also see Allen to Neville Chamberlain, November 2, 1937, ibid.

61. See, for example, Allen's letters to the *Times*, February 4, March 19, 1938, as well as his speeches at Lytham St. Annes (February 22, 1938) and at a church conference (March 12, 1938), reprinted in Gilbert, *Plough My Own Furrow*, 389, 395.

62. Toynbee to Allen, May 16, 1938, and Allen to Toynbee, May 17, 1938, Allen Papers. Also see Allen to Julian [Treveleyan], February 28, 1938, ibid.

63. Cecil to Allen, March 16, 22, 1938, ibid. Archibald Sinclair, leader of the Liberal party, echoed Cecil's view in a letter to Allen, March 22, 1938, ibid.

64. For Catchpool see the admirable biography by Hughes, *Indomitable Friend*, and J. M. Greaves, *Corder Catchpool* (London, 1953). In late June 1938 Catchpool sent a report on the Sudetenland to the Foreign Office, which William Strang called "well worth reading"; see C6425/1941/18 in FO 371/21725.

65. See Gilbert, *Plough My Own Furrow*, 403-04.

66. There is a copy of the proposed letter in C7766/1941/18 in FO 371/21730; the signatories were to have included J. A. Spender, Harold Nicolson, J. A. Hobson, Gilbert Murray, and Lord Cecil.

67. See Allen to J. A. Spender, August 2, 1938, Allen Papers.

68. Murray to Cecil, August 12, 1938, Cecil of Chelwood Papers, British Museum, Add. Ms. 51133.

69. Quoted by Gilbert, *Plough My Own Furrow,* 415. Also see Allen to Lady Allen, August 8, 10, 1936, Allen Papers.

70. Newton to Halifax, August 13, 1938, and minute by Mallet, August 15, 1938, C8301/1941/18 in FO 371/21731.

71. Burger to Foreign Ministry, August 17, 1938, DGFP, D, II, no. 366, 579. Also see Hencke to Foreign Ministry, August 13, 1938, ibid., no. 351, 557-58.

72. Marwick, *Clifford Allen,* 184-87, 202.

73. *Times,* September 19, 1938. Also see Guy Wint to Allen, September 14, 1938, Allen Papers.

74. Allen to Gwen Catchpool, October 7, 1938, ibid. Also see Allen to Hubert Peet, October 3, 1938, ibid.

75. Lady Allen to Professor G. H. Leonard, October 10, 1938.

76. Allen to Bessie [Treveleyan], October 20, 1938, and Neville Chamberlain to Allen, October 17, 1938, Allen Papers. Chamberlain called Allen's argument in favor of Munich "a masterly statement of the case."

77. Halifax to Lady Allen, n.d., and Von Ribbentrop to Lady Allen [April-May 1939], quoted in Gilbert, *Plough My Own Furrow,* 423, 425.

78. Dr. Thomas Hoader to Lady Allen, n.d., quoted in ibid., 429-30.

79. A. J. P. Taylor, *The Origins of the Second World War* (New York, 1966), 189.

80. Carl Heath to Allen, July 27, 1933, Allen Papers.

12
The Failure of Protest against Postwar British Defense Policy

FRANK E. MYERS

The internal history of the British peace movement during the last thirty years must focus on the many controversies over tactics, organization, and program that engaged so much of the movement's energies. Participants in these controversies believed that success or failure in influencing British policy depended upon such choices as whether the movement should be respectable or boisterous, committed to legality or prepared to try direct action, specific in its focus upon a single issue or more ideologically comprehensive. Such questions were hotly debated at many conferences and meetings.

Now that the aggressive days of the movement have entered the world of nostalgia, we might ask, Could the movement ever have succeeded? Could any of these choices, if made differently, have produced the desired impact on British foreign and defense policy? The answer is that there was never much chance of success: the dominant institutions of the Labour party were less accessible than they appeared to be; the government was well equipped to deflect unwanted pressure; the great weapons of public opinion proved too heavy to wield effectively. Moreover, there is some reason to doubt that even if the peace movement had generated much greater support than it did in public opinion polls, the trades unions, and the

*I wish to thank the Research Foundation of the State University of New York, which provided a summer fellowship enabling me to complete some of the research for this essay. I thank also the Gallup Institute of Princeton, New Jersey, for useful help.

Labour Party Conference, the record of British foreign and defense policy would not be much different from the existing one.

But the peace movement believed that that record could have been changed. Its leaders agonized over the issue, for example, of whether effectiveness was inhibited by respectability, which may be defined as a resolve to rely upon legal means only, to have as its spokesmen well known leaders of the professions and arts, and to defer as much as possible to the symbols and institutions that enjoy social prestige, such as the Church and Parliament. We therefore begin with a brief discussion of the movement's internal development over the past thirty years before assessing the nature of its impact on the government, public opinion, and the political system as a whole.

I

Events leading up to World War II, as well as the war itself, destroyed whatever respectability and effectiveness the peace movement of the 1930s had gained. Most of the famous people associated with the Peace Pledge Union, the most prominent British anti-organization of the 1930s, withdrew their support for the peace movement as war with Germany seemed more certain.[1] During the war itself pacifists were accorded better treatment than the brutal handling they had received in 1914-18, but their influence on public life was, if anything, less. Nor did the atomic bomb immediately direct public opinion to a more favorable attitude toward unconventional alternatives in defense and foreign policy. Although pacifist and antiwar groups in the 1940s and early 1950s presented proposals and arguments not much different from those offered in the late 1950s, the early proposals went unnoticed.

The war had also ruptured the tenuous link between respectable and nonrespectable sides of the antiwar movement. The nonrespectable element, faced with declining opportunities for influence through its regular channels of speeches, pamphlets, vigils, and marches, began to consider the efficacy of illegal activity. Gandhi's disobedience campaign, which had been successful in India, seemed to offer a technique of political coercion, or at least strong pressure, that was morally acceptable to some antiwar activists. Debate over the applicability to Britain of a technique developed in the Indian colonial context of bureaucratic absolutism and nonlegitimate dissent delayed any commitment to nonviolent action until 1949 when the Peace Pledge Union established a commission to examine the subject. In 1951 some members of this commission formed a splinter group to conduct an illegal sitdown in front of the War Office.[2] This and subsequent demonstrations produced some arrests, but not much publicity or any hint of significant public support.

Activities of the more respectable elements of the anti-war movement during this period were not much more efficacious. The Labour left in Parliament had no influence on the pro-American foreign policy of the Attlee government, although it strongly pressed its opposition to the alignment with the United States against the U.S.S.R. and, later, to the rearmament of West Germany. Moreover, the electoral defeats suffered by the Labour party in the 1950s had the ironic effect of strengthening support for the foreign and defense policies favored by the party leadership. Under the influence of Hugh Gaitskell, Anthony Crosland, and others in the party's dominant faction, the defeats of 1951 and 1955 were interpreted as public rejections of an outmoded socialist tradition in foreign, as well as domestic, policy.[3] The Labour left's opposition to German rearmament and the British nuclear deterrent was pressed through such organizations as Victory for Socialism and the Hydrogen Bomb Campaign Committee. The respectable antiwar movement reached its perigee of demoralization with the appointment of Aneurin Bevan in 1957 as foreign policy spokesman in the shadow cabinet.[4]

Bevan's defection from the left unexpectedly combined with several other events—the first British hydrogen bomb test, the development of the intercontinental ballistic missile, and the 1957 Defense White Paper announcement that the British military was no longer capable of defending the country from nuclear attack—to reunite the dormant antiwar coalition and produce the largest mass protest against British defense policy seen in this century. The Campaign for Nuclear Disarmament, (CND), which from its establishment in 1958 provided the organizational focus and visible leadership for this movement, was initiated, but never entirely dominated, by respectable opponents of Britain's nuclear policy who had easy access to communication media.[5] The group that founded CND wished to model the organization on the American National Committee for a Sane Nuclear Policy whose strategy was directed solely toward influential establishment figures. Kingsley Martin, Canon L. John Collins, Bertrand Russell, and others on the early CND executive committee possessed the qualities of rather mild radicalism combined with the social prestige necessary to make the success of such a campaign plausible.

From the first, however, the executive committee was unable to repress a mass element in the movement that had distinctly non-respectable implications. From early 1958 on, as Peggy Duff has written, "There was a sense of urgency, a feeling of emergency, almost a fanaticism which made life very uncomfortable for the Executive Committee, and the [CND] office, as well as the Government and opposition."[6] This tendency, absolutist in ideology and unconventional in preferred tactics, first manifested itself in the unexpected rise of local CND groups and later in the growing membership of the Direct Action Committee against Nuclear War and the Committee of 100.

The history of the antinuclear bomb campaign until approximately 1963 was the story of tugging and pulling between these two factions. Their conflict extended to every dimension of protest activity: program, tactics, and organizational structure. CND was initially conceived as a single-issue campaign aimed at converting the Labour party from support of a defense policy that relied upon nuclear weapons to one that did not. In its early communications, CND made no clear statement regarding the implications of this program for British membership in NATO. In fact, it made no clear anti-NATO statement until 1960 by which time the defeat of the Labour party in the general election of 1959 and the abandonment of the Blue Streak missile program (entailing greater British dependence upon the United States) had clearly reduced the viability of the campaign's early antipolitical stance. After 1959, the Labour party's political prospects made it unlikely that that party could soon serve as the instrument by which to change British defense policy. Moreover, Britain's growing military dependence on the United States weakened the plausibility of CND's long-term strategy whereby a unilateralist Britain could work from within NATO to achieve international nuclear disarmament. These considerations were decisive in turning the 1960 CND Conference toward British withdrawal from NATO.

This anti-NATO posture produced two complications for CND at the very moment when the possibility of converting the Labour party to unilateralism was greatest. With its now broadened, anti-NATO implications, unilateralism provoked furious opposition from the dominant Gaitskell faction of the party and caused even a few unions that had declared themselves in favor of unilateralism to waver. Trade union hostility to Gaitskell had generated the votes needed to pass a unilateralist resolution at the Labour Party Conference of 1960. Gaitskell's successful counterattack at trade union meetings and through the newly created Campaign for Democratic Socialism was facilitated to some extent by worries over the extensive foreign policy implications associated with withdrawal from the NATO alliance.

Second, opposition to NATO involved the campaign increasingly in somewhat technical and detailed discussions of foreign policy, discussions that differed fundamentally in tone from the moral absolutism that had provided CND with its original momentum. Large masses seldom march over fine points of policy. Moreover, the CND leadership under Canon L. John Collins was resolute in retaining its respectability and opposed any form of illegal protest, no matter how nonviolent. As the chances of CND's success through the Labour party ebbed along with the party's political fortunes, ever larger numbers of CND supporters joined in illegal demonstrations organized by the DAC (Direct Action Committee against Nuclear War).

DAC antedated CND and indeed had organized the 1958 Aldermaston march along with a series of small, but increasingly well-publicized, demonstrations at government offices and defense installations at which people were arrested for such violations as trespass, blocking traffic, or refusing to obey police orders. As dissension within CND grew, DAC's demonstrations became more impressive. In addition, CND supporters began staging their own illegal demonstrations, sometimes using CND's name, while the leadership forcefully denied to the media that such activities were endorsed by CND's national office. By 1960, this controversy over illegal tactics was causing a serious division in the antibomb movement. In October of that year, the CND president, Bertrand Russell, dissatisfied with his organizaiton's slow progress, irritated at Canon Collins over a variety of issues relating mainly to direct action protests, and increasingly pessimistic about the prospects of nuclear disarmament, took the lead in forming the Committee of 100 Against Nuclear War.

The committee aimed to produce large and highly publicized demonstrations that featured illegal, but not violent, activity. Many famous people, especially in the arts, joined the committee, although most of the hard work was performed by pacifists and antiwar activists whose years of dedication to this and similar causes had brought them little or no public recognition. The committee's demonstrations in 1960 and the first half of 1961 succeeded in directing considerable public attention to the issue of nuclear weapons.

Indeed, throughout the 1959 to 1961 period, controversy over defense policy appears to have been the most discussed and controversial issue of the day in Britain. The demonstrations of CND and the committee grew progressively larger, counting among their participants thousands and tens of thousands of protesters. Nuclear disarmament was the talk of the day in the media. The committee's illegal protests contributed significantly to this public focus, a factor that the committee's leaders believed justified their use of illegal means. They conceived of civil disobedience initially not as a form of direct action—by which the government would be coerced into changing its policy—but rather as a means of drawing further public attention to arguments for unilateral nuclear disarmament that would otherwise be ignored by press and public alike.[7] Civil disobedience thus was seen as a positive contribution to discussion in a democratic debate.

The dynamics of illegal protest activity transformed the committee, displacing its original objective with a more radical, even revolutionary, conception of direct action. By 1962 the committee was calling for direct action to obstruct the routine functioning of the military, either by occupation of military bases, industrial strikes of defense plants, or conversion of armed forces personnel to antiwar thinking. This transformation was produced primarily by two interconnected factors. First, the committee's relationship with CND placed it in a curious position. That both pursued the same goal of converting the public and the government to unilateralism encouraged cooperation between the two groups. But the committee could justify its existence only by showing that its more radical approach attracted more adherents and publicity than did CND's conventional tactics. The committee, after all, drew its following from among the more impatient members of CND. Second, the constant need to prove its radical bona fides encouraged the staging of demonstrations in which ever greater numbers of people participated and were arrested. After a Trafalgar Square demonstration in September 1961, in which over one thousand persons were arrested, the membership of the committee began to change. The arrests, and the increasingly severe punishments meted out by courts, reduced committee size. To sustain its membership, the committee recruited new members, who were generally younger and were less likely to have families or to hold steady jobs than the original committee membership. The famous people associated with the committee at its founding had either publicly or tacitly disassociated themselves from the committee. Under the influence of its new and by and large more radical membership, the committee's internal organization weakened, dissension grew, and ill-conceived demonstrations were scheduled. By 1962, the committee was debating issues of social revolution and reorganizing its internal structure drastically. Its influence declined steadily in the 1960s.[8]

Thus, the heyday of the unilateralist movement extended from 1957 or 1958 to about 1963, a brief but singularly strong and spontaneous outpouring of dissent that neither its opponents nor its own leaders could completely control. After 1963, the decline of the movement was nearly as quick as its rise had been. The general lines of the development after 1963 took a paradoxical form. On the one hand, the concerns of antiwar activists tended increasingly to broaden beyond the single issue of unilateralism to include such issues as Greek political prisoners, the complexities of disarmament after the Nuclear Test Ban Treaty of 1963, problems of housing the poor, and, above all, the Vietnam war. By the 1970s, *Peace News,* the main organ of pacifist and antiwar discussion, was devoting most of its space to gay rights, women's equality, opposition to increases in public transportation fares, Northern Ireland, human rights in such countries as the Soviet Union, Chile, Argentina, and Australia, and opposition to proposed nuclear power stations.

On the other hand, CND leadership was convinced that the organization's success in achieving mass support had been inextricably linked to its concentration upon the moral and practical issues associated with nuclear weapons.[9] It was largely this narrow focus that had originally enabled CND to cut through party loyalties, offset a certain wariness about ideological commitments in the 1950s, and represent itself as a moral crusade. In its effort to maintain its original character, CND severed itself from the ebullient rebelliousness of the 1960s that it had done much to inspire. In May 1964, the controversy over whether CND should dissociate itself from its supporters' activities that were not closely related to the nuclear issue provoked the resignation of Canon Collins as CND president.[10] Two years later, in an attempt to stabilize the organization, CND decided to become a membership organization, forswearing all further claims to being a mass movement and accepting the status of pressure group—and not a very powerfully based one at that. CND's formal membership was necessarily far smaller than the total population of potential antiwar activists. Thus the British antiwar movement lost the organizational focus that so strongly differentiated it from the more cumbersome organization of U.S. protest against the Vietnam war and that had given some promise of ongoing mass pressure upon political decision makers in the formulation of British defense policy.

II

For a time in 1960 and 1961 it appeared that the British peace movement might have significant impact on defense policy. The movement had considerable popular support, and enough trade unions had been won over to unilateralism to influence official Labour party policy.[11] But the victory of 1960 was reversed the following year. Moreover, the Labour government, which began in 1964, conducted defense policy as if the great CND marches had never taken place, as if the great controversy of 1960 and 1961 had been no more than a quibble over rules.

The foreign policy of the Wilson governments of the 1960s was built around the same two factors that had established the parameters for the Conservatives. The first of these was the NATO alliance, which tied American diplomatic influence and military (primarily nuclear) power directly to the defense of Europe. The second was the maintenance of a continental forward defense line against the Soviet Union.[12] Thus, the "special relationship" with the United States and ultimate reliance upon the American nuclear umbrella served Wilson just as they had Macmillan. To be sure, the independence of the British nuclear deterrence was ended, but not the policy connected with it.

The outstanding feature of Harold Wilson's early foreign policy was the effort to assert Britain's world role even while the economic foundation for such a role was rapidly eroding.[13] As Britain's balance of payments forced a progressive reduction in defense spending, the government felt forced to continue its reliance upon NATO for ultimate defense. There is no evidence that the Wilson government ever considered nuclear disarmament and diplomatic neutrality as leading to the solution of its foreign policy problems. At various times Wilson did make some effort to express British independence from the United States, especially when he attempted to mediate the Vietnam dispute. But he failed, bringing confusion rather than order to the situation. The Labour governments of the 1960s applied little or no pressure on the United States to withdraw from Vietnam. Britain's role as a loyal NATO ally was unchallenged.[14]

It is perhaps even more surprising that within the Labour party organization itself, the 1960-61 controversy produced so little continuing dispute on nuclear weapons. Throughout the 1960s and the early 1970s, Labour party conferences gave little challenge to the government's pro-NATO policy. Conferences regularly defeated all proposed resolutions calling for British neutrality and withdrawal from NATO. The 1966 official party policy statement, for example, called for limits to the spread of nuclear weapons, a comprehensive test ban, and a reduction of nuclear armaments. At the same time, it asserted the party's belief "that NATO has played a major part in creating stability in Europe and maintaining peace" and called for continued British membership in the organization.[15]

The 1967 Labour Party Conference featured a strident debate on a resolution calling for the Labour government "to dissociate itself completely from the policy of the United States Government in Vietnam" and join with other nations in trying to persuade the United States "to end the bombing of North Vietnam immediately, permanently and unconditionally."[16] The resolution was passed by a narrow margin over the objection of George Brown, the foreign secretary, that British condemnation of U.S. policy would deprive the government of the influence it had with Washington and Hanoi by virtue of its impartiality in the conflict. Brown's argument provoked laughter.[17] But this brief victory for the Labour left failed to affect government policy to any significant degree and did not lead the way to stronger antiwar conference resolutions in subsequent years.

Indeed, the interest of the conference in foreign policy appears to have declined in the late 1960s in favor of a greater focus on domestic policy. Conference foreign policy debates tended to concentrate less on British defense policy and more on such issues as the Common Market, Rhodesia, Biafra, and Spanish refugees. But the continued opposition of large trade unions to government policy was shown in two resolutions passed in 1972. The first called for the ultimate dissolution of NATO and the Warsaw Pact and "a substantial measure of nuclear and general disarmament." The second declared that "Conference is opposed to any British defence policy which is based on the use or threatened use of nuclear weapons either by this country or its allies and demands the removal of all nuclear bases in this country."[18] This stance was reaffirmed in 1973 along with a demand for "the closing down of all nuclear bases British and American on British soil or in British waters," and "that this pledge be included in the General Election Manifesto."[19] In the following two years this policy was not reaffirmed.

There are several apparently contradictory developments in this historical record. The governments of 1964 and 1966, presumably representing a leftward turn from the Gaitskell years, carried out a foreign policy indistinguishable from that associated with the Gaitskellites. The annual conference oscillated between hostility to nuclear weapons and intense concern with Vietnam on the one hand and tacit acceptance of NATO and support of the Labour government's policy on the other. Almost the only thing that can be said about this record with clarity and relevance to the peace movement is that the peace movement ultimately failed to influence the policy of the government in a significant way.

There are three possible explanations, at increasingly high levels of generalization, for this failure. The first focuses upon the trade unions, whose conversion to unilateralism in the late 1960s gave the peace movement its most powerful political support. Indeed, since World War I the typical failing of Western European and American antiwar movements has been their lack of support from, or even significant communication with, the working-class trade union movements. In Britain the lack of rapport between the unions and the peace movement has been a decisive fact because the voting arrangements in the Labour party, as well as its financial structure, enable the largest unions to set the boundaries of party policy. Until the mid-1950s the unions constituted the main support of the party's right wing. In the middle 1950s, when Frank Cousins succeeded Arthur Deakin as head of the Transport and General Workers' Union, the identification of unionism with the party right began to alter as Cousins became convert to unilateralism and appears single-handedly to have led his powerful union to the left of the party.[20] Until 1959 the party conference did not seriously challenge the party leadership on the issue of nuclear weapons policy. In 1959, however, several unions broke from the official policy of the party or threatened to do so.[21] At the Trades Union Conference in September 1959, the party leadership's position was affirmed only by narrow votes after intense debate.

Thus the leadership was waging a close but successful struggle within the party on defense. In 1959, though, two events—the Labour party's defeat in the general election and the attempt by Hugh Gaitskell to abolish clause four of the party constitution, which states that the nationalization of industry is the primary aim of the party—severely weakened the leadership position on defense policy. The election defeat shook Gaitskell's authority, although it is probably true that, as Lord Pakenham later wrote, he could have "presided indefinitely and without much trouble over a party satisfied with his leadership, if otherwise at a low ebb."[22] Instead, Gaitskell moved at a special party conference to abolish clause four. The conference was hostile to the suggestion, and the party entered a phase of vitriolic divisiveness in which unilateralism became linked with nationalization as questions of principle to be defended against the opportunism of the leadership. Gaitskell at first attempted to compromise with the Labour left, a maneuver that only confused labor unions who were debating defense policy at the spring 1960 meetings. An official party statement on defense policy in the summer of 1960 declared that although Britain could no longer be an "independent nuclear power," its commitment to NATO should be continued, if not increased.[23] This wording may have confused some trade unionists who could not be certain whether unilateralist resolutions up for vote in union meetings were oppposed to the party leadership's policy. The real issue in this debate centered around support for NATO, but the discussion revolved around whether one supported the bomb. CND, after all, had voiced its hostility to NATO only in March 1960. The full implications of the trade union movement against Gaitskell and in favor of unilateralism, therefore, were not realized until after the 1960 Labour Party Conference.

That conference endorsed unilateralism. The relative ease with which this victory for the peace movement was achieved suggests also the reasons for the reversal of the conference vote in 1961. Gaitskell and the party leadership wing launched a vigorous, yearlong campaign within the unions. Several decisive factors worked in Gaitskell's favor. First, in those unions, such as the Amalgamated Engineers' Union, in which rank-and-file support for unilateralism had caught pro-Gaitskell leaders by surprise, the leadership now had ample time to campaign for reversal of the 1960 party vote. Second, the Gaitskellites formed an organization, the Campaign for Democratic Socialism, to lead the counterattack against unilateralism, the CND, and the newly formed Committee of 100. Indeed the latter group's civil disobedience campaign made the unilateralist resolution even more vulnerable to attack on the grounds of its association with political extremism.

Thus the reversal of the trade union vote on the issue of unilateral nuclear disarmament may be explained as a consequence of the relatively low degree of union commitment to unilateralism as such. The issue of the bomb was but an element, and not necessarily the central one, in a transformation of certain unions from traditional support for the Labour party's right wing leadership and toward the more leftward, critical stance that characterized union activity throughout the 1960s and early 1970s.

This raises a somewhat larger question: If control of the annual conference was falling into the hands of the party left, why did the Labour governments not reflect this development in their foreign policies in the 1960s and 1970s? The move of the unions, and with them the party conference, to the left would be expected to produce a more left-oriented and pacifistic Labour government policy. That this did not occur indicates the development of a gap between the constituency upon which the conference is based and that which elects a government. Gaitskell lost on clause four and was only narrowly victorious on unilateralism, yet his position as party leader was stronger in 1962 than ever, perhaps because he was doing well in public opinion polls and seemed likely to restore the party to office. But this points, as David Coates has argued, to a fundamental characteristic of the Labour party: the tendency of the left to win verbal victories only.[24]

Coates finds the reasons for this trait in the history of the party. The left has never been more than a minority within the party, forced constantly to compromise between its socialist objectives and the realities of the party's power structure. Whether influenced by the habit of compromise or some other factor, the Labour left has not offered a detailed and integrated attack on British capitalism or the traditional structure of foreign policy making. The "socialist foreign policy," so often advocated by the left, has remained comparatively vague. Neither the left, nor the party as such, has sought to radicalize the British working class. Neither the working class, nor the electorate at large, has given consistent support to the left, a factor that under-lies all calculations on party policy and that has encouraged the defection of left leaders when faced with hard political choices. No strong, radical base of electoral support exists to ensure that party leaders adhere to the radical party conference decisions. Thus, the Gaitskellites' struggle with the unilateralists tended to strengthen rather than weaken their hold on the leadership.[25]

The death of Gaitskell in 1963 and the rise of Harold Wilson as party leader did not signal the revival of unilateralism. Wilson raised the unilateralists from the position of ignominious defeat, to which Gaitskell probably would have consigned them, to a position of dignified irrelevance. He sought first to build the party's image around issues of modern management and the application of technology to public policy, a focus that deflected attention from ideological splits over clause four and defense policy.[26] He also coopted into the cabinet some leading members of the Labour left, most obviously Frank Cousins and Michael Foot. The effect of this move was not to give unilateralists access to the policy-making process but to cut these influential leaders off from the rank and file of the CND. As government policy responded to the national electorate and public opinion polls, even the influence of unilateralism in the party conference proved to be more a symbolic than a substantial victory.

III

An examination of public opinion polls during and after the heyday of the postwar peace movement supports this interpretation. The polls show a fluctuating pattern of concern with the issues of disarmament and peace but a consistent tendency on the part of the public in general to disagree with the unilateralist and anti-NATO policy endorsed by the peace movement.

Throughout the period in question, the Gallup Poll periodically asked some form of the following question: "What would you say is the most urgent problem facing the government at the present time?"[27] The responses to this question can be taken as indicators of the degree of public concern with various problem areas. Beginning with the period when the CND was formed, the concern with foreign affairs generally, and the H-bomb and disarmament specifically, steadily increased. From March 1959 through May 1961, when CND was at the height of its dynamism and growth, foreign affairs, defense, and nuclear armaments consistently ranked as the most frequently mentioned "urgent problems." In June 1959, 46 percent of the national sample stated that either "foreign affairs" or "H-bomb, disarmament" was the most urgent problem. About 30 percent gave economic issues as the most urgent problem. In November 1960, 49 percent thought that defense or foreign affairs was the most urgent problem, with "defence, armaments, and nuclear weapons" alone accounting for 25 percent. The tendency for defense and foreign policy to be replaced by economic issues as the most urgent problem facing the country is clear by December 1963, when only 17 percent of the Gallup Poll respondents regarded defense and international affairs as the most urgent problem. Economic affairs, housing, pensions, education, and so forth accounted for over 50 percent of the answers. After 1963, concern over foreign affairs, as manifested in the Gallup Poll, declined steeply. In November 1964, 55 percent of the sample stated that they were "not worried at all" about the possibility of an outbreak of nuclear war. Only 9 percent were "very worried." Throughout the post-1964 period, foreign affairs and defense were never regarded as the country's most urgent problem by as many as 20 percent. By 1971, the economic situation of Britain was overwhelmingly the most urgent issue, with Ireland and the Common Market following far behind. In the polls of September and November of that year, defense was not even mentioned. In January 1973, one issue alone—"cost of living, prices"—stood out as the most urgent government problem by 57 percent of those polled. By June 1973, that figure had risen to 70 percent. The concern over foreign affairs and defense, like the unilateralist movement itself, had been a phenomenon of the late 1950s and early 1960s.

The peace movement never gained anything approaching a majority in support of its anti-NATO and unilateralist policies. In 1958 and 1960, about 30 percent of those polled consistently supported a policy of British nuclear disarmament. Thus in September 1958, 30 percent approved British unilateral renunciation of the H-bomb. In a June 1959 poll, 17 percent supported unilateral nuclear disarmament, and another 12 percent supported nuclear disarmament if it was combined with British encouragement "of countries like France to stop all efforts to have nuclear bombs." The 1960 polls show a drop in unilateralist sentiment to about 20 percent, a notable development in the year of CND's outstanding successes within the Labour Party Conference.[28] After 1960, the issue of unilateralism was seldom posed in the polls. The Gallup question on defense policy became more complex and frequently focused on the British relationship with NATO. In September 1960 and April 1961, when the poll sample was given the three alternatives of continuing British nuclear weapons, pooling all nuclear weapons with other NATO countries and relying mainly on American production, or giving up British nuclear weapons entirely, 36 percent of the respondents in each case supported the first alternative, and about 20 percent opted for the third alternative. Pooling with NATO was favored by 31 percent in September 1960 and 26 percent in April 1961. It should be noted that the first alternative did not mean opposition to a pro-NATO policy. Support for NATO was fairly constant and high during the early and mid-1960s. Thus, in October 1966, 60 percent of a Gallup Poll thought that British policy should be to support NATO; only 21 percent preferred a position of independence similar to that adopted by France, and 19 percent did not know what British policy toward NATO should be. The same questiions were asked in March 1968, with similar results: 59 percent supporting NATO, 24 percent favoring independence, and 17 percent having no opinion.

The available data suggest that CND's policy demands were supported by a significant minority of the British public during a period when foreign and defense policies were matters of great national concern. But support never approached a majority of the public. Moreover, the decline of interest in foreign affairs and the growth of concern about economic issues may have had little to do with any objective change in the circumstances of foreign and defense policy. To a certain extent Harold Wilson as leader of the party deliberately attempted to turn attention away from the divisive issues of nuclear weapons and toward neutral questions of technology and modernization. But the drift toward concern with economics in the mid-1960s was probably beyond contrivance.

Anthony Downs has argued that no issue can maintain itself indefinitely as a major topic of public concern.[29] An issue-attention cycle sets limits, according to Downs, on the duration of public concern with any particular topic. The competition of groups for public attention, the concern of experts with different critical problems, and the tendency of the public to become bored with a problem and impatient with its complexities and the difficulties of resolution are factors that encourage the decline of interest in one issue and growing concern with another in an endless cycle of national concerns.[30]

If this is true, it suggests that CND had little hope of success with the public once the complexities attendant upon unilateralism entered the public debate. The decline of public interest in nuclear armaments, which caused the unilateralists so much anguish and which provoked them to change tactics, divide into factions, and alter programs, may have been the result of factors beyond the influence of the unilateralists altogether. Nothing they might have done could have sustained the level of public attention required to turn mass campaign into a change in governmental policy.

It may be, however, that the peace movement's lack of success with the government and with public opinion generally does not indicate a total lack of influence. There is some, though slight, evidence that elements of scientific opinion were moved by unilateralist arguments, as well as the mass antibomb campaign. The Pugwash Conferences of scientists concerned with issues of nuclear arms was originally instigated by Bertrand Russell.[31] Focusing on technical questions relating to nuclear tests and problems of international inspection, the Pugwash Conferences depoliticized much of the debate on weaponry. However much the British political leaders were worried about the political divisiveness of unilateralism, scientific advisers to the government were, according to Terence Price, "privately encouraged to clear our minds on what, if anything, might be possible" regarding disarmament:

We took part in the disarmament conversations at London and Geneva, and were encouraged to go if we wished as observers to Pugwash, or to participate in private meetings of bodies like the Institute of Strategic Studies. There was no intellectual conflict here—it was the problems that were difficult. The more one became acquainted with the issues, the less one felt able to share the certainty of the Aldermaston marchers, admirable though they were as people. And yet they were not wholly without influence: It may have been partly due to their conviction that something ought to be done that it was possible to have a serious, and on the whole reasonably convincing, discussion within Whitehall.[32]

Price, of course, is not arguing that unilateralism or the peace movement directly influenced policy recommendations put forward by scientific advisers. Rather the peace movement contributed to a climate of discussion. This may be a significant point. Governments in general, and the British Foreign and Defence ministries in particular, are insulated by their attitudes, recruitment patterns, and work habits from mass public pressures on foreign policy issues. Expert opinion, on the other hand, may weigh more heavily upon them. The peace movement may thus have made some contributions to the restrictions on nuclear testing and the generally cautious approach to nuclear weapons that has come to characterize the postures of governments possessing them.

IV

Underlying all the confusing and sometimes bitter arguments within the peace movement over tactics and organization is the question of the movement's relationship to the ordinary practices of the British political system. Should the peace movement play by the unwritten rules that govern the activities of pressure groups? Or would the movement be more effective if it abandoned those rules? Throughout the postwar period, powerful forces within the movement sought by strictly legal means to persuade political leaders in the parties (primarily the Labour party) and the Parliament of the virtues of a more pacifistic foreign and defense policy. They preferred to lead organizations with well-defined memberships of articulate and, if possible, prestigious individuals. The decision in 1966 to turn CND into a membership organization marked the organizational triumph of this orientation.

Against this conventional view, there had been persistent challenges, culminating in 1958 in the rise of truly mass activity within the peace movement. This mass element—representing not merely greater numbers of peace movement participants but also a greater degree of impatience, volatility, and unpredictability—challenged the assumption on which conventional antiwar activity had been based.

The dispute between these two orientations has been so noisy that it has compelled interpreters of the postwar British peace movement to concentrate all their attention upon the issues of respectability versus nonrespectability as the road to political effectiveness or upon the related question of the peace movement as an instance of mass, expressive behavior. This has been unfortunate, for in the process the greatest political significance of the postwar peace movement has been drowned out. The issue of respectability or nonrespectability, essential as it is to understanding its internal history, has not had much connection with the peace movement's failure. And focus upon mass behavior within the peace movement has not been a productive line of inquiry.

Let us take the latter issue first. In the collective behavior school of political sociology, the categories of elite analysis originally developed by Vilfredo Pareto are extended to mass political activity, which is seen as irrational activity. According to this view, participants in mass movements seek not to attain specific political goals but rather to express their felt dissatisfaction with some social condition. This condition may be economic deprivation or insecurity. It may be actual or threatened loss of social status. Whatever it is, it need not have any instrumental link to the policy demands urged by the mass movement with which such participants are associated. Mass behavior is, therefore, a form of irrational behavior.[33]

Certain characteristics of the British peace movement, especially after 1958, invited analysis of this sort. The movement was a mass one with much spontaneous activity, especially on the marches and vigils. Indeed, the participation of young people, whose new musical style and preference for direct action and confrontation presaged the cultural rebellion of youth in many countries a few years later, appeared to many to indicate some change in British family structure or disenchantment with the presumbly bland security of the welfare state. The prominence in the movement of freelance artists and intellectuals provoked nearly as much discussion of alienation as it did of national defense. Moreover the ideological inconsistency of the unilateralist movement seemed to indicate some irrationality. An inverted chauvinism was revealed in arguments that Britain, by renouncing nuclear weapons, could regain its status among nations either by assuming moral leadership of the West or political leadership of the nonaligned countries of the Third World. Did not such arguments manifest anguish over Britain's declining world position rather than a clearly thought out foreign policy alternative?

Indeed the most prominent interpretation of the postwar British peace movement argues that it was a symbolic protest. According to Frank Parkin, support for CND "did not derive solely, or even mainly, from opposition to nuclear weapons. Instead protest against the Bomb was often a thinly veiled protest at certain other aspects of the social order which were independent of the Bomb, but which the latter appeared dramatically to highlight. To campaign against the Bomb was thus to a great extent also to campaign against other perceived ills of society."[34] Thus, Christian unilateralists were primarily concerned with revitalizing the Christian community.

Marxists supported it "mainly for the disruptive potential it appeared to open up." Intellectuals were using the movement to attack commercial control of the arts, to resolve their status conflicts, or to make a moral gesture. This analysis is extended to every category of unilateralist support in an effort to grasp the full range of the significance of the antibomb campaign.[35]

Parkin's analysis is by no means an extreme version of the collective behavior approach. His data specifically do not support the theoretical assertions of William Kornhauser or Eric Hoffer, who viewed participation in such movements as CND as pathological. Parkin is explicit in his criticism of the latter view. Nevertheless, the focus on the symbolic or irrational aspects of the unilateralist movement detracts from one's understanding of the latter's internal dynamics as well as its political significance.

The peace movement failed because it lacked the political resources needed to succeed. Its single strength was a tenuous grip on transitory public attention. Given that fact, the internal controversies, splits, and efforts at new tactics and new programs may be seen as rational behavior, not as symbolic protestations. As leaders of the peace movement studied the list of protest actions available, they might have concluded that lean times were ahead. They could try to change policy by attempting to elect a majority of pacifistic members to Parliament, or they could hope to become a sufficiently large minority in the House of Commons or among the public at large that governmental leaders would accept nuclear disarmament for political reasons, if not out of conviction. Or they could attempt to convert political leaders to the rationality and necessity of unilateralism. Or they could attempt to persuade civil servants in the Foreign and Defence Ministries. There were probably other alternatives, too, none very promising. In this light the choice between respectable and nonrespectable tactics is a practical matter. There is no need to question the motives of participants by raising the issue of symbolic protest; probably all political behavior contains expressive as well as instrumental elements. One central fact is that no alternative course of action available to the movement was likely to succeed, given the political resources at the movement's disposal.

What stands out in a review of the British peace movement since World War II is the stability, almost invulnerability, of the system by which foreign and defense policies are made. In a review of the various conceptual approaches to the governmental decision-making process, Richard Rose writes:

Major decisions about diplomacy and defense are consistently made by a single group of people. Ironically, the group consists of public officials: those around the prime minister, the Foreign Office, the Ministry of Defence, and, when financial considerations are significant, the Treasury. To describe these persons as a single group is not to suggest agreement among everyone involved, but rather to note their relative isolation from influences outside a narrow circle in Whitehall.[36]

The implication is that even if public opinion had supported unilateralism more strongly than it did, policy would have changed little, if at all. Even when "balance of power pluralism" or "segmented pluralism" might describe other policy areas, or the system as a whole, such terms, says Rose, do not convey the closed character of decision making in foreign policy. This has probably always been true of foreign and defense policy, but in the post-World War II period the closed quality of the decision-making process was reinforced by the need for internationally coordinated policies among the Western powers and the need to maintain and exchange secret information. Such continuity, coordination, and secrecy could be purchased only at the expense of the deliberative and open organs of government.[37]

By the late 1960s, many observers had diagnosed certain ramifications of this situation as a crisis of the House of Commons, and they called for reforms giving greater control over the cabinet and civil service.[38] (This has been recognized as the British equivalent of the "end of liberalism" often discussed in the United States.)[39] In this view, parliamentary debates and votes, party conference resolutions, public lectures, and speeches are examples of expressive or symbolic, rather than instrumental, behavior. The impression that such deliberative institutions give of public impact on policy is vastly greater than the reality.

The surprising and perhaps most significant quality of the postwar peace movement is the naiveté of so many of its leaders in assuming that the complex and internationally interlocked mechanism of defense and foreign policy could be fundamentally altered in a short space of time through the actions of the Labour Party Conference

and the Parliamentary Labour party. Canon Collins, Kingsley
Martin, Bertrand Russell, A. J. P. Taylor, and the other leaders of
CND, who came to disagree so much among themselves, agreed in
their faith that the liberal description of the British political system was the accurate one.[40] They did not anticipate that even if
some large trade unions moved to the left, bringing the Labour
Party Annual Conference over to their side (which to some extent
did occur in the 1960s) this would have little effect on the foreign
or defense policies of a Labour government. The party's annual
conference resolutions were ignored when they did not support
government foreign and defense policy. The unilateralists overestimated the importance of the House of Commons.

This faith in the validity of the liberal description of British institutions was probably the greatest weakness of the peace movement.
It encouraged the movement to insist that questions of defense
policy be isolated from other issues. If they had recognized the weakness of the deliberative organs they were attempting to influence,
they might more effectively have linked the question of nuclear
weapons to the issues of executive discretion and even domination
and the need for governmental reform. The Watergate scandal
opened this possibility to dissidents in the United States, broadening
the base of support sufficiently to have some effect. But the British
peace movement either failed to see the possibilities of such a broader
campaign or else saw little promise in it. The movement, therefore, withered in the 1960s, leaving only a few seeds for some future
generation to nurture.

NOTES

1. Among the sponsors who resigned from the Peace Pledge Union at the outbreak of war in 1939 were Storm Jameson, Ellen Wilkinson, Maude Roydon,
Rose Macaulay, Cyril E. M. Joad, and Bertrand Russell. Many rank-and-file
supporters did the same. See Sybil Morrison, *I Renounce War: The Story of the Peace
Pledge Union.* (London: Shephard Press, 1962), p. 36.

2. Hugh Brock, *The Century of Total War* (London: Peace News, n.d.), pp.22
ff., and Morrison, *I Renounce War,* pp. 60, 78, and passim.

3. See Socialist Union, *Twentieth Century Socialism* (London: Socialist Union,
1956), and C. A. R. Crosland, *The Future of Socialism* (London: Jonathan Cape,
1956), for examples of Labour party revisionism.

4. Leslie Hunter, *The Road to Brighton Pier* (London: Arthur Barker, 1959), is
a vivid contemporary account. See also Carl F. Brand, *The British Labour Party:*

A Short History, rev. ed. (Stanford, California: Stanford University Press, 1974), chap. 14.

5. The history of the unilateralist movement has been thoroughly told. See, for example, Christopher Driver, *The Disarmers: A Study in Protest* (London: Hodder and Stoughton, 1964); Frank Parkin, *Middle Class Radicalsim: The Social Bases of the Campaign for Nuclear Disarmament* (New York: Praeger, 1968); Peggy Duff, *Left, Left, Left: A Personal Account of Six Protest Campaigns* (London: Allison and Busby, 1971); Frank Myers, "Dilemmas in the British Peace Movement Since World War II," *Journal of Peace Research* (March 1973): 81-90.

6. Duff, *Left, Left, Left,* p. 129.

7. Bertrand Russell believed, for example, that the committee's "purely rational arguments are so strong that they would convince even the Prime Minister if they could be brought to his attention." See *Encounter* (London) 16 (1961): 93.

8. For a fuller account of the committee, see, in addition to references cited in note 5, Frank Myers, "Civil Disobedience and Organizational Change: The British Committee of 100," *Political Science Quarterly* 86, no. 1 (March 1971): 92-112.

9. For example, the CND's opposition to British membership in the Common Market was based solely on the argument that British entry would lead to further spread of nuclear weapons. See *Times* (London), October 18, 1971, p. 1.

10. Duff, *Left, Left, Left,* pp. 220ff.

11. The 1960 conference resolution called for "a complete rejection of any defence policy based on the threat of the use of strategic or tactical nuclear weapons" and "the permanent cessation of the manufacture or testing of nuclear and thermonuclear weapons." Labour Party, *Report of the Annual Conference,* October 3-6, 1960, p. 178.

12. Coral Bell, "The Special Relationship," in Michael Leifer, *Constraints and Adjustments in British Foreign Policy* (London: Allen and Unwin, 1972), pp. 103-119.

13. Leslie Stone, "Britain and the World," in David McKie and Chris Cook, *The Decade of Disillusion: British Politics in the Sixties* (London: Macmillan, 1972), pp. 126-127.

14. See Donald Maclean, *British Foreign Policy Since Suez: 1956-1968* (London: Hodder and Stoughton, 1970), pp. 286-293, where it is argued that the controversies within British Labour in the early 1960s produced a leftward shift in the party leadership, a shift expressed in the Wilson government's efforts to promote détente with the Soviet Union. Wilson and Labour cabinet members made several visits to the U.S.S.R., says Maclean, in response to the domestic political climate.

15. Labour Party, *Report of the Annual Conference* (1966), appendix II.

16. Ibid. (1967), p. 233.

17. Ibid., p. 235.

18. Ibid. (1972), p. 221. An amendment calling for British withdrawal from NATO, however, was defeated. See p. 219.

19. Ibid. (1973), p. 301.

20. A vivid discussion of Cousins may be found in Woodrow Wyatt, *Distinguished for Talent: Some Men of Influence and Enterprise* (London: Hutchinson and Co., 1958). See also Martin Harrison, *Trade Unions and the Labour Party Since 1945* (Detroit: Wayne State University Press, 1960), pp. 175ff.

21. See *Times* (London) of April 1, June 5, June 11, June 15, August 22, 1959, for accounts of unilateralist votes at trade union meetings.

22. *Guardian* (Manchester and London), October 1, 1960.

23. This statement was reproduced in Labour Party, *Report of the Annual Conference* (1960), pp. 13-16.

24. David Coates, *The Labour Party and The Struggle for Socialism* (London: Cambridge University Press, 1975), pp. 177ff.

25. Ibid., pp. 218-230.

26. The manner and consequences of Wilson's effort to deflect Labourite passions from ideology—especially concern with unilateralism—to technology is described in Victor Keegan, "Industry and Technology," in McKie and Cook, *Decade of Disillusion,* pp. 137ff.

27. George H. Gallup, ed., *The Gallup International Public Opinion Polls: Great Britain, 1937-1975.* (New York: Random House, 1976). All references to Gallup Polls are from the two volumes of this compilation, which presents poll results by date.

28. In July 1965, however, one poll asked respondents: "Are you sympathetic with propaganda against the H-bomb or not?" Twenty-nine percent said that their sympathies were with the propaganda, a large percentage considering that the wording of the question may be regarded as hostile to this position. "Propaganda" usually carries a negative connotation. Forty-six percent were not sympathetic to the anti-H-bomb propaganda.

29. Anthony Downs, "Up and Down with Ecology—The 'Issue-Attention Cycle,' " in *The Public Interest* 28 (Summer 1972):38-50.

30. Downs applies his argument directly to the ecology movement in the United States, but the terms of his argument would apply to most, if not all, issues. The question one might raise about Down's argument is its failure to explain the very long predominance of economic issues as objects of British public attention after 1965.

31. J. Rotblat, *Science and World Affairs: History of the Pugwash Conferences* (London: Dawsons of Pall Mall, 1962).

32. Terence Price in *Nature* 234 (November 5, 1971):19.

33. Vilfredo Pareto, *Sociological Writings* (New York: Praeger, 1966); Herbert Blumer, "Collective Behavior," in Alfred McClung Lee, *Principles of Sociology* (New York: Barnes and Noble, 1962); William Kornhauser, *The Politics of Mass Society* (Glencoe, Ill.: Free Press, 1959); Neil Smelser, *Theory of Collective Behavior* (New York: Free Press, 1963); Eric Hoffer, *The True Believer* (New York: Harper and Row, 1951). For critical views, see William A. Gamson, *The Strategy of Social Protest* (Homewood, Ill.: Dorsey Press, 1975), esp. pp. 130-143, and Anthony Oberschall, *Social Conflict and Social Movements* (Englewood Cliffs, N.J.: Prentice-Hall, 1973).

34. Parkin, *Middle Class Radicalism,* p. 108.

35. Ibid., pp. 108-109. See also John Rex, "The Sociology of CND," *War and Peace* 1, no. 1 (January-March 1964).

36. Richard Rose, "Politics in England," in Gabriel A. Almond, *Comparative Politics Today: A World View* (Boston: Little, Brown, 1974), p. 184.

37. For examples of discussions of these general developments, see Claus Offe, "Political Authority and Class Structure—An Analysis of Late Capitalist Systems," *International Journal of Sociology* 2, no. 1 (Spring 1972):73-108; Murray Edelman, *The Symbolic Uses of Politics* (Urbana, Ill.: University of Illinois Press, 1964); Frank Myers, "Social Class and Political Change in Western Industrial Systems," *Comparative Politics* 2, no. 3 (April 1970):402ff.

38. See R. H. S. Crossman, *The Myths of Cabinet Government* (Cambridge: Harvard University Press, 1972); Bernard Crick, *The Reform of Parliament* (London: Weidenfeld and Nicolson, 1964); Max Nicholson, *The System: The Misgovernment of Modern Britain* (New York: McGraw-Hill, 1967).

39. See, for example, Theodore Lowi, *The End of Liberalism* (New York: Norton, 1969); Henry S. Kariel, *The Decline of American Pluralism* (Stanford, Calif.: Stanford University Press, 1961); and Edelman, *Symbolic Uses of Politics.*

40. The attempt to make real the liberal ideal of a democratic foreign policy was the effort of the Union for Democratic Control, established in 1914 as the first antiwar organization to be formed during World War I. The UDC, unable to pay its debts, went out of existence in 1966.

13
Pragmatists and Visionaries in the Post-World War II American Peace Movement: SANE and CNVA

MILTON S. KATZ AND NEIL H. KATZ

The United States' participation in World War II inspired the formation of a new American peace movement. The large, nebulous peace movement of the 1930s ostensibly had failed; it had not prevented the outbreak of hostilities, and it had not developed effective means to thwart American war involvement. Nevertheless, peace activists, committed to a world vision of both peace and justice, took advantage of two war-related developments to generate a new, dual-thrust movement. These two developments—the use of atomic warfare and the use of nonviolent resistance among conscientious objectors—provided an issue for one wing of the new peace movement, known as nuclear pacifists, and provided a methodology for the other wing, the radical pacifists.

Nuclear pacifists, who concentrated on the dangers of nuclear war, emphasized public opinion, credentials, and political expediency in attempting to influence policy makers on specific issues. Radical pacifists, opposed to all wars and committed to major societal changes, concentrated on developing a nonviolent action methodology that allowed pacifists and others to work for peace and to combat injustice by nontraditional means. At a 1957 organiza-

---

*SANE is an acronym for the National Committee for a Sane Nuclear Policy; CNVA an acronym for the Committee for Nonviolent Action. Milton Katz authored the section on SANE and Neil Katz that on CNVA. The introductory paragraphs and the conclusion were jointly authored.

tional meeting these two wings of the peace movement were formally established. The nuclear pacifists were housed in an organization that would become the National Committee for a Sane Nuclear Policy (SANE); the radical pacifists were linked to the network that later became the Committee for Nonviolent Action (CNVA).[1]

SANE

The first use of the atomic bomb in 1945 generated a wide public controversy and spawned a new group of pacifists who agreed with Norma Cousins, editor of the *Saturday Review,* that "man's survival on earth is now absolutely dependent on his ability to avoid a new war."[2] Nuclear pacifism emerged from the traditional internationalist groups composed of writers, intellectuals, university faculty, scientists, and other professionals who had supported World War II.

Nuclear pacifists were comprised initially of two main groups: advocates of world government and atomic scientists. Out of these two groups emerged the United World Federalists and the Federation of Atomic Scientists, both of which became influential in American life in the relatively friendly postwar atmosphere.[3] As relations between the United States and the Soviet Union deteriorated into an East-West polarity, however, the nuclear pacifist movement waned. Already reduced to insgnificant proportions by the Cold War, their troubles deepened when McCarthyism became an overriding fact of American life. The loyalty mania of the early 1950s left nuclear pacifism nearly impotent. "Seven years ago, when world law was mentioned, people said it was too soon," complained Cousins in late 1952. "Now when it is mentioned, they say it is too late."[4]

Despite the inaction of the Cold War and McCarthy period, hope within the nuclear pacifist camp remained alive. By 1956, with the Albert Einstein-Bertrand Russell appeal for an end to Cold War hostilities and with the thaw in the Cold War following Stalin's death and denunciation at the Soviet Union's Twentieth Party Congress, the potential developed for a new force within the peace movement. The profound misgivings generated by the nuclear policy of building bigger and better bombs finally united the nuclear pacifist and radical pacifist wings of the peace movement. In the spring of 1957, consequently, the American peace movement underwent a significant revival. The National Committee for a Sane Nuclear Policy and the Committee for Nonviolent Action led the way. Although they eventually focused criticism upon thermonuclear weapons and other forms of violence, their immediate concern was the atmospheric testing of hydrogen bombs.

These two organizations were formed in the spring of 1957 when Larry Scott, American Friends Service Committee (AFSC) peace education director in Chicago, became "obsessed with nuclear testing and began agitating constantly for an end to it."[5] He went to New York and won over such leading pacifists as A. J. Muste, Bayard Rustin, and Robert Gilmore, the New York secretary of the AFSC. Using their names to attract other leading pacifists, Scott called them together for a late April meeting in Philadelphia. These pacifists talked about a "Proposed Committee to Stop H-Bomb Tests," and decided that the committee would be "broadly based with both pacifists and non-pacifists included."[6]

Two very important questions were discussed at this April meeting: how to deal with the differences between the radical pacifists and the nonpacifists and whether to work for disarmament or to focus only on the nuclear testing issue. The first question was settled when they decided to form two groups: one for the radical pacifists, who would use Gandhian nonviolent resistance as their major tactic, and the other for the nuclear pacifists, who would stress conventional tactics, such as education and lobbying. The second question was easily answered when it was agreed that both groups should focus on the nuclear testing issue as the first step toward disarmament. Finally, it was decided to operate through a three-pronged organization: an ad-hoc liberal, nuclear pacifist organization that would later be known as SANE; an ad-hoc radical pacifist, direct-action oriented organization, which would become CNVA; and the older peace organizations (such as AFSC and the Women's International League for Peace and Freedom), which would focus increasingly on the nuclear testing issue, thus giving support and encouragement to the two ad-hoc committees.

Scott made it clear, however, that although there would be two separate committees, he wanted a close working relationship be-

268   MILTON S. KATZ AND NEIL H. KATZ

tween them. "While the two groups are not organizationally tied together," he said, "I hope there will be some organic and spiritual relationship between the two aspects within a larger movement of Creative Truth." Scott, a radical pacifist, had more sympathy with that wing. He and A. J. Muste organized CNVA. Robert Gilmore, who worked well with both kinds of pacifists, Norman Cousins, and Clarence Pickett, secretary emeritus of the AFSC, organized SANE.

In the fall of 1957, SANE placed an advertisement in the *New York Times* that "started a movement."[7] The copy began, "We Are Facing a Danger Unlike Any Danger That Has Ever Existed," and ended with a call for an immediate suspension of nuclear testing. The response was overwhelming. By the summer of 1958, SANE had about 130 chapters representing approximately 5,000 Americans.[8] One SANE official suggested that "this response was evidence of a vacuum in the American peace movement. No group was then urging politically relevant action on specific issues of the arms race." He concluded that "SANE gave anxious citizens from varied backgrounds a single meaningful issue on which to act—the cessation of nuclear weapons testing."[9]

Yet this view seems only partially correct. SANE did attract many young people and liberals; however, it also drew upon the peace movement's more traditional sources of strength. As sociologist Nathan Glazer observed, SANE "was actually based on a coalition of two major groupings, both of which had their origins in older issues: the proponents of world government on the one hand and the pacifists on the other."[10] For example, prominent SANE spokesmen like Norman Cousins, Oscar Hammerstein, and Walter Reuther had all been officers in the United World Federalists (UWF). In addition, Donald Keys, SANE's first full-time executive director, had been on the UWF staff. Because of the latter's desire to avoid "eyebrow raising" activities, SANE received little cooperation from the world government organization.[11] Although a considerable number of SANE leaders were moderate and traditional pacifists, including Clarence Pickett, Robert Gilmore, and veteran peace activist Norman Thomas, SANE itself was "pragmatic, not absolutist."[12] Radical pacifists like Muste gave SANE strong support in the beginning, but most became involved in the more direct-action oriented groups such as CNVA.

As the peace movement reasserted itself, the nuclear testing issue gave way to an emphasis upon the dangers of nuclear weapons themselves. For some time, SANE's leaders had considered expanding the organization's scope. In June 1958, pondering what would happen if the United States did ban nuclear weapons tests, Norman Cousins maintained that such an action would "not represent the be-all and end-all of world peace and nuclear sanity. A truly sane nuclear policy will not be achieved until nuclear weapons are brought completely under control."[13] Consequently, in 1958, when both the Soviet Union and the United States voluntarily suspended nuclear weapons tests, SANE turned its attention to intercontinental ballistic missiles and to the threat of nuclear annihilation. At a fall 1958 national conference, the organization resolved to broaden its goal from a nuclear test ban to general disarmament.

As Americans became more conscious of the potential for nuclear disaster, SANE grew rapidly in size and influence. During the 1958-59 Geneva talks on disarmament, the committee gathered thousands of signatures on petitions urging a test ban, inaugurated peace demonstrations patterned after Britain's Aldermaston march, and worked in support of a Senate resolution endorsing efforts to secure a test-ban treaty. In May 1960, at the height of its influence and prestige, SANE held a major rally in New York City to coincide with the planned summit conference between President Eisenhower and Premier Khrushchev. The rally was successful despite the fact that the summit was cancelled. Twenty thousand persons heard a roster of distinguished citizens speak about the human right to live without the fear and danger of fall-out and nuclear disaster.[14] "For a moment," one critic observed, "it looked as though SANE might grow into a really powerful force in American politics."[15] But this prediction never came true. The reasons for this failure tell us a great deal about the difficulties that faced the American peace movement.

SANE's troubles began on the eve of the rally, when Senator Thomas J. Dodd (D-Conn.), temporary chairman of the Senate Internal Security Subcommittee, demanded that SANE "purge their ranks ruthlessly" of communists. He charged that "the unpublicized chief organizer of the rally was a veteran member of the Communist Party," and that "the Communists were responsible for a very substantial percentage of the overflow turnout." While

admitting that SANE was "headed by a group of nationally prominent citizens about whose integrity and good faith there is no question," Dodd contended that "evidence" existed "of serious Communist infiltration at chapter level."[16]

Although the threat of being identified with the communist issue
had long concerned its leadership, the Dodd crusade precipitated a
minor panic within SANE. The board reacted by stating that the
organization resented the Senate investigation. At the same time,
however, it adopted a resolution welcoming into membership only
those persons "whose support is not qualified by adherence to Communist or other totalitarian doctrine."[17] The Greater New York
SANE Committee was totally reorganized in order to eliminate local
affiliates that the national board considered dominated by actual or
potential communists. About half the chapters in the New York
metropolitan area, which comprised half the chapters in the nation,
refused to take out new charters and were expelled from the organization. Thus, SANE cleaned its own house before the Dodd committee could do it for them. SANE's leaders felt compelled to maintain a respectable image whatever its cost in influence within the
peace movement. As one participant explained: "SANE was still
proving credentials at the time. The McCarthy period was not
over then."[18]

To A. J. Muste, Robert Gilmore, and the others who resigned
from the organization, however, this policy was absolutely destructive. Muste pointed out, and most of the SANE board agreed, that
Dodd's charge of communist infiltration was an attempt to stifle
the nuclear test-ban movement and, with it, SANE. "The Senator
was aiming to kill two fat pigeons with one shot," Muste explained,
"to show Vice-President Nixon and the public on the eve of the
Presidential election campaign that no one was going to outdo the
Democrats in hunting out Communist heretics and stooges; and to
strike a blow against a conservative peace organization which was
gaining a considerable number of adherents."[19] By its expulsion of
alleged communists, SANE played into the hands of its enemies. As
Homer Jack, then executive director, explained: "Ironically, SANE
helped continue what it was supposed to be fighting against: McCarthyism and the Cold-War hysteria."[20]

Although SANE survived as one of the largest and most influential
peace groups, it was badly shaken. Its hopes were raised, however,

the following year with the establishment of the semiautonomous Arms Control and Disarmament Agency and with the announcement of the American-Soviet accord on a nuclear test-ban treaty in 1963. SANE and other peace groups worked feverishly to mobilize public opinion behind Senate ratification. They saw the treaty as the first step toward defusing the potentially explosive East-West confrontation. To make the moment even more satisfying, Jerome Wiesner, President Kennedy's scientific adviser, gave public acclaim to the national committee as one group that helped bring about the treaty and to Norman Cousins for playing an important role in the test-ban negotiations. Many consider this particular episode to be SANE's greatest triumph. As Kennedy began to adopt the rhetoric of the peace movement, talking of a "world safe for diversity," and of a "peace race," many people in SANE believed they had achieved a breakthrough at the highest levels of power.[21]

Following the signing of the test-ban treaty, the national board of SANE met to consider the organization's future course. Some directors, including Norman Cousins, thought that SANE should be discontinued since its primary objective had been achieved. The majority of the directors, however, wanted to continue to work for more substantial agreements.[22] Vietnam soon made the argument moot, for if the test ban had weakened SANE and the nuclear pacifist movement, the war in Southeast Asia brought both back to life.

SANE AND THE VIETNAM WAR

After the bombings of North Vietnam began in early 1965, SANE placed a full-page advertisement in the New York Times asking Americans to mobilize public opinion. The committee called for a stop in the widening of the war, a cease-fire, and a negotiated international settlement.[23] In the spring, SANE, with the help of other moderate peace organizations, sponsored an "Emergency Rally on Vietnam." At this event, speaker after speaker assailed U.S. policy and called for negotiations with all concerned parties, including the Vietnamese National Liberation Front.[24]

SANE again took an active role in the American peace movement, but new problems quickly emerged. In April 1965, after the organization boycotted a Students for a Democratic Society

(SDS) rally, SANE began planning its own demonstration. The coordinator of the SANE march, Sanford Gottlieb, declared that his objective was to keep "kooks, Communists, or draft-dodgers out of the Washington Demonstration."²⁵ Again, SANE felt compelled to keep its centrist position that only a responsible peace demonstration would influence the American public and the administration on Vietnam.

On November 27, SANE sponsored a march on Washington for peace in Vietnam. Publicized as "A Call to Mobilize the Conscience of America," the action attracted an estimated crowd of 35,000 (most of them middle-class adults) and was, in the organization's words, "moderate and responsible." A disagreement over who could participate almost took place between the SANE liberals and the SDS radicals, but the two groups agreed before the march that SDS, in return for its participation, could issue its own call and add its own spokesmen to the official program.

Although the April SDS march included all organizations that wished to join, the November SANE march was designed to exclude not only communists, but the more radical and militant antiwar activists as well. This development highlighted the growing division within the movement. Afterwards Sanford Gottlieb stated the reasoning behind SANE's approach: "It should not have been necessary to prove [i.e., by having this demonstration] that ordinary Americans favor a negotiated settlement in Vietnam, but in the view of the chauvinistic climate whipped up by the radical demonstrations, an abject lesson was necessary just to get our message heard." He concluded by saying that "before November 27, it was all too easy for the hard-liners to dismiss the substance of what we were saying by intoning that only extremists were saying it."²⁶

SANE kept its march moderate, middle class, and responsible. The committee acted as internal policemen and not only kept the protesters moving and out of trouble but enforced a ban on unauthorized placards. Thus, SANE effectively isolated and controlled the extremists. In this way it strove to moderate both the demonstration's tone and to preserve its general atmosphere of dignity and restraint. It also loaded the speakers' program with moderates who, as SDS President Carl Oglesby said later, were so eager "to show their 'responsibleness' to criticize both sides equally that some of the speeches would hardly have been wrong for a pro-war rally."[27] Placed at the end of the program, Oglesby delivered a speech that was a public and symbolic break between the liberals and radicals in the peace movement. Although the subject was Vietnam, he denounced corporate liberalism for its imperialist policies abroad and its oppression at home, and demanded revolution to overthrow it.

For his efforts, Oglesby received the only standing ovation of the day. SANE, however, was not impressed. Instead, they were proud of the effect their march had on the news media. According to Sanford Gottlieb, the newsmen were "victms of their own propaganda," for they "expected a crowd of 'beats' and found middle-class America. One could almost hear the gasps of surprise in their reports." As a result, the news stories tended to concentrate on the marchers rather than on the content of the speeches. "Yet," Gottlieb added, "this had importance. In middle-class America, the neatly-dressed, the well-groomed, and the restrained simply have greater acceptability, and their acceptability is 'transferrable' to the realm of ideas. To recognize this," he concluded, "is not to make value judgements about physical appearance, but to understand how to communicate."[28]

The growing division between the radical students and SANE became even more pronounced the following spring when SANE initiated a "Voter's Peace Pledge Campaign." This campaign was to culminate with a hugh May rally to hand in contributions for the congressional candidates who had pledged to work for a peaceful settlement in Vietnam. The project was not as successful as the earlier demonstration. This led John Gerassi, writing in *Liberation,* to state that SANE had "done the peace movement a disservice" by again attempting to keep its demonstrations "moderate and responsible, and dogmatically accepting the Administration's own definition of responsibility." Gerassi argued that students were disenchanted by the SANE marches in November and again in May and began to realize that "the march did not represent them." He concluded that "it is not enough to be a well-meaning protestor; one must also know what one is protesting against." Thus, those 40,000 who went to Washington in November and failed to return in May were those "who could be fooled once—but not again."[29]

SPLIT IN SANE

In 1967 the break between SANE and the more radical groups in the peace movement, and within SANE itself, became complete. When the Spring Mobilization to End the War in Vietnam was being organized by a peace coalition, Benjamin Spock and Martin Luther King, Jr., were asked to be cochairmen. Spock, then serving as cochairman of SANE along with Harvard history professor H. Stuart Hughes, viewed the demonstrations with enthusiasm. His opponents on the SANE board, however, viewed the march with apprehension. "We didn't like the style of the thing," said Norman Cousins. "Some of the leaders had black racist tendencies streaked with violence. Some were Vietcong supporters. Some were opposed to negotiations. We couldn't control what those people would say or do, and we didn't want SANE to be taxed with ideas that most of us didn't share."[30] Seymour Melman, later cochairman of SANE, stated that "the central issue was the prospect of violent behavior in marches that were not going to be politically effective."[31] Spock, although deploring violence and supporting negotiations as the way to end American involvement in Vietnam, argued that only by participating in such protests could SANE exert any influence over them. He cautioned that disqualifying selected elements from the peace alliance would encourage dissension in the ranks: "I believe in going in with other groups as long as their aims are roughly those of SANE," said Spock. "I believe in solidarity."[32]

Spock's decision to become cochairman of the march without consulting SANE's national board increased tension within the organization. The board passed a resolution stressing the need for SANE to concentrate on its own program and declared that the organization would remain in communication with the planners of the mobilization. However, SANE support for the march was not forthcoming.[33] Although many SANE members individually took part in the mobilization, the organization's main activity was the Negotiations Now Campaign, "a search . . . for millions of the as-yet uncommitted citizens to join with the leaders who have broken with the President over Vietnam."[34] Supported by the moderates in SANE as well as establishment liberals such as John Kenneth Galbraith and Arthur Schlesinger, Jr., Negotiations

Now was designed to rally wide middle-class support to end the bombing of North Vietnam and to begin talks with the National Liberation Front.

The turbulent events of 1967 prompted the resignations of key SANE officials. Norman Cousins and Donald Keys, for example, resigned because they feared that the committee had strayed too far to the left and was now unwilling to antagonize the militants within the movement. Benjamin Spock, on the other hand, resigned because he thought that SANE had not radicalized nearly enough.[35] One thing was clear, however: SANE had lost badly needed support and leadership from both sides of the political spectrum. It became evident to those who remained within SANE that the organization's "middle-of-the road position was being eroded on both sides. . . . they had no choice but to stay in the middle."[36]

As the war in Vietnam continued unabated, SANE became increasingly frustrated and outraged. When it finally called for a unilateral withdrawal of American troops in September 1969 and supported the moratorium and March on Washington in October and November, it joined the rest of the peace movement in direct action protest. But for the organization itself, SANE's all too moderate radicalization came too late to be really effective. By the end of the decade, SANE's reputation within the antiwar movement was badly damaged.

CNVA

Radical pacifism emerged out of the direct action experiences of a small group of conscientious objectors (COs) who, with the advent of conscription in 1940, were brought together in Civilian Public Service (CPS) camps or in federal prisons.[37] A number of these COs had been inspired by new interpretations of the philosophy and actions of Mahatma Gandhi and by the recent successful nonviolent struggles waged by the American labor movement.[38] Armed with new knowledge and strategies, CPS assignees conducted work slowdowns, fasts, strikes, and walkouts to protest the camps' demeaning work, lack of wages, and military climate. In federal prisons, militant pacifists refused to work, fasted, and engaged in other forms of noncooperation to win struggles against prison censorship, restrictions on parole, and racial segregation.

During the war years the radical pacifists were isolated in their struggle both physically and emotionally. Established pacifist organizations, such as the American Friends Service Committee and the Fellowship of Reconciliation, joined the vast majority of the American population who supported the Allied war effort in condemning the militant pacifists' response against CPS camps and federal prison policy. By the time of their release after the war, the radical pacifists had succeeded in reducing the martial atmosphere of the camps and in ending segregation in some prison mess halls.

These small but important successes gave them unity and determination to continue and develop the use of nonviolent action in the postwar period. Radical pacifists demonstrated in favor of amnesty for COs and campaigned against the atomic bomb, a permanent conscription law, and militarism in general. "These demonstrations," War Resisters League member Jim Peck recalled, "constituted our attempts to apply effectively on the outside the nonviolent method we had used in prison . . . somehow it seemed a continuation of the same struggle—a struggle against what we believed to be injustice."[39]

During the late 1940s the radical pacifists were active in organizations such as the Congress of Racial Equality, the Committee for Nonviolent Revolution, the Peacemakers, and the War Resisters League. In these organizations, they set up nonviolent communities and demonstrated against segregation, the peacetime draft, war taxes, and other war-related developments. Though the number of active radical pacifists dwindled during the Korean War and the McCarthy period, pacifist militants publicly called for mediation instead of military intervention in Korea and continued to protest the denial of civil liberties to dissident Americans.

In the mid-1950s radical pacifism, like nuclear pacifism, experienced a rebirth. *Liberation,* a radical pacifist journal dedicated to publicizing and developing the use of nonviolent action, began publishing in 1956. The success of the Montgomery bus boycott the same year proved the efficacy of sustained nonviolent struggle. New York pacifists claimed victory when their refusal to cooperate with civil defense drills gained increasing public support from 1955 onward. (In 1961 compulsory civil defense drills were terminated in New York State.)

These new efforts to publicize, develop, and use nonviolent action gained the radical pacifists more acceptance and support from individual pacifists. Nevertheless, the established peace organizations, such as the Fellowship of Reconciliation and the American Friends Service Committee, feared loss of financial and active support from their diverse constituency if they endorsed militant nonviolent action, including civil disobedience. The radical pacifists, therefore, enthusiastically supported Larry Scott when he called the 1957 organizational meeting in Philadelphia to create new structures to serve as the public education (SANE) and direct action (CNVA) arms of the peace movement. For the next ten years, while SANE provided leadership for the traditional peace advocates, CNVA served as the base for the radical pacifists to organize and implement their dramatic nonviolent efforts toward peace and justice.

CNVA CAMPAIGNS

CNVA's first significant action occurred in August 1957 on the twelfth anniversary of the Hiroshima bombing. Eleven pacifists were arrested at an Atomic Energy Commission bomb test project in Nevada for deliberately trespassing onto military territory.[40] CNVA actions against testing of nuclear weapons continued the next year. One project failed when a group of CNVA pacifists were denied entry into the Soviet Union to plead their case for halting bomb tests before the Russian government and people. Another effort was more successful: four CNVA members sailed a small ketch, *The Golden Rule,* into the Pacific Ocean in a symbolic protest against the H-bomb tests. Refusing to comply with a government-issued injunction, the pacifists attempted two sailings into the forbidden area and were arrested twice. In this project CNVA was noticeably supported by SANE and other pacifist groups who led popular protests to "stop the bomb tests, not *The Golden Rule.*"[41]

Media coverage and public outcry in support of the pacifists increased when Earl Reynolds, a former Atomic Energy Commission anthropologist, and his family, joined a resident of Hiroshima to promote the pacifists' cause. They successfully sailed their small boat, the *Phoenix,* into the nuclear test zone. The favorable publicity resulting from the conversion of five nonpacifists into strident opponents of nuclear testing was the first indication of the radical pacifists' potential influence.

Later that year, Brad Lyttle, a young scholar and advocate of Gandhian nonviolent action, joined other militant pacifists in radicalizing CNVA's goals and tactics. Like their counterparts in SANE, CNVA moved from protesting bomb tests to opposing the construction of intercontinental ballistic missiles (ICBM). Educational witness activities designed to inform and persuade were replaced by obstructionist tactics designed to confront and coerce. At the first ICBM base at Cheyenne, Wyoming, CNVA militants staged repeated sit-ins at the entrance and temporarily prevented vehicles from entering the base.

These confrontational tactics against nuclear weapon production continued in subsequent projects. In 1959, CNVA pacifists demonstrated at the Mead Intercontinental Ballistic Missile Base near Omaha, Nebraska. After being ignored by the media and denied the opportunity to talk to Mead employees or to address townspeople, the CNVA team concluded that only civil disobedience would attract attention to their cause. Led by the American peace movement leader, seventy-five-year-old A. J. Muste, they defiantly climbed over the base's entrance fence and were summarily arrested.

The Cheyenne and Omaha projects confirmed CNVA's shift from the bomb-test issue to a more inclusive antimilitarism stance. In addition, the group now emphasized coercive nonviolent methods. As a result of these changes, Lyttle and Muste replaced Scott as the official leaders of CNVA. Lyttle, with Muste's blessing, conceived the next two projects: action against Polaris weapons and the San Francisco to Moscow walk.

These two projects were the most ambitious and prolonged CNVA undertakings to date. In New London, Connecticut, in 1960, pacifists tried to convince the local citizens of the physical and moral danger of building and supporting Polaris submarines bearing nuclear-tipped missiles. Direct action techniques, such as picketing missile-carrying ships, were combined with a person-to-person educational campaign aimed at townspeople and at workers involved in manufacturing nuclear submarines. Initially most townspeople were hostile. Pacifists were harassed or assaulted, and some of their office furniture and files were destroyed. After several months, however, some citizens expressed support for the pacifists' actions, and CNVA gained entry into at least five churches. CNVA felt its courageous and sustained efforts had borne fruit. They had "shattered public apathy about the arms race," and New London residents had been stimulated to think about the "significance and . . . consequences of creating machines of mass annihilation."[42]

The same year CNVA began another major project, the San Francisco to Moscow walk, which signaled several changes. The goal of the radical pacifists' actions moved from opposition to nuclear weapons to a call for unilateral disarmament. Also, the audience broadened to include non-U.S. citizens. In December 1960, eleven pacifists left San Francisco on a nine-month walk that took them 3,000 miles across the United States and another 3,000 miles across Europe to Moscow. After rallies, speeches, and interviews at numerous cities and military installations in the United States, England, France, East and West Germany, Poland, and Russia, the walk team entered Moscow on October 31, 1961. Most of those who arrived in Moscow had walked well over 1,000 miles. News of this protest reached millions of people, several thousand of whom participated as walk supporters by marching part of the way with the official team. The pacifists' call for unilateral disarmament, however, became embroiled in elaborate international politics: governments responded favorably to the concept but were quick to ask another nation to make the first move.[43] Even so, the walk did extend CNVA's appeal to various countries and successfully underscored the importance of civil liberties by emphasizing freedom of speech. Most newspapers echoed the *New York Post*'s editorial comment that the radical pacifists' "spirit and endurance evoke our respect; so does their consistency in raising the same plea in the U.S.S.R. that they voiced in the U.S.A."[44]

Two years later, CNVA again shifted goals and tactics. The increasing militancy displayed by the disputants in the civil rights struggles and repeated United States-Cuba confrontations forced CNVA to reassess its perspective on the relationship between nonviolence and liberation. Deciding that the two goals were, in fact, compatible, the radical pacifists proposed to demonstrate the efficacy of nonviolent action for revolutionary change. In designing the 1963 Quebec-Washington-Guantanamo walk for peace, CNVA was heeding A. J. Muste's call to "radicalize the peace movement . . . and to adopt direct action and civil disobedience as the major strategy and to relate nonviolence primarily to the dynamics of social change rather than to a personal philosophy or way of life."[45]

CNVA thus implemented an action that linked protest against the United States' diplomatic oppression in Cuba with protest against domestic segregation. It planned to send an integrated walk team from Quebec to Washington to Miami and then to sail to Cuba. Along the walk route, the pacifists would demonstrate at military bases, ending at Guantanamo.

The project in Cuba was cancelled, however, after CNVA became entangled in a major civil rights struggle in Albany, Georgia. Fourteen pacifists were jailed for up to fifty-six days for their refusal to comply with a court order prohibiting an integrated protest march through the major white downtown area. After eight weeks of publicized fasting by the pacifists (intravenous feedings cost the city about $500 per day), a compromise was reached allowing an integrated five-member team to march through the forbidden area.

Because of State Department passport bans on travel to Cuba, exhaustion of the walk team, and increasing American involvement in the Vietnam war, the international aspects of the Quebec-Washington-Guantanamo walk were aborted. However, America's role in the Vietnam war gave CNVA the impetus needed to develop another international project.

CNVA AND VIETNAM

Unlike SANE and the traditional peace organizations, CNVA had actively protested American involvement in the war since 1963. In 1966, though many of its members had joined in coalition activity, CNVA decided to send its own six-member team to Saigon to show the Vietnamese that some Americans opposed the war. The Americans held cordial meetings with the underground South Vietnamese peace movement, but were harassed by Vietnamese youth at public meetings. The pacifists believed that they had evidence that the harassment had been ordered by the South Vietnamese government, with the approval of the United States. However, since the American press generally implied that shouts of "Pacifists, go home; go to the Communists,'' and other provocations were all honest and spontaneous, the pacifists felt they must take their protest home to minimize the chance of distortion.[46]

In the United States, CNVA continued to organize some of its own anti-Vietnam war actions, while it also participated in coalition activities. Before and after the Saigon trip, pacifists intensified their tax resistance campaigns, draft refusal efforts, and protests at munition plants. Members participated in numerous teach-ins on college campuses, organized a speakout at the Pentagon, and, in three instances, immolated themselves in a witness action modeled after those of the Vietnamese Buddhist monks. After 1965, radical pacifists led small-scale protest actions such as draft-card burnings and picket lines at induction centers.

Acts of nonviolent resistance proliferated within the entire peace movement. CNVA proudly declared in its bulletin that "now more people are emphasizing themes traditionally of CNVA for their own actions such as refusal of military service, protest at war transportation industries, tax refusal, and confrontation of war symbols like at Armed Forces Day."[47] Whether as a result of CNVA's past protest actions, their participation in coalition activites, or, more subtly, because of CNVA's consolidation of peace and justice issues with the ideas and methods of nonviolent action, CNVA was influencing the expanding and increasingly powerful American protest movement.

Like SANE, CNVA's major dilemma in the mid-1960s was how to relate to the progressively popular anti-Vietnam coalition demonstrations. CNVA's decision to move from independent to joint political action ensured it some impact on the greatly enlarged peace movement. The resolution to ally CNVA with the new left groups who did not share the same commitment to nonviolence, however, caused much controversy within CNVA and the entire peace movement.

The main issues of contention with CNVA were threefold. First, by joining the "nonexclusionist" coalitions, CNVA would be allied with some Maoist and Marxist groups that clearly did not share a principled commitment to nonviolence. Second, CNVA's participation in the coalitions meant that it could not publicize its total anti-war message but must accept the common, though narrower, goal of the coalitions of getting the United States out of Vietnam. Third, CNVA's time, energy, and financial resources were limited; joining the coalitions meant sacrificing some of its independent actions.

The anticoaliton forces within CNVA were led by Connecticut College chemistry professor and CNVA officer, Gordon Christiansen, who felt that CNVA's participation would "dilute, muffle, and distort the pacifist message."[48] His prediction proved correct. Traditional pacifist concerns—a commitment to principled nonviolence for meaningful social change and a condemnation of all wars and violence as destroyers of physical and spiritual life—were subsumed by the coalitions' search for a common cause to build a mass movement. The radical pacifists' role in the coalition was downplayed by the more flamboyant and glamorous new left groups and was ignored by the media. By investing so much energy in coalition activity, CNVA was unable to garner enough emotional and financial commitment from its supporters to keep itself afloat as a separate organization. These factors, combined with CNVA's realization that militant nonviolent direct action was now widely used, brought CNVA to merge with the War Resisters League in December 1967.

Brad Lyttle and A. J. Muste were the prime movers behind CNVA's decision to participate actively in mass antiwar protests. Lyttle shared Muste's belief that the Vietnam war protest movement was an "exceptional and fateful movement in history which required an unusual response."[49] Lyttle argued that the coalition was an "experiment," with "the stopping of the war in Vietnam the main purpose." Alliance with the left, rather than with the liberals, was preferable to Lyttle, for the left would "confront and inhibit the administration's military ambitions, not just encourage the administration to be more enlightened." In addition, "the hard core activists [i.e., civil rights workers, new left students, the old left, and the radical pacifists] had withstood persecution and repression and had not accepted political compromise."[50]

Muste and Lyttle also believed that CNVA's joining of the coalition would have two other advantages. First, by defending "nonexclusionism," CNVA would help lay to rest in the peace movement the "sub-human anti-communist propaganda" that had severely hurt SANE in 1960. Second, pacifists could influence the coalition.

They could help keep the demonstrations nonviolent "by becoming monitors and assuming an active role in civil disobedience and serving as a witness to nonviolent responses to police, arrest, bail, etc."[51]

Many of Muste's and Lyttle's contentions were borne out. Mass demonstrations played an authoritative role in the antiwar movement. While confrontational tactics invited repression, they did force change. "Red-baiting" the demonstrators failed to divide the movement. And CNVA activity in the coalitions successfully influenced the dynamics of the demonstrations since the radical pacifists were excellent conciliators and enjoyed the trust of competing factions. They helped keep communications open, not only among the groups of protesters but also between the protesters and the police. By displaying their commitment to nonviolence, they provided an example and an atmosphere in which people could explore alternatives to the violent confrontational model for forcing change. One such instance occurred during the fall 1967 Pentagon demonstration when radical pacifists averted violence by successfully organizing a teach-in for the soldiers.[52] Some of the mass coalition participants, such as writer Norman Mailer, were deeply affected by the pacifist actions and sense of community.[53]

CNVA'S ACHIEVEMENT

The most important achievement of CNVA was to popularize and refine the use of nonviolent action, not only as a means of self-expression but also as an important tool to bring about needed change. CNVA initially concentrated on attainable goals (the bomb test issue) and persuasion methods designed to educate the public and/or enlighten the decision makers. Throughout their ten-year history, the radical pacifists broadened their goals and escalated their nonviolent tactics. They moved from protesting bomb tests, to opposing the construction and use of nuclear weapons, to calling for unilateral disarmament. By 1963 they had adopted a platform that advocated revolutionary nonviolence in order to obtain justice as well as peace. Their nonviolent methods became more coercive and confrontational and often included civil disobedience. These changes moved the radical pacifists too far away from SANE and most of the other traditional peace organizations for them to co-ordinate activities. Also, CNVA failed to lead the mass coalitions and redirect their goals to a general condemnation of violence and injustice.

Nevertheless, CNVA's flexibility and vision allowed it to function as the cutting edge of the peace movement. By engaging in militant actions and asking for revolutionary changes, CNVA not only prodded SANE and the other traditional peace advocates to broaden their goals and tactics, but also gave these groups more room to operate since both the government and the general public viewed them as safer and more rational than CNVA.

Because of their flexibility and vision, the radical pacifists also served as an important link between the peace and the civil rights movements. As a result they influenced the means that the new left groups employed to wage their struggles. Overall, the radical pacifists shaped and directed the peace movement's use of non-violence and infused it with a recognition that a massive direct action component could supplement standard forms of political discourse, broaden the power base, and bring pressure to bear on important public policy.

CONCLUSION

Though SANE and CNVA were partners in an overall American peace movement and shared some common dilemmas, their different sociopolitical assumptions dictated different strategies. SANE was "founded on the premise that mistaken United States policies can be remedied and set right, and that in order to do so, the imperatives are effective communication, dialogue, public education, and direct political action."[54] Given certain facts on an issue, SANE believed the government had the intelligence, courage, and willingness to change. Thus, the organization limited its direct action methods to persuasion and protest; it made no attempts to use noncooperation or civil disobedience. SANE's leaders chose specific goals, at least partially, because they were "moral, realistic, politically possible and pragmatically feasible next steps."[55]

CNVA operated under different sociopolitical assumptions. These radical pacifists viewed true peace in terms of both the absence

of violent struggle and the presence of social justice, and felt war
was not an aberration or an error in judgment but a manifestation
of a broad and more pervasive violence. Necessary and major atti-
tudinal and behavioral changes could come only through dramatic
actions that would not only educate and persuade the general public
and decision makers but would also challenge and confront them
with moral and political choices. CNVA's campaigns usually contained tactics of economic, political, and social noncooperation
and often included civil disobedience. Those methods frequently
brought change through coercion rather than persuasion. When
necessary, radical pacifists would resort to "unrespectable massive
dislocation efforts" to "jam the gears of the war machine."[56] To
the radical pacifists, the final arbiter of peace and justice was a
citizenry that was not only knowledgeable about issues but also
able and willing to act on its beliefs through nonviolent action.

SANE has continued to exist and exert impact on public policy.
Although its influence was damaged by internal and external dissension over its role in the antiwar movement, the organization
recovered to help form the "Dump Johnson" coalition in 1967 and
spearhead the Eugene McCarthy presidential campaign in 1968.
By the end of the 1960s, SANE had developed a long-range strategy
to scale down the power and wealth of the military and its governmental and industrial allies. In addition, the organization drew up
plans to channel resources into life-serving pursuits. The balanced
strategy between advocacy and acceptability that served SANE in
the post-McCarthy period helped it bring about achievements
such as the Arms Control and Disarmament Agency and the Nuclear
Test Ban Treaty. That same strategy, however, limited its vision
and methods and curtailed its impact on the anti-Vietnam war
movement. Nevertheless, SANE continues to function as a base
for those seeking a liberal, pragmatic organization to lend legiti-
mization and direction to their work for disarmament and peace.

Although CNVA officially merged into the War Resisters League
in 1967, its legacy still wields influence. CNVA gave up its organizational identity partly because of a lack of resources, but, more
importantly, "because the nonviolent action it had pioneered had
long since been adopted by the movement as a whole."[57] CNVA's
methodology, developed through daring and challenging action

and a constant reevaluation of its position and strategy, provides numerous groups today with an effective means of struggle consistent with their ethical and humanistic ends. People who have traditionally exercised little political power find in this legacy encouragement and nonviolent strategies to participate in peacefully and influence domestic and foreign policy.

NOTES

1. The Committee for Nonviolent Action (CNVA) was initially an ad-hoc group known as Nonviolent Action Against Nuclear Weapons. In 1959 CNVA was established as a permanent organization. For simplicity, we will refer to the group as CNVA throughout the article.

2. Norman Cousins, *Modern Man Is Obsolete* (New York: Viking Press, 1945), p. 10.

3. The Federation of Atomic Scientists was formed in Chicago in November 1945 when thirteen local groups came together "to promote the use of scientific discoveries in the interest of world peace and the general welfare of mankind." Leaders included Albert Einstein, Leo Szilard, and Eugene Rabinowitch. *Bulletin of the Atomic Scientists* 1 (December 10, 1945):1, 2.

The United World Federalists was founded in February 1947 in Ashville, North Carolina. Cord Meyer, Jr., was elected the first president. In 1952, Norman Cousins succeeded him. The organization was tremendously successful in attracting members; by the end of 1948, its membership rose to 40,000 people in 659 chapters. United World Federalists, *Unity and Diversity* (New York: World Government House, 1947).

4. Norman Cousins, "The H-Bomb and World Federalism," *The Federalist* (January 1953):15. For more information concerning the peace movement in the postwar period, see Lawrence S. Wittner, *Rebels Against War: The American Peace Movement, 1941-1960* (New York: Columbia University Press, 1969).

5. Robert Gilmore, interview, October 13, 1971.

6. Lawrence Scott, "Memo One—Shared Thinking," April 30, 1957, National Committee for a Sane Nuclear Policy Manuscripts, Swarthmore College Peace Collection, Swarthmore, Pennsylvania, Document Group 55, Box 4 (hereafter cited as SANE MSS).

7. Arlo Hurth, "Response to the First Statement Issued by the National Committee for SANE Nuclear Policy: November 15—December 31, 1957," January 1958, SANE MSS, box 4.

8. SANE's members were generally upper class, professional and semiprofessional, white collar, Protestant and Jewish, and white. Sanford Gottlieb, interview, January 19, 1972.

9. Sanford Gottlieb, "National Committee for a Sane Nuclear Policy," *New University Thought* 2 (Spring 1962):156.

10. Nathan Glazer, "The Peace Movement in America," *Commentary* 31 (April 1961):290.

11. Donald Keys to Bertram F. Willcox, March 2, 1959, SANE MSS, box 23.

12. Homer Jack, "What SANE Is and Is Not," *Sane World* 1 (December 15, 1962):2.

13. Minutes of the Executive Committee Meeting, June 8, 1958, National SANE Manuscripts, Washington, D.C., log 1958.

14. For a review of the rally, see "The Other Summit Conference," *Nation* 190 (June 4, 1960):482.

15. Glazer, "Peace Movement," p. 290.

16. U.S. Senate, Internal Security Subcommittee of the Judiciary, "Communist Infiltration in the Nuclear Test-Ban Movement," 86th Cong., 2d sess., 1960, pt. I, and 87th Cong., 1st sess., 1961, pt. II.

17. "Standards for SANE Leadership," statement of policy passed by the National Board of Directors, May 26, 1960, National SANE MSS, log 1960.

18. Gottlieb, interview.

19. A. J. Muste, "The Crisis in SANE: Act II," *Liberation* 5 (November 1960): 5-8. See also Muste, "The Crisis in SANE," *Liberation* 5 (July-August 1960):10-14.

20. Homer Jack, interview, January 29, 1972.

21. Gottlieb, interview. For Cousins's role in the negotiations, see Arthur Schlesinger, Jr., *A Thousand Days: John F. Kennedy in the White House* (New York: Fawcett Crest, 1967), pp. 817, 819.

22. Norman Cousins to Homer Jack, March 7, 1963, SANE MSS, box 36, and Homer Jack, "SANE: Tasks Ahead," *Sane World* 2 (October 15, 1953):2.

23. *New York Times,* February 19, 1965, p. 21.

24. "SANE's Vietnam Rally Fills Garden," *Sane World* 14 (July 1965):1.

25. Kirkpatrick Sale, *SDS* (New York: Random House, 1974), p. 240.

26. Sanford Gottlieb, "35,000 March for Negotiations," *Sane World* 5 (January 1966): p. 1.

27. Sale, *SDS,* p. 242.

28. Gottlieb, "35,000 March for Negotiations."

29. John Gerassi, "SANE, Civil Rights and Politics," *Liberation* 11 (June 1966):44.

30. Walter Goodman, "War in the Peace Camp," *New York Times Magazine,* December 3, 1967, pp. 49, 177.

31. Seymour Melman, interview, January 5, 1972.

32. Goodman, "War in the Peace Camp," p. 177.

33. "April 15 Demonstrations of Spring Mobilization Committee," Resolution Passed by the National Board of SANE, February 12, 1967, National SANE MSS, log 1967.

34. "U Thant Advances SANE Campaign," *Sane World* 6 (May 1967):1.

35. Donald Keys, Executive Director, to Members of the Board of SANE, November 13, 1967, National SANE MSS, log 1967, and interview, January 5, 1972. Norman Cousins, interview, January 6, 1972, and Benjamin Spock, interview, March 6, 1972.

36. H. Stuart Hughes, interview, January 7, 1972.

37. During World War II there were approximately 12,000 conscientious objectors in CPS camps and over 6,000 in federal prisons. Mulford Q. Sibley and Phillip E.

Jacobs, *Conscription of Conscience: The American State and the Conscientious Objector, 1940-1947* (Ithaca: Cornell University Press, 1952), pp. 168, 332.

38. See Krishnalal Shridharani, *War Without Violence* (New York: Harcourt Brace and Co., 1939); A. J. Muste, *Nonviolence in an Aggressive World* (New York: Harper and Co., 1940); and Richard Gregg, *The Power of Nonviolence* (Philadelphia: J. B. Lippincott Co., 1943).

39. Wittner, *Rebels Against War,* chap. 3, and James Peck, *We Who Would Not Kill* (New York: Lyle Stuart, 1958), p. 174.

40. Information on Nevada and other CNVA projects is from the CNVA Manuscript Collection, Swarthmore College Peace Collection, Swarthmore, Pennsylvania (hereafter cited as CNVA MSS). I will cite specific documents only when quoted.

41. "May 7 Press Release," Voyage of the *Golden Rule,* CNVA MSS, box 3.

42. "Reports," Polaris Action MSS, box 1, Swarthmore College Peace Collection.

43. For further explanation, see Bradford Lyttle, *You Come with Naked Hands— A Story of the San Francisco to Moscow Walk for Peace* (New Hampshire: Greenleaf Books, 1961).

44. "A Long March," *New York Post,* October 6, 1961, "The San Francisco to Moscow Walk," CNVA MSS, box 2.

45. A. J. Muste, "Let's Radicalize the Peace Movement," *Liberation* 8 (June 1963): 26-30.

46. "The Saigon Project," A. J. Muste Mss, box 43, Swarthmore College Peace Collection. See major American newspapers for April 21-22, 1966.

47. CNVA *Bulletin,* December 27, 1965.

48. Gordon Christiansen, "Coalition," *WIN* (May 26, 1967):6-10.

49. A. J. Muste to Martin Luther King, Jr., March 30, 1965, "Saigon Project," A. J. Muste MSS, box 43.

50. Brad Lyttle to George Lakey, December 3, 1965, "Releases, Literature," CNVA MSS, Box 1.

51. Brad Lyttle, "Why I Am Working for the Coalition," *WIN* (May 12, 1967): 9-10.

52. Brad Lyttle, interview, July 20, 1973, Syracuse, New York. These statements were corroborated by several other interviewees.

53. Norman Mailer, *Armies of the Night* (New York: New American Library, 1968), p. 319.

54. "Statement of National SANE Regarding Spring Mobilization," 1967-1968 File, SANE MSS, box 2.

55. Donald Keys, "What Is SANE to You?" *Sane World* 5 (June 1966):4.

56. Dave McReynolds, "Teaching Pacifists a Lesson," *WRL NEWS* (July-August 1963).

57. "Merger," *WRL NEWS* (March-April 1968).

Index

290

Association of Catholic Youth
(Italy), 158
Austrian Christian Social Party, 27
Austrian Peace Society, 21, 23
Austrian Social Democratic Party.
See Socialism, in Austria
Atomic bomb, 266
Atomic Energy Commission (AEC),
277-278
Attlee, Clement, 242
Aulard, Alphonse, 122
Avanti!, 157, 167-168

Baker, Newton D., 209
Balabanoff, Angelica, 167
Balance of Power, 163, 175; theory
of, 3-5
Baldwin, Stanley, 226
Balfour, Arthur James, 88
Balkan Wars (1912-1913), 60, 99,
181
Banca d'Italia, 163
Barberis, Francesco, 167, 170
Barthou, Louis, 110, 114, 119, 124
Beck, William, 210
Benedict XV, Pope, 158-159, 169-
170
Berber, Fritz, 221-222, 228, 229, 232
Berchtold, Count Leopold, 63-65,
69
Berliner Tageblatt, 230-231
Berne Conference, 198
Bernstein, Edouard, 100
Bethmann-Hollweg, Theobald von,
51
Bevan, Aneurin, 242
Bismarck, Otto, von, 49-50
Bissolati, Leonidza, 168, 172
Bolshevik Revolution. *See* Russian
Revolutions
Borah, Senator William E., 204-205,
212

Bordiga, Amadeo, 169, 172
Boselli, Paolo, 165, 171
Bourgeois, Leon, 45
Brailsford, H. N., 180
Briand, Aristide, 110, 119, 123-124
British Expeditionary Force (1914),
103
British Socialist Party (BSP). *See*
Socialism, in Britain
Brockway, Fenner, 186
Brooke-Hitching, Sir Thomas, 92
Brown, George, 249
Browne, Edward Granville, 97
Bryan, William Jennings, 45
Bülow, Prince Bernhard von,
Imperial German Chancellor
(1900-1909), 50-51, 66, 162
Buozzi, Bruno, 167-168
Burns, John, 85, 105
Butler, Nicholas Murray, 131-132,
135
Buxton, C. R., 187-188, 190

Cadorna, Luigi (General), 156, 171
Caillaux, Joseph, 117, 122-124,
169, 172
Campaign for Democratic Socialism
(Britain), 244, 251
Campaign for Nuclear Disarmament
(CND), 358-359, 365, 367-368,
242-246, 247-248, 251, 253-261
Campbell-Bannerman, Sir Henry,
45, 88
Camporeale, Prince di, 162
Capelli, Raffeale, 162
Caporetto, battle of, 167, 171
Carnegie, Andrew, 131, 136
Carnegie Endowment for Interna-
tional Peace, 128, 131-132, 203,
207-209
Carranza, Venustiano, 129, 133-134,
145

War Resisters League, 276, 282, 285
Warsaw Pact, 249
Watergate scandal, 261
Wedel, Count Karl von, 67, 70
Wickersham, George, 209-210
Wiesner, Jerome, 271
Wigram, Ralph, 225
Wilkinson, Ellen, 186, 236n, 261n
William II, Emperor, 58
Williams, John Sharp, 137-138, 218
Wilson, Harold, 248-249, 252, 255,
    263n, 359-360, 367, 371, 384n
Wilson, Henry Lane, 130, 132,
    210-212
Wilson, Woodrow, 130-131, 133-
    134, 136, 138-140, 143-147, 170-
    172
Women's International League for
    Peace and Freedom, 210, 213, 267

World Court, 208-209
World government, 268
World Peace Foundation, 127, 131,
    136
Works, John, 138, 218
Württemberg, 46, 99

Young, George, 92
Yvetot, Georges, 115-117, 119

Zapata, Emiliano, 145, 227
Zaragosa, Morelos, 134, 215
Zocca, Elvira, 168
Zimmerwald Conference (1915),
    167-168, 181, 185-186
Zweig, Stefan, and conscientious
    objection in Austria, 23. *See also*
    Conscientious objection

About the Contributors

ROGER CHICKERING teaches history at the University of Oregon. He was educated at Cornell University and Stanford University. His publications include *Imperial Germany and a World Without War: The Peace Movement and German Society, 1892-1914.* He is currently at work on a study of patriotic societies in Germany prior to World War I.

CHARLES DEBENEDETTI teaches history at the University of Toledo. A graduate of the University of Illinois (Urbana), he has written on the interplay between the American peace movement and foreign policy makers in the 1920s for *The Historian, Political Science Quarterly,* and *The South Atlantic Monthly.* He is the author of a forthcoming book, *Origins of the Modern American Peace Movement, 1915-1929,* and is currently preparing a survey, "The Peace Reform Movement in American History."

MILTON S. KATZ teaches American studies at the Kansas City Art Institute. He was educated at Rockford College and St. Louis University, where he completed a doctoral dissertation on SANE and the American peace movement from 1957 to 1972. Recently he participated in a National Endowment for the Humanities seminar at Vanderbilt University on society and politics in modern America.

NEIL H. KATZ is director of the program in nonviolent conflict and change at Syracuse University and assistant professor of social science in the Maxwell School. He was educated at the University of Illinois and the University of Maryland where he completed his doctoral dissertation, "Radical Pacifism and the Contemporary American Peace Movement: The Committee for

Nonviolent Action, 1957-1967." Professor Katz has published articles in *Peace and Change—A Journal of Peace Research* and *New America:A Review.*

THOMAS C. KENNEDY teaches history at the University of Arkansas. He was educated at Arizona State University and the University of South Carolina. Professor Kennedy has published articles on British social history and minority movements in the twentieth century in *The Journal of British Studies, The Canadian Journal of History,* and other periodicals.

RICHARD R. LAURENCE is a member of the Department of Humanities at Michigan State University. He studied at the University of Tennessee, Middlebury College, the University of Vienna (as a Fulbright scholor), and Stanford University, where he received the doctorate in history and humanities. His research interests include the problems of Habsburg Austria, the history of pacifism, and popular culture in Eastern Europe and the Soviet Union.

MICHAEL A. LUTZKER teaches history and archival management at New York University. He received his doctorate from Rutgers University and helped edit the Woodrow Wilson Papers at Princeton University under a fellowship from the National Historical Publications and Records Commission. Professor Lutzker has published an essay on the formative years of the Carnegie Endowment for International Peace in an anthology, *Building the Organizational Society*, and an article, "The Pacifist as Militarist: A Critique of the American Peace Movement, 1898-1914," in *Societas.*

A. J. ANTHONY MORRIS currently is head of the School of Politics, Philosophy and History at Ulster College (Northern Ireland). He was educated at the London School of Economics where from 1967 to 1973 he was senior research officer in the Government Research Division. In 1973 he was Robert Lee Bailey Visiting Professor of History at the University of North Carolina. Professor Morris has published in academic journals on both sides of the Atlantic and is editor of *Moirae,* a journal of politics and history. His most recent book is *C. P. Trevelyan, 1870-1958: Portrait of a Radical.*

FRANK E. MYERS teaches political science at the State University of New York at Stony Brook. He was educated at the University of California at Berkeley and at Columbia University. His articles have appeared in *Comparative Politics, Political Science Quarterly*, the *Journal of Peace Research*, and *New Society*. He is now working on a study of twentieth-century political thought.

DAVID E. SUMLER is the assistant to the commissioner of higher education for the state of Maryland. After completing his graduate studies at Princeton University, he taught twentieth-century French history at the University of Illinois-Urbana (1967-73) and at Washington College (1973-76). The author of *A History of Europe in the Twentieth Century*, he has also published articles on French politics and society in *French Historical Studies, Ethnicity*, and *Comparative Studies in Society and History*. His current research focuses on the social bases of French political cleavages.

SOLOMON WANK teaches history at Franklin and Marshall College. He received the doctorate from Columbia University and has published numerous articles on Austro-Hungarian foreign policy in, among others, *Austrian History Yearbook, Mitteilungen des Österreichischen Staatsarchivs, Slavonic and East European Review*, and *Intellectual and Social Developments in the Habsurg Empire*. He is currently working on a biography of the Austro-Hungarian diplomat and foreign minister, Count Alois Lexa von Aehrenthal.

HOWARD WEINROTH (1929-76) taught history at McGill University. He was educated at Stanford University and Kings College, Cambridge, England. Professor Weinroth wrote articles on the English Radicals and British foreign policy for *The Historical Journal, Journal of Contemporary History, European Studies Review*, and *Canadian Journal of History*. He contributed an essay, "Radicalism and Nationalism: An Increasing Unstable Equation," to *Edwardian Radicalism 1900-1914* and a chapter on Victorian society to a forthcoming volume on Western civilization to be published by D. C. Heath.

JAMES A. YOUNG teaches history at Edinboro State College in Pennsylvania. He was educated at Ohio University, the University of Toledo, and Case Western Reserve University. Professor Young has lectured in Britain and the United States on Italian foreign policy matters during the World War I period. He is currently working on a history of the Italian Left in the twentieth century.